The Skills of Helping, 5e
Wayne State University Custom Edition

Lawrence Shulman

THOMSON

WADSWORTH

Australia · Canada · Mexico · Singapore · Spain · United Kingdom · United States

The Skills of Helping, 5e
Lawrence Shulman

Custom Editor:
Steve Korb

Project Development Editor:
Colin Manly

Marketing Coordinator:
Sara Mercurio

Production/Manufacturing Supervisor:
Donna M. Brown

Project Coordinator:
Bree Main

Pre-Media Services Supervisor:
Dan Plofchan

Rights and Permissions Specialist:
Kalina Ingham Hintz

Senior Prepress Specialist:
Deanna Dixon

Cover Design:
Krista Pierson

Cover Image:
© Getty Images

Printed in the United States of America
1 2 3 4 5 6 7 8 9 10 11 12 13 14 09 08 07 06

For information about our products, contact us at:
Thomson Learning Academic Resource Center
(800) 423-0563

For permission to use material from this text or product, submit a request online at **http://www.thomsonrights.com**. Any additional questions about permissions can be submitted by email to **thomsonrights@thomson.com**.

The Adaptable Courseware Program consists of products and additions to existing Wadsworth products that are produced from camera-ready copy. Peer review, class testing, and accuracy are primarily the responsibility of the author(s).

Student Edition: ISBN 0-495-20570-2

Thomson Custom Solutions
5191 Natorp Boulevard
Mason, OH 45040
www.thomsoncustom.com

Thomson Higher Education
10 Davis Drive
Belmont, CA 94002-3098
USA

Asia (Including India):
Thomson Learning
60 Albert Street, #15-01
Albert Complex
Singapore 189969
Tel 65 336-6411
Fax 65 336-7411

Australia/New Zealand:
Thomson Learning Australia
102 Dodds Street
Southbank, Victoria 3006
Australia

Latin America:
Thomson Learning
Seneca 53
Colonia Polano
11560 Mexico, D.F., Mexico
Tel (525) 281-2906
Fax (525) 281-2656

Canada:
Thomson Nelson
1120 Birchmount Road
Toronto, Ontario
Canada M1K 5G4
Tel (416) 752-9100
Fax (416) 752-8102

UK/Europe/Middle East/Africa:
Thomson Learning
High Holborn House
50-51 Bedford Row
London, WC1R 4L$
United Kingdom
Tel 44 (020) 7067-2500
Fax 44 (020) 7067-2600

Spain (Includes Portugal):
Thomson Paraninfo
Calle Magallanes 25
28015 Madrid
España
Tel 34 (0)91 446-3350
Fax 34 (0)91 445-6218

CUSTOM CONTENTS

Part I: A MODEL OF THE HELPING PROCESS

1. An Interactional Approach to Helping   2

Part IV: SOCIAL WORK WITH GROUPS

8. The Group as a Mutual Aid System   266
9. Group Formation   282
10. The Beginning Phase in the Group   305
11. The Work Phase in the Group   360
12. Working with the Individual in the Group   383
13. Endings and Transitions with Groups   450

A Model of the Helping Process

Part I consists of a single, major chapter that introduces and illustrates the major themes of the interactional approach to social work. Chapter 1 sets the stage for the rest of the book with a discussion of the underlying assumptions of the model, the history of the profession, underlying theories of oppression and resilience, and the importance of integrating the personal and professional selves. A brief summary of other theoretical approaches—elements of which can be integrated into the interactional model—provides a wider perspective.

CHAPTER ONE

An Interactional Approach to Helping

CHAPTER OUTLINE

Social Work Practice Theory

The Client-System Interaction

Underlying Assumptions
in the Interactional Model

The Social Work Profession:
A Historical Perspective

Social Work Skill
and the Working
Relationship

The Integration of Personal
and Professional Selves

Oppression Psychology

Resilience Theory

Additional Social Work
Perspectives

This chapter introduces some of the central ideas of the interactional social work practice theory. A discussion of theory building in social work will place this effort in context. The client will be viewed in a dynamic interaction with many important social systems, such as the family, school, and hospital. The chapter also presents the underlying assumptions about the nature of the relationships between people and their social surroundings.

Our discussion of the assessment process will center on a strengths perspective rather than on client pathology (the medical model). The role of the social work profession as mediating the individual-social engagement will be traced to the roots of the profession, which has historically been concerned with both "private troubles" and "public issues."

Social work practice skill will then be described as the method by which the social worker strives to develop a positive working relationship with the client, a relationship that allows the social worker to help the client. The impact of the social worker's personal self—that is, the effect of his or her feelings, ethics, or values—on her or his professional practice will be examined. Finally, the chapter presents alternative views of social work practice.

Social Work Practice Theory

This book centers on the **interactional model** of social work practice, which we shall explore shortly. This model has developed from many diverse theories guiding the helping professions. By the late 1980s the helping professions were in what Kuhn described as a "pre-scientific stage" (1962). The social work profession had just begun to use theories to translate empirical research into practice. In a scientific stage, by contrast, the results of research are used to modify theories, which are then used to guide new research. In the 1990s the profession was moving toward a scientific stage and beginning to follow an **empirically based practice theory.** Today, I believe that the helping professions have made the transition and are now in the early phase of a scientific stage. As such, this book integrates recent research results from both quantitative and qualitative methods.

Because social work professionals are just beginning this crucial theory-building process, there is room in the profession for a wide range of views. In recent years social work has seen a significant expansion of efforts to strengthen theory building by employing empirical approaches. I have completed my own effort to develop a holistic, empirically based theory of social work practice, which has at its center the interactional approach to helping (Shulman, 1991). Ideas from that model have been included in this book, as have findings from the study associated with that effort. In particular, I emphasize resilience theory and the strengths perspective as models for understanding human behavior.

All practitioners eventually develop their own practice frameworks, some more and some less explicit, and judge them by how well they explain their practice. The framework for social work described in this book has been most helpful to me in my practice, my theory building, and my research. It is not engraved in stone, however. Having evolved for over 30 years, it will continue to be used as a framework just as long as it appears to do the job. You should test its ideas against your own sense of reality and use those portions that seem helpful. Many of the skills and intermediate models are not bound by one approach and can easily fit into other theoretical frameworks. Ideas from other models, some of which are identified and briefly summarized in this chapter, are integrated whenever they help to enrich the core framework. For example, strategies and interventions from solution-focused models join the list of available practitioner tools.

Because I refer to practice theory, models, and skills throughout the text, a brief explanation of how I use these terms may be helpful. In developing his framework, Schwartz (1961) defined a *practice theory* as

> a system of concepts integrating three conceptual subsystems: one which organizes the appropriate aspects of social reality, as drawn from the findings of science; one which defines and conceptualizes specific values and goals, which we might call the problems of policy; and one which deals with the formulation of interrelated principles of action. (p. 27)

A practice theory, then, first describes what we know about human behavior and social organizations. The social worker then establishes a set of specific goals or outcomes based on these underlying assumptions. Finally, a description of the worker's actions to achieve these specific goals completes the practice theory. This approach to theorizing about practice is used throughout the text. For example, when we examine the beginning phase of work, assumptions about how people behave in new situations are related to outcomes the worker wishes to achieve in first sessions. These outcomes, in turn, are linked to specific activities of the worker, described as *contracting.*

The term *model* is used to describe a representation of reality. One would construct a model to help simplify the explanation or description of a complex process or object. In this text, models are used to describe helping processes (such as the dynamics and skills required in a beginning, middle, or ending phase session), individual and social psychologies (such as resiliency theory), and the entities with which professionals work (such as families, groups, communities, or organizations).

The term *skill* refers to a specific behavior that the worker uses in the helping process. Many of the skills described in this text are core relationship skills, useful in the performance of professional as well as personal tasks. For example, empathic skills are needed by parents, spouses, and friends. The focus here will be on their use in relation to social work helping functions.

Finally, although I have been conducting empirical testing of the hypotheses contained in the practice theory, this work should be seen as an ongoing process. The **grounded theory** approach to theory building, first described by Glaser and Strauss (1967) in the field of sociology, guides this work. Formal and informal observations from practice are used to develop constructs of the theory. Formal research is conducted both to test propositions and to generate new ones. Some of the most interesting findings of my earlier study did not support my initial hypotheses. These helped me to expand the theoretical constructs, leading to the development of the more general and **holistic theory** presented in the text that complements this book (Shulman, 1991).

Many of the core findings about skill from my earlier research have been supported by research in social work and related fields. Some propositions have begun to reach the stage at which they may be described, in Rosenberg's term (1978), as **theoretical generalizations**. These propositions have received repeated support from many research efforts. As these ideas are presented, I shall provide citations to the supportive literature. However, even these propositions must be open to modification as further empirical efforts direct. It is in this spirit of evolution that the ideas in this book are shared.

● --

The Client-System Interaction

A critical factor in the helping process is the way one views the client. In early attempts to conceptualize this process, the helping professions borrowed the medical model developed by physicians. The term *medical model* has also been used in recent years to characterize a view of the client that focuses on illness and pathology; however, I use it here in another sense. The **medical model** is defined here as the four-step process of thinking about practice commonly described as study, diagnosis, treatment, and evaluation. In this framework, the knowing professional studies the client, attempts to make an accurate diagnosis, develops a treatment plan, and then evaluates the outcome.

It is entirely possible that practitioners who are preoccupied with illness or pathology and those who use other models of viewing clients (such as systems or ecological approaches or a strengths perspective) may still be employing a medical model in the way they conceptualize their practice. Even practitioners who reject what they call "Band-Aid" help, and who advocate social action and advocacy, often employ the medical model in their thinking. The only difference, in their case, is that it is the "system" that is studied, diagnosed, and treated.

One of several problems with this model has been the heavy emphasis on the study phase, in which the social worker attempted to obtain a great deal of information about the client (such as family history, work history, medical history), in order to develop what was called the psychosocial study on which the diagnosis and resulting treatment plan were developed. Obtaining such information in the early stage was important and, in some settings, essential for reimbursement of the service, yet the question-and-answer format could lead workers to ignore the equally important processes required to engage the client and to begin to develop the working relationship.

The following example illustrates how a social work student begins to connect with her new client during their first session, loses the client as she switches to taking the family history, and then catches herself as she reconnects with her client on an emotional level.

WORKER: Come on in and sit down. If you get too cold, just tell me and I'll close the window.

CLIENT: No, that's fine, it's very nice outside. So, what is your experience, your specialization? They tell me this is an important question to ask.

WORKER: Well, I'm a second-year graduate student at the School of Social Work. This is my second internship. My first one was at a child welfare office. I could tell you all of the theories I have learned and books I have read, but I think it is more important for you to see how comfortable you are with me.

CLIENT: I never had therapy before so I guess we'll make a good team.

WORKER: What brought you here today?

CLIENT: I felt like driving my car into the canal. I left my husband in Florida, and I came home. I feel like this is where I belong. Basically, I feel like I'm drowning. (Tears fill her eyes.)

WORKER: Sounds like this is a very painful time for you. (Client is silent, head down.) When did you leave Florida?

CLIENT: Two and a half weeks ago. I went to Florida a year ago to save my marriage. I gave up everything for him—my friends, family, job—and I realize the sacrifice is not worth it. I'm going through the empty-nest syndrome without the children. I had to adjust to his family, his way of living. There was no communication between us. I got scared! I felt more like his roommate. I always have to take care of everyone!

WORKER: You sound angry.

CLIENT: Yes, and I'm tired of it!

WORKER: Because this is an intake I need to ask you some questions in order to complete the paperwork portion of our meeting.

CLIENT: Oh, I'm sorry. Go ahead.

WORKER: Don't be sorry. I just wanted you to know we needed to shift gears for awhile.

CLIENT: Go ahead; that's fine.

WORKER: Tell me about your family.

CLIENT: I have five grown children: Pam, Jane, John, Cathy, and Tina. She's my baby. She recently had a baby and (tears fill her eyes). That's another subject.

WORKER: Seems like babies are a tough subject for you to talk about.

CLIENT: (Beginning to cry) It's OK. Go ahead, ask your questions.

WORKER: They are not as important as your feelings are right now. We'll have plenty of time later to complete the forms.

When the example was discussed in class, the student worker recognized that she had switched to the questioning format just when the client expressed strong feelings of anger. Other students in the class acknowledged that having a structured first interview in which they could focus on asking a series of questions made them feel more comfortable, while possibly making the client feel less comfortable. They could also see how important it was to stay close to the feelings of the client. Many of the questions would be answered in the course of the interview, and the social worker could always leave some time at the end to obtain the missing data.

Because assessment schemes are usually integrated into the practices of social agencies, I try to help my students develop a workable approach while recognizing its limitations. We develop creative approaches for obtaining the required information and skillfully engaging the client in the first interview. Involving the client actively in the process, discussing the reasons for the information gathering, and making sure that the study phase does not substitute for contracting work are essential elements. Students are also encouraged to find ways of relating to the team when discussing specific clients, such as in a case conference, which may affect a shift in attitude toward clients from pathology to strengths. In later chapters we examine assessment models and systems work in more detail.

Another problem with the medical model is that it has tended to present clients in static terms. The model emphasizes attributing descriptive characteristics to the client (such as resistant, hard to reach). In extreme cases, workers refer to clients as diagnoses, as in "I'm working with a borderline" rather than "a client with a borderline diagnosis." Even the term *therapy*, often used by social workers to describe work with individuals, families, and groups (such as family therapy) implies that something is wrong with the client that requires fixing. For many years now, dynamic systems theory has profoundly influenced the way helping professionals view their clients. One central idea has been the emphasis on viewing a client in interaction with others. Instead of seeing a client as the object of analysis, workers began to focus on the way in which the client and the client's important systems were interacting. In fact, according to this viewpoint, one can never understand the movements of the client except as affected by the movements of others.

This shift in thinking can be illustrated using the example of a depressed middle-aged woman admitted to the psychiatric ward of a hospital. One could choose to focus only on her depression and other symptoms. In fact, current knowledge about the biological sources of some forms of depression requires that professionals be aware of treatment possibilities that can include the use of psychotropic drugs.

An alternative framework would also seek to identify those important systems in her life that she has had to deal with: her husband, her children, her job, her peer group, her parents or siblings, her society and its many sexist attitudes, and so on. In addition, one could include the hospital, her doctor, ward staff, and other patients. A diagrammatic way of viewing this is shown in Figure 1.1.

This important change in perspective alters the kind of questions the worker mentally asks. Instead of simply focusing on the state of the patient's mental health,

Relationship of Client and Systems

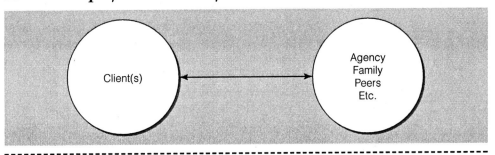

the degree of the depression, and its possible cause (such as early childhood trauma or substance abuse), the worker is equally curious about the state of the interactions between the patient and each of the relevant systems. What is the nature of the relationship between the woman and her husband? Can they talk to and listen to each other? Is the relationship emotionally or physically abusive? The worker would also be interested in the relationship between the patient and the hospital. How well is the patient integrating into the ward? Is she reaching out to other patients, creating an informal support group, or is she cut off and isolated?

These are not questions the worker will be asking the client in the early interviews (the structure of first sessions will be discussed later). Rather, they are examples of the potential areas of work on which the helping process may focus. Furthermore, the worker will not focus only on the client's part in the interaction. As stated earlier, the client's movements can only be understood in relation to the movements of those around her. How well do the family, friends, and the other clients reach out to her? Part of the outcome of these interactions will be determined by the client's input, but other parts will be a result of the system's responses. In fact, the relationship will be reciprocal, with the movements of each constantly affecting the movements of the others.

The self-in-relation theory emerged from efforts to rethink women's psychology initiated by Miller (J. B. Miller 1987, 1988; J. B. Miller & Stiver, 1991, 1993) and Gilligan, Lyons, and Hammer (1990) as part of the Harvard Project on Women's Psychology and Girls' Development, as well as by others at the Stone Center in Wellesley, Massachusetts (for example, Fedele, 1994; Jordan, 1991, 1993). If we were to apply some of this theory, we might rethink this client's situation in terms of paradoxes. For example, in an article on the use of relational theory in group work practice, Fedele describes a central paradox first identified by Miller as follows:

> This paradox states that during the course of our lifetime, in the desire to make connections and be emotionally accessible, we all experience harm or violation that leads to a need to develop strategies to keep large parts of ourselves out of connection. In the face of intense yearning for connection and in order to remain in the only relationships available, we develop strategies that keep more and more of ourselves out of connection. Simply put, the paradox is that in order to stay in connection, we keep parts of ourselves out of connection.
> (J. B. Miller, 1988)

The paradox of maintaining connection through disconnecting offers some additional insights into the potential causes of a client's depression, rooted in current and possibly past experiences. It also suggests how to help clients find ways of making new connections (with family members, the hospital, other women in a mutual aid support group) without the need for maintaining the disconnection defenses. (The relational model will be discussed in more detail in Chapter 12.)

In addition, to truly understand clients, workers need to understand clients' interactions in the context within which they take place. We are much clearer now about how our society's stereotypes of women and men affect relationships. In many examples, when one looks beneath the depression of some middle-aged women, one finds an understandable anger, even rage, related to sex-role stereotyping and oppression by a male-dominated society. Does the woman experience herself as able to influence her social environment, or does she feel powerless (Weick & Vandiver, 1982)? Has she experienced significant victimization in her life (Berlin & Kravetz, 1981)? Is this a situation where it is important to empower the client (Smith & Siegal, 1985)? Does the view of her situation change if workers apply one of the many feminist models more recently summarized by Saulnier (1996, 2000), such as "liberal feminism," "radical feminism," or "postmodern feminism"?

If the client is also a person of color and economically disadvantaged, then we have the classic triple oppressions related to gender, race, and class. A severe depression may well represent an understandable defensive reaction in response to the oppressive conditions imposed by the increasing "feminization of poverty" or the impact of welfare reform efforts that require recipients to find work when jobs are unavailable and resources are limited.

Oppression psychology, as described by Fanon and elaborated by Bulhan (1985) is discussed in more detail later in this chapter. Fanon suggested that prolonged exposure to oppression could lead clients to internalize the "oppressor without," adopting negative self-attitudes and self-images. Internalized rage, often masked by depression, can lead clients to behavior that is maladaptive and destructive to themselves and others. "The oppressor without becomes an introppressor—an oppressor within" (p. 126). Such a person, according to Fanon, becomes an "autopressor" by participating in her or his own oppression. Ironically, and conveniently, the maladaptive behavior that results from prolonged experience of oppression is then used by the majority group to justify continued stereotyping and oppression, maintaining a vicious cycle.

If the client is also a **vulnerable client**—for example, lacking a strong social support system of family or friends—then the essentially maladaptive responses of the client become all the more understandable. In addition, given the client's situation, one has to be impressed by the strength the client has shown in simply surviving and continuing to struggle. By viewing the client from a strength perspective and a resiliency model as well as incorporating solution-focused strategies, discussed later in this chapter, the social worker can focus on the part of the client that has demonstrated a capacity to deal effectively with life.

A worker starting from this perspective will be more interested in identifying what is right than what is wrong about clients. The worker will want to help them identify times in their lives when they effectively coped and the resources they needed then. For example, rather than focusing only on the causes of relapses in substance abuse recovery, the worker will want to help clients focus on how they maintained their recovery between relapses. The subtle signs of life and strength are what the worker will reach for in trying to help clients overcome the effects of oppression.

To return to our earlier example, as the client-system interactions are identified, the woman's depression may take on new meaning. The sadness and passivity are not the problems; rather, they are the symptoms of the breakdown in these important interactions and the result of the experienced oppression. The depression is not the illness to be cured, but rather a signal that important areas of interaction in the life of this woman have broken down. The worker will not try to "cure" the client, but rather to affect the client's capacity for coping and change, the way she thinks about her feelings and problems, and how she and these important systems interact. The cure for the "problem" will emerge not from the professional's treatment plan, but rather from the client's increasing understanding of her situation and her own efforts to find new ways to interact with the systems that matter to her—either reaching out to them or cutting herself off from them and finding new sources of support. Similarly, the systems (such as the family) may have to find new ways to reach out to this client in order to reengage her. Both the client and the systems may find implementation of this process difficult. Here, the job of the social worker plays a crucial role.

At this point, you may have many questions and possibly some objections. What if the client is too weak to deal with the system, doesn't want help, and refuses to work on the interaction? Perhaps the problem is with the system. As mentioned earlier, what happens if the depression is related to biological factors for which pharmaceutical treatment is needed, perhaps in conjunction with counseling? These and other objections are pursued in some detail in the discussions that follow. For the moment, try to set them aside. At this point, the most important concept to grasp is that the client to be helped is viewed as an interactive entity, often ambivalent, acting and reacting to the various demands of the systems she must negotiate. The systems will be viewed in this way as well.

Each client is a special case within this general model. The unwed pregnant teen in a child welfare agency might be dealing with the systems of the agency, the child's father, family, friends, societal attitudes as reflected in recent welfare legislation, prejudices towards women and sexuality in general, and so on. Of equal concern to her may be issues of income (welfare or work), housing, child care, and the medical system. If she lives in a group care home, the house parents and other residents become part of the active systems in her life. Her feelings about herself as a woman, her reactions to society's norms, and her own, often harsh, judgments of herself (the oppressor within) may all be part of her agenda, but always in relation to the way in which she deals with those systems that matter to her. Whatever the category of client discussed in this book—the child in the residential center, the husband in marital counseling, the student who is failing, the client with a terminal illness, the client learning to live with AIDS, the client in the early stages of recovery from substance abuse, or the member of a citizens' community action group—all will be viewed in the context of the interaction with their social surroundings and an understanding of their potential strengths.

Underlying Assumptions in the Interactional Model

All models of social work practice are based on underlying assumptions about people and their social surroundings. These are the starting points for theory building, and they need to be made explicit. While many assumptions about people and the helping process will be examined throughout this book, three core ideas underlying the interactional model are presented here. The first is the **symbiotic assumption:** a belief in the essential symbiotic relationship between people and their social surroundings. The second is the assumption that this mutual need is systematically blocked by obstacles, some raised by the client and others by the systems the client must negotiate. The third basic assumption is that the social worker must always assume and reach for the client's (and system's) strengths for change. These assumptions are explored in the sections that follow.

Assumption of Symbiosis

Now that we have placed clients in interaction with the various systems that impinge on them, we need to examine the nature of this relationship. If we return to the example in the previous section of a depressed, middle-aged woman, our view of how to help this client will depend on our assumptions about the individual-social engagement. If we examine her interactions with her environment, we can perceive a certain amount of ambivalence. Some part of her will seem to be reaching out, however faintly, toward life and the people around her. On the other hand, her withdrawal, depression, and general communications appear to signal a retreat from life. She may have experienced life as being too difficult, her feelings too painful to face, and the demands seemingly impossible to meet.

A part of her seems to be giving up and saying that the very struggle seems useless. She can be observed placing barriers between herself and these systems, including that part of the system (the worker) that is reaching out to help her. She is simultaneously reaching out for life, growth, and the important systems around her and moving away from each.

The assumption that a part of us is always striving toward health lies at the core of the practice theory formulated by Schwartz. Borrowing a "symbiotic" model of human relationships, he views the individual-social interaction as

> a relationship between the individual and his nurturing group which we would describe as "symbiotic"—each needing the other for its own life and growth, and each reaching out to the other with all the strength it can command at a given moment. (Schwartz, 1961, p. 15)

The term *symbiotic* is used to describe the mutual need of individuals and the systems that matter to them. This woman's needs can best be met in interaction with the world around her, not through complete withdrawal from it. Similarly, society has a stake in maintaining this client as an active, involved, unique, integrated individual. The idea of symbiotic striving fits comfortably with the constructs of the relational model described earlier.

Unfortunately, the term *symbiotic* has taken on a professional connotation of unhealthy mutual overdependency, as between a mother and child. In the world of biology, symbiosis actually describes two organisms living in a mutually beneficial relationship. The exploitation of one organism by another would be described as a parasitic relationship.

Schwartz uses the term to underline our mutual dependency and our essential interest in each other. It is a statement of the interdependence that is fundamental to a belief in social responsibility for the welfare of each individual. It also recognizes that each individual finds life's needs best satisfied in positive relationships with others.

You may be wondering at this point how this assumption of a symbiotic model relates to experiences where individual-social interaction appears to be far from symbiotic and, in fact, has been defined as often oppressive. Schwartz points out that

> in a complex and often distorted society, the individual-social symbiosis grows diffuse and obscure in varying degrees, ranging from the normal developmental

problems of children growing into their culture to the severe pathology involved in situations where the symbiotic attachment appears to be all but severed. (1961, p. 15)

The very fact that the mutual self-interest of people and their surrounding systems is often obscured creates the working ground for the helping professional. The observation that people and their systems often appear to be acting against each other's self-interest is not an argument against the symbiotic model; rather, it is an argument for some helping person to help both system and client regain their sense of mutuality.

Following this model, the worker will search not only for the part of the client that is reaching out toward systems, but also for the part of the family, friends, peer group, and hospital system that is reaching out toward the patient. For instance, if the husband appears to turn away from his wife during the family session, closing off his feelings, then the worker might reach for the underlying sense of loss and hurt that he attempts to hide even from himself. When the hospital rules, procedures, and services seem to work against the best interests of a patient, the helping person will attempt to influence the part of the system that cares about the people it serves; in doing so, the worker will employ several strategies such as mediation, brokering, or advocacy.

In example after example throughout this book, you will observe that the helping person's movements with the client, the moment-by-moment interventions, are affected by the worker's view of the individual-social relationship. At critical moments in the interactions, connections will be discovered between husbands and wives, parents and children, students and teachers, community groups and politicians, individual group members and the group, and so forth, because the helping person was searching for them. This idea will be termed the **two-clients construct**, in which the social worker will always be seen as having two clients. The second client will change in each situation. In the current example, it may be the woman's family, the hospital system, friends, and so on.

The practical implications of this philosophical assumption are important. For example, in the case of our female client, the worker's belief in the importance of helping her find her connections to people around her and the belief in this woman's partial striving for this connection will cause the worker to search for faint clues that the client is still emotionally alive and trying. The worker will not be fooled by the defenses thrown up by the client but will concentrate instead on the spark of life that still exists, often associated with the anger, even rage, buried under the depression and apathy. The work of the helping person is not to remotivate the client, but rather to discover and develop the motivation already there. Helping the client understand the nature of her internalized oppressor is an important step in helping her take control over her life and begin dealing with the oppressor without.

Belief in this symbiotic model does not necessarily exclude the existence of important tensions and real conflicts of interest between the individual and the systems. Interactions in life involve conflict and confrontation. Not all interests are mutual. Oppression happens for a reason. The effective helping person brings these underlying differences into the open so that the engagement is a real human process invested with a range of feelings. Examples abound in which the skilled helper challenges the illusion of agreement between the parties in conflict by reaching for and demanding real work. What the model does is provide the worker with a sense of the potential common ground on which both the client and the important life systems can build.

For workers to be effective in this role, they need to recognize that oppression clearly has some psychological and concrete payoffs for the majority group in any situation. For example, when a man uses battering and intimidation to attempt to control a woman in his life, he receives psychological and concrete benefits from the interaction. If we consider the "master-slave" paradigm developed by Hegel in 1807 (1966), elements of which underlie oppression theory, the insecure "master" seeks to "recognize" or define himself through the unreciprocated recognition by the "slave" (Bulhan, 1985). In effect, the male batterer uses the subjugation of his female partner to bolster his sense of self by his partner "recognizing" him without his having to "recognize" her.

In considering such relationships, social workers' first concern should be protecting oppressed clients and holding the oppressors accountable for their actions. Battering is a criminal offense and must be treated as such. Work with a battered woman often involves helping her find her own strength and the social resources needed to leave the abusive relationship safely. However, when also working with the male batterer, workers would need to recognize that this use of violence for control can have significant negative effects on him, including legal consequences, emotional damage to the self, and precluding of an intimate relationship based on mutuality and equality—a relationship of mutual recognition.

We can extend this individual psychology to a social psychology if we recognize that the wider sexist attitudes that support this brutal form of oppression can be explained by the same psychological dynamics. The payoffs for sexism are not only psychological but concrete and financial as well. When women are consistently paid less than men for the same jobs, profits are higher, even in nonprofit organizations. When a "glass ceiling" stops women (and other minority groups) from advancing in business or government agencies, more senior positions are available for men and members of the majority groups. Even these gains, however, are offset by the long-term social, moral, and economic prices paid as a result of such shortsighted practices.

On a broader scale, oppression by all majority groups against all minority groups—such as people of color, women, immigrants, Jews, gays and lesbians, or people with mental illness, mental retardation, or significant physical disabilities—results in specific economic and psychological benefits for the majority group. However, the significant personal, social, and even economic costs are often ignored. For example, when the AIDS epidemic was viewed as a problem affecting only gays, Haitians, and intravenous drug users, many of whom live in inner-city ghettos, the U.S. government largely ignored it. Some groups actually pointed to this disease as retribution for "immoral" behavior and saw the growing numbers of deaths as a "cleansing" of society. Although these views were extreme, they may have represented a more general undercurrent of racism and homophobia that fostered lethargy and inaction by the larger community. One has only to imagine the difference in the response if such an epidemic had initially struck middle-class, heterosexual whites instead of these minority populations.

The differential provision of medical research and support to minority populations represents a deadly form of oppression. Only now is the majority group coming to grips with the incredible social and health-related costs associated with the increase in this epidemic and its spread to the majority population. The same is true if one considers the true costs of the inadequate health care services provided in the United States to the poor and the oppressed. Lack of a universal health care system in this country stands in stark contrast to programs developed in Canada and Europe. These examples can be added to the list of the many documented incidents of racism in medicine, including the "shocking and scandalous recently halted Tuskegee experiment on syphilis among blacks in Macon County, Alabama" (Bulhan, 1985, p. 87), in which the effects of the untreated disease on 400 black men and their families were observed for more than 40 years without the knowledge of the study participants or the provision of available treatments. It was only in 1997 that President Clinton publicly acknowledged and apologized for these actions on behalf of the American people.

The existence of the many powerful examples of oppression and exploitation of vulnerable populations in U.S. history does not change the essential, symbiotic nature of the relationship between people and their social surroundings. These instances instead reveal how much we have lost sight of these connections. They also provide a rationale for the unique functional role of the social work profession described later in this chapter.

Assumption of Obstacles in the Engagement

Thus far we have focused on the client's interactions with important environmental systems. Both the individual and the systems are vitally linked through mutual need. Each is seen as reaching out to the other with all the strength available at the moment and with the capacity to reach out more effectively. The next logical question is this: What goes wrong? The mutual dependence can be blocked or obscured by any number of obstacles. We now briefly examine three potential obstacles to interaction between the individual and the social system: changing social systems, conflicts between self-interest and mutual interest, and the dynamics of interpersonal communication.

The Increasing Complexity of Human Social Systems One problem is the increasing complexity of human social systems, such as the family. The relationships between parents and children and husbands and wives (or same-sex partners) have become increasingly difficult. Important sources of social support across generations have diminished as modern nuclear families tend to live apart from grandparents and other relatives. As society's norms and values change more rapidly than they did in past generations, parents are forced to reconcile their own beliefs with the newer values of their children. Further, the world of work absorbs more time and energy, often leaving parents less opportunity to foster family stability.

Middle-aged parents find themselves attempting to provide support for their adolescent (and often young adult) children, while simultaneously feeling responsible for the well-being of their aged parents. Called by some the "sandwich generation," they often ask, "When will I have time for me?" Is it any wonder that family members at times find dealing with one other quite complicated?

Our definition of *family* has changed dramatically. The typical two-parent family of a generation ago has been replaced by an ever-higher percentage of single-parent families. These families, as well as low-income two-parent families, face increasing stress because of the breakdown of the formal support network—the government "safety net"—as a result of budget cuts. The full impact of the 1996 Welfare Reform Act has just begun to be known, but early indications suggest that at least some of the families cut off from welfare have not been able to make the predicted transition to work and independence and are now far worse off than they were before.

The availability of day care, low-cost housing, financial subsidies, and adequate health care has decreased almost in proportion to the increase in need. Some political and economic leadership has stressed a "me-first" ethic that has encouraged the majority to ignore the needs of disenfranchised populations. We were at first shocked by the appearance of the homeless on our urban streets, then encouraged to be angry at them by political leaders who suggested that shelter was available for anyone who really wanted it.

Periodically, we have experienced severe problems in the economy that have undermined employment stability. Employment patterns relying on temporary workers and corporate restructuring that lay off midlevel managers are more common now than before. The increased globalization of the economy and the ability of corporations to "outsource," move jobs to other counties to increase profits, has led to fears that unemployment in the United States may be an ongoing problem even when the economy appears to be robust. When higher-paying jobs are lost and replaced by lower-paying ones, often without benefits, a larger portion of our population moves into poverty and vulnerability rather than into economic and social security. The high levels of unemployment and uncertainty have led to increased family tension. In one of my early research projects (Shulman, 1991), Canadian workers in British Columbia reported significant increases in the number and severity of child abuse cases, which appear to be linked to economic stress—either loss of a job or fear of such a loss. Normal family tensions, such as parent-teen conflicts, become exacerbated when parents face economic stress or must cope with the "earthquake" of unemployment.

Even during stable economic conditions, a politically divided federal government, debates over a balanced budget, pressures to provide tax breaks (which mostly benefit the wealthy), the rising costs of health care in general and prescription drugs in particular, demands for "smaller government," and the abandonment of federal responsibility to be replaced by state control over health and social welfare programs—all have led to an increasing gap between the rich and the poor, the healthy and the sick, the fully participating members of our communities and those who are left out.

More generally, as the poor collect in cities, and as the institutions (welfare, medical, educational) designed to serve them grow more complex, the basic relationship between people and these important systems is bound to become obstructed. One need only think of one's reactions to the first day at a new school or to entering a busy hospital in order to remember how strange, overwhelming, and impersonal the system can seem. The obstacles related to complexity are inherent, and they often emerge inadvertently from the realities of the system.

Divergence in Self-Interest and Social Interest A second set of obstacles is associated with the divergent interests of people and the systems that matter to them. Life does not consist only of mutual interest and interdependence. There are times when self-interest directly conflicts with the interests of others. In fact, each individual, as part of the growth process, must learn to set aside his or her own immediate needs in order to integrate into the social order.

For example, in marriage or partnerships, the man may believe he has some stake in maintaining a traditional and privileged gender role. The rules of behavior, norms, and the traditional structures in such relationships provide some payoffs for the male partner. A confident woman who is able to develop a sense of her self differentiated from her husband and her family may be a more interesting person, but she may also intimidate a partner who is struggling with his own sense of worth. Obstacles to the symbiotic relationship can be generated by the ambivalence family members feel toward change. Rapid changes produce anxiety for all in our society, so we often attempt to maintain the status quo and preserve continuity.

Complex systems are also ambivalent toward the people they serve. For example, politicians may view community action pressure groups as thorns in their sides. As these groups expose important unmet needs, they also reveal problems that are difficult to handle. Government bodies face demands from many sources for a share of the economic pie, and to have this pressure heightened by citizen groups creates new difficulties.

While society has a fundamental stake in strengthening and incorporating its most vulnerable populations, it also has an element of economic self-interest in maintaining the poor and in fostering a stereotype that blames them for their own problems. It is easy to see how the need for strong, active, community pressure groups as sources of feedback for our society can be obscured by the immediate need for peace and quiet. Similarly, large institutions such as schools and hospitals find it easier to deal with students and patients who conform, make no trouble, and go along with the present order. They often fail to realize the price they pay in terms of effective teaching and healing.

Problems of Interpersonal Communication A third major set of obstacles involves problems of interpersonal communication. Sharing and understanding painful or taboo thoughts and feelings is hard. People find it difficult to speak of feelings about sex, authority, intimacy, dependency, loss, sexual orientation, and so on. The powerful norms of our society are brought to bear in each interpersonal relationship, often making achievement of mutual understanding difficult. Most important conversations between people take place through the use of indirect communications that can be extremely hard to decipher.

For example, the husband who feels hurt and rejected by his wife's apparent lack of interest in sexual relations may express this through hostile or sarcastic comments in a totally unrelated area. The wife, in turn, may be expressing her own reactions to the husband's continual criticism through lack of interest in sexual contact. Each may be feeling a powerful and important need for the other that is obscured by the built-up resentment developed by their immature means of communication.

Students who feel the teacher is always on their back, or is racist, or does not like them, respond with failure, lack of preparation, and cutting classes. The teacher, out of frustration at not being able to reach the children, responds with increased exhortation or punishment, or in some cases by developing stereotypes based on race, class, ethnicity, or gender. To the children, the message is that the teacher does not care. To the teacher, the message is that the children (or their parents) do not care.

In most cases, they are both wrong. The children's stake in the successful completion of their education and the teacher's stake in helping students through a difficult learning process may be overwhelmed by their mutual misconceptions. Instead of strengthening the relationship, the student and the teacher turn away from each other. The difficulty of overcoming these obstacles is heightened when reduced financial support for education results in larger classes, diminished support services, and reduced resources for children with special needs. The teacher might not recognize the community and family issues that are profoundly affecting the student. Substance abuse, physical and sexual abuse, vicarious trauma from witnessing community violence, and so forth can severely impact the healthiest people. Often, behavior problems in school are a cry for help.

The gay man previously rejected by his family for being gay but who has been diagnosed as HIV-positive may feel a strong need to repair a fractured family-of-origin relationship. Having been hurt deeply by his family, he may be reluctant to contact his parents and inform them of his illness. For the family, the crisis of their son's illness may be the very catalyst needed to break the cycle of rejection and allow for some form of family reunification and healing. An understandable fear of another painful rejection may cut a client off from his ability to communicate his need for renewed family relationships.

In the relationships between parent and child, hospital ward and patient, student and school, the person with AIDS and his family, individual and group—that is, in each special case of the individual-social engagement—the essential mutual need is fragile and easily obscured by the complexity of the situation, by divergent needs, or by the difficulty involved in communication.

Out of this ever-present possibility of **symbiotic diffusion**, the loss of a clear sense of the symbiotic striving, the need for the social work profession emerged (Schwartz, 1961). The profession's tasks relate directly to the fact that obstacles can easily obscure the mutual dependence between the individual and important systems. When both sides have lost sight of this important connection, a third force is needed to help them regain this understanding. According to Schwartz, the social work profession, with its historical roots firmly planted in two streams—concern for individual well-being and social justice—is uniquely suited to play this role. This idea of the third force leads to the mediating function of the social work professional described later in the chapter.

Assumption of Strength for Change

Belief in the existence of symbiotic striving is closely linked to another assumption about the individual-social engagement: that both the individual and the system contain within them the strength to implement this mutuality. This assumption depends on a view of people (and complex systems) as being able to act in their own interest without being bound by their past experiences. An alternative approach considers that people fundamentally act according to the sum of the strengths and skills accumulated by past experiences. Causal links can be drawn between a person's present apparent immobility and earlier traumatic events.

While it seems logical that past experiences affect the way in which an individual attempts to negotiate new surroundings, the danger exists, with this view, of pre-judging and underestimating a client's (or the system's) resiliency, strength, and capacity for change. Within the framework presented here, the individual is best described by actions and is as strong or as weak as he or she acts in the present moment. The practice implication of this attitude is that the worker must believe that the individual or the system has the capacity to move in its own self-interest, even if only by small steps, and that this movement will lead to increased strength and more change. These strengths and resiliency perspectives will be discussed more fully later in this chapter.

With this basic assumption in mind, the interactional perspective calls for the helping person always to place a "demand for work" before the client. The **demand for work** occurs when the worker exhorts the client to work effectively on her or his tasks and to invest that work with energy and affect. The work itself, the goals of the process (even with mandated clients), must be shared by the client, not merely imposed by the worker. Also, this demand must be integrated with support in what could be called an empathic demand for work. A similar demand will be placed on the system.

A familiar expression in this connection is "reach for the client's strength," suggesting that the very act of reaching for strength—that is, believing in the potential of the work and refusing to accept even the client's own self-description of weakness—is a central part of what helps a client to act. Possibly the client has reached the present impasse precisely because all the signals received from important "others" have reinforced belief in the client's own impotence. The social worker, by contrast, will operate on a basic principle: No matter how hopeless it seems, there is always a next step.

In an example from my own practice, I confront a group of people with AIDS in early recovery who have apparently given up on their ability to have nonexploitive and drug- and alcohol-free intimate relationships with others; I tell them that they must set aside their own concerns and issues and become a mutual support group for each other. This demand for work is rooted in the belief that even these clients, who have experienced years of polysubstance abuse, prison sentences, prostitution, and traumatic childhood experiences, still have the strength to reach out for each other within the group, which serves as a microcosm of larger society. The group members' ability to care for others is a tribute to themselves and an affirmation of the strengths perspective.

The assumptions just demonstrated will interact in important ways in the models and examples shared in this book. Workers will always search for subtle connections and will always demand that clients and systems act on their potential for change. This view of practice is built on a deep investment in the concept of interdependence; a view of the client as the source of energy for change, healing, and growth; a belief in client strength; and a preoccupation with health rather than sickness.

This stance does not negate the fact that some clients and some systems, for many complex reasons, will not be able to use the worker's help at a given moment. The helping process is interactional, with workers carrying out their parts as best they can. As such, clients have a part to play, and their strength helps to determine the outcome. For example, no matter how skillful the worker, he or she may not be able to reach a substance-abusing client until the client enters detox and stops using cocaine. Using findings from my own research and that of others, we shall throughout this book explore the ways in which stress, acceptance of a problem, and motivation affect the client's ability to receive and use help at any given moment.

Socioeconomic factors, such as income, housing, and employment trends, also profoundly affect social work outcomes. Social workers must therefore be concerned with social policies that affect the human situation. Becoming aware of and working for changes in social policies is part of the task of helping. Recognizing that a particular client may be unable to use help at that time, the worker will nevertheless always attempt to reach for the client's strength because this is the way in which help is given.

The Social Work Profession: A Historical Perspective

Thus far in the discussion, we have tried to view each client as a special case of the more general individual-social interaction in our society. The issue we explore in this section is the role that the social work profession plays in this process. Although providing a detailed discussion of the complex history of the development of the profession lies beyond the scope of this book, a general understanding of its unique historical roots will place the helping role in perspective.

The Roots of the Profession

The profession, as we know it now, was created through the merger over the years of two basic streams of thought about the helping process. One was rooted in the work of those interested in issues of social change. An example was the early settlement house movement, most often associated with the work of Jane Addams at Hull House, founded in 1889 (Addams, 1961). This movement, which began in England, was one of the many established at the turn of the century to cope with the stresses created by urbanization, industrialization, and the large-scale influx of immigrants to North America. The mission of these early, community-oriented social agencies included attempting to help immigrant and other poor families integrate into U.S. society more effectively. At the same time, the leadership of these movements, mostly middle and upper-class liberals of the day, waged a fight against the social conditions facing these populations. Poor housing and health services, child labor, sweat-shop conditions in urban factories—all became targets for social change.

While Jane Addams was known for her relatively radical approach to working with and involving actively oppressed people, many in the settlement house movement incorporated a "doing for" approach to the populations with which they worked. Little effort was directed at actually organizing the poor, through an empowerment process, to fight effectively against the forces of oppression related to class, gender, race, ethnicity, and the like. An **empowerment process** involves engaging the client (individual, family, group, or community) in developing strengths to personally and politically cope more effectively with those systems that are important to them. It is likely that if the leaders of these early social movements had attempted to mobilize client groups in this way, they would have been viewed as too radical and would have themselves faced political repression.

In addition, this early movement saw as one of its major roles the acculturation of the poor to the values and beliefs of their own upper-middle-class society. Developing an appreciation of the arts, such as classical music and literature, and participating in other "refined" activities were seen as paths for self-improvement and "building character." Workers often lived with clients in the settlement houses; helping was seen as practical in nature. For example, if cities were overcrowded and unhealthy, then children needed to be removed to camps in the country during the summer. Not until the 1930s did this social-change orientation join the mainstream of the emerging social work profession. This early driving concern for social justice for vulnerable populations gave the social work profession an important element of its current identity. The early roots of the group work and community organization methods can be traced to these professional pioneers.

The other major stream of professional development was rooted in a focus on fulfilling individual needs. The founder of this stream is often identified as Mary Richmond, whose work at the Charities Organization Society made a major contribution toward the professionalizing of social work (1918). Her efforts were directed at moving social work beyond the notion of "friendly visitors" who were charitable to the poor toward a systematic, professional approach to helping. Richmond was interested in the helping process and wanted it to be recorded, analyzed, and then taught.

By the 1930s, two new specializations in social work had developed: group work and community organization. Group work was closely associated with the informal education and socialization movements. Early leaders included Grace Coyle (1948) and Gertrude Wilson and Gladys Ryland (1949). The work focused on using the peer group to help people cope with the normative tasks of life. A typical group might consist of teenagers forming a social club in a community center, with the group worker assigned to help them learn to work effectively together. Activities such as games, singing, crafts, or bowling provided ways through which group members could enjoy recreation and work on appropriate individual and group developmental tasks.

The early community organization activity was designed to coordinate social services through, for example, councils of social agencies. A second function was to raise funds for private social welfare activities through organizations such as community chests, the forerunners of today's United Way campaigns. It would not be until the late 1950s and early 1960s, reflecting the social activist themes of the times and the civil rights movement, as well as borrowing from community action and organizer models developed by activists such as Saul Alinsky (Reitzes & Reitzes, 1986), that community organization practice would shift to an approach that emphasized organizing and empowering clients and other members of the community to achieve social changes.

Specht and Courtney (1993) describe the convergence of the three streams of casework, group work, and community organization in the mid-1930s as creating the social work trinity:

> Social work practice had evolved into specializations: social casework, social group work, and community organization. Each drew on different theories. Community organization was related clearly enough to the organizational frameworks within which social casework was practiced to make the relationship practical even though it was not compatible philosophically and theoretically. Social group work began with a philosophical concern for social improvement and moral uplift of disadvantaged people. However, social casework focused on individual causes of problems, while social group work concentrated on citizen education for social action and social development. (p. 36)

Thus, these three major modalities of practice, each defined by the targeted client (individual, family, group, and community), merged to become the modern-day social work profession.

This creation of a unified profession was consummated in 1955, when seven separate social work organizations—the American Association of Group Workers, the American Association of Medical Social Workers, the American Association of Psychiatric Social Workers, the American Association of Social Workers, the National Association of School Social Workers, the Social Work Research Group, and the Association for the Study of Community Organizations—united to form a common professional organization, the National Association of Social Workers (NASW). While sharing a code of ethics, a value system, knowledge, and skills, social workers still differentiated themselves into groups by methodology, describing themselves as caseworkers, group workers, or community organizers.

For the caseworkers, the "friendship" of the friendly visitors became the "relationship" of the clinician with the client. The strong influence of psychoanalytic theory was evident at schools of social work, and with few exceptions, the diagnostic model of medicine—the three-phase process of study, diagnosis, and treatment—was seen as a model of professionalism worthy of emulation.

In more recent years, the three modalities of practice have been subsumed under two more general categories. Casework, family work, and group work are often combined into "micro-" or "clinical" practice. Community organization practice has become more closely linked to policy and management-oriented social work in a "macro" subgrouping. A trend toward the deemphasis of specialization has led to the wider use of the term **generalist practice**, which has come to describe a social work practitioner whose knowledge and skills encompass a broad spectrum and who assesses problems and their solutions comprehensively. The term **generic social work** is often used interchangeably with *generalist practice,* although the former refers more specifically to the social work orientation that emphasizes a common core of knowledge and skills associated with social service provision.

This historical review presents an oversimplified description of the development of the social work profession. For our purposes, the main point is that the profession is the product of a unique merger of interest in individual healing and social change for social justice. This is the basis for what will be presented as the "two-client" idea, which is central to the interactional model of social work. In the complex interaction between the individual and her or his social surroundings (such as society, community, family, small group), the social work professional will always be identifiable because of her or his attention to both clients. While common values, knowledge, beliefs, skills, professional associations, codes of ethics, and so on help to unify the profession, it is the shared sense of social workers' function in society that makes their profession unique.

The Function of the Social Work Profession

In developing his view of the social work profession's function in society, Schwartz (1961) did not accept the broadly held idea that the profession was defined solely by a base of shared knowledge, values, and skills. He also rejected the notion that one could describe the profession's function solely in terms of aspirations for positive general outcomes, such as "enhancing social functioning" or "facilitating individual growth and development." He understood that a profession required a general and yet unique functional statement that would direct the actions of all social workers regardless of the setting in which they practiced. While many variant elements of practice would be introduced by the particular problems facing the client, the mission of the agency or host setting, the modality of service (such as individual, group, or family counseling), the age and stage of life of the client, and so forth, Schwartz viewed professional function as a core element of any social work practice theory.

Function is defined here as the specific part the profession that each social work professional plays in the helping process. To understand the term better, consider how an automobile engine might work if all the parts were like people. If we defined the function of the carburetor as "helping to make the car move," we would be defining function in terms of outcome. This would not provide specific direction to the carburetor, which would be left on its own to figure out how to play its part in the process. On the other hand, if we specifically defined the carburetor's function as mixing air and gasoline to create a vapor that could then be ignited by a spark plug, our anthropomorphic carburetor would have a clear idea of how to do its part. If all parts of the engine understood clearly their functional roles, and if all parts implemented that role effectively, the car would start to move.

This kind of functional preciseness is what Schwartz felt every social worker needed in order to understand his or her role in the many complex situations faced in everyday practice. This professional role would travel with the social worker to any agency or host setting and would, in part, define the social worker's interventions at any given moment. We would be able to recognize a social worker in action, and distinguish him or her from other professionals with similar knowledge, values, and skills, because we would see the functional role in action. Schwartz's definition of the function of the social work profession was based on the earlier described underlying assumptions about the essentially symbiotic nature of the individual-social relationship. He examined the history of the profession and tried to identify the essential functional assignment that might define a unique role for social work.

His definition of the professional function is "to mediate the process through which the individual and his society reach out for each other through a mutual need for self-fulfillment." To the earlier diagram of a hypothetical client attempting to deal with several important systems, a third force is introduced (see Figure 1.2).

With the addition of the worker, the basic triangular model is complete. On the left is the client reaching out with all available strength, attempting to negotiate important systems while often simultaneously throwing up defenses that cut him or her off from the needed systems. On the right are the systems reaching out to incorporate the client but often reaching ambivalently. At the bottom is the social worker, whose sense of function and skills are mobilized in an effort to help client and system overcome the obstacles that block their engagement.

One could argue that this functional statement is too limited. I have already indicated that the term *mediation* is used in a broad sense and can include other activities such as confrontation and advocacy. There are times when the crucial work in the area between the helping person and the system requires conflict and social pressure. In one example, the social worker helps a tenant group confront the political system because of the unresponsiveness of the housing project administrator (see Chapter 16).

Even with a broad interpretation of mediation, one might still argue that this functional statement is too limited. However, if the helping person is clear about the helping function and that function is specifically defined, then the chance of consistently

FIGURE 1.2

Relationship of Client, Systems, and Worker

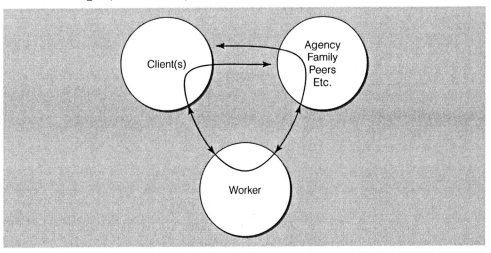

performing it improves. Jessie Taft (1942), one of the early leaders of the functional school of social work practice, stressed this view. In addition, the client who understands what the helping person does—the way in which help is given—will be better able to use the worker's services.

Couple's counseling provides a good illustration. The division between the given couple has caused most people they know (family, friends, coworkers) to take sides with one or the other. An early, often unstated question on the minds of both partners as they enter the counseling process is "Whose side will the social worker be on?" Only through explanation and demonstration can the skillful worker help the couple understand that the worker must be on both sides at the same time in order to help them. Practice experience has taught most workers that the moment they identify with one side versus the other, they have lost their usefulness to the client who feels cut off.

Clarity about one's professional function and role in the helping process is essential for effective practice. When a social worker is clear about his or her part in the interaction, the worker will be less likely to take over the client's part—for example, doing things for the client instead of with the client. Once a social worker has integrated a sense of professional function, then the communications, relationship, and problem-solving skills become the tools through which the social worker puts her or his function into action. I have long believed that most students and new practitioners already have many of the basic human relations skills needed to be helpful. Once they have integrated a clear sense of their general function as social workers, and the specific way it emerges in a particular setting with a particular client, in a particular modality of practice, then developing more sophisticated skills will follow. Clearly knowing one's role, then, matters a great deal; beginning workers can do well from the start with a clear purpose in mind.

Again, a profession is differentiated from other professions by its functional role, not by its knowledge, values, and skills. For example, in a hospital, empathy skills are important for the social worker, the doctor, and the nurse. Each professional must harness these skills in pursuit of his or her separate functions. In the scores of examples included in this book, you will see that social workers often get in trouble in their practice when they lose their sense of functional clarity. For example, you will see incidents in family work in which the social worker identifies with the children and loses the parents. Such a worker can no longer help the family work on its issues. In another example, a new worker who claims he has "solved" the client's problem by taking him to church on Sunday may once again be unclear about the role. One might see ongoing professional development as a continual deepening of the social worker's understanding of the helping function as well as a developing understanding of those situations that may lead to functional confusion and diffusion. *Functional diffusion* occurs when the social worker tries to be everything for everyone, losing sight of the core job. This is not a terminal illness, however, and is usually cured by a dose of functional clarity.

At this point, you may be wondering how generally applicable this mediation assignment can be. In the rest of the book, we shall work toward the answer, drawing illustrations from a range of settings with varying types of individuals, families, groups, and communities. In each example, you should mentally step into the shoes of the worker. The argument is that the worker's sense of the next step at specific moments of interaction will be vitally affected by an internalized sense of function.

These introductory comments have laid out the general model applied in each step of analysis throughout the book. A further elaboration of this function and worker tasks will be shared in the context of practice illustrations.

Social Work Skill and the Working Relationship

At the core of the interactional theory of social work practice is a model of the helping process in which the skill of the worker helps to create a positive working relationship. In turn, this relationship is the medium through which the worker influences the outcomes of practice. This simple model can be visualized as in Figure 1.3.

While the model suggests that applied skill leads to relationship, which then influences outcomes, the double-pointed arrows imply that the model is dynamic. For example, a change in the working relationship will affect the worker's use of skill. A worker may be influenced in her or his interaction with a client by the changing nature of the relationship (for example, a positive relationship leading to more empathy on the worker's part). Similarly, positive or negative outcomes for the client may influence his or her sense of the relationship.

Another model incorporated into this theory has to do with the relationship between clients' ability to manage their feelings and their ability to manage their problems. These ideas were developed as part of the theory-building effort I have described in other publications (Shulman, 1978, 1981, 1991). The construct is based on the assumption that how we feel powerfully affects how we act. The relationship between feelings and action is reciprocal: How we act also influences how we feel.

To this feeling-behavioral connection we can add a third element: cognition. *Cognition* refers to the way clients think about themselves and their environment. The contributions of cognitive-behavioral theory (Berlin, 1983) have helped us to broaden our understanding of how a client's perception of reality can have a powerful impact on self-image, identification of the nature of a problem, and self-assessment of the ability to cope. I argue throughout this book that how clients think affects how they feel, which affects how they act, in a circular and reciprocal manner. The model presented could be termed a cognitive-affective-behavioral framework without confusing it with other models that incorporate cognitive-behavioral approaches.

For example, some female survivors of childhood sexual abuse describe themselves as "damaged goods" as they enter their teenage years. These clients may respond to the oppression they have experienced by internalizing a negative self-image and assuming some form of responsibility for what was done to them. They may express feelings of guilt and concern that they may have been seductive toward the offending adult, thus shifting responsibility for the problem to themselves—a form of self-blaming the victim. This is an example of the internalized oppressor at work. Symptoms of depression and personal apathy often cover an underlying rage that the child learned to suppress in order to survive. The use of alcohol and drugs provides an escape, a flight from the pain associated with the abuse, and is an

FIGURE 1.3

Worker Skill and the Working Relationship

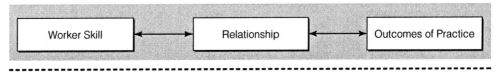

example of the self-destructive behavior, described earlier, in which oppressed clients become autopressors.

The association between these perceptions of low self-image and the feelings (such as shame) that they can generate may lead these teenage survivors to enter into relationships and life patterns that perpetuate their exploitation. For example, a low sense of self-esteem may lead to relationships with exploitive men who use physical, emotional, and sexual violence to maintain control over the lives of women. The use of drugs and involvement in the street culture may lead to prostitution. These actions on the client's part, related to the client's feelings, may in turn deepen the sense of being "damaged." Thus, negative reciprocal relationships among how the client feels, thinks, and acts result in a deepening of the problems in living. Of course for many survivors, protective factors, described later in this chapter, may mitigate the impact of the abuse on their lives.

An intervention is needed to disrupt this vicious cycle. In the example of the survivor, as the worker helps the client to examine the underlying pain and rage, and to face the oppressor within, the client can begin to take control of the emotions and more effectively manage them rather than being managed by them. Effective practice can help the client reframe the source of the problem and begin to perceive herself as a survivor rather than a victim. Techniques associated with solution-focused practice, also described later in this chapter, can also help the client see his or her strengths and begin the healing process. The principle of dealing with feelings in pursuit of purpose, discussed further in later chapters, will cause the worker to help the client connect her feelings and perceptions with her actions. Being aware of the connections between how we think, feel, and act is an early step in taking control over these thoughts and feelings and over our resultant behaviors. As the client better manages these feelings and develops a more accurate assessment of herself and her situation, she can begin to manage her life problems more effectively. Success with her life's problems, in turn, will influence her thoughts and feelings.

For example, the teenage survivor in this illustration may begin to change her self-destructive behavior by taking some first step on her own behalf. Obtaining help with her addiction, leaving the streets for a shelter, or attempting to break off from an abusive and exploitive relationship may be the first step in breaking out of her trap. Each step that she takes in her own self-interest, however small, can contribute to a more positive feeling about her self and strengthen her to take the next step. Thus, managing her feelings helps her to manage her problems, and managing her problems helps her to manage her feelings.

As this model is explored, we shall see that if the worker is to help clients manage their feelings, the worker must be able to manage his or her own emotions. For example, feeling the client's pain, a worker who is helping a survivor of sexual abuse may prematurely attempt to reassure her that she is not damaged. Or the worker may take on the woman's anger against the men who have exploited her, which may preempt the client's essential work in facing her own anger. Both of these understandable emotional reactions by the worker may block the client's ability to manage her own feelings. The worker would need to share his or her sense of the client's pain without trying to relieve it. For example,

> As I listen to you I'm feeling how much pain you are in, how damaged you must feel. A big part of me wants to say, "Don't feel that way! You are a person of value." But I know that no matter what I say the pain is there, and I can't make it go away.

The anger against the exploitive men—for example, a sexually abusive father—can also be shared, but in a manner that helps the client face her own anger rather than doing the work for her. For example,

> It makes me angry when I think of what was done to you by people you expected to take care of you and to protect you. But from what you are saying to me, it seems that your feelings are mixed right now. It sounds like a big part of you wishes your family could be different, could change, and that you could still be like a real family.

Sharing the worker's feelings, in an integration of personal and professional selves, is a crucial element in this model.

The eight skills examined in my study (Shulman, 1991) were drawn from those that proved to be most important in my prior research (1979b, 1978). Twenty-two specific skills were examined in the earlier research, with 10 of the 22 associating at a significant level with developing a positive relationship and worker helpfulness. While all of these skills and others are discussed in the chapters that follow, a particular emphasis is placed on the eight skills examined in the more recent work. (For a clearer understanding of methodology, findings, and limitations, review a more detailed outline of this research in Appendix A on the book's companion page on the Wadsworth website.) These eight skills have been organized into two groupings. The following list summarizes the two sets of skills:

Workers' Skills for Helping Clients Manage Their Feelings

Reaching inside of silences

Putting the client's feelings into words

Displaying understanding of the client's feelings

Sharing the worker's feelings

Workers' Skills for Helping Clients Manage Their Problems

Clarifying the worker's purpose and role

Reaching for client feedback

Partializing concerns

Supporting clients in taboo areas

All of these skills are important in all phases of practice. However, each skill may have various meanings or impacts at different stages in the relationship. Because the helping process is so complex, it helps to analyze it against the backdrop of the phases of work. The four phases of work described in this book are as follows:

- Preliminary (or Preparatory) Phase
- Beginning (or Contracting) Phase
- Middle (or Work) Phase
- Ending and Transition Phase

Each phase of work—preliminary, beginning, middle, and ending-transition—has unique dynamics and requires specific skills. Jessie Taft (1949), referring to the beginning, middle, and ending phases, was one of the first to draw attention to the effect of time on social work practice. Schwartz (1971) incorporated this dimension into his work, adding the preliminary phase and modifying the ending phase to the "ending and transition" phase. The **preliminary (or preparatory) phase** is the period prior to the first encounter with the client. The **beginning (or contracting) phase** refers to the first sessions in which the worker develops a working contract with the client and begins developing the working relationship. The **middle (or work) phase** is the period in which the work is done. Finally, in the **ending and transition phase,** the worker prepares the client to bring the relationship to an end and to make transitions to new experiences.

Another way of thinking about these phases is that the client (individual, family, group, or community) must make a first decision in the beginning phase about whether or not to face the problems and engage with the worker. Even mandatory clients (such as child welfare or probation) must make that decision in order for the work to be effective. The second decision comes as the client makes the transition to the middle phase and decides to deal with the more difficult and often painful issues. The third decision is made by the client as she or he prepares for the termination of the relationship and, in a manner often described as "doorknob therapy," raises the most powerful and difficult issues of the work. These processes are identified in the balance of this book using examples of micro- (clinical) and macropractice.

We begin the exploration of these constructs in Chapter 2, which focuses on the preliminary phase of practice in work with individuals. The phases of work serve as an organizing principle for the rest of the book as well.

The Integration of Personal and Professional Selves

In the history of social work, another carryover from the medical model was the importance placed on maintaining one's professional self. Most helping professions stressed the professional role and the need to suppress personal feelings and reactions. For example, in order to work with stressful patients, one might have to keep one's real reactions in check so as to avoid appearing judgmental. A professional worker was described as one who maintained control of emotions and would not become angry or too emotionally involved, would not cry in the presence of a client, and so forth. The injunction to the worker appeared to be "Take your professional self to work and leave your personal self at home." This image of professionalism was (and still is) widely held, with many of my social work students starting their careers wondering if they would have problems becoming a social worker because they "felt too much."

The practice model presented in this text will suggest that we are faced with a false dichotomy when we believe we must choose between our personal self and our professional self. In fact, I will argue that we are at our best in our work when we are able to synthesize the two by integrating our personal self into our professional role.

The conflict of views about what defines the professional self was brought home dramatically in a workshop I led on direct practice. One pediatric oncology social worker described an incident in which a mother appeared at her door after being referred by the attending physician. The mother had just been told that her 7-year-old daughter had a terminal illness. After explaining this to the social worker, the mother broke down and cried.

When I asked the worker what she did, she described how overwhelmed she felt by the mother's grief. All that the worker could do was sit and hold the mother's hand, softly crying with her. I maintain that while there would be much work to be done in this case (such as helping the mother to deal with the dying daughter and her family over the next few months), at this point what the mother needed most was not advice but someone to be with her. In fact, as the worker partially experienced the mother's pain, and shared it with her through her own tears, she was giving that client an important gift of her own feelings. The worker was being professional in the best sense of that word. Other workers, who might not cry with a client, might make the same gift in other ways—through facial expressions, a respectful silence, or a hand on the shoulder—each worker responding in a way consistent with his or her own personality. The crucial factor would be the worker's willingness to be honest and to share his or her own feelings.

In my example, the worker continued her story by telling us that her supervisor passed the open door, called her out, and berated her for unprofessional behavior. The supervisor said, "How could you let yourself break down that way? You can't help your clients if you become overwhelmed yourself." When I asked the worker what she took from the experience, she replied, "I learned to keep my door closed."

While many who hear that story are upset with the supervisor, I am not. I realize that she may have been trained, as I was, in a time when personal expressions of emotion were considered to be unprofessional. I encouraged the social worker to talk to her supervisor, because I felt it was crucial for her to obtain support from her supervisor and colleagues if she was to continue to provide this kind of help to clients. My research (Shulman, 1979b) has emphasized the importance of formal and informal sources of social support for social workers. This worker was making a gift to the client of her willingness to "be with" her at a terrible moment in her life. The worker's capacity to continue to be there for the client depends somewhat on her having someone—supervisor, colleague, or both—there for her.

This artificial split between personal and professional selves was created because of the profession's understandable concerns over the inappropriate use of self by helping professionals. For example, concern arose about *countertransference,* a process in which workers might project onto clients their own unfinished family business (relating to a father in a family as if he were one's own parent, for instance). The profession was troubled by workers who used the argument of spontaneity to justify acting out with clients, such as getting inappropriately angry or judgmental or sharing personal problems ("If you think you have troubles with your kids, let me tell you about my family"). Unethical behavior with clients, such as abusing the powerful forces of the helping bond to sexually exploit a vulnerable client, is another example. Each of these examples illustrates a lack of integration of personal and professional selves. The concerns about the use of the personal self were and continue to be well founded. Unfortunately, the solution to separate personal from professional led to more problems than it resolved.

The argument advanced throughout this text will be that each of us brings our own personal style, artistry, background, feelings, values, and beliefs to our professional practice. Rather than denying or suppressing these, we need to learn more about ourselves in the context of our practice, and find ways to use our self in pursuit of our professional functions. We will make many mistakes along the way, saying things we will later regret, having to apologize to clients, then learning from these mistakes, correcting them, and then making what I call more sophisticated mistakes.

In other words, we will be real people carrying out difficult jobs as best we can, rather than paragons of virtue who present an image of perfection.

As we demonstrate to our clients our humanness, vulnerability, willingness to risk, spontaneity, honesty, and lack of defensiveness (or defensiveness for which we later apologize), we shall be modeling the very behaviors we hope to see in our clients. Thus, when workers or students ask me, "Should I be professional or should I be myself?" I reply that the dualism implied in the question does not exist. They must be themselves if they are going to be professional. Fortunately, we have the whole of our professional lives to learn how to affect the synthesis.

Oppression Psychology

Social workers need to draw on the social sciences and the large theory and knowledge base about human development, behavior, and the impact of the social environment. This theory base can help the practitioner understand the client in new ways and to hear underlying client communication that might otherwise be missed.

As one example of a theory that can guide social work practice, I have selected the **oppression psychology** of Frantz Fanon. A brief introduction to the life, views, and psychology of Fanon will help to set the stage for the use of his central ideas and those of others who have built on his work. Fanon, an early exponent of the psychology of oppression, was a black, West Indian revolutionary psychiatrist who was born on the French-colonized island of Martinique in 1925 and who died at age 36. His short life was chronicled by Bulhan (1985). At age 17, Fanon enlisted in the French army to fight against the Nazis in World War II. He later became interested in and studied psychiatry. While working as a chief of service at a psychiatric hospital in Algeria, he secretly provided support and medical services to the national liberation front (FLN) fighting against the French colonial government. When he resigned his position, he became a spokesperson for the FLN and was based in Tunisia. These experiences and others shaped his views of psychology, which challenged many of the constructs of the widely held, European American, white, male-dominated psychology of the day. Bulhan states,

> In the first chapter of his classic *The Wretched of the Earth* (Fanon, 1968), Fanon elaborated the dynamics of violence and the human drama that unfolds in situations of oppression. He boldly analyzed violence in its structural, institutional, and personal dimensions.
>
> Fanon analyzed the psycho-existential aspects of life in a racist society. He emphasized the experiential features and hidden psycho-affective injuries of blacks and the various defensive maneuvers they adopted. Another unstated objective was quite personal: He himself had experienced these injuries, and writing about them was a way of coming to terms with himself. (p. 138)

While Fanon's psychology emerged from his analysis of race oppression, particularly oppression associated with white, European colonial repression of people of color, many of the key concepts apply to any oppressed population. In such an application, workers need to recognize the significant differences in degree and types of oppression experienced by clients. The results of the oppression of African

Americans, for example, rooted in the unique experience of slavery, must be seen as one of the most critical, major social problems still facing urban areas in the United States.

In addition, we must be cautious in how we think about the impact of oppression, because we might inadvertently ignore the significant strengths and resiliency demonstrated by oppressed clients and communities. Such a one-sided view can lead to a practice that does not recognize or work with existing sources of support (such as the extended family, the church, community leadership). The next section of this chapter complements this oppression model with a summary of a resiliency model that helps uncover clients' strengths for coping.

If social workers think about issues of oppression, vulnerability, and resiliency broadly, then they can use such a model in understanding many of their clients. People with mental illness, female survivors of sexual abuse, people with AIDS, people with significant physical or mental disabilities, long-term unemployed people, people of color, the homeless, aged nursing home residents, neglected and abused children, clients addicted to substances or in recovery—all of these clients and others can be understood using a framework that takes oppression, vulnerability, and resiliency into account.

These concepts will be illustrated in the examples of practice explored in this book. Strategies for social worker intervention, based on understanding emerging from this psychology, will be directed toward helping clients deal with both the oppressor within and the oppressor without. In fact, it will be argued that unless they broaden their understanding of many of their clients' problems by seeing them as dynamic and systematic in nature and related to oppression, then the social agencies, social work departments, and helping professionals who are trying to help these clients can themselves inadvertently become part of the system of oppression.

The Master-Slave Paradigm

We have already noted the influence of Hegel's (Hegel, 1966) formulation of the master-slave dialectic, which described relationships in which two people, each depending on recognition of the self by the other, struggle to determine a hierarchy. The winner of the struggle (the master) is recognized by the loser (the slave) without having to reciprocate the recognition. While the complete exposition of the dialectic is more complex than presented here, the central idea of gaining one's sense of self through exploitation of others can be seen in many different oppressive relationships. The abusing parent and the abused child, the battering husband and his wife, societal male-female sexism, the scapegoating of religious groups (such as Muslims and Jews) and ethnic and racial groups (such as Southeast Asian immigrants, Hispanics, African Americans, Native Americans), the treatment of people with physical or mentally disabilities, the "normal" population and people who are mentally ill, and the straight society's repression of homosexuals—all are examples in which one group (usually the majority) uses another group for enhancing a sense of self.

Repeated exposure to oppression, subtle or direct, may lead vulnerable members of the oppressed group to internalize the negative self-images projected by the external oppressor—the "oppressor without." The external oppressor may be an individual (such as the sexual abuser of a child) or an aspect of society (such as the racial stereotypes perpetuated against people of color). Internalization of this image and repression of the rage associated with oppression may lead to destructive behaviors toward oneself and others as oppressed people become autopressors participating in their own oppression. Thus, the oppressor without becomes the oppressor within. Evidence of this process can be found in the maladaptive use of addictive substances and the growing internal violence in communities of oppressed people, such as city ghettos populated by people of color.

Oppressed people may develop a victim complex, "viewing all actions and communications as further assaults or simply other indications of their victim status. This is an example of 'adaptive paranoia' seen among the oppressed" (Bulhan, 1985, p. 126). The paranoia is adaptive because oppression is so omnipresent that it would be maladaptive not to be constantly alert to its presence. For the white worker with a client of color, the male worker with a female client, the straight worker with a gay or lesbian client, and so forth, this notion raises important implications for the establishment of an effective and trusting working relationship. These implications are explored in later chapters dealing with the dynamics and skills involved in developing a positive working relationship between worker and client.

Indicators of Oppression

Bulhan (1985) identifies several key indicators for objectively assessing oppression. He suggests that "all situations of oppression violate one's space, time, energy, mobility, bonding, and identity" (p. 124). He illustrates these indicators using the example of the slave:

> The male slave was allowed no physical space which he could call his own. The female slave had even less claim to space than the male slave. Even her body was someone else's property. Commonly ignored is how this expropriation of one's body entailed even more dire consequences for female slaves. The waking hours of the slave were also expropriated for life without his or her consent. The slave labored in the field and in the kitchen for the gain and comfort of the master. The slave's mobility was curbed and he or she was never permitted to venture beyond a designated perimeter without a "pass." The slave's bonding with others, even the natural relation between mother and child, was violated and eroded. The same violation of space, time, energy, mobility, bonding and identity prevailed under apartheid, which in effect, is modern-day slavery." (p. 124)

The model of a slave is an extreme example of the violation of space, time, energy, mobility, bonding, and identity as indicators of oppression. One can find current examples of these restrictions. Institutionalized racism in North America toward people of color (for example, African Americans, Native Americans) currently offers examples of restrictions on all six indicators. Not long ago, as Bulhan's comments attest, an oppressive, white government dominated South Africa through apartheid.

While the slavery experience of African Americans in North America must be considered as a unique example of oppression, the indicators may be used to assess degrees of oppression for other populations as well. In this way, a universal psychological model can help us to understand the common elements that exist in any oppressive relationship. Consider these six indicators as you read the following excerpt of a discussion among battered women in a shelter, as they describe their lives:

> Candy said one thing that she didn't like was that her husband had to be number one all the time. He felt he should come first even before the children. She said, "The man's got to be number one. Just like the president.

He's a man and he's number one. You don't see no female presidents, do you?" I said, "Are you saying that a man has the right to abuse his partner?" She said no and then turned to the women to say, "But, who's the one who always gives in in the family? The woman does." All the women nodded to this remark. Linda said, "To keep peace in the family." Candy said, "In the long run, we're the ones who are wrong for not leaving the abusive situations." She said she finally came to the realization that her man was never going to be of any help to her. In the long run, she felt that her children would help her out if she gave them a good life now. She feels very strongly about her responsibilities to her children.

Another woman, Tina, said that when she called the police for help, they thought it was a big joke. She said when she had to fill out a report at the police station, the officer laughed about the incident. The women in the group talked about their own experiences with the police which were not very good. One woman had to wait 35 minutes for the police to respond to her call after her husband had thrown a brick through her bedroom window. I said, "Dealing with the police must have been a humiliating situation for all of you. Here you are in need of help and they laugh at you. It's just not right."

Joyce said that she wanted to kill her husband. This desire had been expressed by an abused woman in a previous group session. Other women in the group said it wouldn't be worth it for her. "All he does is yell at me all the time. He makes me go down to where he works every day at lunch time. The kids and I have to sit and watch him eat. He never buys us anything to eat. Plus, he wants to know where I am every minute of the day. He implies that I sit around the house all day long doing nothing." Marie said her ex-husband used to say that to her all the time. She said, "But now I'm collecting back pay from my divorce settlement for all the work I never did around the house."

Then Joyce said she was going to tell us something that she had only told two other people in her life. Joyce said that she had been molested from the ages of 5 to 7 by her next-door neighbor, Pat. She said that Pat was friendly with her parents. Her mother would say, "Bring a glass of lemonade over to Pat." The first time she did this, he molested her. After that incident, when her mother told her to bring something over to Pat, Joyce would try to get out of it, but her mother insisted that she go over. Pat had told Joyce not to tell anyone what went on. At this point in the session, Joyce began to cry. I said that I understood this was a difficult situation for her to talk about. Candy said, "Joyce, it wasn't your fault." Joyce said she had kept this incident to herself for approximately 25 years. Finally, when she told her husband, he said, "You probably deserved it." Joyce said she felt like killing him for saying that.

Candy said she watched while her father beat her mother. She said she used to ask her mother why she put up with it. She said now she sees that it's easier to say you want to get out of a relationship than it is to actually do it. Candy said that leaving was better in the long run. By staying, the children will see their father abusing their mother. "What kind of example is that going to set for the children?" She felt her children would be happier by their leaving. Joyce said her children were happy to leave their father. She said, "They're tired of listening to him yell all the time." She said her son was more upset about leaving the dog behind than he was about leaving his father. Linda said another good reason for leaving is self-love. She said, "It comes to a point where you know he's going to kill you if you stay around."

Careful reading of the preceding excerpt provides examples of the violation of these women's space, time, energy, mobility, bonding, and identity—the six identified indicators of oppression. Other examples with differing numbers of indicators violated, and different degrees of violation, could include an inpatient in a rigidly structured psychiatric setting; a wheelchair-bound person constantly facing buildings that are not accessible; an African American woman who is the only person of her race in an organization and who is held back from advancement by the "glass ceiling" and excluded from the "old boys' network"; an unemployed, 55-year-old man who cannot get a job interview because of his age; an elderly person in a home for the aged who is tied to a chair or tranquilized all day because of staff shortages; a large, poor family, forced to live in inadequate housing, a homeless shelter, or on the street. To one degree or another, space, time, energy, mobility, bonding, and identity may be violated for each of these clients.

Alienation and Psychopathology

Bulhan believes that Fanon's complete work suggests five aspects of alienation associated with the development of "psychopathology." *Alienation* is a term commonly used in psychology and sociology to describe a state of withdrawal or estrangement. Fanon's five aspects of alienation are

- Alienation from the self
- Alienation from the significant other
- Alienation from the general other
- Alienation from one's culture
- Alienation from creative social praxis

Fanon's work emphasized alienation from the self and from one's culture. These were the inevitable results of prolonged oppression and the "deracination" (uprooting) of people of color by the oppressor. The destruction of the culture, such as the forced use of another language, is an assault on the oppressed person's sense of self, which is already alienated by the internalization of the negative self-image. Alienation from the general other refers to the estrangement between the oppressed group and the oppressor, such as the majority group. Significant others include family, friends, neighbors, and so forth. The creative social praxis refers to organized activities of society, such as employment.

An example illustrating wide-scale oppression and these five aspects of alienation can be found in the experience of Native American groups in the United States and Canada. These "first peoples" were displaced by the immigration of European, white settlers; eventually forced off their traditional lands; resettled on reservations; and cut off from their traditional forms of activity, such as hunting and fishing. Efforts on the part of Native people to fight back were met with brutal repression. During one period in U.S. history, their children were removed from their families and sent to white boarding schools. Native children in many of these boarding schools report being told to "speak white" and punished for using their native language. More recent shocking revelations have indicated that in some schools many of these children suffered physical and sexual abuse by staff and administrators.

Even social welfare services, such as those designed to protect children, participated in the alienation process by removing Native children whom they saw as neglected or abused (by certain white, middle-class, cultural standards) and then placing these children in white foster or adoptive homes. This was often done without first making a serious effort to use the formal and informal support system that existed in the Native American community. The results of these assaults on a whole people, and the resultant alienation, can be seen in high levels of family violence, alcohol addiction, and suicide among some groups of Native Americans. The alienation is reversible, however, and significant progress has been made by Native people in opposing and changing many of the oppressive influences on their culture. For example, in British Columbia, Canada, several bands (tribal subgroups) take full responsibility for child welfare services and have maximized the use of native resources for children in need. An emphasis on traditional values and a reintroduction of traditional ceremonies and events, such as the potlatch, a large-scale meeting and celebration that is attended by different bands within a tribe and that includes healing circles, have served as important vehicles for reversing the alienation process.

In working with clients who are members of groups that have experienced long-term oppression, workers must understand the potential impact of alienation as an underlying cause of and contributor to the current problems. Cultural awareness on the part of the social worker can make a major difference in developing intervention approaches that use the strengths of the culture to decrease the alienation. Examples of this approach to practice can be found in the chapters that follow.

Methods of Defense Against Oppression

A final element of the oppression psychology theory concerns methods of defense used by oppressed people. Bulhan (1985) summarizes these as follows:

> In brief, under conditions of prolonged oppression, there are three major modes of psychological defense and identity development among the oppressed. The first involves a pattern of compromise, the second flight, and the third fight. Each mode has profound implications for the development of identity, experience of psychopathology, reconstituting of the self, and relationship to other people. Each represents a mode of existence and of action in a world in which a hostile other elicits organic reactions and responses. Each also entails its own distinct risks of alienation and social rewards under conditions of oppression. (p. 193)

Bulhan sees these modes of defense as implemented in stages, although it is possible for individuals and whole groups to be stuck in a stage or take decades for a transition to take place to a new stage. The first stage involves capitulation, in which the oppressed people identify with the oppressor without and assimilate into the majority culture. This is associated with a rejection of one's own culture—the alienation mentioned earlier. The second stage, which he calls revitalization, involves a rejection of the dominant culture and a "defensive romanticism of the indigenous culture" (1985, p. 193). The third stage, in which a clear commitment toward radical change is made, is termed the radicalization stage. Individuals and whole populations can move with a different timing through these stages, and some may become fixed in one or the other. For an individual or a group, whatever stage is in effect will have a profound effect on all aspects of alienation as well as on the mode of reaction of the dominant culture.

While the model just described is most directly related to issues of cultural identity, a wider model of defensive reactions to oppression can be understood when one applies certain elements to cases. Examples in the chapters that follow will illustrate how oppression can lead to capitulation, resulting in symptoms that are then viewed as pathological. In one illustration, a group of survivors of childhood sexual abuse describes the pattern of capitulation that led to their loss of self-identity and their identity as women. The resultant internalizing of the belief that they are "damaged goods," as well as their willingness to feel guilty about what was done to them, profoundly affects their current lives and relationships. A revitalization of their selves and their sense of their identity as women can be seen developing, enhanced by the social support of the group. Finally, a form of radicalization is noted when the group decides to join a "Take Back the Night" march in the community, protesting actively against violence toward women. This leads to their making a commitment to work toward changing community understanding and attitudes toward children who have been sexually abused.

This brief summary of some central ideas in oppression psychology theory sets the stage for the use of these constructs in later chapters. Although there are many other models that can help workers understand their clients and develop effective intervention strategies, it is a very useful model for thinking about work with oppressed and vulnerable populations, which makes up a large part of the social worker's practice. As we consider the impact of oppression, we must also understand the elements of resilience that help individuals, families, communities, and entire population groups survive and often thrive in the face of adversity.

Resilience Theory

During the 1970s and 1980s, developmental research focused on risk factors that appeared to be associated with negative outcomes for clients. A child growing up in an inner-city neighborhood besieged by drugs and violence faced a degree of risk in attempting to negotiate the passage to young adulthood and beyond. If the same child also had experienced childhood trauma (physical or sexual abuse, abandonment, and so on) and had parents and family members who were active abusers of drugs and alcohol, research indicated that the degree of risk for the child's negative developmental outcome increased exponentially.

Yet, a recurring anomaly in social work practice experience and literature indicated that not all children exposed to high degrees of risk and trauma had negative developmental outcomes. As Butler (1997), examining the "anatomy of resilience," pointed out,

> A growing number of clinicians and researchers were arguing that the risk-factor model burdens at-risk children with the expectation that they will fail, and ignores those who beat the odds. Broad epidemiological studies, they say, don't explain why one girl, sexually abused by a relative, becomes an unwed mother or a prostitute while another becomes an Oprah Winfrey or a Maya Angelou. Retrospective studies can't explain why one man, raised in a harsh, crowded household in impoverished Richmond, California, becomes addicted to crack cocaine and dies of AIDS, while his younger brother—Christopher Darden—graduates from law school, and goes on to prosecute O. J. Simpson. It's time, they say, to see what the Dardens and Winfreys of the world have to teach. (p. 25)

Given the widespread nature of substance abuse, the evidence of substantial emotional, physical, and sexual abuse, the increase in the nature and degree of violence in many communities, and the growing numbers of children living in poverty, it is little wonder that research shifted toward understanding why some children, families, and communities can still thrive under these conditions, given the risks that they face. This focus lends itself to the development of both preventative and curative approaches to clients at risk.

Rak and Patterson (1996, p. 369) identified four major groupings of protective factors associated with the "buffering hypothesis": that is, variables that may provide a buffer of protection against life events that affect at-risk children:

1. The personal characteristics of the children (e.g., an ability from infancy on to gain others' positive attention)
2. Family conditions (e.g., focused nurturing during the first year of life and little prolonged separation from the preliminary caretaker)
3. Supports in the environment (e.g., role models, such as teachers, school counselors, mental health workers, neighbors, and clergy)
4. Self-concept factors (e.g., the capacity to understand self and self-boundaries in relation to long-term family stressors such as psychological illness)

Garmezy, Masten, and Tellegen (1984) suggested three models for understanding the relationship among risk, vulnerability, and resilience. These were the compensatory model, in which protective factors simply outweigh risk factors; a challenge model suggesting that limited risk factors enhance competency; and the conditional model, which focuses on personal factors that increase or decrease the impact of the risk factors.

Masten (2001) reviewed the existing resilience models and research and identified two major streams of thought. One is the variable-focused study, which suggests that parenting qualities, intellectual functioning, socioeconomic class, and so forth correlate with positive adaptive behavior. The second line of inquiry is the person-focused study, which tries to understand the whole individual rather than specific variables. Researchers using this latter approach seek to identify groups of individuals with patterns of good versus poor adaptive functioning in life contexts of high versus low risks and then compare outcomes. After reviewing studies using both approaches, Masten drew the following conclusions:

> The accumulated data on resilience in development suggest that this class of phenomena is more ordinary than one was led to expect by extraordinary case histories that often inspired the study. Resilience appears to be a common phenomenon arising from ordinary human adaptive processes. The great threats to human development are those that jeopardize the systems underlying these adaptive processes, including brain development and cognition, caregiver-child relationships, regulation of emotion and behavior, and the motivation for learning and engaging the environment. (p. 238)

Developmental Psychology Theory and Research

A landmark study in this area involved 698 infants on the Hawaiian Island of Kauai who, in 1955, became participants in a 30-year, longitudinal study of "how some individuals triumph over physical disadvantages and deprived childhoods" (Werner, 1989, p. 106). Werner described the goals that she and her collaborators shared as follows: "to assess the long-term consequences of prenatal and perinatal stress and to document the effects of adverse early rearing conditions on children's physical, cognitive, and psychosocial development" (p. 106). She described their growing interest in resilience as follows:

> But as our study progressed we began to take a special interest in certain "high risk" children who, in spite of exposure to reproductive stress, discordant and impoverished home lives and uneducated, alcoholic, or mentally disturbed parents, went on to develop healthy personalities, stable careers, and strong interpersonal relations. We decided to try to identify the protective factors that contributed to the resilience of these children. (p. 106)

The researchers identified 201 "vulnerable" children (30 percent of the surviving children) as high-risk if they encountered four or more risk factors by the age of 2 (severe perinatal stress, chronic poverty, uneducated parents, or troubled family environments marked by discord, divorce, parental alcoholism, or mental illness). Two-thirds of this group (129) developed serious learning or behavior problems by the age of 10 or had delinquency records, mental health problems, or pregnancies by the time they were 18.

It was the other third (72) of these high-risk children, who "grew into competent young adults who loved well, worked well, and played well" who attracted the researchers' attention (Werner, 1989, p. 108). They identified several constitutional factors as sources of resilience (high activity level, low degree of excitability and distress, high degrees of sociability, ability to concentrate at school, problem-solving and reading skills, and effective use of their talents, for example). They also identified environmental factors (coming from families with four or fewer children, spaces of two or more years between themselves and their next siblings, the opportunity to establish a close bond with at least one caretaker who provided positive attention during the first years of life, and so forth). These resilient children were found to be "particularly adept at recruiting such surrogate parents when a biological parent was unavailable or incapacitated" (p. 108). These children were also able to use their network of neighbors, school friends and teachers, church groups, and so forth to provide emotional support in order to succeed "against the odds" (p. 110).

The researchers concluded on a hopeful note:

> As long as the balance between stressful life events and protective factors is favorable, successful adaptation is possible. When stressful events outweigh the protective factors, however, even the most resilient child can have problems. It may be possible to shift the balance from vulnerability to resilience through intervention, either by decreasing exposure to risk factors or stressful events or by increasing the number of protective factors and sources of support that are available. (Werner, 1989, p. 111)

Researchers and theorists have built on this basic set of ideas: Life stressors can lead to negative outcomes for people at high risk; however, personal and environmental factors can buffer the individual, providing the resilience to overcome adversity.

For example, Fonagy, Steele, Steele, and Higgitt (1994) examined attachment theory, which focuses on the impact of early infant-caregiver attachments on a child's development and the security of such attachments. They examined the intergenerational transmission of insecure attachments, focusing on factors that might disrupt a negative cycle: in other words, ways to help mothers who had themselves experienced insecure attachments avoid transmitting these to their own children.

Other researchers have applied the basic model to specific populations (as defined by race, ethnicity, and so forth) or economic status (poverty), or community variables (inner-city, level of violence). For example, Daly, Jennings, Beckett, and Leashore (1995) make use an "Africentric paradigm" to describe an emphasis on collectivity, expressed as shared concern and responsibility for others: "Scholarship using this perspective identifies positive aspects of African American life richly embedded in spirituality and a world-view that incorporates African traits and commitment to common causes" (p. 241)

As an example on the individual level, referring to the resilience of successful African American men, the authors cite research findings (Gary & Leashore, 1982; Hacker, 1992) that suggest the following:

> Much of their success can be attributed to individual and family resilience, the ability to "bounce back" after defeat or near defeat, and the mobilization of limited resources while simultaneously protecting the ego against a constant array of social and economic assaults. To varying degrees, success results from a strong value system that includes belief in self, industrious efforts, desire and motivation to achieve, religious beliefs, self-respect and respect for others, responsibility toward one's family and community, and cooperation. (Daly et al., 1995, p. 242)

In another example, researchers examined age, race, and setting by focusing on risk and resilience for African American youths in school settings (Connell, Spencer, & Aber, 1994). They developed a theoretical model that they tested with data from two large samples in two cities: New York and Atlanta. Their findings confirm that family involvement is an important target for these interventions. This study's results also support efforts to develop intervention strategies for increasing poor African American youths' belief in their own abilities and capacities to affect their academic outcomes and for improving their relationship with peers in the school context. Further,

> perhaps the most intriguing and disturbing implication of this study for our understanding of risk and resilience is that disaffected behavior in low-income African-American youth can lessen parental involvement, which in turn contributes to negative appraisals of self that exacerbate disaffected patterns of action and contribute to negative educational outcomes. (p. 504)

Christian and Barbarin (2001) also examined the importance of parental involvement on the adjustment of low-income African American children. They found that children of parents attending church at least weekly had fewer behavior problems than did those that attended less frequently. This supported the importance of religiosity as a sociocultural resource in African American families with children potentially at risk for behavioral and emotional maladjustments related to growing up in poor families and communities. In a second and related line of inquiry, the researchers hypothesized that parents who reported a positive racial identity, as well those who tended to externalize by attributing the causes of negative African American life outcomes to external forces, would have children with fewer behavioral problems. While these two variables might be related to parental self-esteem, they did not directly affect the children's incidence of behavioral problems. In fact, parents who tended to internalize explanations of poor outcomes (such as not working hard enough, lack of persistence) had children with fewer behavioral problems. The authors concede that the limitations of the study do not allow wider generalizations; nonetheless, this finding was both unexpected and intriguing.

Richters and Martinez (1993) offer an example of resilience research that examines the impact of community violence on childhood development. They examined factors contributing to resilience on the part of 72 children attending their first year of elementary school in a violent neighborhood of Washington, D.C. Their findings indicate the following:

> Despite the fact that these children were being raised in violent neighborhoods, had been exposed to relatively high levels of violence in the community, and were experiencing associated distress symptoms, community violence exposure levels were not predictive of adaptational failure or success. Instead, adaptational status was systematically related to characteristics of the children's homes. (p. 609)

The authors point out that only when the environmental adversities contaminated the safety and stability of children's homes did their odds of adaptational failure increase.

In a study of the risk and protective factors associated with gang involvement among urban African American adolescents, the researchers found that youths with current or past gang membership documented higher levels of risk involvement, lower levels of resilience, higher exposure to violence, and higher distress symptoms than did youths with no gang affiliations (Li et al., 2002). The findings persisted when controlled for age, gender, and risk involvement. The authors suggest that gang membership itself is associated with increased risk and ill effects on psychological well-being. They also found that strong family involvement and resiliency protects against gang involvement.

Garmezy (1991) focused on the resilience and vulnerability of children in relation to the impact of poverty. He states,

> The evidence is sturdy that many children and adults do overcome life's difficulties. Since good outcomes are frequently present in a large number of life histories, it is critical to identify those "protective" factors that seemingly enable individuals to circumvent life stressors. (p. 421)

The author points to a core of variables. These include "warmth, cohesion, and the presence of some caring adults (such as a grandparent) in the absence of responsive parents or in the presence of marked marital discord" (p. 421). Similar findings in studies examining the resiliency of children exposed to poverty and other traumas have identified emotional responsivity in the parent-child relationship as a buffering factor (Egeland, Carlson, & Sroufe, 1993).

In one example of a study focusing on children from maltreating homes, Herrenkohl, Herrenkohl and Egolf (1994) report on a longitudinal study of the effects of abuse and neglect on 457 children. The study began in 1976 and continued with follow-up studies of 345 of the children in 1980–1982 (elementary school age) and again, in 1990–1992 (late adolescence). The 1980 phase included children receiving services from the local child welfare agencies for abuse ($N = 105$) or neglect ($N = 86$), as well as a control group of children in day care ($N = 52$), Head Start programs ($N = 52$), and private nursery schools ($N = 50$). All of the children were rated on several variables and then grouped into high-functioning, low-functioning, and middle-functioning categories. School success (as in attendance, graduation) was one of the key outcome measures for determining success.

The authors suggest that their findings, although based on a limited final sample, indicate that "at least average intellectual capacity is a necessary, though not sufficient, condition for minimal success for abused and neglected children" (Herrenkohl et al., 1994, p. 304). Chronic physical abuse by one parent, without intervention or protection from another parent, created "insuperable obstacles to academic success" for children who remained in such an environment (p. 304). Their data also suggested that "the presence of at least one caretaker throughout childhood appeared to be a necessary, although not sufficient, condition for school achievement" (p. 304). Finally, positive parental expectations for self-sufficiency on the part of parents with children who experienced severe physical health problems appeared to "stimulate the child's goal-setting and determination, with good effect on their academic work" (p. 304). Unger and Wandersman (1985) explored the importance of neighbors and neighboring as sources of both informal support and social networks that helped children cope with stress.

In a more recent study examining resilience among abused and neglected children (who reported the information as adults), McGloin & Widom (2001) matched 676 abused and neglected children (substantiated cases between 1967 and 1971) with a control group of 520 non-abused and non-neglected children. The two groups were matched by gender, age, race, and approximate family social class. Both groups were administered a 2-hour in-person interview, including a psychiatric assessment, between 1989 and 1995. Of the original group, 1,307 (83 percent) were located and 1,196 (76 percent) interviewed. The authors' definition of resilience required success in eight domains of functioning: employment, education, and social activity; lack of homelessness, psychiatric disorder, and substance abuse; and two domains assessing criminal behavior. Significant differences in favor of the control group were found for the domains of employment, no homelessness, education (high school graduation), no psychiatric disorder, no arrest, and no self-reported violence. Only in the domains of no substance abuse and social activity were the results similar for both groups. When the sample was analyzed by gender, the only difference was that the control group of men had significantly less substance abuse.

In a review of the literature on resilience and poverty, Garmezy (1993) suggests that

> these findings provide new questions and new avenues for research. What factors are involved in the seeming diminution over time of resilience in some hitherto adaptive children and adults? Prolonged and cumulated stress would appear to be a prime candidate for examination. Another factor worthy of consideration would be the absence of a support structure and its availability over time. Other candidates for effecting change may be critical modifications in the child's environment such as the physical dissolution of the family. (p. 130)

Other examples of resilience studies that are population specific include research on youths with high incidence disabilities (Murray, 2003), homeless students (Reed-Victor & Stronge, 2002), and adolescents who experience marital transitions (Rodgers & Rose, 2002).

Resilience and Life-Span Theory

Resilience theory does not apply only to children and families. Staudinger, Marsiske, and Baltes (1993), working in the area of aging, have attempted to integrate the notion of resilience with work concerning developmental reserve capacity emerging from the field of life-span psychology. Life-span theory suggests that development throughout life is characterized by joint occurrence of increases (gains), decreases (losses), and maintenance (stability) in adaptive capacity (p. 542).

They suggest this theory challenges a one-dimensional model in which aging, for example, might be seen as simply the loss of capacity. Plasticity, which can be positive or negative, is another central notion of life-span theory. *Plasticity* can be defined as the individual's ability to be flexible in response to stress. This idea suggests that variable components of change can be attributed to individuals or populations and may be associated with cross-cultural or historical differences. The degree of an individual's plasticity may depend on the individual's reserve capacity, which is constituted by the internal and external resources available to the individual at a given point in time. Cognitive capacity and physical health are examples of internal resources; one's social network and financial status are external ones. Note that an individual's resources need not be fixed but may change over time (p. 542).

The authors describe two types of reserve capacity. *Baseline reserve capacity* is the individual's current "maximum performance potential" with existing internal and external resources. *Developmental reserve capacity* refers to resources that can be activated or increased. The life-span theory argues that as reserve capacity increases, so does the potential for positive plasticity.

Social work intervention activities, such as case management, may be seen as focusing on helping elderly clients, for example, to use their baseline reserves while intervening to activate their clients' developmental reserves. For example, increasing the client's social network (external reserves) through involvement in a senior citizens' program could directly improve the internal reserve capacity (health, emotional state, cognitive capacity), which in turn strengthens the client's capacity for developing stronger social networks. This client would have demonstrated positive plasticity in the area of social relationship.

Staudinger et al. (1993) attempt to merge these two streams—resilience theory and life-span theory—as follows:

> Mapping definitions of resilience onto the concepts of reserve capacity and plasticity suggests that resilience can be conceptualized as one type of plasticity. While plasticity, in principle, can be seen as encompassing the potential for any change in adaptive capacity (including increase, maintenance and decrease), resilience refers to the potential for the maintenance and regaining of levels of normal adaptation; that is, resilience is a subtype of the broader range of changes in adaptive capacity encompassed by plasticity. Like reserve capacity, resilience implies the presence of latent resources that can be activated. Unlike resilience, however, reserve capacity is not only relevant to maintaining or regaining normal levels of adaptation. Reserve capacity also refers to factors and resources that promote growth beyond the normal level of functioning. (pp. 543–544)

More recently, researchers have examined the concept of "cognitive hardiness" and coping style as buffering or moderating variables between life stress events and trauma and psychological and somatic distress (Beasley, Thompson, & Davidson, 2003). The study involved analysis of questionnaires completed by 187 students who had returned to the university as mature adults. In general, findings supported a direct effect on outcomes of life stress and psychological health. Cognitive hardiness, coping style, and negative life events also impacted outcomes. Several cases supported the concept that cognitive hardiness moderated the impact of emotional coping styles and adverse life events on psychological distress. The researchers used Kobasa and Pucetti's (1983) definition of cognitive hardiness as a personality variable; specifically, the quality of hardy individuals who

> (1) believe that they can *control* or influence events, (2) have a *commitment* to activities and their interpersonal relationships and to self, in that they recognize their own distinct values, goals and priorities in life, and (3) view change as a *challenge* rather than a threat. In the latter regard, they are predisposed to be cognitively flexible. (p. 841)

Implications for Social Work Practice

This growing interest in resilience theory and research, along with the concepts of life-span theory, fits nicely with evolving theory and practice in social work and with the interactional model. For social workers who have long held a psychosocial approach to understanding and working with clients and who have more recently embraced ecological models and a strengths perspective, these theoretical models and research findings tend to confirm what their practice wisdom and research has told them. These models also reinforce the first practice principle I was taught in graduate school: "Always reach for the client's strength!"

The strong emergence of a resilience model, with its concepts of reserve capacities and plasticity, together with the life-span idea of cognitive hardiness, can influence social work practice on many levels. For example, we have just seen in this chapter, through our own exploration of theory development, how theories provide underlying propositions about people and their behavior that can guide our interventions. Gilgun (1996) provides one example of an effort to integrate resilience theory with social work practice theory—what has been commonly described as **systems or ecological approach** or framework. She suggests that this framework leads to social work interventions that are "wide-ranging, covering research, program development, direct practice, and policy formulation, implementation, and evaluation" (p. 399). She points out that developmental psychopathology introduces social work to a language full of generative concepts and theory, while social work provides the ecological framework, strengths-based focus, and phenomenological perspectives. In combination, social work and developmental psychopathology can greatly advance knowledge to inform research, program development, practice, and policy.

We can find one example of the use of resilience theory and research in its implications for child welfare practice with African American families. Scannapieco and Jackson (1996) review the historical response of African American families to separation and loss, starting with slavery and continuing through the reconstruction period, World War II, the civil rights years, the 1970s and 1980s, and on to the 1990s. In each stage, they describe the resilience of the African American family and the ways in which it coped with life stresses brought about by racism in U.S. society. Current stresses associated with poverty, AIDS, child abuse and neglect, and reductions in services have elevated childhood risks to crisis proportions. These authors point to "kinship care" placements where the resources of the extended African American families are used to provide some of the resilience factors described in the previous discussion of the research. The authors suggest that all members of the extended family should be involved in case planning, because any of them may need to take over as full- or part-time caregivers:

> Social work practice within kinship care programs must recognize the resilient nature of the African-American family and work with the "kinship triad," made up of the children, the biological parents, and the caregiver relatives. A system of services should be directed at this union of three to ensure a permanent living arrangement for the children. (p. 194)

This same example could be conceptualized in life-span theory terminology as focusing on resources (internal and external, baseline and developmental) that have increased the positive plasticity of the African American family, thus allowing not only for recovery from trauma but also for the optimizing of individual, family, and community growth and development.

For the purposes of this chapter, I suggest that resilience and life-span theory and their related research provide an important framework for understanding and engaging any client. If we understand that clients—even those who appear to be totally overwhelmed—have the potential for overcoming adversity, we will always be looking for what is right with them rather than what is wrong. By doing so—and by representing to the client a professional who believes in the client's capacities for growth, change, and adaptation—the social worker becomes a source of resilience for the client. This strengths perspective also provides a rationale for the integration of solution-focused interventions, discussed later in this chapter.

Additional Social Work Perspectives

The social work profession is still in a stage of development with many emerging theoretical frameworks to draw on. Many professionals are engaging in theory building and empirical testing of constructs about practice to develop evidenced-based practice. While this book offers one perspective on the role of the profession and the processes of helping, other perspectives compete for attention. This is healthy. The approach taken in this book will be to borrow practice concepts and ideas from all of the models described in this chapter and to integrate them into the general framework of the interactional approach. The emphasis will be on finding "what works" rather than on maintaining ideological purity. The sections that follow briefly summarize some of the models that have made major contributions or are under active consideration by the profession. They were also selected because of elements that have been integrated into the interactionist approach. Constructs from these models will be referenced in the chapters that follow.

Solution-Focused Practice

A more recently developed model of practice that has elements that fit nicely within the interactional framework is called solution-focused practice. While not advocating the practice of the model itself, I suggest that several of its underlying assumptions and intervention techniques can be useful, particularly in the beginning phase of work. Further, these interventions may not be appropriate for all clients and in all situations. The practitioner needs to discern when they might be suitable or not. This section provides a brief introduction to the model and identifies core techniques.

Major Assumptions on the Nature of the Helping Relationship The solution-focused model is built on the strengths perspective, described earlier. As a form of "existential" practice, it focuses on the client's current issues and assumes that, with the help of the social worker, the client can identify and make use of inherent strengths that might be overlooked in a pathology-oriented practice. Put in simple terms, the social worker is thinking about what is right with the client rather than what is wrong. The social worker also believes that the source and methods of change will come from the client. This model emerged from an integration of the strengths perspective with interest in short-term treatment (deShazer, 1988; deShazer & Berg, 1992).

Some of the specific assumptions in the model that are clearly compatible with the approach advanced in this book include the following:

- Intervention should focus on the present and what clients bring with them to the process.
- Achieving behavioral changes takes place in and affects the present, rather than resolving problems of the past.
- While focusing on the present, the model recognizes that longer-term treatment may require examination and resolving of issues in the past (as for survivors of sexual abuse).
- When engaging the client, workers might acknowledge the person's discomfort but they do not engage in a prolonged discussion of etiology and pathology.
- Individuals have within themselves the resources and abilities to solve their own problems.
- Clients are often caught in feelings of powerlessness regarding their problems in living.
- Clients need to be helped to imagine what their future would look like without the problem, that is, if they were unstuck.
- When working with mandated clients, the involuntary nature of the relationship must be acknowledged and becomes the starting point for the work.

Prior to the engagement the worker will make minimal use of history and agency records, preferring to let the client tell the story. This can help the worker avoid stereotyping the client from the judgments of previous workers. In the classic example, a new worker's colleagues chime in, "They gave you the Jones family!" The worker's perception that this will be a difficult family helps to create the conditions that can lead to a self-fulfilling prophecy.

With mandated clients, the worker typically asks the clients to share their views about the mandating agency's expectations and requirements. The worker recognizes that while the agency or court can demand certain changes, clients serve as the final "authority" on what they want or need to change in their lives. When the worker asks what the client wants and the response is "Get the god-dammed agency off my back!" the worker can respond, "OK, let's start with what you have to do to get the agency off of your back." Essentially, the client is invited to be the "expert" who informs the worker about her or his situation.

Defining Techniques Several specific techniques have been identified as associated with this model. All of them share a common focus on the client's strengths and capacity for coping with adversity.

- *Asking about presession changes:* The worker recognizes that change may have occurred even before the first session. The fact that a client has made an appointment, voluntarily or not, may begin a change process. The worker will be curious and inquire about how the client made these changes and who was responsible for them.

- *Asking about between-session changes:* The worker recognizes that the client has a life between sessions. Many factors will have influenced the client's life, and the worker will want to explore these at the beginning of the session. For example, the worker may ask, "What's better this week, compared with last week?"

- *Asking about exceptions:* This technique asks the client to begin to examine when the problem did not occur in the past and what the conditions were that created these exceptions. For example, "You've relapsed and started drinking again at least three times over the past five years, but you've also been able to maintain your recovery for longer and longer periods. What was going on during the time you maintained your recovery, and how were you able to do that?" A variation on this question would be to ask about times when the problem was not that serious or severe, was less frequent, or lasted a shorter time. The goal would be to search for and reinforce factors that made a difference. This is a subtle yet important shift from focusing on the problem to identifying potential solutions.

- *The miracle question:* While there are different forms of the "miracle question," the most common is this: "Imagine you were to wake up tomorrow and a miracle had happened." The miracle would be that the client's life had changed for the better and the "problem" had been resolved. Questions such as "How would you first know that things were different?" or "What would others notice that would indicate the problem was gone?" are designed to help the client conceptualize the desired change. A variation includes "Imagine this isn't so much of a problem" or "This appointment has helped you in just the way you thought it would" or "It is 6 months in the future and we have been working together and problems have been resolved. How would you know this? What would be different?" The one caveat that the worker has to include in asking the question is that the client cannot answer that the problem itself did not exist. For example, a grieving widow cannot wake up the next day and find that her husband had not died.

- *Scaling questions:* This technique asks clients to identify the degree of the problem by thinking about zero representing the worst end of a continuum and some other number being the ideal. The worker can then ask clients what number represents where they are in respect to this problem at a certain point in the work. In this way, clients may be able to identify incremental changes rather than seeing a problem as "solved" or "not solved."

- *Coping questions:* Another technique that emphasizes the clients' strengths and helps clients see themselves in new way is to ask "coping" questions. For example, after acknowledging the problem, the worker might ask, "How have you managed to cope?" Another question might be "Given how bad things are, how come they are not worse? How have you kept things from getting worse?"

Radical Social Work Practice

In a second model, there are social work theorists who call for a more radical social work approach. This model emerged with some force and impact during the 1960s and 1970s when movements for social change, such as the civil rights movement, were active. Advocates for radical social work practice rightly point to persistent social problems and the lack of social justice, particularly for oppressed and vulnerable populations. These challenges to the profession were and still are healthy in that they have reminded us of our historical concern with social change as well as individual adaptation. This "social" aspect of social work can easily be lost as the profession moves to become more "clinical," taking on models of practice used by other professions—such as psychotherapy or psychology. They have also provided a needed reminder of our unique professional role, which can easily be lost if we allow our function to be solely defined by the job description written by our agency or host setting.

For a segment of this group of radical social work theorists, at times identified with what might be called "critical theory," direct practice with clients, by definition, is ineffective. For example, Galper (1967) views social services as failing to be effective because they derive from the existing social order, and play a role in maintaining it. Problems are defined in terms of economic, political, or social contexts. These theoreticians point to the very real problems in approaches to practice that seemed to ignore social realities and issues of oppression. The reason they have had such a powerful impact on faculty, students, and workers is that they focused on aspects of our practice about which we were already feeling defensive. Workers who feel oppressed by their own agencies and somewhat overwhelmed by their clients' life situations are responsive to the charge that they are involved in "band-aid" work rather than bringing about real social change.

However, practitioners know that when they work with real clients, employing a critical analysis of the clients' problems is often just a first step. Such an analysis can lead to new and more helpful ways to intervene in the process with clients who need help now—today—in this interview, family session, or group meeting. However, the client often cannot wait for the major changes in our society that will be needed to modify institutionalized oppression. Thus, while we need a conceptualization of practice that reframes our way of viewing client troubles and requires us to act on injustices in our society (and agencies and institutions), we simultaneously must provide services to the victims of these injustices. The real task is technical in nature. How can we integrate radical views of society, psychology, and interpersonal relationships into our ongoing practice, and how can we develop the skills to have an impact on systems as well as clients? The use of oppression psychology in this book is one example of an effort toward integration.

While one is free to differ with the particular interventions, these "radical" approaches contribute to the general professional development by providing models that can be applied to practice with oppressed and vulnerable clients. In fact, many of the intervention constructs of the model would constitute good practice principles for any worker-client intervention. The important point is that these theory builders have not given up on the idea of social workers playing an influential role with individual clients as well as dealing with issues of social justice.

Feminist Practice

A third group of models influencing our professional development is the emergence of a body of literature related to what is termed "feminist practice." While this view can also be considered a form of radical practice, and it draws heavily on social and political issues related to gender oppression, its proponents tend to translate their ideas into specific method theory that helps to connect ideas to the realities of day-to-day practice.

Feminist approaches to practice have diverged into identifiable streams. As I mentioned earlier, Saulnier (1996, 2000) has attempted to identify these various viewpoints. Her typology includes the following models: liberal feminism, radical feminism, socialist feminism, lesbian feminism, cultural and ecofeminism, womanism, African American women's feminism, postmodern feminism, and global feminism. While some may disagree with the specific categorization of the models and the associated descriptions, analysis, and critiques, Saulnier's contribution highlights this important area of theory development and identifies implications for social policy and social work practice.

Sands and Nuccio (1992) specifically address the emergence of postmodern feminist theory and its implications for social work. The authors describe how the feminist literature has identified three general categories of philosophical and political feminist orientations: liberal, socialist, and radical feminism. *Liberal feminism* emphasizes the attainment of political rights, opportunities, and equality within the existing political system. *Socialist feminism* attributes women's oppression to the interaction among sexism, racism, and class divisions, which are produced by patriarchal capitalism. *Radical feminism* finds patriarchy an omnipresent influence that needs to be dismantled (p. 490).

They then trace the emergence of postmodern feminism from its postmodern philosophical and French feminist theoretical roots. While identifying differences in the roots and the emergent thinking of this model, they point to a shared political agenda with American feminism:

> Regardless of whether a feminist has a liberal, socialist, radical or other perspective, she has a desire to change the social and political order so that women will no longer be oppressed. Thus, organizing and taking political action to redress injustices are significant dimensions of postmodern feminism. (Sands & Nuccio, 1992, p. 492)

An example of the specific application of this shared principle can be found in Chapter 13, in which a social worker approaches the ending phase of work with a group of survivors of sexual abuse. After many months of difficult and powerful work on the impact of the abuse on their lives, the worker suggests that they consider attending a local march against sexual violence directed toward women.

> Then group members asked me to review information about the local "Take Back the Night" march with them. We had told them about the march against sexual violence against women a few weeks before and, after some exploration of their fears about participating in a public demonstration, they decided to march as a group. I supported the group's readiness to act independently and support each other in new experiences. I shared with them how good I felt that they wanted to march together and gave them the information they needed.

At the Next Session

We supported the group's growing independence and shared our feelings with them. As the group processed how the march had felt for them, Jane and I shared how powerful it had felt for us to see them there, marching, chanting, and singing. We also shared that it was hard for us to see them and know that the group was ending. The group was special for us and it would be hard to let it go.

After their experience with the march, the group members decided to contribute samples of their poetry and art to an exhibit dealing with issues of violence toward women. They also decided to contribute proceeds from the sale of their art to a fund devoted to support groups for survivors like themselves. This represents an example of combining the personal and political, and choosing which part of their work was more "therapeutic" would be difficult. The cake they shared in their last session had written on it, "Survivors—Striving and Thriving!"

Another model that brings a feminist perspective to social work practice emerged from efforts to develop a new psychology of women. Much of the rapidly evolving work in this area is rooted in the publications and a series of working papers from the Stone Center in Wellesley, Massachusetts. This framework is often referred to under the general rubric of self-in-relation theory, mentioned earlier. In one application of this theory, Collins (1994) "reconstructs" the concept of codependency using a feminist social work perspective to analyze the concept and its underlying assumptions about recovery and relationships.

Many of the core constructs of this theory and, in particular, the group work implications of the model fit well with the interactional framework presented in this book. For example, Schiller (1993) uses the self-in-relation framework to rethink a classic theory of group development known as the Boston Model (Garland, Jones, & Kolodny, 1965) and adapts it to a feminist perspective.

In another example of an application of feminist theory to practice, Holmes and Lundy (1990) present what they term a feminist perspective on work with men who batter. They provide specific prescriptions for intervention that are based on feminist theoretical and ideological assumptions. Other examples that draw on feminist perspectives include Berman-Rossi and Cohen (1989), focusing on work with homeless, mentally ill women, and Breton (1988), providing an example of a "sistering" approach in a drop-in shelter for homeless women. O'Brien (1995) identifies the self-empowerment of a group of African American women, who were long-term public-housing residents and activists, as contributing to their resilience and effective mothering.

In an effort to merge a feminist perspective with a cognitive-behavioral approach (discussed later in this chapter), Srebnik and Saltzberg (1994) describe how internalized cultural messages negatively affect a woman's body image. The authors then propose interventions to influence thought patterns and dysfunctional behaviors.

In another example, Collins (1994) uses feminist theory to challenge the concept of codependency in substance abuse practice. The author refutes the view that women need to view their relational strengths as pathology. Instead, she argues that they can get well by naming and discussing the injustices in their relational context.

In more recent work in this area, Wood draws on feminist and social constructionist positions, anthropology, and narrative ideas to describe and illustrate a framework for social work with groups of women who are being battered and raped by husbands and boyfriends. She emphasizes the role of resistance and protest in developing self-representation and proclaiming it in definitional ceremonies (Wood & Roche, 2001).

In another example, Westbury and Tutty (1999) conducted a small, quasi-experimental study comparing women who were sexually abused as children and who were receiving individual and group treatment that included feminist techniques with women on a wait list who were receiving only individual counseling. They found that the treatment group had significantly improved depression and anxiety scores, when compared with the wait list group, as well as a near significant improvement in self-image.

Social Work as Psychotherapy

A fourth model, associated with the growth of private practice and the certification of social workers as eligible to receive third-party insurance payments, has intensified another influence on the profession—the "social worker as therapist" model. While many social workers applaud this recognition of the competency of the profession, some have raised a serious concern about social work's continued commitment to oppressed and vulnerable populations. Many social work clients are economically disadvantaged and do not have the medical insurance required to use private services. Social workers have traditionally found their place working in social agencies or social work departments in host institutions (such as hospitals, schools, and residential centers). A real fear exists that the profession may abandon its important and unique roles in these settings in the search for increased status, income, and professional autonomy.

As ever more social workers describe themselves as therapists or psychotherapists, sometimes even avoiding the use of their social work title, they blur the distinctions between their profession and others engaged in private-practice counseling. The very existence of a unique profession of social work could be jeopardized if we do not keep clear what it is that makes social work different. Because this private-practice movement is growing, one solution may be for the profession to identify and research the elements in the work of private-practice colleagues that maintain their unique identity as social workers. Identifying themselves as social workers and affiliating with certain professional associations are examples. A willingness to intervene with other professionals and systems, on behalf of a client, might be another.

Cognitive-Behavioral Therapy

A fifth emerging and promising model is related to interest in constructs borrowed from cognitive-behavioral psychology and therapy. In cognitive-behavioral therapy, the therapist uses strategies and techniques designed to help clients correct their negative, distorted views about themselves, the world, and the future, as well as the underlying maladaptive beliefs that gave rise to these cognitions (Beck, Rush, Shaw, & Emery, 1979; Elkin, Parloff, Hadley, & Autry, 1985).

Earlier in this chapter, I pointed out the powerful interaction between how we feel and how we act. Essentially, cognitive-behavioral approaches, building on social-learning theories, suggest that how one thinks also interacts with one's behavior. When feelings and cognitive distortions combine, they can result in maladaptive behaviors, which in turn strengthen the distortions, which then continue to affect the behavior. In cognitive-behavioral treatment models, the therapist would help the client identify and modify cognitive distortions and would reinforce behaviors that were more adaptive for the client.

Concepts drawn from a widely recognized and researched cognitive therapy model based on the work of Beck, who explored the causes and treatment of depression

(Beck et al., 1979), can be usefully incorporated into the interactional model of practice. Oei and Shuttlewood (1996) summarize the three dimensions of Beck's theory.

First, life experiences lead people to form assumptions about themselves and the world ("schemata" or "underlying predispositions") that are then used to interpret new experiences and to govern and evaluate behavior. "Some assumptions reached on the basis of past negative experience may become rigid, extreme, and resistant to change and, hence, are termed dysfunctional or counterproductive." (p. 93)

Second, Beck posed the existence of "automatic thoughts," short pieces of "internal dialogue" that are associated with negative emotions and can lead to self-statements such as "I am a failure." According to Beck, a pattern of frequent and "highly negative automatic thoughts" can develop into a vicious cycle leading to depression, which then leads to more depressive cognitions.

Third, automatic thoughts are seen as containing "errors of logic," which Beck termed "cognitive distortions." These could include overgeneralizing, disqualifying the positive, catastrophizing, minimization, and personalization.

Beck's treatment approach "disrupts the vicious cycle of depression by teaching the patients to question negative automatic thoughts and then to challenge the assumptions (schemata) on which they are based" (Oei & Shuttlewood, 1996, p. 94).

There are many examples of how one can incorporate constructs from the cognitive-behavioral model into the interactional framework. Albert (1994) writes about a mutual aid support group for chronic mental patients using a cognitive approach. He describes a patient in a day treatment center, which had so many groups that patients often felt "grouped out," surprising staff by suggesting another group:

She said, "We need to talk just about being mental patients, what it means, what it feels like." One patient after another seconded the motion. They wanted to address the mental patient identity. How were they thought of in their families and neighborhoods? How should they think of themselves? Was the mental patient stigma justified? Where did it come from? What were its effects? Although their "patienthood" was at the heart of what the patients had in common, it seemed to have remained an oppressive presence, at once too obvious and too painful to mention. (p. 109)

In one example from the group, patients are dealing with the ideation of permanent thinking—that when they are depressed, for example, treatment can seem "interminable and futile." This sense of failure and permanency, in turn, affects their ability to continue to cope.

Sharon said, "I had the leaves raked into piles. Then the wind blew them all around the yard again. I thought, 'What's the use? They'll never get done. There will always be leaves.' Then I went back to bed. My body started feeling heavy. I couldn't get out of bed." I (the worker) pointed out that Sharon had used the word "always" when speaking about her hospitalization, too. ["I'll always go back to the hospital."] I asked, "Is it true that there will always be leaves? Is the job never done?" Sharon said, "That's one way of looking at it." I asked the group for other ways. Members suggested that Sharon think about other tasks she has completed. [Disputation] Nick said, "Maybe you would have to redo the raking once or twice; maybe even three times—But not forever. [Disputation] I mean, you do what you can, then it snows and you're done." [laughter] I repeated, "You do what you can." (Albert, 1994, p. 110)

Cognitive-behavioral approaches represent good examples of how related disciplines can provide powerful ideas that can be integrated into a social work practice model. In addition, the emphasis by the cognitive-behavioral social work theoreticians on a **practitioner-researcher** model, in which the social worker is continuously evaluating his or her own practice, is also healthy for the field as it accelerates the movement toward development of a more empirically based practice.

While contributing to professional theoretical and research growth, the expansion of cognitive, behavioral, or cognitive-behavioral models in social work practice raises two concerns. The first is evident in efforts by some theoreticians to propose such models as a unified social work practice theory (Thyer, 1987). Such an effort would substitute a model borrowed from a foreign discipline, one that is not rooted in the same history as the social work profession, for its unique sense of professional function.

Examination of the literature of this approach, for example, indicates it has been applied most often to very specific populations and problems (such as anxiety disorders, anger management, parenting training, and depression), while social work has developed a broader constituency, including specific attention to oppressed and vulnerable populations.

In addition, the model is generally built on a base of individual psychology. This is evident in its lack of attention to the social change aspects of practice that have been central to the social work profession. In an example of an exception to this criticism, Stern and Smith (1995) report on a study of family processes and delinquency in an ecological context. They tested a model "hypothesizing that family content influences parenting, which in turn influences adolescent behavior" (p. 703). Their results for 804 adolescents and their families showed that "the family's disadvantaged neighborhood, life distress, social isolation, and lack of partner support were associated with dysfunctional parenting that increases delinquency" (p. 703).

Stern and Smith (1995) reviewed the literature and identified several behaviorally focused interventions that have proved helpful in, for example, providing tools for parents to identify the sources of stress from their children's behavior and to find parenting methods for coping with that stress. However, as they also point out,

> Our research supports the growing recognition of the importance of multidimensional approaches to intervention with delinquents and their families. It seems clear that intervention focused solely on the micro-processes in families will generally be inadequate to address the complex problems that juvenile delinquency presents. If we look at parents without considering the complex contexts in which they operate and the multiple stresses operating in them, we are likely to promote ineffective intervention models and high levels of treatment dropout. We also run the risk of blaming and re-victimizing families struggling with considerable adversity who are already victimized by a society that does not adequately support disadvantaged and distressed children and families. (p. 722)

In my view, if social work can hold on to the core of its unique role, which always recognizes the two-client concept, then workers can incorporate ideas from a wide range of models and theories. The task for the profession is to treat frameworks from foreign disciplines with appropriate respect and to borrow constructs that can enhance the work, while guarding against substituting these constructs for the profession's own model-building efforts.

A second issue related to the growth of this model is the apparent co-optation of the term *empirically based practice* by some proponents of this specific framework. This has occurred somewhat by default as social work as a profession was slow in developing a solid body of research focused on practice method—what it is the social worker actually did with clients. While many outcome studies existed, they were usually weak in defining the independent (predictor) variables. For example, in Fischer's (1973) well-known article on the effectiveness of social work practice, out of more than 40 studies reviewed, not one described what it was the social worker actually did while spending time with the client. Operational definition of the worker's intervention is one of the strongest points of cognitive-behavioral practice models, allowing this framework to move quickly to attempt to fill this research vacuum.

Empirical work can be undertaken from a range of theoretical perspectives, including some that could be termed interactional. The early work of the psychotherapy researchers associated with the client-centered approach of Carl Rogers (Truax, 1966) broke ground in this area. More recently, empirical work that involves specifying worker interventions has been more evident in the field, with a wide range of research approaches and methodology emerging. The work reported in this book is one example of the use of quantitative and qualitative research methods for building social work practice theory (for example, statistical analysis and content analysis of interviews, respectively). One contribution of the feminist practice movement has been to focus our attention on qualitative models of practice research that are useful for exploring worker-client interactions in ways that enhance the practice knowledge base.

Finally, the profession must guard against the tendency of proponents to oversell a particular framework or model, often by first attacking the efficacy of models currently in use. In reality, as pointed out by Oei and Shuttlewood (1996), there are many unanswered questions about what makes any form of therapy effective. Their review of the literature indicates that the evidence does not yet support the superiority of any particular form of therapy, and the debate still rages over whether specific therapy-related factors or else nonspecific or more general factors produce the positive results of therapy when compared with no treatment at all. They point to the most researched nonspecific factor, the therapeutic alliance, as an example of a variable that, while defined variously, may nevertheless cross models of treatment and account for some measure of effectiveness. This concept closely parallels the idea of the working relationship at the core of the approach described in this book.

In summary, developing a model of social work practice involves incorporating as many ideas as are helpful while still holding onto a unique professional identification. Many emerging theoretical models compete for social workers' attention. We are far from being ready to vote, as a profession, on which one will best suit us in the years to come. More likely, an integration of many of the universal constructs developed from differing points of departure will provide us with a unified practice theory. The interactional model discussed in this book may provide some of these constructs.

The framework described in this book will allow you to view relationships between clients and their important systems in an ecological context. Real conflicts between clients and systems will be identified; however, emphasis will be placed on attempting to identify areas of common ground. Practitioners will be described as trying to deal directly with clients, as well as trying to influence families, agencies, political systems, and so on. These practitioners will at times function in different roles, mediating where appropriate, confronting and advocating when necessary. In whichever role they play, however, they will keep in mind the essential common ground between the individual and society. This is the basis from which change can be brought about, and it is the real challenge for developing a radical social work practice.

Chapter Summary

The interactional theory of social work practice views the client as being in a symbiotic relationship with his or her social surroundings. The mutual need between the individual and the social surroundings is blocked by obstacles that often obscure it from view.

A historical perspective of social work shows the profession rooted in the twin streams of concern for individual well-being and for social change. As such, the functional assignment for the social work profession is that of mediating the engagement between the client and the systems important to that client. Practice methods and communication and relationship skills are the tools that enable the social worker to put his or her function into action. Practice skills are the instruments for developing a positive working relationship that serves as the medium through which the social worker influences the client.

Central to the effectiveness of the worker is her or his ability to integrate the personal self with the professional self. The social worker's practice is guided as well by a set of professional and personal values and by a well-defined professional code of ethics.

An oppression and vulnerability psychology model, as well as a resilience framework, can be helpful for understanding clients. This model assumes that the strength for change is always present although not always possible to engage.

Many other social work practice perspectives—such as solution-focused practice, radical social work practice, feminist practice, social work as psychotherapy, and cognitive-behavioral therapy—help place the interactional perspective in context.

Related Online Content and Activities

 Visit *The Skills of Helping* Book Companion Website at www.socialwork.wadsworth .com/Shulman06/ for learning tools such as glossary terms, InfoTrac College Edition keywords, links to related websites, and chapter practice quizzes.

The website for this chapter also features additional notes from the author.

Social Work With Groups

In Part IV we explore the interactional model of practice in the context of social work with groups. In Chapter 8 we discuss the group as a mutual-aid system, and in Chapter 9 we review the principles of group formation. In Chapter 10 the beginning phase of group work practice is examined in detail. Then, Chapters 11 and 12 explore the middle phase of practice, with special emphasis on the importance of working with two clients: the individual and the group. In Chapter 13 we examine the ending and transition phase of practice in relation to groups, and in Chapter 14 we look at variant elements of contracting introduced by different types of groups.

CHAPTER EIGHT

The Group as a Mutual-Aid System

CHAPTER OUTLINE

The Fear-of-Groups Syndrome

The Dynamics of Mutual Aid

Obstacles to Mutual Aid

The Function of the Group
Leader

In Part IV we explore the dynamics of mutual aid that can occur when a group of clients with common concerns is brought together for the purpose of helping one another. You will find that many of the processes and skills discussed in Parts II and III can be used in the group context. We also explore some of the unique features of group method, as well as specific obstacles to mutual aid. In this chapter we outline the mutual-aid processes and examine the function of the social worker in the group. We also look at the concerns often experienced by workers as they prepare to lead their first group session.

In our previous discussions of the underlying assumptions of the general helping model, we focused on the client in interaction with the various surrounding systems: family, agency, school, and so on. Perceiving the similarities between individual and group work is easier when one realizes that the group is a special case of the general individual-social interaction. In a sense, the group represents a **microsociety**, a special case of the larger individual-social interaction in our society. The potential for the "symbiotic" relationship described in the first part of this book is also present in each small-group encounter. In a seminal article entitled "The Social Worker in the Group," Schwartz (1961) defined the helping group as follows:

> The group is an enterprise in mutual aid, an alliance of individuals who need each other, in varying degrees, to work on certain common problems. The important fact is that this is a helping system in which the clients need each other as well as the worker. This need to use each other, to create not one but many helping relationships, is a vital ingredient of the group process and constitutes a common need over and above the specific tasks for which the group was formed. (p. 18)

The idea of the group as a mutual-aid system in which the worker helps people to help each other is an attractive one. However, workers with experience as members and leaders of groups have raised many legitimate questions about the potential effectiveness of such work. Exactly how can a group of people sharing the same set of concerns help one another? Isn't it a bit like the blind leading the blind? How will clients be able to talk about their most intimate concerns before a group of strangers? What about the coercive power of the group? How can individuals stand up against the odds? What is the job of the group leader if the members are helping one another?

My response is that the potential for mutual aid exists in the group, but simply bringing people together does not guarantee that it will emerge. Many obstacles can block the group members' ability to reach out to one another and to offer help. Many of these are similar to the obstacles described in earlier chapters; however, the group context can magnify their effect. Because all members will bring to the group their own concepts based on past experiences with groups (school, camp, committees, and so forth), and because many of these experiences may have been poor ones, the group worker is needed to help the group members create the conditions in which mutual aid can take place. The tasks of the group worker in attempting to help group members develop the required skills are related to these obstacles. Creating a mutual-aid group is a difficult process, with members having to overcome many of their stereotypes about individuals, groups, and helping. They will need all the assistance they can get from the group worker. Further, because the worker has also been affected by past group experiences, one of the worker's early tasks requires facing her or his own feelings and examining stereotypes. Without this self-examination, the worker may be unable to convey to the members a belief in their potential for helping one another. Faith in the strength of the group contributes greatly to the members' success.

Before we list the processes of mutual aid, let us discuss the common concerns experienced by students and workers when they first make the transition from working with individuals and families to work with groups.

The Fear-of-Groups Syndrome

In every one of my workshops for group work training, a moment arises, usually early on the first morning, when I sense a general unease in the group. Sometimes the first clue of what I call the **fear-of-groups syndrome** emerges during the introductions, when participants indicate they have never led a group, expressing this fact in a tone of voice that suggests that, if they had it their way, they would never lead one. When I explore these clues, I often hear that the workers were sent to the workshop by an administrator or supervisor who decided that group work would be a good idea. More recently, the pressures of managed care have led agencies to try to expand their group services, often for the wrong reasons.

Whether the participants are in the workshop voluntarily or not, and whether they are experienced workers or new workers, the underlying feelings are often the same: They are scared stiff of leading a group. As one experienced social worker said of group clients, "There are so many of them and only one of me!"

A common concern is having to practice with a group of people who are judging your work. Group work practice is seen as more exposed than individual work. If an individual client does not return after a few interviews, the worker can always chalk it up to the client's "lack of motivation." If ten clients fail to return to a group session, however, the worker feels he or she has failed.

Another concern involves the potential for direct negative feedback from clients. Anger from a single client or couple is one thing, but an angry group is something else. Of even greater concern is the possibility of a boring group. Workers feel completely responsible for the success of a group and dread the possibility of long silences, rambling conversations, individuals who dominate the discussion, or the sight of ten pairs of eyes glazing over.

Beginning group workers often raise their fear of lack of control. One workshop participant put it this way:

> When I'm conducting an individual interview, I know where it is going and can keep track of what is happening. In a group session, the members seem to take control of the session away from me. It feels like I am on my motorcycle, pumping the starter to get going, and the group members are already roaring down the road.

It takes some experience for a group worker to realize that moments such as these, when the group members take over the group, mean precisely that the group is well on its way to success. One of the benefits of caseworkers facilitating groups is that they begin to realize they can also let go of control in their one-to-one interviews.

The complexity of group work also intimidates workers. Whereas before they needed to concentrate on the relationship between themselves and the client, they now have to also concentrate on the relationships among group members. As they gain group work experience they become more conscious of the entity called the group-as-a-whole, which I will discuss in detail in a later chapter. In their one-to-one interviews they have to concentrate on the individual only, but now they must also pay attention to the group and somehow develop the ability to observe both the one and the many at the same time.

Such concerns are understandable. On reflection, however, experienced practitioners soon realize these concerns are similar to those they experienced when they first began to practice. Skills in work with individuals, which they now take for granted, seemed out of reach in their first interviews. They are continually learning more about the dynamics of the relationships between themselves and clients, as well as the dynamics of family relationships or couples. With some confidence in the skills they have, they worry less about those they need to learn and tolerate areas of ambiguity better. In learning the skills for working with groups, workers often start with no confidence at all; as in individual practice, they will build confidence through experience.

Further, I try to reassure these workers that they already know more about group work than they realize. Much of what they have learned about helping can be applied in the group situation, as chapters that follow illustrate. The areas of uncertainty represent exciting opportunities for new learning that can take place during the rest of their professional lives.

For the new worker or student, I suggest starting with individual work to develop some beginning confidence in basic practice skills, and then broadening these skills in the group context. Of course, students can also begin their learning with group work practice; I have seen many students develop quickly while working in the group medium. Nonetheless, talking to one client at a time makes the worker's task of beginning practice easier and more comfortable. If this can be supplemented with an opportunity to work as a coleader or observer with a more experienced group worker, then the learner has the best of all learning possibilities.

With both the new and experienced worker, I try to point out that the root of their fear is a misconception about their complete responsibility for the group work process. When they realize that they only have responsibility for their part, and that group members will do some of the most important helping, workers can view group work in its proper perspective. Certainly they will grow more helpful throughout their careers as they develop group skills and gain knowledge and confidence. They can, however, still give a great deal to their first groups.

Recall that new workers tend to underestimate the amount of help they can give to their clients. Group workers face this same problem. Continued group experiences help correct this misconception. The marvelous feeling a worker gets when he or she sees the power of mutual aid in group work helps to make up for the worker's anxiety along the way.

Finally, fear-of-groups must not interfere with the clients' right to receive the modality of service that is most appropriate to their particular needs. Consider, for example, populations of oppressed and vulnerable clients, as well as oppressors, for whom mutual-aid groups may well be the service modality of choice, providing a crucial complement to individual counseling. These clients should not be restricted to what may turn out to be less effective agency service simply because their social worker did not receive training in group work practice or feels more comfortable facing one client at a time. As you explore the many examples of mutual aid in the chapters that follow, the obvious healing power of groups will make the case for overcoming fear-of-groups.

The Dynamics of Mutual Aid

This section presents an overview of the mutual-aid process through several illustrations of specific dynamics. These will set the stage for understanding the more detailed discussions and examples of mutual aid in the chapters that follow.

Sharing Data

One of the simplest and yet most important ways group members can help one another is by **sharing data**. Members of the group have had different life experiences, through which whey have accumulated knowledge, views, values, and so forth that can help others in the group. For example, in a married couples' group (described in detail in Chapter 10), one of the couples was in their late sixties. They had experienced many of the normal life crises as well as those imposed by societal pressures, such as the Great Depression. As other group members who were in their fifties, forties, thirties, and twenties described their experiences and problems, this couple often shared insights that came from being able to view these crises from the perspective of time. As the group leader, I often found myself learning from the experiences of this couple. We created in the group a sort of extended family in which one generation passed on its life experiences to the next. In turn, the older couple used the group not only for their immediate problems but also as a place for reviewing their 50 years together. (This may be an important part of their work at this stage in their life cycle.)

In another group, working mothers shared ideas that had proved helpful in organizing their daily routines. The power of the Internet allows many clients to have access to information about resources that would never have been available before. Members shared the names of community services that they had discovered, and each mother tapped the experiences and the ingenuity of the others. Whether the data consisted of specific tips on concrete questions (jobs, available housing, money management, and so on), values, or ideas about relationships, each member contributed to the common pool of knowledge. The worker also contributed data that rounded out a rich resource for the members.

A group of clients with AIDS who were in early recovery from substance abuse (referred to as an AIDS/Recovery group) regularly shared specific information about the recovery process and coping with AIDS and its treatment. For example, one client told another, "This is the start of your second year in recovery—the feelings year—so don't be surprised about all of the pain you are feeling because you don't have the drinking and drugging to cover it up." At another meeting, clients shared their experiences with the new triple-drug therapy and provided information for those who were not in the trial groups about how to get connected. In the example that follows, group members provided tips on how to increase one member's chances for acceptance into a special housing program for people with AIDS. My job as group coleader was to help connect the group to the member to facilitate this form of mutual aid.

> I pointed out that, earlier, Theresa had mentioned her interest in getting into this independent living facility. I wondered if we might help her just by addressing that issue, as well. She told us she was concerned about putting an application in because she didn't think she had established enough credibility in her single-room occupancy housing. At this point, Jake and Tania started suggesting strategies and ideas about how to approach the living facility and what would maximize her ability to get in. They strongly encouraged her to make an application right now, since there were openings, and a few months down the road these openings might close, and there would be no place for her. They said they thought it would be wonderful if she could move into the building.
>
> Tania pointed out that the building—if you looked at it—the building was supposed to be for people with AIDS, but, if you took a look at it, your guess would be that it was essentially for gay men. She said she was the only woman in the whole building—the only single woman in the whole building. She said

to Theresa that if worse came to worst, you could always tell them it's discrimination, and that'll get their attention. She said, "That's how I got in."

They continued to talk with Theresa about ways she could demonstrate her responsibility, things that she had done, her commitment to recovery, the fact that she wanted to leave the place she currently lived in. Even though it was supposed to be a safe building, everybody knew drug dealing was going on there all the time, and it was scary to be there. She took it all in, thanked them for their advice, and said she was going to apply.

The Dialectical Process

The **dialectical process** is a mutual-aid process in which group members confront each other's ideas in an effort to develop a synthesis for all group members. An important debate can take place as each member shares views on the question under discussion. Group members can air tentative ideas by using the group as a sounding board—a place for their views to be challenged and possibly changed. Challenging ideas in the group is not always easy; I discuss later how such a culture for work can be developed. When this kind of group culture is present, the argument between two or more members becomes dialectical. Group members can listen as one member presents the "thesis" and the other, the "antithesis." As each member listens, he or she can use the discussion to develop a personal "synthesis."

For example, in a couples' group I co-led, one couple in their fifties discussed a problem they were experiencing with their grown, married children. They described their negative perception of the way in which their children were handling their marital difficulty. As they spoke, I could see anger in the eyes of a younger couple in their twenties. They were experiencing difficulty with the wife's parents, whom they viewed as "meddling" in their lives. When I reached for the verbal expression of the nonverbal cues, the battle was on. The older couple had to defend their perceptions against the arguments of the younger couple, who could see the problem through the eyes of the older couple's children. In return, the younger couple had to look at their own strained relationships with the wife's parents through the eyes of the older couple. For each couple, the debate led to some modification of their views and new insights into how the respective children and parents might be feeling. It was obvious from the discussion that other group members were making associations to their own experiences, using the dialogue taking place before them.

Confrontation is a part of mutual aid. Instead of being suppressed, differences must be expressed in an arena where they can be used for learning. Group members often present strongly held views on a subject precisely because they have doubts and desperately need a challenging perspective. The skills involved in helping group members to use these conflicts constructively are explored later. Further, the group can be a laboratory for developing skills such as asserting oneself, so that the individual members can become more effective in their relationships outside of the group. In our example, the conversation between the older and younger couples constituted a rehearsal for the important discussion that needed to take place with their respective children and parents. The group members were able to use the experience for this purpose after the leader pointed this out.

Discussing a Taboo Area

Each group member brings to the group the norms of behavior and the taboos that exist in our larger culture. *Norms* are the rules of behavior that are generally accepted by a dominant group in society. These norms can be recreated within a social work group or other system. The existence of the norms is evident when the group members behave as if the norms exist. For example, one norm of group behavior may be to avoid discussion of a generally taboo area such as money.

In the beginning phase of work, the group recreates in this microsociety the general community culture, consisting of norms, taboos, and rules that the group members have experienced outside the group. Thus, direct talk about such subjects as authority, dependency (on people or drugs), death and dying, and sex is experienced as taboo. One of the tasks of the group leader will be to help the group members develop new norms and feel free to challenge taboos so that the group can be more effective. This helps the group develop a culture for work. The concept of a **culture for work** will be discussed in more detail in Chapter 12. For now, the term refers to an explicit or implied set of values, taboos, rules of interaction, and other concepts that are shared by the group members and that positively affect the group's ability to work at its tasks. Each client will feel the urgency of discussing the subject somewhat differently from the others, and each will experience the power of the taboo differently. As the work proceeds and the level of comfort in the group increases (the skills for helping this to happen are discussed in later chapters), one member may take the first risk, directly or indirectly, that leads the group into a difficult area of discussion. **Discussing a taboo area** is the mutual-aid process in which one member enters a taboo area of discussion, thereby freeing other members to enter as well. By being first, the member allows the more fearful and reluctant members to watch as the taboo is violated. As they experience positive work, they can see it as permission to enter the formerly taboo area. Thus, all the group members benefit from the particular sense of urgency, the lower level of anxiety, or the greater willingness to risk of the member who leads the way.

In my AIDS/Recovery group, one member spoke about her own abusive past history and how she had escaped her family and turned to the streets and "to every kind of drug and drink you could imagine." She described working as a prostitute in order to raise money for drugs and how she was not proud of herself or what she did. She said, "While I was on the street I was with many men but I was really with no man." These revelations opened the door for other members to share their own sexual experiences, often degrading and exploitive, as they went on "coke dates" to raise money for their drugs. The ability to discuss their emotions in a supportive, nonjudgmental environment appeared to have a cathartic effect, creating a culture in which other taboo issues were discussed, such as their own illnesses, their rejection by friends and family, painful losses of people close to them, and their own fears of debilitation and death associated with AIDS.

The "All-in-the-Same-Boat" Phenomenon

The **"all-in-the-same-boat" phenomenon** is a mutual-aid process in which group members gain support from discovering that other group members have similar problems, concerns, feelings, and experiences. After the group enters a formerly taboo area, the members listen to the feelings of the others and often discover emotions of their own that they were unaware of, feelings that may have been powerfully affecting their lives. They also discover the reassuring fact that they are not alone in their feelings, that group members are "all in the same boat." Knowing that others share one's concerns and feelings somehow makes these feelings less frightening and easier to deal with. When, as a group member, one discovers that one is not alone in feeling overwhelmed by a problem, or in being worried about one's sexual adequacy, or in wondering who one is and where one comes from (as a foster teenager might), or in experiencing rejection because of "the virus," one is often better able to mobilize oneself to deal with the problem productively.

Discovering that other members of the group share his or her feelings often helps release a client from the power of the feelings. Guilt over "evil" thoughts and feelings can be lessened and self-destructive cycles broken when one discovers they are normal and shared by others. For example, a parent of a child with a physical or mental disability who hears that other parents may also feel that their child's condition represents "God's punishment" may be better able to cope with guilt. This can be one of the most powerful forces for change resulting from the mutual-aid process. A worker in individual work may reassure the client that others share the same feelings. However, it cannot compare with the impact of hearing them articulated by others in group sessions.

In another example from the AIDS/Recovery group, one member talked of her fears of being rejected by her boyfriend because she had AIDS and he did not. Even though the boyfriend knew about her AIDS and seemed to accept it, she was afraid to ask for a stronger commitment from him, because she thought he would turn her down and she would lose him. Although she was an attractive young woman, she feared that no one else could ever love her because of "the virus." A male member of the group responded, saying, "That's the thing you fear most—the rejection. I just disconnect my telephone and stay in my room because I know if I get close to someone, I'm just going to be rejected again."

Developing a Universal Perspective

Developing a universal perspective is a mutual-aid process in the group in which members begin to perceive universal issues, particularly in relation to oppression, thus allowing them to view their own problems in a more social context and with less personal blame. Expanding one's perspective is a special case of the all-in-the-same-boat phenomenon just described. Many clients, particularly those belonging to oppressed and vulnerable populations, may internalize the negative definitions assigned to them by the larger society. Thus, battered women, survivors of sexual abuse, people of color, the mentally ill, or people with AIDS may see their difficulties as a product of their own shortcomings. Mental health professionals who focus on personal pathology while ignoring the socioeconomic factors that created and constantly reinforce the negative self-image can reinforce this self-blame.

As members of a mutual-aid group share their common experiences of oppression, clients find it easier to recognize that a source of their problems may be external to them. For example, early in the women's movement, "consciousness-raising" groups arose to help women become more aware of gender stereotyping and oppression issues that affected their lives. A more universal perspective on one's problems can lift the burden of taking all of the blame for one's troubles. The anger against the oppression—anger that often lurks just beneath the outward signs of depression, submission, and apathy—can be released and converted into positive energy for dealing with personal as well as social issues.

In an example described in some detail in Chapter 13, a group of young female survivors of sexual abuse supported one another in recognizing the social roots of the gender oppression and violence they experienced. In a pivotal meeting, the worker announced that a "Take Back the Night" march would occur in their town the following week and wondered if group members might want to participate. An important discussion between the women, which highlighted how these women had been taught to accept their "victim" status, led to their decision to attend the march as a group. This experience, resulting from their ability to universalize their perspective, may well have been one of the most therapeutic aspects of the group practice.

In an example from the AIDS/Recovery group, one woman talked about the sexual exploitation she experienced both from her "Johns" while prostituting and from her boyfriends over the years. A transgender female member of the group angrily declared that, in her experience, sex is all most men are interested in and they will use and exploit you and your feelings, if they can, in order to get it. To underscore her point, she declared, "And I know, because I have been both!" After the group members stopped their good-natured laughing at her comment, there followed a discussion among the men and women of the group about intimate relationships, how hard it is to find people who really care, and how painful it is to lose someone who does.

Mutual Support

Mutual support occurs when group members provide emotional support to one another. When the group culture supports the open expression of feelings, members can empathize with one another. The group leader sets the tone through expression of personal feelings and understanding of others. Because group members share some concerns, however, they often understand one another's feelings in a deeper way than the worker. This expression of empathy facilitates healing for both the group member who receives it and the one who offers it. Specifically, as group members understand the feelings of the others, without judging them harshly, they begin to accept their own feelings in new ways. For a member struggling with a specific concern, the acceptance and caring of the group can be a source of support during a difficult time.

The idea of the acceptance and caring of the group introduces a new concept. It implies that the entity created when people are brought together—the group-as-a-whole—involves more than just the simple sum of the parts (members). For example, support from the mutual-aid group often differs from support received from a single empathic person. This is more than just a quantitative difference of more people equaling more empathy. At crucial moments in a group, one can sense a general tone or atmosphere, displayed through words, expressions, or physical posture, that conveys the caring of the group for the individual. This seems to have a special meaning and importance to the individual member. (See Chapter 12 for more on this and other properties of the group-as-a-whole.)

In the following example, also from the AIDS/Recovery group, the client who is reluctant to confront her boyfriend for fear of losing him asks the transgender member how she looks:

> Once again, Theresa asked Tania how she looked. She said, "You're a woman. I know, as a woman, you will be honest with me and just tell me what you think. Do you think I look OK?" Tania seemed confused and said, "Well, sure, you look wonderful." I said, "I wonder if Theresa is really asking, 'Am I pretty enough? Am I attractive enough? If my boyfriend leaves me, can I find someone else who could love me even though I have AIDS?'" She said, "That's it," and came close to tears. She said, "I'm so afraid, if I lose him, I won't find anyone else." She said, "I know I could have guys, and I know I could have sex, and I like the sex. I sure missed it during the time I was in prison, but can another guy love me?"

The group members tried to reassure her that she was a wonderful person, and Tania said, "It's not what you look like on the outside, it's what you're like on the inside." And she said, "And you honey—you've really got it where it counts."

Mutual Demand

Earlier in this book, we saw how the helping relationship consisted of elements of both support and demand, synthesized in unique, personal ways. The same is true in the group context. In **mutual demand**, group members offer each other help by making demands and setting expectations on personal behavior. One illustration is the way group members confront one another. For example, in my couples' group two male members challenged a third who was maintaining that the source of the problem was his wife, that she was the identified patient, and he was coming to group merely to help her out. Both of the confronting group members had taken the same position at our first session and had slowly modified their views. They had lowered their defenses and accepted the idea that the problem was a "couples" problem. Coming from group members, this demand on the third member had a different quality from any that the group leader might have made.

As the group culture develops, it can include expectations that members will risk their real thoughts and ideas, listen to one another and set their own concerns aside at times to help one another, and so on. Such expectations help develop a productive culture for work. For example, the group may expect members to work on their concerns. At moments when clients feel overwhelmed and hopeless, this expectation may help them take a next step. The group cares enough about them not to let them give up. I have witnessed group members take some difficult action, such as confronting a boss or dealing more effectively with a close relative. When the action was discussed the following week, they indicated that one of the factors that had pushed them to make the move and take a risk was the thought of returning to the group and admitting that they had not acted. Mutual demand, integrated with mutual support, can be a powerful force for change.

In my AIDS/Recovery group, members often used their insights and understanding about the recovery process, gained through participation in 12-step groups such as Alcoholics Anonymous (AA) and Narcotics Anonymous (NA), to confront one another when their behaviors threatened their recovery. In one example, a group member who had just spent 2 weeks in a detoxification program after relapsing into cocaine use described how hard it was for him not to "hang around" the pool hall where all his friends were. He described how he wavered each day, wondering if he could connect up with them and not relapse again. Using an analogy obviously known by the group, one of the other members said, "You know, John, if you hang around a barbershop long enough" and then he paused. The rest of the group, in a chorus, replied, "You're going to get a haircut!" Everyone laughed, and John replied, "I know, I know, you're right, I would definitely be risking my recovery."

Individual Problem-Solving

A mutual-aid group can be a place where an individual asks for assistance with a particular problem. The group members help one member to solve a particular problem, receiving help themselves while offering it to another. For example, in one group a young mother discussed the strained relationship between her mother and herself. Her mother lived nearby and was constantly calling and asking to come over.

The group member had been extremely depressed and was going through periods where she neglected her work at home (dishes piling up in the sink and so on). Each time her mother came over, she felt, because of her mother's actions, that she was being reprimanded for being a poor housekeeper and a poor mother to her young children. The resulting tension produced many arguments, including some between the husband and wife. The client felt her mother still treated her like a child even though she was 27.

When the client presented the issue, at first indirectly and later with much feeling and tears, the group members reached out to offer support and understanding. They could use their own experiences to share similar feelings. The older members of the group provided their own perspective on the actions of the client's mother. They could identify with her feelings, and they pointed out how uncertain she might feel about how to help her daughter. When the group discussed conversations and incidents described by the client, they offered new interpretations of the interactions. It became clear that the client's perceptions were often distorted by her own feelings of inadequacy and her harsh judgments of herself. The worker also provided a new perspective by describing the problem as a normative crisis in life as the young couple sought new ways to relate to her parents, and the parents, in turn, struggled to find ways of being close while still letting go. There were other issues involved as well, related to some of the reasons for the client's depression, such as her feelings of being trapped at home and trapped as a woman. These emerged in later sessions.

Note that as the group members offered help to the individual with the problem, they were also helping themselves. Each member could make associations to a similar concern. All of them could see how easily the communications between mother and daughter were going astray. As they tried to help the client clarify her own feelings, understand her mother's reactions in new ways, and see how the mutual stereotypes interfered with the ability to communicate real feelings, the other members could relate these ideas to their own close relationships. This is one of the important ways in which giving help in a mutual-aid group is a form of self-help. It is always easier to see the problem in someone else's relationships than in your own. The general learning of the group members can be enhanced through the specific problem-solving work done with each member. The group leader can help by pointing out the underlying common themes.

Rehearsal

Another way in which a mutual-aid group can help is through **rehearsal**, in which the group provides a forum wherein members can try out ideas or skills. In a sense, the group becomes a safe place to risk new ways of communicating and to practice actions the client feels may be hard to do. To continue with the previous example, as the session neared the end, the group leader pointed out that the client seemed hesitant about taking up the issue with her mother. The following excerpt from the process recording starts with the client's response.

ROSE: I'm not sure I can talk with my mother about this. What would I say?
WORKER: That's a good question. How about trying it out right here? I'll pretend to be your mother calling to ask to see you. You can practice how you would respond, and the group can give some ideas about how it sounds. Does that sound all right?
ROSE: (She stops crying now and is sitting straight up in her chair with a slight smile on her face.) OK. You call me and tell me you want to have lunch with me and that I should keep the kids home from school so you can see them.

WORKER: (Role-playing) Hello, Rose, this is Mom.

ROSE: Hi, Mom. How are you and Dad feeling?

WORKER: Not so good. You know, Dad gets upset easily, and he has been feeling lousy. (The client had indicated that her mother often used her father's health to try to make her feel guilty.)

ROSE: That's it! That's what she would say to make me feel guilty. (The group members are laughing at this point.)

The discussion picked up, with the group members agreeing about how easy it is for others to make us feel guilty. The worker asked how Rose would feel at that point in the conversation. It became clear that the rest of the discussion would consist of her indirect responses to what she perceives as her mother's "laying on a guilt trip." After some discussion of what the mother might have been really feeling and having trouble in saying (such as how much she and her father really care about Rose and how much she needs to see her), the group brainstormed ways to break the usual cycle of indirect communications. The key moment in the role play came when the mother asked Rose to keep her children home for the mother's lunch visit. Rose had complained that the mother never wanted to see her alone—it was always with the children. She was always asking to have them at home when she visited. She thought her mother didn't trust her with the kids and was always checking up on her.

WORKER: (Speaking as the mother) I wonder, Rose, if part of the reason I always ask to have the kids there is that I'm uncomfortable when we get together. I'm not sure what I would say to you for a whole two hours. I want the kids around to help fill the conversation.

ROSE: You know, I'm not sure what I would say to my mother either. I really don't know what to talk to her about.

FRAN: (Another group member) Can you try to tell your mother that you get upset when she asks to keep the kids home because you want to have some time alone with her? Maybe your mother could understand that. (Silence)

WORKER: Rose, do you really want to spend some time with your mother?

ROSE: I'm not so sure I do.

WORKER: Then that's the first step. When you're sure, I think the words will come more easily. If you tell your mother how you really feel, it could be the start of some honest talk between you. Perhaps she could share some of her real feelings in response, instead of always doing it indirectly and in ways which are open to misinterpretation. Maybe if you could do this, then your mother would see this as a sign of your maturity.

Rose tried to articulate her feelings more clearly but was obviously still having difficulty. She reported the following week that she had talked with her mother about how it made her feel when the mother tried to do things for her (such as wash the dishes when she came over), and the mother had responded by describing how she never really knew what to do when she came over—should she help out or not? Rose felt it cleared the air, even though other issues and feelings were not discussed. The interesting thing about the role-playing device as a form of rehearsal is that is often reveals the underlying ambivalence and resistance that the client feels but has not expressed in the discussion. The rehearsal not only offers the client a chance to practice, it also reveals to the group, the worker, and the client some of the feelings that need to be dealt with if the client is to succeed in his or her efforts.

In the AIDS/Recovery group, the client who had raised boyfriend problems used the group at one point to consider how to approach him with her concerns. One member helped by role-playing how Theresa could handle the conversation:

> We returned to Theresa, and I said, "Is the question really, Theresa, that you're afraid that he might not stay with you—that, if you actually confront him on this issue of the other women, he might leave you?" She agreed that it was her concern. At this point, I wondered if it might help Theresa to figure out what she might say to her boyfriend. Theresa said that would be helpful because she didn't know when and how to say it. Then she laughed and said, "Maybe I should say it in bed." Tania said, "Oh no. Don't say it before sex and don't say it after sex." And I added, "And don't say it during sex." Everyone laughed at this point, and Tania, a stand-up comedian, did an imitation of having a conversation with Theresa's boyfriend, while pumping up and down as if she were in bed having sex with him.
>
> Tania said, "You have to find a quiet time, not a time when you're in the middle of a fight, and you have to just put out your feelings." I asked Tania if she could show Theresa how she could do that. She started to speak as if she were talking to Theresa's boyfriend. I role-played the boyfriend and said, "Oh, but Theresa you're just insecure, aren't you?" Tania did a very good job of not letting me put her off and, instead, putting the issue right where it was—whether I was prepared to make a commitment or if I was too insecure.
>
> Theresa said, "I know I have to talk to him, but, you know, he's told me that he's not sure he wants to be tied down, that he likes to have his freedom." Jake nodded his head and said, "Yeah, that's the problem, they want their freedom and they don't want to make a commitment, and you're afraid, if you push him, he'll leave you because you got the virus." Theresa said she realized she had to sit down and talk to him because it couldn't keep up the same way. She would just get too angry and do something crazy and screw up her recovery. She said when she had a fight with him on Thanksgiving he did call his sponsor and came back much more gently. She felt she had gotten through to him, but she had to find another way to get through to him and talk to him. Otherwise, this thing was just going to continue and it was going to tear her up inside.

The "Strength-in-Numbers" Phenomenon

Sometimes it is easier to do things as a group than as an individual. The **"strength-in-numbers" phenomenon** is a mutual-aid process in which group members are strengthened to take on difficult tasks through the support of other group members. In one example, described earlier, a group of female survivors of sexual abuse attended a "Take Back the Night" march. In another example, described in Chapter 16, individual tenants in a housing project found it difficult to stand up to the housing authority on issues of poor maintenance service. When organized into a tenants' group, the "strength-in-numbers" phenomenon worked to decrease their feelings of isolation and individual risk, which encouraged the group members to make demands for their rights. An individual's fears and ambivalence can be overcome by participation in a group effort as his or her own courage is strengthened by the courage of others.

I have shared several examples to illustrate how the dynamics of the mutual-aid process can work. These examples should not suggest that working in groups is a preferred method. The choice of individual or group work is influenced by many factors, particularly the comfort of the clients in dealing with their concerns on a one-to-one basis as opposed to within a group setting. A client often finds both kinds of work helpful at the same time. Each would have a slightly different focus, and each could be expected to provide important stimulation for the other. For many clients, the group can offer unique forms of help in dealing with their life problems. I have attempted to identify some of these mutual-aid processes, but it is important to realize that groups will not provide this kind of help just because they have been brought together. In the next section, we briefly examine some of the obstacles that can make mutual aid a difficult process. These obstacles and others will be explored in detail in later chapters.

Obstacles to Mutual Aid

In the early phases of a group's development, one potential obstacle to mutual aid is the apparent divergent interest each group member brings to the engagement. Even in a group with a narrow, clearly defined purpose, group members might not identify their common ground. Various group members may feel their concerns and feelings are unique and unrelated to those of other members. The symbiotic attractions among members may be partial, subtle, and difficult to perceive.

In many ways, the small group is a microcosm of the larger society. The apparent diffusion of interest in the group between self and other group members is a reflection of the same inability to see the connections in our larger society. Thus, as each member becomes oriented to the group engagement, that member will be asking, "How am I the same or different from the other members?"

Given these concerns, one of the early tasks of the group leader will be to help group members begin to identify their common ground. As the group develops a mature way of relating, individual members can begin to understand that they can learn and grow by giving help as well as receiving it. As each member develops the skills required to offer help and to take help, these same skills will be found to be related to their individual concerns outside of the group. For example, group members who learn how to identify their feelings and to share them in the group may be able to apply these skills in other intimate relationships. Nevertheless, at the beginning stage and periodically during the life of the group, the inability of members to perceive their connections to the others will present an important obstacle.

A second set of obstacles emerges from the fact that even a small group can be a complex system that must deal with many developmental tasks if it is to work productively. As soon as more than one client is involved, a new organism is created: the group-as-a-whole. As we have seen, this group is more than the simple sum of its parts (that is, the individual members). For example, this new organism needs to develop rules and procedures that will allow it to function effectively. Some will be openly discussed, while others may operate beneath the surface by mutual consent. Roles such as scapegoat, deviant member, and internal leader may be subtly distributed to group members. Some of these role assignments allow the group-as-a-whole to avoid dealing directly with a problem. For example, the group gatekeeper may intervene to distract the group each time the discussion approaches a painful subject. Many of the unstated rules for relating will be counterproductive to the purpose of the group. Such factors are properties of this complex organism called the group and must be dealt with by the leader if the group is to function effectively.

A final major source of potential problems for the group is the difficulty of open communication. I have already discussed some of the barriers that make it difficult for clients to express their real feelings and concerns. These are related to a social culture that has implicitly and explicitly developed certain norms of behavior and identified taboo areas in which honest communication is hard to achieve. Each group member brings a part of this culture into the group, and thus the group culture, in early phases of work, resembles the culture of the social surroundings. This often makes it difficult for group members to talk with and listen to one another in areas of central concern. With the group leader's help, members will need to develop a new culture in which norms are modified and taboos lose their power, so that members may freely communicate with one another.

I have just outlined three major obstacles to mutual aid: the difficulty individual members have in identifying with other group members, the complex tasks involved in creating a mutual-aid system, and the difficulties in communicating honestly. Such obstacles define in part the job of the group leader. They do not argue against the use of groups as mutual-aid systems; rather, they represent an agenda for the group worker. If groups were not faced with these problems, and if people could easily join together to offer aid and support, then there would be no need for a group worker. The small group is a special case of the larger individual-social engagement described in Chapter 1; as such, it essentially carries the same potential for diffusion of the symbiotic relationship. Once again, the functional role of mediation will be used as a starting point for describing the tasks of the helping person—this time, however, in the context of group work.

The Function of the Group Leader

In the earlier discussion of Schwartz's mediation practice theory, the function of the helping person was illustrated using three circles (see Figure 1.2). The client was on the left, the systems to be negotiated on the right, and the worker in the middle. Because the group is a specific case of this larger engagement, the same diagram can be drawn with the individual on the left and the group on the right.

The general function of mediating the individual-social engagement is now translated into mediating the individual-group interaction. This leads Schwartz to present one of his most central and useful ideas about group work: that the group worker always has two clients—the individual and the group. The function of the worker is to mediate the engagement between these two clients. As the group process unfolds, the worker is constantly concerned with both. For example, when an individual raises a specific concern, the worker will help the member share that concern with the group. Chapter 4 detailed how difficult it often can be for clients to describe their concerns. All the worker skills described earlier—such as reading indirect communications and helping clients move from the general to the specific—can be employed to help individuals express their concerns to the group. As the leader helps the one talk to the many, she or he will also monitor the interaction to see if the members appear to be listening and relating to the individual. If they seem to be turned off, the worker will explore their feelings and reactions. Perhaps the individual's problem is painful to the group members, raising related feelings of their own and making it hard for them to listen. In any case, the group worker, with a clear sense of function, will pay attention to both clients at exactly the same time.

Like the first client (the individual), the second client (the group) needs help from the worker in dealing with the obstacles described earlier. For example, if the group culture is making it difficult for members to discuss their real feelings about a specific issue, then the worker can call this to the attention of the group. Bringing the obstacle out in the open is a first step in helping the group members become more conscious of their own processes. With the assistance of the worker, members can discuss how the blockage of open communication in a sensitive area frustrates their work. With understanding comes growth as the group becomes more sophisticated about its ways of working. A new agreement, including new norms that are more productive, can be openly reached. In many ways the group worker serves as a guide for the group members faced with the complex task of developing an effective mutual-aid system. The important point is that this is the members' group: The work to strengthen it is theirs, and the group worker is there to help them to do it.

In a general way, these two areas of work characterize the group leader's responsibilities: helping the individual and the group relate effectively to one another, and helping the group become more sophisticated about the group's way of working, so that it releases the potential for mutual aid. Of course, this process is more complicated than this simple explanation implies. In the remaining chapters of Part IV, we shall explore the underlying assumptions about how mutual-aid groups work and the tasks and skills required of the group worker.

Chapter Summary

Common fears of new group leaders, referred to as the fear-of-groups syndrome, are understandable and may be overcome. Clients have many ways of helping one another in mutual-aid groups. These include sharing data, the dialectical process, discussing taboo areas, the "all-in-the-same-boat" phenomenon, developing a universal perspective, mutual support, mutual demand, individual problem-solving, rehearsal, and the "strength-in-numbers" phenomenon. Three major areas of obstacles to the mutual-aid process in groups are the difficulty in identifying common ground, the tasks required to develop a positive culture for work, and the general difficulty of open communication. The role of the group leader is an extension of the mediating function into the group context. The group leader mediates between two clients: the individual and the group-as-a-whole.

Related Online Content and Activities

 Visit *The Skills of Helping* Book Companion Website at www.socialwork.wadsworth.com/Shulman06/ for learning tools such as glossary terms, InfoTrac College Edition keywords, links to related websites, and chapter practice quizzes.

The website for this chapter also features additional notes from the author.

Group Formation

CHAPTER OUTLINE

Preparing for Group Work

Work With the Staff System

Group Composition, Timing, and Structure

Work With Prospective Members

I n this chapter, we explore in detail the steps required to establish a group and to increase its chances for success. Work with the staff system is dealt with first, because much that follows depends upon these efforts. Next, issues related to group formation (timing, composition, and so on) are explored. The impact of ethnicity and culture in the group formation stage is discussed, as well as problems of recruitment. Finally, we return to the tuning-in skill, this time applying it to a first session in the group context.

Preparing for Group Work

Because several crucial issues must be dealt with before the first meeting takes place, the preparatory phase can be one of the most complicated in work with groups. The literature on group work pays surprisingly little attention to the problems of this phase, beyond discussion of group type (as in educational, therapeutic, support), structure (as in frequency and number of sessions), group composition, and so on. For example, one problem that is often ignored concerns staff dynamics. It is not unusual for a worker to decide that a group would be helpful for clients and then to approach colleagues for appropriate referrals. A staff meeting might bring general agreement to support the group; however, the worker waits 2 months without getting a single referral. In analyzing examples of this kind, I have consistently found that the worker had left out the important step of involving the colleagues in a meaningful way. I could often determine the moment in the staff meeting when the groundwork was laid for the frustration that followed.

Similarly, a worker may launch a group and prepare for a first meeting with ten members who have promised to attend. The evening of the meeting arrives, and after waiting 35 long and painful minutes for latecomers, the worker must face the reality that only two members have come. Once again, the source of the disappointment can often be traced to steps that were left out in the preparatory work with clients as the worker or other workers began the referral process. In analysis of interviews and telephone conversations, one can often identify the moment the worker sensed the ambivalence of the prospective group member but did not reach for it.

In the sections that follow, these and other group formation issues will be discussed, with an emphasis on describing and illustrating strategies for launching effective mutual-aid groups.

Work With the Staff System

An important first principle is that a group in an agency or institution must be related to the service. If a worker attempts to establish a group because of a desire to develop new skills or because he or she has decided (without involving the rest of the staff) that there is a need for such a group, the work may be doomed to failure. A common example is the student who is placed in an agency for practicum experience and is taking a course in group work practice. A requirement for the class is to have a group, so the student endeavors to set one up in the field. Quite often the group never has its first meeting, because the student's need for it is not a sound reason for developing a group. The idea for a group must begin with the identification of an area of clients' unmet needs that the group method might meet. The group must reflect the consensus of the department or team involved so that it is not seen as being personally "owned" by the group worker.

The difficulty or ease involved in establishing a group may depend on the group experience of the agency. In those settings where groups are a common form of service and where all staff members take their turn at leadership, many of the problems of formation can be minimized. In agencies that usually do not offer groups as a service, such problems may be intensified. For example, a worker who attempts to introduce group work into a setting that has never had groups must recognize that such a move might threaten staff. As we saw in the previous chapter, many workers are frightened by the idea of facing more than one client at a time. If they do not have a fund of good experiences to draw on or if they unsuccessfully attempted to establish a group when they were students, they may be hesitant about working with groups. The worker attempting to initiate a group service must recognize that colleagues may wonder whether they will be asked to carry a group next, especially if the first succeeds. This fear is often expressed indirectly with comments such as "Groups would be great in this agency, but do we really have the time?" The development of group service can have an important impact on the staff system, and the worker should make use of the tuning-in skill in preparing to negotiate the establishment of the group.

Staff resistance also occurs when the administration of an agency or organization, because of the pressures of managed care or other cutbacks in resources, has decided to move into group work as a measure of **cost containment.** In reality, group practice may actually increase costs, because it rarely serves as a substitute in those situations where individual work is required. In many cases, issues that emerge in the group for one client may generate the need for more intensive individual work, rather than less work, for other group members. Group work should be the practice modality of choice only if it is the best modality for the particular population and problem. When cost cutting is the only rationale offered, staff resistance due to fears about competency is often masked by staff anger at the "top-down" imposition of group practice. Whether the reasons for developing group work practice are sound or spurious, the use of group work has expanded explosively. Further, a documented decrease in group work content in social work education programs has accompanied this expansion. Any system considering moving into group practice must also consider the need for staff training and consultation to ensure the quality of the practice.

In the rest of this section, excerpts from an effort by a hospital social worker to establish a ward group illustrate the dynamics and the skills involved in preparatory work with staff.

Achieving Consensus on the Service

The idea of a group may emerge in an agency in many ways: client feedback, a worker discovering a common concern among individual clients, or a staff team discovering an important gap in the service. Wherever the idea starts, all staff involved must have the opportunity to comment honestly on the potential service. A common mistake is for workers to decide on the need for a group and then to set about "selling" colleagues on the idea. Rather than presenting their own views on the need for it and inviting feedback and discussion, workers may try to influence their colleagues, creating the illusion that they are involving others in the process. In the following illustration, a young social worker, relatively new to the hospital, approaches a long-time head nurse about forming a group on the ward. The nurse has a reputation for being tough and uncooperative on projects such as this, so the worker has steeled herself for the task of convincing the nurse of the need for the group. The illustration demonstrates the problems generated when one tries to "sell" an idea.

> I said to Miss Ford that I had been doing some thinking which I would like to share with her. I told her that I had been on the ward quite a bit and felt quite at home on it. I said to her that I, as everyone else on the ward, am here to try to service the patients to the best of my ability. I then asked her what she thought of a group having any value on the ward. She said that it has been

suggested before, so that it was nothing new. She said that the room full of ladies could do with something of that sort but that that's the only ladies' room there is. I asked if she thought that only ladies could benefit from a group experience and she said no, but that she was thinking in terms of room number 1403. She asked what the group would be about and for. I said that I'm open to suggestions but that perhaps the basic purpose could be for the patients to discuss their hospitalization, frustrations, etc. It would be open to all patients.

Although the worker said she wanted to explore the nurse's views, she really did not mean it. The nurse quickly sensed her purpose when she did not explore the suggestion that the patients in room 1403 might benefit from a group. The worker was still reacting, on an emotional level, to the nurse's first comment that the idea had been suggested before and that it was nothing new. Had the worker not been so set on convincing the nurse, she could have asked for an elaboration of the nurse's first comment. What had that earlier effort been like? Had there been any problems? The worker is new on the ward, and the nurse might have shared some past experiences that could have provided helpful feedback. Because the worker has already pegged the nurse as resistant, however, she did not reach past this first comment. The same lack of genuine interest in the nurse's views is demonstrated when the worker challenges her suggestion that the women in room 1403 might need the help. As the worker will find out later, this room contains patients with terminal cancer. It represents a room full of problems for which the nursing staff has genuine concern but few ideas for helping. It could represent an important area of missing service, but the worker does not know this because she has cut off the nursing supervisor's participation in the process.

After the nurse received the signals confirming her own stereotype of workers as outsiders who do not really appreciate the problems of the ward, she responded rather perfunctorily, asking crisp questions about the worker's proposed group:

Miss Ford asked how the patients would know or how I would tell them. I told her that in order to make it a voluntary thing, perhaps written invitations to each patient would be a good idea. She asked when and where it would be held. I told her that I hoped she could help make that decision, especially the time, because I realize they are busy. As far as the room goes, I suggested, perhaps an empty bedroom or the sunroom. She said that by October 16th all rooms should be filled up. I suggested we could decide on that at a later date. I asked if she could, however, talk to the doctors and staff about this, get some ideas, and we could discuss it again next week at rounds. She said that would be fine.

At the end of the worker's process recording, she included the following comment:

Miss Ford did not seem too enthusiastic and was quite resistant (mentioning no rooms, how would patients know, etc.). However, I feel she can see some value in a ward group. Next week I plan to give her some examples of why I can see a need for the group.

If the worker had done that, she likely would have met the same resistance. If she had continued to accept the nurse's superficial agreement, she would have proceeded to set up her group and probably been surprised on the day of her first meeting. Either the room would have been unavailable or the worker would have discovered that half the patients she had selected for the group session had been "inadvertently" scheduled for blood tests, X-rays, or other medical procedures that took them off the ward. The nursing staff would have apologized, and the problem would have repeated itself the following week. The worker would eventually have given up, adding one more story to the collection of examples of how "resistant" Miss Ford was to any new ideas.

The missing skill in this interview was described in Part II as "looking for trouble when everything seems to be going the worker's way." In this case, the worker sensed the underlying negative reaction in the interview but did not reach for it. For example, she could have said, "Miss Ford, you don't seem too enthusiastic about this group. Can you tell me why not?" This direct response to the indirect cue would have opened up Miss Ford's real feelings and reactions and might have turned a one-way selling job into an honest exploration of mutual thoughts about a new service. In many ways, the nurse's fair amount of directness about her feelings should have been an aid to the worker. At least her feelings were almost out in the open. By contrast, there are many instances, as when a worker is describing a group to other workers at a team meeting, when the worker might find an artificial agreement expressed through apparently unqualified support. Once again, the skilled worker would not leave the session without first reaching for the underlying reservations. For example, the worker might say, "It's great to see such quick support for my idea, but you know, it's going to cause some problems and inconveniences for the rest of you. Don't you think we should also talk about those?"

The worker often senses the underlying resistance but fears reaching for it. The belief is that if one leaves the negatives unexpressed, they might go away. They never do. These reservations, negative reactions, fears, and the like all come back to haunt the worker in the form of conscious or unconscious sabotage of the worker's plans. To establish a group successfully, the worker must insist that it be a service of the staff, not just the worker. It is not the worker's personal group that happens to be taking place in this setting. Without real support from the rest of the staff, the worker will be alone when problems emerge. I have seen excellent work done with school principals, for example, when after the principal has given perfunctory agreement to allow a group to meet in the school, the worker has asked, "Would you be very upset if we couldn't offer this group to your kids?" After a moment's pause, the principal has responded, "The only reason I OK these groups is that the people at the board like to see them in the schools. Actually, staff and I often find they are more trouble than they are worth." Only at this point does the real discussion begin, and the worker can start serious contracting with the agency or setting. If this stage is skipped over in the worker's eagerness to gain a toehold, then the lack of real investment will hurt when the going gets rough in the group.

Fortunately, as in work with clients, workers can usually go back after making a mistake and try again. After some consultation and discussion of the first process recording of the interview with the nurse, the worker returned to Miss Ford; instead of trying to convince her, she owned up to her mistake and tried to start over again. You will notice the change in the nurse's attitude as the discussion becomes real:

> I told Miss Ford that I felt I may have been too pushy about the ward group. I said that I had asked for her participation and interest, yet I hadn't given her a chance to express herself, and I wasn't really listening to her. I then apologized and suggested that we might go back to the beginning. I said I was interested in knowing her true feelings regarding the group. She said she thought the group would be very good for most patients, but she was worried about the manpower of nurses. She said it was difficult enough to get all the nurses to attend her

ward conference without having them attend a patients' group. I asked if she was thinking in terms of all the nurses going to the group at once. She said she didn't know and wondered what I thought. I said that the decision of nurses was up to her. I suggested that it might be just as effective to have one nurse drop in on the group or have the nurses rotate.

This may have been the issue on the head nurse's mind when she commented on the group having been tried before. The worker needs to pay attention to the problems that the group creates for the ongoing system. The worker must be able to empathize genuinely with the day-to-day difficulties of other staff members. Often, the recognition of these problems can lead to alternative solutions or to the willingness of the staff to extend themselves. As in all human relationships, the worker must truly understand how the other staff member feels. The discussion in the interview turned to the issue of purpose and contract:

I suggested that one important gap existed between patients and doctors or patients and nurses. I explained further that I believed that if a patient could release some of his anxieties or fears about his medical problems or share his hostilities in the group, he might be an easier patient to cope with. Rather than expressing his feelings in an undesirable way, he might be happier on the ward and easier to deal with. Miss Ford agreed with this and then asked about the resident on the ward. How could we keep him involved? We discussed this for a while.

Although the worker's contract statement is still unclear—reflecting her own lack of clarity—the general sense of the group dealing with issues related to hospital and illness and with communication between patient and staff is clearly suggested. This is important, because workers who do not connect the purpose of a proposed group to the general service of the agency are often seen as simply requesting space. When administrators and staff members perceive the connection between their service and the purpose of the group, they will be more likely to invest themselves in the group's development. A worker offering to lead a group for children who have been identified by teachers as having trouble at school will be more easily accepted by the staff than one asking to lead groups for general discussion (for example, "I would like to work with children who need a socialization experience").

As the discussion with Miss Ford continued, her more active involvement showed:

Miss Ford asked how the patients would know about the group, who would go, etc. I suggested that the nurses see all the patients, and they could tell who could benefit from a group experience, and who was ready to go. She asked how patients would find out about the group. I suggested we stick notices to their bedside tables. She said it would not be a good idea because the tables must be washed. She suggested we put them in the bathrooms where the beauty salon advertises. I said it was a good idea, and we went to the bathroom to select the best spot. I then brought up the subject of confidentiality.

The worker has used her tuning-in preparation to anticipate another sensitive area for discussion—the issue of confidentiality. Although the nurse has not raised this issue, she is likely wondering what would happen if patients complained about the nursing staff. This issue is often difficult for workers. It often lies under the surface when a worker proposes a group in a hospital, school, or residential setting, or when the worker is sharing clients with another worker but the first worker will continue to see the client on an individual basis. The group worker often suggests to the staff the need to maintain confidentiality, not reporting group discussion, so that the group members will feel free to talk. When group members talk negatively about staff, they often hope the worker will help improve a bad situation. They are also concerned about how the information will be used (the possibility of retribution from the teacher, nurse, and so forth). They are not, however, raising the concerns just for the sake of venting feelings.

Acting as a communication bridge between clients and the agency system—the mediating approach—is very much a part of the work. When the two-way flow of communication is not acknowledged, trouble results. For example, if the worker begins work with staff by stating they will not be included in discussion of group content, their fears and anxieties may lead to direct or indirect efforts at sabotage. In one such case, a worker in a home for unmarried mothers had completely ignored the housemother's concerns, particularly her fear of complaints, and had indicated that all discussions would be confidential. When the worker arrived, the housemother rang a bell and shouted, to the worker's consternation, "Group therapy time." In other examples, the worker's colleagues have described the group to their individual clients in a way that served to heighten the clients' fears of involvement: "We are going to offer this group for single mothers, but you don't have to go if you don't want to."

Clearly, the work of setting up a mutual-aid group involves careful contracting with staff, especially regarding confidentiality. That is, because the worker's sense of function involves communicating between client and system, including the agency, this must be part of the contract. Nurses, child care workers, teachers, and other counselors must be viewed as colleagues, with each having a part in the operation. Discussions should focus on how the group worker and the other staff members will handle feedback. The meaning of the feedback and the way in which clients might use either the individual worker or the group worker as a channel must be recognized. The agreement can include ways to achieve the optimum outcome, in which each will attempt to assist the clients' efforts to provide direct feedback to the other. I have found that this discussion often takes much of the threat out of the possibility of negative feedback and turns it into an important technical issue for both workers.

When I explore why workers are reluctant to follow this course of action—that is, to treat staff as colleagues and work out agreements for mutual sharing of relevant information—they raise several objections. First, they usually express concern about the client's acceptance of such a contract. Next, they express their own fears about confronting a colleague with "bad news." How do you tell a staff member with whom you have coffee each day that his client doesn't feel he understands her? Setting up a contract regarding what sort of information is to be shared—and in particular, obtaining agreements from colleagues to be open with each either even in regard to negative feedback—serves to protect the group worker from such scenarios. Finally, workers often reveal that they have developed stereotypes of their colleagues as "lousy" workers (poor teachers, insensitive doctors, and so on), so what good would sharing be? I can understand their reticence to take on this function, yet if the group worker accepts that the nurse on the ward, the teacher, a fellow social worker, or whoever is actually closed to change, such acceptance means that an important part of the service to clients will no longer be available. The worker will inevitably be in a serious quandary when the "strength-in-numbers" phenomenon leads the group members to share their real feelings. A situation will have been set up that makes it impossible for the worker to do anything about the problem except empathize, ignore it, or defend the system. This often leads to apathy and disengagement on the part of the group members.

The question of confidentiality has broadened during this discussion to encompass a much larger issue: the function of the helping person within his or her own helping system. This will be explored in detail in Part V. Clearly, this concern is often a central issue for staff members when group formation is discussed. It is best discussed out in the open, and contracting should take place with both staff and group members for freedom of communication of group content in a responsible manner. Returning to the interview, we find that this is precisely what our worker on the hospital ward does.

> I then brought up the subject of confidentiality. I asked how Miss Ford felt it should be handled. For example, if one patient or more complained about a certain nurse or herself, would she like to know or not? Rather than directly answering, she told me about a patient on the ward who would complain of different shifts of staff and play one against the other. I asked her if the gist of her story was that it was better to know the complaints so that they can be investigated and dealt with. She said yes. I told her I felt the same way and that I would like to know when patients made complaints about me.
>
> We then talked about where the group could be held. I again suggested the sun porch. This time, Miss Ford said that it would be all right because patients used it anyway. We then discussed further clearances in the hospital and set up a meeting with the nursing staff to clarify the group's purpose and to select members.

The result of this effort was active involvement on the part of Miss Ford in the establishment of the group. The frontline nursing staff quickly picked up the message of positive support for the group and offered their assistance to the social worker. The group was established and became integrated into the program on the ward, with nursing staff becoming involved as coleaders.

Identifying Group Type and Structure

Staff colleagues can also be helpful in considering the question of the group type and structure. For example, will it be a group of fixed membership meeting over a period of time, or will it be an **open-ended group** in which different members arrive and leave each week? Special problems and dynamics associated with open-ended groups will be discussed in Chapter 14; however, for some purposes and settings they provide a better alternative than a fixed-membership group. One ward group in a hospital consisted of women who arrived for a 2-day preparatory stay, a 1-day exploratory operation to determine the possibility of cancer, and a 2-day recovery period. Participation of both pre- and postoperative patients lent itself to the mutual-aid process, as those who had just gone through the experience were helpful to those preparing for it, and those who were newly admitted began the process of preparing to leave the hospital by helping those who were leaving.

In contrast, a group for teenage survivors of sexual abuse would need some time to establish the levels of trust required to explore painful and formerly secret experiences. An open-ended group with a continually changing membership would not be appropriate for such a population. Some members might join after the initial sessions, but at some point, such a group would need to be closed.

Groups are sometimes formed from ongoing natural groups, such as a group home. This living group operates 7 days a week, 24 hours each day. For 2 hours twice each week, house meetings are held at special times within the ongoing group life to focus on issues of group living, such as problems among residents and between residents and staff. These meetings represent structured incidents in the life of the ongoing group designed to improve their ability to live and work together.

Another issue is related to the content of the group meeting. People can provide mutual aid not just through talking but also through other "mediums of exchange" between people (Shulman, 1971). For example, senior citizens in a residential center might use activities that they have developed to structure their time, to provide enjoyment or education, to acquire new skills, or just to enjoy the company of others. In the formation stage, workers must consider whether interaction through activity represents an important part of the purpose of the group and fits within the general function of the setting.

A ward group in a psychiatric hospital involved in planning recreational activities for patients provides an example in which activities relate both to patients' needs and to the service of the setting. On the other hand, social activities offered during the school day to a group of children who are not doing well in their classes may be viewed by the school staff as a "reward" for acting badly, even if the worker argues that the students are helped indirectly. However, when such activities are used as a substitute for discussions about class problems or because the worker is concerned that the children will not come to a "talking group," they may frustrate the essential work rather than assist it. A decision on group type (talk, activity, or both) needs to relate directly both to the service of the agency and to the needs of the group members.

One widely used framework for describing group types was developed by the group work faculty at Boston University (Bernstein, 1965, 1970). The researchers identified four general types:

1. *Support and stabilization groups* are best suited for people experiencing a life crisis such as divorce, bereavement, or economic instability. As the name implies, group support is used to help members stabilize and begin to cope with the stress.

2. *Growth and education groups,* more familiar in traditional group service agencies, are applicable to people experiencing major life developmental challenges or transitions (such as teenagers) or people with delayed development of skills because of isolating, regressive, or stagnating influences (such as long-term chronic care mental patients). The focus of the group is on learning specific competencies and social skills related to the developmental tasks.

3. *Task and action groups* include committees, grassroots community organization groups, hospital ward governments, and so on. Their focus is on tasks to be accomplished, rather than support or individual development of the group members.

4. *Recapitulation and restitution groups* are more closely related to the classical psychoanalytically oriented insight groups for adults or play therapy groups for children. Their focus is on recapitulation of life events and restitution of member strengths and positive self-esteem.

While the various types of groups are helpful in conceptualizing the central purposes of the group, Bernstein points out that no group is ever a pure form of the model. In fact, most groups can be seen to contain elements of two or more of these "classical models."

Group Versus Individual Work With Clients

Another issue that can create problems for the group worker is the compatibility of group and individual work. Some group workers believe that group members should not be seen individually because that will lessen the intensity of the group experience. Individual counselors, as well, worry that clients will use their group session to discuss central issues. This can lead to a struggle over "who owns the client," a misunderstanding of the interdependence of individual and group work and an unacceptable attitude to client participation in decisions about service.

Clients may use both individual and group help for different issues, as they see fit. For example, as the group works on the concern of a particular member, the discussion may raise a similar concern for the client, who may want a chance to discuss a special case of the general problem and may not have enough time in the group to do this. Individual sessions can provide this opportunity. Rather than robbing the individual work of its vitality, group discussion often enriches the content of the individual sessions. As clients listen to issues and understand how others are experiencing problems, they may be put in touch with feelings of their own that were not previously evident. For example, finding out that others have fears related to taboo areas, such as sex, may greatly speed up clients' willingness to discuss their own concerns in individual work.

Similarly, the work in the individual sessions can strengthen a client to raise a personal concern in the group. For some clients, sharing their most private feelings and concerns with a group may be too difficult at first. As they find they can share these with an individual counselor and not be harshly judged, they may be more willing to share them in the group. Thus, the group and individual work can be parallel and interdependent, with the client free to choose where and when to use these resources for work.

Note here again that such choices, at any particular moment, rest with the client. Only clients can discern where they feel most comfortable dealing with a particular issue. Workers may share their opinions, offer support, and even provide concrete help (role-playing in an individual session to show how the client might raise an issue in the group), but the client decides in the end.

With two and possibly more helping people working with the same client, good communication between the helpers becomes essential. They should establish structures that guarantee regular communication, so that each understands how the client is choosing to deal with issues and so that the workers can help each other in their related work. For example, in a couples' group that I led, the two coleaders were also seeing most of the couples on an individual counseling basis. In the tuning-in session we held prior to each group meeting, they summarized the specific concerns dealt with in the individual sessions. We used this preparatory work to anticipate potential group issues. I maintain a policy of not directly raising concerns in the group that were discussed in the individual work unless the couples wish them raised. Through the tuning-in process, I became more effective at picking up their indirect cues. Because the coleaders sat in on each of the sessions, they could incorporate content from the group experience into their individual work. If they were not able to sit in, I shared copies of my group process and summary reports so that they would be aware of the couples' progress. When sessions were videotaped, the tapes were also available for their use. Rather than competing for client ownership, we had three professionals, each providing a service through different modalities. As pointed out in the earlier discussion on confidentiality, without freedom to share information, this open communication would not have taken place.

Agency Support for Groups

In addition to support from colleagues, help from the agency administration may also be needed. For example, special expenses may be incurred in carrying out a group program. Mothers' groups held during the day may require babysitting services. Recruitment publicity, transportation, coffee, and other items may need to be paid for in some group programs. In addition, the worker developing a group may need a reduced individual caseload and group work consultation from an outside consultant if one is not available on staff. These issues should be discussed when the group is formed.

In some settings, where groups have not been an integral part of the service, the approach to group work programs may require the worker to take personal responsibility for their implementation. For example, workers are encouraged to develop groups if they can do so "on their own time." Many workers, eager to see the service begin or to develop new skills in work with clients, accept this responsibility but soon regret it. If a service is part of the agency function, it should not have to be carried as a personal "hobby" by the worker. Groups take time, and if workers do not foresee the full extent of their responsibilities, the additional demands on them and their feelings about them will often negatively affect their work with the group.

Even when agencies support the development of group services, they sometimes do so for the wrong reasons. Administrators may believe that seeing clients in groups can save time and so encourage a swing to group programs as a way of providing more service to clients without increasing staff. With cost-containment programs on the rise, there are situations in which seeing clients in groups does save time. For example, orientation meetings for prospective adoptive parents or new foster parents can be an effective way of starting communications. As pointed out earlier, however, more often than not the development of group services tends to increase the staff's workload, because new issues and concerns that require additional individual work may be discovered. Groups should be viewed as an important service in their own right rather than as a service substitute. A worker in a group will need time to follow up with individual members, to meet with other staff, to develop a system for recording the group work for agency accountability, and to pursue personal learning.

To start a group service on a sound agency footing is best, even though the formation process may be slower and more frustrating. Time taken by the group worker to interpret the group's purpose as well as to identify the special needs and potential problems related to instituting new group services will pay off in the long run. In those cases where doubts exist about the benefits of group practice, the worker can propose the group as an agency experimental service to be closely evaluated. Records can be kept on the costs and benefits. The agency staff and administration can use the first groups as a way of developing experience with a new form of service. The important point is that the service be "owned" by the agency, not be the personal project of a concerned worker. With the latter, it is not unusual to have a good first group only to discover that the service dies when the worker can no longer provide it personally.

Group Composition, Timing, and Structure

A conversation I had with a group of students and health professionals helps illustrate some of the myths and questions involved in planning a group. I led a group for five couples in marital difficulty; sessions were videotaped and simultaneously observed on a monitor in another room. (Transcript excerpts appear in Chapter 10.) After each session, I met with the observers and my coleaders to discuss the session. At the end of a first session, which was marked by excellent group member involvement, the students and professionals peppered me with questions on how the group had been formed. The first request was for my principles of group composition, which had led to such a lively, interactive group. One couple was in their twenties, another in their thirties, a third in their forties, a fourth in their fifties, and the oldest couple was in their late sixties or early seventies. I explained, much to the disappointment of the group, that these were the only five couples referred for the group.

Another student asked how I had decided on five couples. I pointed out that we were using a studio for videotaping, and with myself and my coleaders, there was only enough room for five couples. Another effort to tease out principles followed as they inquired how we decided on the number of sessions. I pointed out that there were many long-standing issues involved, and a short-term group did not seem to offer enough time. "How did you settle on exactly twenty-three sessions?" was the next question. Once again I disappointed the group by explaining that we could not start the group before October 15, because we needed time to do the advance work, and we simply counted the weeks until the end of the academic year. We then went on to discuss the differences between what I felt to be the myth of scientific group composition versus the reality of how decisions were made.

The students wanted prescriptions and rules, and I argued, perhaps more strongly than was needed, that the rules were not really that clear. In reality, we often "take what we can get." Our experiences, and some research findings, have provided us with some guidelines. For example, we know that extremes often lead to problems. Groups can clearly be too large to provide an opportunity for everyone to participate or too small to provide a consistent core of members. While groups can tolerate some degree of age range, as in my married couples' group, extremes for some populations, such as teenagers, can create serious problems. For example, a 12-year-old foster child faces life tasks that differ significantly from the concerns of a 17-year-old who is preparing to leave the care of the agency at 18. One person of color in an all-white group, what I call the "only one" problem, may experience a sense of isolation that the addition of another might well alleviate. A group of survivors of sexual abuse may have significant difficulty in achieving intimacy if the group is open-ended, with new members constantly joining the group and other members leaving it.

The literature provides a fund of observations on questions of group composition and structure, but unfortunately it also provides conflicting scientific evidence in support of rules. For example, there are conflicting studies on the optimum size for effective discussion groups, with support for different numbers argued persuasively.

A balance has to be struck between ignoring these issues completely and depending too much on rigid rules and structures.

The position argued here is that each setting must develop its own rules, based on its experiences as well as those of others. As such, a worker must address several questions, using the experiences of colleagues and of other settings to develop tentative answers. Each group represents an experiment that can contribute to the fund of experience the worker will draw on in starting new groups. The remainder of this section highlights some of these questions. Rather than providing definitive answers, the discussion will offer a way of exploring the issues.

Group Member Selection

The crucial factor in selection of members is some common ground between their individual needs and the purpose of the group. Whether this purpose has been defined broadly or narrowly, each member must be able to find some connection between a personal sense of urgency and the work involved. Even if this common ground is not apparent to the prospective members at the start, the worker should have some sense of its existence. In the example of the couples' group, each couple was having severe marital problems. Another point in common was that all five couples had some commitment at the start to strengthen their marriages. Couples who had already decided to separate and who needed help in doing so without causing additional pain to each other or their families would not have belonged in this group.

In an AIDS/Recovery group I co-led, the five members included one white, gay man; a transgender woman; a heterosexual woman; and two African American men. Although their life experiences differed significantly, all the members had AIDS and all were in relatively early recovery from polysubstance abuse. Group members differed in their status with respect to AIDS. Two members were on an experimental treatment that had lowered their AIDS viral loads (counts) to almost zero and had raised their T-cell (protective) counts to near normal. One client was waiting for her viral load and T-cell count to reach the point at which she could enter the clinical trials with the new drugs. Another client was eligible but refusing treatment. The health of the fifth had been damaged so badly by her use of hormones and illegal substances that she was too ill for the treatment. This client's viral load was climbing each week, her T-cell count was nonexistent, and she was experiencing a range of infections common to late-stage AIDS. In spite of these significant differences, each member could eventually relate to the others on the basis of their shared struggle with AIDS, with early substance abuse recovery, and with the interaction between the two.

As the group leader defines the purpose of the group and considers potential members, common sense can help to identify potential differences that might create difficulty in reaching group consensus on the focus of the work. As mentioned previously, for example, although 12-year-old and 17-year-old wards may share their foster status, their issues and concerns may differ greatly. Combining these two age groups in a group to discuss life problems and issues related to being "foster" could create unnecessary obstacles. On the other hand, this may not be a problem, depending on the group's purpose. For example, I have seen groups developed by a child welfare agency to promote better communication between teens and staff and to provide social and recreational activities; here, a wide age difference between teens appeared to have a less negative impact. The older teens provided leadership for the group and looked on themselves as "big brothers" and "big sisters" to the younger ones.

As this example suggests, workers should consider group purpose when thinking about age and group composition. In the couples' group described earlier, the differences in the ages of the five couples also provided unexpected dividends. Each couple was experiencing the crises somewhat associated with their particular phase of life and phase of their marriage; however, common themes cut across all phases. In many ways, the older couples were able to share their experiences and perspectives with the younger ones, and the group often took on the appearance of an extended family. After one session in which some of the problems associated with the older couples' life phases were clearly delineated, the husband in the youngest couple said good-humoredly, "I'm beginning to wonder if this is what I have to look forward to going through!" The wife of the oldest couple, who had been married 49 years, responded, "But you will have the advantage of having had this group to help you face these problems."

Whether to include male or female members or both will similarly have to be determined according to the group's purpose. However, I find some of the other factors often discussed when deciding on group membership, such as judgments about a member's "personality," somewhat questionable. For example, I have seen a group meticulously assembled with the supposedly proper number of relatively passive schoolchildren balanced by a manageable number of active ones. The theory was to guarantee interaction, with the active members stimulating the passive ones. In addition, some limit on active members was thought to help the leader with potential problems of control. Unfortunately, nobody informed the group members about their expected roles. The leader was observed in the first session desperately trying to deal with the acting-out behaviors of the "passive" members while the "active" members looked on in shock and amusement. Clients simply do not act the same in every situation. A client who acts passively in an individual interview or classroom may act differently in a different context. Clients will not remain in the "diagnosed" box long enough to be clearly identified. Their reactions will somewhat depend on the actions of those around them, particularly the group leader.

Workers also need to consider race, ethnicity, and language issues when composing a group. Davis (1979, 1981, 1984, 1999; Davis & Proctor, 1989) has addressed the impact of race on group composition and practice, basing his observations on anecdotal as well as empirical evidence. In reviewing the literature on the impact of racial composition, Davis identifies several observed processes that emerge when a racial ratio changes and minority membership increases. These processes include cleavage, tipping points, and white flight. In **cleavage**, the group splits into distinct racial subgroups. The **tipping point** is the number that creates majority members' anxiety, resulting in aggression toward members of the "out" group. He suggests that white people are so often in the majority that when they are placed in a group in which they are in a smaller-than-usual majority—for example, with more than 10 percent to 20 percent people of color—they may experience a mental state of being in the "psychological minority," at times leading to a **white flight** reaction (Proctor & Davis, 1994). Conversely, members of the minority group faced with this ratio may experience being in the "psychological majority" even though their absolute numbers represent less than 50 percent.

As with many such observations, these concepts of psychological minority and majority may not significantly affect the decisions related to the composition of a group. Rather, they serve to attune the group leader to potential dynamics resulting from a composition that may affect the group's functioning. Awareness of the process by the group leader, as well as a willingness to address these issues when and if they emerge, may help the group cope more effectively.

In summarizing the literature on race and group, Davis and Proctor (1989) suggest the following:

> There is some evidence that whites and minorities may prefer different racial compositions: neither whites nor minorities appear to like being greatly outnumbered. The language spoken in the group may also be important. For example, if some members speak Spanish, while others do not, the non-bilingual speakers may become isolated. (p. 115)

Davis and Proctor also summarize the findings on group leadership:

> Leaders who differ in race from their group members may receive less cooperation. Biracial co-leadership may enhance communication in racially heterogeneous groups. However, biracial co-leaders must remain alert to the possibility of one leader being perceived as the leader and the other as his helper. (p. 116)

Finally, in addressing the paucity of empirical research, they suggest the following:

> There is no evidence which suggests that group treatment is more or less suitable for any particular ethnic group. Furthermore, there is little evidence that either racially homogenous or racially heterogeneous groups are superior in their outcomes. Very few studies have attempted to assess the effects of the group leader's race on group member outcomes. Furthermore, reports from studies involving the race of the leader are mixed. However, these studies are consistent in that they have found that prior group leader experience in working with minorities appears to have beneficial effects for the group. (p. 117)

Group Timing

When setting up a group, workers need to consider many time-related factors. How often will the group meet? How long will the meetings last? For how long will the group meet? Each of the answers must draw on common sense, the experience of the agency, and the literature, and all must be related to group purpose.

In the married couples' group, we chose to meet once each week, for 2 hours each session, for 23 weeks. Meetings had to be held in the evening so that the working partners could attend. The group was designed to provide long-term support to the couples as they dealt with their marital problems. The alternate option of intensive weekends was not considered. For couples in crisis, it seemed that the intensive, short-term experience might open up more problems while leaving the couples unable to deal with them. On the other hand, weekend workshops for marital enrichment groups, in which the relationships are strong to begin with, may provide successful educational and skill-development experiences. The decision to meet weekly was based on the recognition that longer breaks between meetings might diffuse the intensity of the experience, making each session seem like a new beginning. Two hours seemed to be enough time to allow for the development of central themes and issues in the beginning phase of each meeting, while leaving enough time to deal effectively with specific individual and group concerns. More than 2 hours might wear out group members and workers alike.

In every case, discussing and clarifying the plan with group members is important. Group members have a sense of the group's time frame and will be affected by the particular phase of the meeting or the phase in the life of the group. As pointed out earlier, the "doorknob" phenomenon can accelerate the presentation of important issues; however, the members need to know when the time to reach for the door is close at hand. Group members sometimes work more effectively if they have less time to carry out their tasks. Reid and Shyne (1969), for example, discuss the impact of time on both the worker and the client in their work on short-term treatment. There is a limit to how much can be dealt with; workers must balance the group's needs against the time limit, allowing the right number of sessions to deal with the anticipated themes of concern. This limit will come from experience as an agency evaluates each group, using the group members as part of the evaluation process. Before a group is established, workers can gain much help from group members by exploring their reactions to time proposals. Feedback on the day of the week or the specific time for starting may help a group worker avoid unnecessary conflicts.

An expression borrowed from architecture, "Form follows function," is useful in thinking about time in the group formation stage. The form of the group in relation to time needs to be connected to group purpose. Agency conceptions about time can change as experiences with new group services are evaluated. In one example, I served as a consultant to an agency providing extensive group services to people with AIDS as well as their friends, lovers, and family members. Under the original plan developed by the agency, a group would start with clients diagnosed as HIV-positive and continue as members progressed through the stages of the illness. The group would continue as a sort of community as members became progressively more ill and most finally died. This structure seemed to make sense if the purpose of the group was to provide an alternative source of support for its members, many of whom felt cut off from other systems in their lives (such as family, work, and friends). In reality, the groups did not work this way. Most of the groups began to dissolve as some members died or became seriously ill.

The experience caused a rethinking of group purpose. Rather than thinking of each group as a substitute community, the agency conceptualized the groups as time limited, with a focus on helping the members deal with transitions to the various stages of the illness. That is, one group would be for recently diagnosed HIV-positive clients, while another group would serve clients facing the onset of serious medical problems. This was not always easy to do, as the course of the illness was neither smooth nor predictable. However, instead of the agency attempting to provide the substitute community—a task that would eventually overwhelm the agency, given the number of potential clients involved in the pandemic of AIDS—the focus changed to one of helping group members mobilize existing support in their own friendship, family, and community systems. Analysis of process in the groups indicated that group leaders had been too quick to accept their members' contention that such support was closed to them and that only the group could provide it. Work in the groups became more demanding, and members were asked to look closely at their own efforts to connect with their social support systems. The move to time-limited groups greatly changed the nature of the work for the better. Once the "function" of the group had been clearly defined, the questions of "form" were easier to resolve.

In my more recent experience co-leading a group for people with AIDS in early recovery from substance abuse, new issues of timing presented themselves. For example, with several of our group members on the triple-therapy drug regime, and with their resulting improvement in health, we were viewing the group as one of the ongoing support systems designed to help members cope with living with AIDS rather than dying from AIDS. Also, the substance abuse recovery issues required more long-term support than if the members were dealing with AIDS alone. This group began in October, focusing on helping members get through the extremely stressful holiday season of Thanksgiving, Christmas, and New Year's Eve. The group reconvened in the new year and agreed to continue until a summer break period, with the understanding that the members would assess the need to reconvene in the fall. Individual group members received ongoing support from my coleader, who served as their substance abuse counselor.

Group Structure, Setting, and Rules

The formation stage raises many questions related to group structure and setting. For example, where should the group meet? Ease of access by public and private transportation might be a factor. Holding a session on sensitive and potentially embarrassing work (such as child abuse) in a public setting where members might fear being identified could be a mistake. The room itself should offer group members privacy and face-to-face seating (in a circle, around a table). Comfortable chairs and surroundings often add to the group members' comfort. On the other hand, work with children may require facilities that are relatively "activity proof," so that members and the group worker can relax without constant worries about order and decorum.

Group rules also need clarification prior to the first group meeting. For example, limits on physical activity may be set with children's groups. Some adult groups require boundaries regarding the use of physical force. In a group session for prison parolees, for example, one member pulled out a knife and begin to clean his fingernails in a manner meant to be threatening to another member. In this case, the worker must recontract with the members on the issue of bringing knives to the session. Many other "rules" need attention as well. Attendance requirements should be clear. Members' expectations regarding the agency and the group, as well as the worker's expectations regarding the members, should be discussed, especially concerning confidentiality. In my couples' group, we discuss three rules in the first session: (1) each member is expected to come each week as long as he or she is not ill, (2) a couple wanting to quit the group will come back for one additional week to discuss it, and (3) group members will agree to confidentiality. In my AIDS/Recovery group, meetings were held in a "clean and sober" residence. Members were not to bring substances to the group or be under the influence of substances when they attended.

There are many differences of opinion on the question of group rules. For example, some argue that group members should not have contact with each other outside the meetings. The field of group work is far from agreement on these questions. My general bias is that group members own their own lives and that my group is simply an incident in their week (I hope, an important incident). I would therefore have difficulty insisting on a rule preventing them from having contacts outside the group. In fact, in many groups the bonds of mutual aid that have developed through telephone calls and informal contacts outside the group have provided powerful support for individual members. Workers in some groups, who fear that group members may get involved in "acting out" outside of the group (having sexual contact, for example), appear to me to take more responsibility for their lives of the members than they should. Even so, in some groups, such as the AIDS/Recovery group, such outside activity could definitely threaten the members' recovery at a particularly vulnerable time in their lives. These issues need to be discussed as part of the structure of the group.

In addition, group members should be free to bring their outside interactions with each other into the group if they wish; such interactions can serve as an important entry into the content of the group work. In general, the rules stated in the beginning of the group should be firmly rooted to the reality of the situation rather than the arbitrary authority or personal preferences of the group leader. Group members should see them as emerging from the necessities of the work.

Issues related to group composition, timing, setting, rules, and structure have been raised here to show you some of the questions requiring consideration prior to the start of any group. I have shared my opinions on these questions merely to illustrate how one practitioner develops his own views from his experiences and those of others. As with all the ideas shared in this book, you will have to test them against your own sense of reality and ongoing group experiences.

Work With Prospective Members

After agency administration and staff support have been mobilized, potential obstacles to cooperation identified and discussed, and formation questions considered by the worker, then one more step remains: recruitment of group members. In contrast to individual and family work, a group of clients rarely arrive at the agency and request services. It may happen with some naturally formed groups, as when a group of teens in a school or a group of tenants in a housing project approach the social worker for help. These are the exceptions, however, rather than the rule. Most group work practice requires an **outreach process**, through which the social work service is brought to the potential clients. Recruitment of group members is therefore a crucial element in the formation stage.

This process can also be complex, because clients feel the general ambivalence about taking help (described in Parts II and III) as well as unique concerns related to the group context. Of course, workers who deal with groups in settings less focused on personal problems, such as community centers or community organization agencies, do not have to deal with the same reluctance to join a group activity. Nevertheless, when people consider joining any group, they face some degree of ambivalence. This discussion will focus on examples of mutual-aid groups designed to deal with problems of living—marital difficulties, parenting skills, alcohol or drug addiction, school difficulties, and the like—in the belief that some of the principles can be applied to other types of groups as well.

Clients may become prospective group members by identifying with advertisements for the group. They might respond to posters or newspaper stories, a letter from the agency, or other publicity of a group service. If handled well, the steps involved in making potential group members aware of the group can help to turn the potential client toward the service. For example, posters or letters should be worded clearly, without jargon, so that the prospective member has a clear idea of the group's purpose. It may be helpful to identify some of the themes of concern that may be related to the client's sense of urgency.

The embarrassment of the workers in being direct about the problem, discussed in the chapter on contracting with individuals, or the workers' concern that direct statements about the problem may turn potential clients off can result in the use of euphemisms or vague and general descriptions of the group. The result of this lack of clarity and directness may actually reduce the interest of the potential member in attending. Workers can test the letters or posters with colleagues and clients to get their sense of the meaning and suggestions as to how to make the wording direct but nonthreatening.

Other clients are referred by colleagues or other helping professionals or are selected by workers from their caseloads. Whatever the circumstance, even when the client has initiated the contact, the gap between thinking about joining a group and arriving at the first meeting can be a big one. Many of the skills already identified can increase the chances of a successful start. Two other skill sets, which we shall now examine, center on work with colleagues after they have agreed to recruit group members and telephone or in-person contacts between the worker and prospective members.

Strategizing for Effective Referrals

A worker may have done an effective job with other staff members regarding the establishment of a group but still be disappointed by a relatively low number of referrals. An important question often overlooked is how the colleague will conduct a referral interview. It is a mistake to assume that even a motivated colleague will be able to make an effective referral without some joint work and strategizing as to how it might be done. For example, the colleague may have a general sense of the group contract but be unable to articulate it clearly. One who has not worked with groups may not be sensitive to some of the underlying feelings and ambivalence that the client may share indirectly, thereby missing a chance to help overcome obstacles to group formation.

In a tuning-in session, either one-on-one or with a staff group, workers can pool their efforts to sensitize themselves to the concerns clients may have about joining the group and the indirect ways these may emerge. Staff can then share strategies for reaching for the underlying concerns. In addition, a brief role-play of the referral interview may reveal to the group worker that some colleagues cannot yet articulate the group purpose, and work can then proceed on that skill. Such a process may also bring to the surface any ambivalent feelings or unanswered questions that need to be dealt with prior to the actual referral interviews.

To see this process in action, consider a referral workshop that I conducted for social service professionals in connection with the establishment of a new and (at that time) experimental group service for men who had physically abused their partners. Recognizing the importance of professional referrals to launch the program and knowing that the referral process might be extremely difficult in this situation, we provided an opportunity for tuning in and joint strategizing. To keep the discussion focused on skills, I asked for examples of difficult referrals of a similar nature.

One worker described a referral he had recently attempted with the common-law husband of a client. The client was a prostitute who had been beaten by the husband who was also her pimp, but she had refused to report the incident or leave him. As the worker's interaction with the husband was analyzed, it became clear that the worker had never mentioned the physical abuse to the husband, attempting instead to lead him indirectly to agree to seek help. When this was mentioned during the analysis of the example, the worker revealed that he had feared angering the husband and risking that the husband might then take the anger out on the wife. An important discussion followed in which other workers spoke of their fears of possible retribution not only on the partners but also themselves. Their dilemma was discussed and strategies were developed for broaching the subject directly without exacerbating the partner's defensiveness. Without this preparatory work, workers would have been blocked in their attempts to offer this group.

The problem of stating group purpose came up for our group in another way as well. In a role-play, one of the workers described the group in a way that would lead the prospective member to believe his worst fears—that the group was designed solely to chastise him for his behavior and to educate him to appreciate his impact on his woman. When I pointed out that the worker seemed angry at the prospective group member, my comment released a flood of feelings, echoed by many in the room, of anger at the men. All of the professionals had agreed earlier that these groups could not be effective unless the men could both be held accountable for their violent actions toward women and also see the group as designed to help them as clients in their own right. This intellectual agreement evaporated in the role-play to reveal an essentially punitive and thereby ineffective offer of service. Enabling workers to discuss and be in touch with these natural yet often denied feelings might ensure a presentation of the group that will turn prospective members toward the service rather than reinforce their resistance. In this case, the workers recognized that, for many of these men, even the most effective offer of service might not elicit a response. Some of them would not come to the first meeting unless their partner left them or they received a court order. Although this group example may be extreme, I believe that in most cases the worker forming a group would be well advised to take some time with colleagues to discuss the technical aspects of making the referral.

Worker Skills in the Initial Interviews

Before the first meeting, group workers often contact individual members, in person or by phone, to discuss their participation in the group. These interviews can be seen as part of the exploratory process in which the worker describes what the group has to offer and checks with the client to determine what may be needed. The skills of clarifying purpose, clarifying role, and reaching for feedback are useful in this interview (see Part II). Describing the structure of the group (how it will work) as well as timing helps to provide the information needed for the prospective member to make a decision about using the service.

In addition to tuning in to the client's feelings about beginning a new relationship, the worker must also tune in to the specific concerns related to beginning in a group. For example, the public image of helping groups, ranging from group psychotherapy to encounter groups, might affect potential clients' attitudes. In addition, clients may bring other stereotypes of groups based on their past experiences (such as class groups at school, camp experiences) that will affect their feelings about attending.

Questions about how people with the same problems can help each other will also be on their minds. Much of this hesitancy and fear may lie just beneath the surface. The worker must listen and reach directly for any indirect cues. In the following example, a worker has been describing a foster parents' group to an agency foster parent, and the parent seems receptive. The cues of resistance emerge when the worker gets specific about the dates.

WORKER: We are going to have our first meeting in two weeks, on a Wednesday night. Can I expect you there?

FOSTER PARENT: (Long pause) Well, it sounds good. I'll try to make it if things aren't too hectic that week at work.

If the worker quits right there and accepts the illusion of agreement, she may be guaranteeing that the parent will not show up. Even though workers can sense the ambivalence in the client's voice, they often refrain from reaching for the negative attitude. When I ask why workers refrain, they tell me that they are afraid that if they bring the doubts out in the open, they will reinforce them. They believe the less said, the better. In reality, the client's doubts and questions are valid, and the worker is missing an opportunity to help the client explore them.

Without this exploration, the client may simply not show up at the first meeting, despite having promised to attend. When the worker later calls, then, the client will feel guilty and offer profuse explanations for his absence (as in "I really meant to come, only it got so hectic that day it just slipped my mind").

Returning to the interview with the foster parent, note the turn in the work when the worker reaches for the cue.

WORKER: You sound a bit hesitant. Are you concerned about attending the group? It wouldn't be unusual; most people have a lot of questions about groups.

FOSTER PARENT: Well, you know I never do too well in groups. I find I have a lot of trouble talking in front of strangers.

WORKER: Are you worried that you would have to speak up and be put on the spot?

FOSTER PARENT: I don't mind talking about fostering; it's just that I get tongue-tied in a group.

WORKER: I can appreciate your concern. A lot of people feel that way. I can tell you right now that except for sharing your name no one will put you on the spot to speak. Some people always talk a lot at the early meetings while others prefer to listen. You can listen until you feel comfortable about speaking. If you want, I can help you begin to talk in the group, but only when you're ready. I do this all the time with people who feel this way.

FOSTER PARENT: You mean it's not just me who feels this way?

WORKER: Not at all. It's quite common and natural. By the way, are there any other concerns you might have about the group?

FOSTER PARENT: Not really. That was the biggest one. Actually, it doesn't sound like a bad idea at all.

Once again we see the importance of exploring the indirect cue so that the worker has a clearer idea about the source of the ambivalence. Many workers hesitate to explore the cue, because they see it as a polite rejection of the group (and the worker). When asked why they see it this way, they often reply that they are unsure about their own competency and the quality of the group. They respond to the client's ambivalence with their own similar feelings. In the case just cited, the fear of speaking in the group needed to be discussed. Knowing that the worker understands and that it is all right to feel this way can help the client overcome the obstacle. Other obstacles might stem from memories of bad group experiences, horror stories recounted by friends or relatives about harsh and confronting group encounters, or embarrassment about sharing personal details with strangers. Workers need to clarify what will actually happen in the group, as compared with what the potential member may fear. The worker also needs to empathize genuinely with the fears, and still attempt to help the client take the first difficult step. With this kind of help from the worker, many prospective group members overcome their fears and doubts and give the group a try. A source of great support for the client lies in knowing that the worker understands his or her feelings.

Another type of resistance occurs when a group is offered to the caretaker, support person, or relative of a client. In one example, a worker was recruiting a group for relatives of elderly Alzheimer patients who were caring for these patients at home. In the face of the initial, hinted reluctance, the worker said, "You sound hesitant about coming to the group, Mrs. Smith. Can you tell me why?" The client responded, with some feeling, "Just one more thing on the list for me to do to take care of my mother. I don't have time for myself!" The worker replied, "Mrs. Smith, I think I can appreciate how demanding caring for your mother must be. But I don't think I made the purpose of this group clear when I described it. This group is not for your mother. This group is for you. Other group members will also be feeling overwhelmed by the demands made upon them by their relatives with Alzheimer's, and part of what we can discuss is how you can get the support you need." By reaching for the lurking negatives and the ambivalence, the worker creates an opportunity to clarify group purpose to a potential member.

A common trap that workers fall into when they hear the indirect or direct cues of reluctance is to try to "sell" the group even harder. Consider the following example of a worker in a convalescent home who is recruiting an elderly resident. In this case, the worker's honest caring and enthusiasm may well help the potential member consider the group, but her work would be stronger if she explored and acknowledged the obvious resistant responses. Also, the worker's focus on discussion of the "good old days" brings a response that surprises the worker but may actually suggest a different group purpose: to talk about both the good and the bad old days.

Purpose of the Interview

To explain the group and to invite 92-year-old female resident to attend. The prospective member is white, with a diagnosis of progressive dementia and agitated depression. She has been living in the nursing home for 3 years.

The Interview

Mrs. Franks was sitting up in a chair listening to music upon my arrival. I knocked on her door, entered, and introduced myself. She asked me to have a seat, which I did. I asked her how she was doing. She responded rather cheerfully that she was OK, but a little tired. I asked her if she generally napped in the afternoons (a common practice in the nursing homes). She replied, "Well, on Sundays I don't really have anything to do." "Oh," I replied, "so Sunday is your day of rest." We both laughed, and she agreed. "What do you do during the rest of the week?" I asked her. "I have my duties," was her reply. "Do you ever get down to any of the activities?" "Oh sure," she said.

"One of the reasons that I stopped by was to invite you to an activity that I am organizing. Beginning next week, we are going to be having a group called 'Jog Your Memory.' There will be five or six women in the group and we'll spend some time talking about the good old days. Do you think that you might be interested in something like that?"

"Well, I didn't have any good old days."

"Nothing good happened in your life?"

"Oh, sure," she said, smiling. "There were many good times. Some days were good, some days were bad."

"Each week there will be a different topic and we'll see what kinds of memories it brings back."

"Well, it sounds nice, but I don't think that it's for me."

"Well, it's going to be a small group of ladies, and we'll meet for about a half hour each Tuesday, just down the hallway in the nursing office."

"Oh, it sounds nice. We need something like that."

"Do you think that you'd like to come? I would pick you up and bring you back, so you wouldn't have to worry about that."

"Oh, wonderful; I might be older than some of the others though."

"Don't worry about that, Mrs. Franks. All of the ladies are in their eighties and nineties, and one woman is even over 100."

"My goodness." We laughed.

"Mrs. Franks, I am glad that you are interested in the Jog Your Memory group. I think you will enjoy it."

"Oh yes, it sounds like a wonderful opportunity. Thank you so much for thinking of me." I smile at Mrs. Franks and touch her hand. "You're welcome. Today is Friday. I will come back Tuesday morning to remind you about the 'Jog Your Memory' group. I will also let the nurse know, so she'll be sure that you are up."

Once again, the worker's caring comes through and may well lead to Mrs. Franks attending the group. The odds are good, because this is a residential setting.

Now that the worker has completed the group formation tasks and the clients are ready to attend, the worker needs to pay attention to the beginnings and the dynamics of first sessions. These topics are explored in the next chapter.

Chapter Summary

Three major areas of work are involved in the formation stage of group work practice. The first focuses on the skills required to work with one's setting and colleagues in order to engage them as active partners in the development of the group service. Several strategies help workers cope with underlying obstacles that can sabotage group work efforts. The second area involves issues of group composition, timing, and structure. Exploring issues in advance can maximize the possibility of success in forming the group. The final area of work centers on the skills required to recruit members who may be ambivalent about attending a group session. In particular, the skill of looking for trouble when everything is going the worker's way can help avoid the illusion of agreement, in which the client promises to attend but does not show up.

Related Online Content and Activities

Visit *The Skills of Helping* Book Companion Website at www.socialwork.wadsworth.com/Shulman06/ for learning tools such as glossary terms, InfoTrac College Edition keywords, links to related websites, and chapter practice quizzes.

The website for this chapter also features additional notes from the author.

The Beginning Phase in the Group

CHAPTER OUTLINE

The Dynamics of First Group
Sessions

The Couples' Group:
An Illustration

Variations on First Group
Sessions

Recontracting

Coleadership in Groups

In this chapter we examine the dynamics of the first group session. The contracting issues explored in Parts II and III with individuals and families will be revisited, but this time we also explore the variant elements of practice introduced by working with a group. A detailed example of a first session with a married couples' group will illustrate the concepts. Next, we discuss five variations on first group sessions, relative to the age and relative articulateness of the members, the authority of the worker, the specific concerns of the clients, and the impact of the setting and time. We then examine the issue of recontracting when the initial contract was not clear, looking at examples of social workers modifying their working agreements with their own groups as well as with ongoing groups. Finally, the chapter ends with a discussion of coleadership.

Many of the issues related to beginning work that we described in Chapter 3 apply equally to first sessions with groups, with an important difference: The individual client must also deal with a new system—the group. The first two central questions for the client in the individual context were "What are we doing here together?" and "What kind of person will this worker be?" In the group context, a third question is added: "What kind of people will these other group members be?" Many of the uncertainties and fears associated with new beginnings will be increased by the public nature of a first group session. For example, the client's fear of being manipulated by someone in authority may increase at the thought that peers will witness any display of inadequacy, along with the resultant humiliation. For this reason and others, workers must pay special attention to first sessions in order to set a proper stage for the work that will follow.

This chapter provides an overview of the general structure of a first group meeting, reviewing some of the underlying assumptions outlined in Chapter 3 and considering some of the unique dynamics associated with group work. The tasks of both the worker and the group members are outlined, and specific skills are identified. With this overview as a backdrop, the dynamics of a first group session are illustrated through a detailed analysis of a first session of a married couples' group. Then, several variations on first group sessions are presented. We look at work with children and adolescents to see the impact of age and articulateness, then we examine involuntary groups to see how the authority of the worker affects group work. The specific concerns of the clients, as well as the impact of the setting and time, also present special challenges to workers and clients alike.

Next, we explore the issue of recontracting. This is the process in which the worker reopens the issues of contracting by providing a clearer statement of purpose or exploring the group members' resistance or lack of connection to the service. The skills in working with the coleaders and the group in initiating a recontracting process are illustrated using a detailed example from a student's experiences. The chapter ends with a discussion of the potential problems involved in coleadership and strategies for dealing with them.

The Dynamics of First Group Sessions

As in all new encounters with people in authority, clients begin first group meetings tentatively. Their normal concerns about their own adequacy may be heightened because the encounter is taking place in public view. Most clients bring to first meetings an extensive fund of group experiences, many of which are associated with painful memories. For example, we have all either witnessed or experienced the excruciatingly difficult moments in a classroom when an individual student has been singled out to answer a question or solve a math problem on the board. We have felt the embarrassment of a classmate exposed to sarcasm from an insensitive teacher. Whereas new encounters in a one-to-one counseling situation generate fears of the unknown, new group encounters tend to reawaken old fears based on past experiences.

As in individual work, early clarification of purpose is central in the group context. The clients' first question will be "What are we here for?" Once the boundary of the group experience has been clearly described, members will find selecting appropriate responses easier. When the expectations of the group worker and the setting or agency within which the group takes place are clear, the group members feel much safer than when the purpose remains ambiguous.

As the group starts, the members will watch the worker with keen interest. Having experienced the impact of powerful people in authority, they know it is important to "size up" this new authority figure as soon as possible. This leads to the clients' second central question: "What kind of person will the worker be?" Until the group members can understand clearly how this worker operates and will affect them, they will need to test the worker directly or indirectly. Defenses will remain in position until members are certain of their individual safety.

All these dynamics are similar to the ones described in Chapter 3. Again, the main difference in the group setting involves the presence of other clients. As the group session proceeds, each group member will also be appraising the others. Many questions will arise: "Who are these other people? Do they have the same problems that I do? Will I be embarrassed by finding myself less competent than they? Do they seem sympathetic and supportive, or are there people in this group who may attack and confront me?" While the client's primary concern in the first session is the group leader, questions about the other members follow closely behind. Not only do members wonder what they can get out of the experience to meet their own needs, they also wonder why it is necessary to get help in a group: "How can other people help me if they have the same problems I have?"

Groups also present a unique dynamic regarding leadership. The social work group leader is now the **external leader,** deriving his or her authority from external sources such as the sponsoring agency. This is in contrast to the **internal leader,** who is a member of the group. The internal leader assumes a leadership role in a situational or ongoing basis. That is, he or she leads in terms of one issue but not others or else leads in an overall way. Internal leaders cannot ultimately impose themselves on a group that is unwilling to accept them in this role.

With some of these issues in mind, the worker should design the structure of first meetings to meet the following objectives:

- To introduce group members to each other.
- To make a brief, simple opening statement that clarifies the agency's or institution's stake in providing the group service as well as the potential issues and concerns that group members feel urgently about.
- To obtain feedback from the group members on their sense of the fit (the contract) between their ideas of their needs and the agency's view of the service it provides.
- To clarify the group worker's task and method of attempting to help the group do its work.
- To deal directly with any specific obstacles that may obstruct this particular group's efforts to function effectively: stereotypes group members may hold concerning group work or people in authority, or group members' anger if attendance is involuntary.
- To begin to encourage intermember interaction rather than discussion only between the group leader and the group members.
- To begin to develop a supportive group culture in which members can feel safe.
- To help group members develop a tentative agenda for future work.

- To clarify the mutual expectations of the agency and the group members. For example, what can group members expect from the worker? In addition, what expectations does the worker have for the members (regarding regular attendance, meetings starting on time, and so forth)? Such rules and regulations concerning structure are part of the working contract.

- To gain some consensus on the part of group members as to the specific next steps; for example, are there central themes or issues with which they wish to begin the following week's discussion?

- To encourage honest feedback and evaluation of the effectiveness of the group.

At first glance, this list of objectives for a first meeting may appear overwhelming. Actually, many of them can be dealt with quickly, and most are interdependent—that is, work on one objective simultaneously affects the others. Obviously, however, these objectives cannot be achieved in the first session unless a clear structure for work is provided. The approach to creating such a structure, which is illustrated in detail in the remainder of the chapter, is offered as a general statement recognizing that the order of elements and the emphasis may vary depending on the worker, the group members, and the setting. Once again we see that a perceived dichotomy between structure and freedom is a false one. Freedom only comes with structure, and the structure must be of the type that encourages freedom.

The Couples' Group: An Illustration

This section illustrates a first meeting using excerpts from a videotaped recording of the first session of a married couples' group that I led. The group was conducted under the auspices of a community mental health setting. Five couples were referred from a variety of sources. All had experienced problems in their marital relationships, and in each of the five couples, one partner was the identified patient. The youngest were John and Louise, in their twenties, with two young children. Rick and Fran were in their thirties and had been married for 7 years with no children. Len and Sally were in their late forties, had been married for 20 years, and had borne children in their late teens and early twenties. Frank and Jane, in their fifties, were recently married after prior marriages and divorces. Jane's teenage sons were living with them at this point. Finally, Lou and Rose were in their sixties with several married children who had children of their own. Louise and Rose had recently been inpatients at a psychiatric hospital. Sally had been seen at the hospital and was considering entering as an inpatient. Frank, Jane, Rick, and Fran had been referred to the group for marital counseling. Each of the couples had been interviewed individually by one of my two coworkers in the group; however, they were meeting me, the senior group worker, for the first time that evening. My two coworkers, one male and one female, were also present.

The Initial Work

The group meeting room was carpeted and had comfortable chairs set in a circle. The session was recorded on video cameras placed in an adjoining studio. Cameras and cameramen worked on the other side of one-way glass partitions. The couples had met the coworkers in another part of the clinic and had been escorted to the meeting room so that they all arrived at once. The purpose of the videotaping had been explained to the couples, and they had signed consent forms prior to the first session. The group workers had tuned in to the impact of the videotaping and had developed a strategy to reach for their reactions at the beginning of the session.

As the couples arrived, I met them at the door, introducing myself to each partner and encouraging them to take a seat. Len, Sally's husband, had to miss the first session, as he was out of town on business. Frank and Jane, who had expressed the most ambivalence and uncertainty about attending the group during the week, were not present at the beginning of the session. After everyone was comfortably settled, I began by suggesting that we go around the room so that the members could share their names, how long they had been married, and whether they had any children. I said this would be a way for us to get to know each other.

LOUISE: I am Louise Lewis. We have been married six years, and we have two children.
WORKER: Go ahead, John (speaking to Louise's husband sitting next to her), please share it with the group members. (Leader points to the rest of the group.)
JOHN: My name is John. (Pause)
WORKER: (Smiling) With the same kids!
JOHN: (Laughing along with the rest of the group) Yes, I hope so.

The group members continued around the circle, giving their names and the data on their families. The advantage of introductions is that they help group members break the ice and begin to speak from the start. In addition, the worker conveys to them the sense that knowing each other will be important. Often during these introductions someone will make a humorous comment followed by nervous laughter; however, even these first contributions can help the members settle down. Because the contract has not been discussed, workers should request only a minimum of relevant information at this point. Later, clarification of group purpose will provide the necessary structure for the members to share why they have come. An alternative approach would be to make a brief statement of purpose before asking for introductions. This could be particularly important if group members had no idea of the purpose of the group.

Following the introductions, I brought up the videotaping issue:

WORKER: I realize you discussed the taping with my coworkers, but I thought I would like to repeat the reasons for taping these sessions and also to give you another opportunity to share your reactions. As you know, this is a training institution and we are involved in teaching other health professionals a number of skills, including how to work with groups. We find it helpful to use videotapes of groups such as these so that new group leaders can have examples to assist them in their learning. In addition, the coleaders and I will use these tapes each week as a way of trying to figure out how to be more effective in helping this group work well.

I went on to explain that if segments of the tape were kept, they would have an opportunity to view them and could decide if they wanted them erased. I asked if there was any response, and after a few moments of silence and some verbal agreement that there was no problem, I proceeded. I believed the tapes were still on their minds and would come up again; however, they were not quite ready at this point to accept my invitation.

With this acknowledgement of the taping issue, I moved to begin the contracting process. The first skills involved were similar to those described in Chapter 3: clarifying purpose, clarifying role, and reaching for client feedback. I had prepared an opening statement in which I attempted to explain the stake the clinic had in providing the group, to identify their potential interest in the work of the group, and to state our roles as workers. My coleaders and I had reworded this statement several times until we felt it was jargon-free, short, and direct.

WORKER: I thought I would begin by explaining how we view the purpose of this group and the role that we would be playing, and to get some feedback from you on what you see the sessions to be all about. All of the couples in the group—and there may be one more here later this evening—are experiencing some difficulties in their marriages. This is a time of crisis and not an easy time. The way we see it, however, is that it is also an opportunity for change, for growth, and a chance to make a new marriage right within the one you presently have. Now we know that isn't easy; learning to live together can be tough. That is why we have organized this group. Essentially, the way we see it, it will be a chance for you to help each other—a sort of a mutual-aid group. As you listen to each other, as you share some of the problems, some of the feelings, and some of the concerns, and as you try to help each other, we think you will learn a great deal that may be helpful in your own marriages. So that's pretty much the purpose of the group. Now, for our role as group leaders, we have a couple of jobs. The first is that we are going to try to help you talk to and listen to each other, since it's not always easy to do that, particularly with people you don't know. Secondly, we will be sharing our own ideas along the way about close relationships, some of which may be helpful to you. Does that make sense? Do any of you have any questions about that? Does that sound like what you thought you were coming to? (Most heads were nodding and there were murmurs of "yes.") I thought to get us started it would be worthwhile to take some time to do some problem swapping. What I would like you to do is to share with each other, for a little while, some of the problems and difficulties you have found between you as couples. I would like you also to share some of the things you would like to see different. How would you like the relationship to be? We can take some time to find out the kinds of issues that you're concerned about and then move from there. Would someone like to start?

The purpose of the problem swapping is twofold. First, it provides the feedback necessary to begin to develop the client's side of the working contract. These issues and concerns will be the starting point for the work of the group. In the initial stage, group members may share near problems, which do not bear directly on some of the more difficult issues. This is their way of testing, of trying to determine how safe it is to use the group. The group worker has to respect and understand their defenses as an appropriate way to begin a new experience. The second function of the problem-swapping exercise is to encourage intermember interaction. For most of their lives clients have participated in groups where the discussion has essentially been between the group member and the leader, the person in authority. This is a long-standing habit. They will need to learn new ways of relating in a group, and the problem-swapping exercise is a good way to start.

As each individual member shares a problem or a concern, the group worker pays attention to his two clients. The first client is the individual who is speaking at the moment. The second client is the group. The worker monitors their reactions as revealed by their eyes, their posture, and so on. The mediation function of the group worker can be seen in action during this exercise as he encourages individual members to speak to the group and share the concerns they are bringing to the forefront and at the same time helps group members respond to the individual. As group members hear others describing problems, they become better able to identify those issues for themselves. In addition, when they hear their own concerns echoed by other members, they feel relief at finding out that they are "all in the same boat." The onus that each member may feel over having somehow failed as a human being and as a partner in a marital relationship can begin to lift as they discover that others share their feelings and concerns.

Silence is not unusual at this point in the first group session. This silence can represent a different communication for each member. Some may be thinking of what they are willing to share with the group at that time. Others may be shy and afraid to be the first one to speak. Still others may be expressing their wariness of being put on the spot if they raise a concern, because they do not know how other members or the leader will react. These are the moments that inexperienced group leaders dread. The silence, they feel, confirms a recurring nightmare they have had about their first group session. They worry that, after they have made their opening statement and invited feedback, nobody will speak. At this moment the group leader will often think, "Why didn't I bring a film?" This anxiety may cause the group leader to take over the group and to offer subjects for discussion or, in some cases, to give a presentation on the topic. This, of course, leads to a self-fulfilling prophecy, where the message conveyed to the members by the worker is that although their participation is being asked for, there is no willingness to wait for it.

An alternative, after a brief delay, is to explore the silence by acknowledging beginning anything is difficult, as is discussing such subjects with people one does not know. Often, this supportive comment frees a member to risk speaking. If not, the group leader can ask if members would discuss what makes it hard to talk in a first group session. As the members discuss why talking is hard, they inevitably start the problem swapping as well.

In the case of this couples' group, Lou, the member in his sixties, had a strong sense of urgency about beginning to work and was ready to jump right in. He sat directly to my left. As he spoke, he directed his conversation to the other members. He began by describing the problem as his wife's depression. His voice was flat, and his wife sat stone-faced next to him. She stayed this way almost until the end of the session, not saying a word, although she appeared to be hearing everything said by others. She would speak at the end of the session in a powerful and moving way. As Lou spoke, the rest of the group listened intently, obviously relieved that he had started.

Lou: To begin with, as you heard, we have been married for 45 years. Our relationship has been on a rocky road due in a great degree to tragedies that have happened to our family. While that was a real contributing factor, social conditions, economic conditions, and family relationships were also contributing factors. I'm making this very brief because most of this will come out later on. I think the outline on this will be enough for us to get our teeth into. As a result of the things I have mentioned, Rose, particularly, went into some real depressions. All the threads of her family seemed to go. As a result, it became difficult for her to operate. The problems were so strong she decided she had to go to a psychiatrist. She went and I went with her for two and one half years. The psychiatrist opened up some doors for her but not enough to really make her free to operate.

The unfortunate thing about her depression is that it developed into hostility toward me and the children. Now as soon as the depression lifted, as far as she was concerned, things straightened out. As soon as her depression lifted, we had no problems. (This is said emphatically, facing the group worker.) We had differences of opinion, but we had no problems.

WORKER: It sounds like it has been tough for her and also tough for you.

LOU: Oh, yes! The unfortunate thing as far as we were concerned is that we did not have a psychiatrist who understood what the relationship was. He took our problems as a family problem. His suggestion after a while was that if we weren't getting along together, we should separate. I felt I really didn't like that because I knew that wasn't the problem. The problem was getting Rose out of her depression.

Lou had begun presenting the problem the way one partner often does in a couples' group. The problem was essentially the other partner who, in some way, needed to be "fixed." This is the way one partner often experiences things, and the group worker must attempt to understand and express that understanding of the members' feelings as they are presented. When I show this tape to students, one often confronts me for "allowing" Lou to talk about his wife as the identified patient. Many students in the class identify with his wife and become angry with Lou for not taking responsibility for his part in the problem. I point out that in the first few minutes of this session this couple is acting out the very problem they have come to get help with. Lou is in effect saying, "Do you want to see how I deny the problem and blame it all on Rose? Just watch me!" Rose is saying, "Yes, and watch how I sit here passively, letting Lou talk about me." I point out to the student that it does not make sense for me to get angry at these clients for acting out the very problem the group was established to deal with. Also, before I confronted Lou, I had to build up a fund of support. In this case I attempted to do that by my comment about this experience being tough on his wife and on himself. He talked about his wife, but I came back to him. Later in the session, this same client dropped some of his defenses.

Some observers also wonder about my letting Lou continue to talk instead of immediately involving other members. It seemed obvious to me that the second client, the group, was listening to what Lou had to say and did not mind his going on at some length. Group members begin first sessions with various patterns of behavior. Those who are used to being withdrawn in new situations will begin that way. Those who are used to speaking and jumping in quickly, such as Lou, will begin that way. Each member is entitled to his own defenses in the beginning, and the group leader needs to respect them. When a group member speaks for a while, keeping to the subject, usually only the leader feels nervous. The other members are often relieved that someone else is talking. In this case, the tuning-in work from the individual session had alerted us to Lou's strong feelings toward helping professionals, who he felt had not been helpful. I had decided to reach directly for the authority theme if I felt there were indirect cues related to us, the group workers. I did so at this point in the following way:

WORKER: Are you worried that I and the other group leaders might take the same position with you and Rose?

LOU: Well, I don't know (voice slightly rising with annoyance). I'm not worried; I'm past that stage (accompanied with a harsh laugh). I'm just relating what happened, because I know where I'm at (said emphatically). To be very frank, my opinion of psychiatrists is very low, and I can cite for two hours experiences of what I have been through, my friends have been through, to show you exactly what I mean. This was a good case in point, his making a suggestion that we should separate because of the problem.

WORKER: After 45 years I can imagine that must have hit you as a terrible blow.

LOU: Well, sure it did.

WORKER: Lou, do you think we could move around the circle a bit and also hear from the others as to what they see some of the problems to be?

In retrospect, I think Lou responded somewhat angrily partly because of the way I made my statement, "Are you worried that I and the other group leaders might take the same position with you and Rose?" I wanted to open up Lou's concerns about what kind of workers we would be; however, my effort was not direct or clear enough. Instead of asking for further elaboration from Lou, or asking if others in the group had similar experiences or relations, I suggested we allow others to exchange problems by "moving around the circle." Encouraging such an exchange of problems was important; however, further exploration of the authority theme was also important. Fortunately I had an opportunity to "catch my mistake" later in the session when I returned to the initial concerns raised by Lou. He responded to my suggestion that we "hear from the others" by turning to his wife:

LOU: Sure, you're on. Go ahead, dear. (He turns to his wife.)

ROSE: I think I'll pass right now (said in a slow, even way, with no evidence of affect).

WORKER: That's fine. How about some others? You don't have to go in order, and you know, you can also respond to what Lou just said if you like, as well as adding some of your own issues. We won't solve all of the problems tonight; I hope you realize that. (Some laughter by the group members.) But what we would like to try and do is get a feel for how they seem to you right now. That can help us get a sense of what we need to talk about, and I think Lou has helped us get started. (At this point, John takes off his coat and seems to settle back in his chair.)

LOUISE: (John's wife, who is now speaking directly to Lou) I can understand what Lou means because depression has been our problem as well. I have gotten into such a state of depression that I can't function as a mother or a wife. I feel I have lost my identity. (This is all said with a very flat affect.) And I don't think that separation is the answer either. And I have had some pretty bad psychiatrists as well, so I can really feel for you when you say that, Lou. I can understand that. But the problem is to be able to sort out and find out what feelings I really have and recognize them for what they are and try to get myself out of the hole that I fell into, and that's the tough part.

WORKER: How does it affect your relationship with John?

LOUISE: It's very strenuous. There is a lot of strain and tension when I'm sick and down and I put the responsibility for taking care of the household on John's shoulders. There is a breaking point for him somewhere there; I want to catch it before we get there. (Pause, worker is nodding and other members are listening intently.) That's about it. (Brief silence.)

JOHN: Our biggest problem, or Louise's biggest problem, is due to her migraine headaches. She's had them ever since she was five years old. This is where the whole problem stemmed from, those migraine headaches, and this new depression which she seems to have gotten in the last few months.

WORKER: Anything special happen within the last few months?

JOHN: No, it has been actually a very quiet time this summer.

LOUISE: I think it is things that have been festering for a long time.

WORKER: For example?

LOUISE: I don't know. I can't put my finger on what they are.

WORKER: (Speaking to John) This depression came as a surprise to you, did it?

JOHN: Yes, it did.

WORKER: How do you see the problem, John? What would you like to see different in the relationship?

John went on to describe how they do not do much together as a couple anymore and that he would like to see Louise get back on her feet so they can have some fun the way they used to. Discussion continued around the circle, with Fran and Rick looking at each other as if to ask who would go first. I verbalized this, and Fran begged off, saying that she did not feel comfortable starting right away and that she would get in a bit later. Her husband, Rick, responded to my question by saying he was wondering why he was there, because he knows that he has—or rather, they have—a problem, but what the problem is, is hard to define. Fran coached him at this point by whispering in his ear the word *communication*. They seemed to agree that that was the problem, but when I asked for elaboration, Rick said, "That's not my problem, that's Fran's problem." Rick then took a further step for the group by entering a taboo area.

RICK: I guess if you get right down to basics, it would have to be sexual intimacy. I have been going along for a little over seven years, and now I find that I'm all alone. Fran's gone on a trip, and we're really in the very rocky stages of breaking up. (There is shaky emotion in his voice as he is speaking.) For the last six months, we have sort of been trying to recover, but it's still pretty shaky.

WORKER: It must feel pretty dicey for you right now.

RICK: Right. (With resignation in his voice.)

WORKER: What would you like to be different? What would you like to see changed in your marriage?

RICK: (After a deep sigh to get his breath) There are times when everything is just fine, it seems to be going along smoothly, but just to say what I would like would be tough to put my finger on.

WORKER: How would you like the relationship to be with Fran?

RICK: I think I would like it to be peaceful at all times. We have been getting into a lot of fights and just recently we have been getting into a lot of physical fights. A peaceful relationship, that's what I would really go for.

WORKER: How about you, Fran, do you have any ideas now?

FRAN: No, can we come back to me?

WORKER: Sure.

The discussion continued with Sally talking about her marriage. This was difficult because her husband, Len, was not present. She described it from her perspective. Her description was filled with interpretations that had obviously been gleaned from years of involvement in various forms of analysis. The group listened intently to her stories. She also responded to Louise's comments about migraine headaches, mentioning that she had had them as well, and then she and Louise exchanged some mutual understanding. After Sally finished her description, there was a long silence as the group seemed unsure about where to go.

WORKER: (Turning to Lou) I didn't mean to stop you before, Lou, if you want to get in again.

LOU: No, that's OK (laughing). I could go on for hours.

WORKER: Oh, they won't mind, you know (pointing to the group), they would be glad. (Most of the group members laugh at this.)

LOU: I want to give others the opportunity to speak because, after all, I have been married over 45 years, so I have an accumulation of incidents.

During the problem-swapping exercise, I had attempted to express my empathic responses to the concerns as they were raised, taking care not to express judgments on the members' feelings and actions. Even this brief period had built up a fund of trust large enough to let me reach for some discussion on this difficult theme. For the group to develop as a healthy organism, it would need to begin to sort out the authority theme—its relationship to me as the leader and the person in authority. Because this is a taboo subject, I would have to work hard to open the topic for discussion. When I invited Lou to speak again, I decided to return to the theme of helpers who had not helped. Note that I returned to this issue directly by pointing out to the group members that I thought such a discussion might be important, so that they could be involved with full knowledge of the process. The group discussion that followed was led by Lou, an internal leader on this issue; it contributed to a striking change in the group atmosphere and to its successful beginning.

WORKER: I have noticed a theme that has cut across a number of your presentations that I think is important for us to talk about. A number of you have commented on helping people who have not been very successful—psychiatrists you have had in the past, doctors, and so on. (Group members all nod, saying yes.) Can you stay on that for a minute in terms of the things in your experiences that you found difficult? The reason I think it is important is because it would be a way of your letting me and my coleaders know what you would not find helpful from us.

This is the second time I reached for comments about the group members' concern about us. This time, because a relationship was beginning and because I reached in a way that was less threatening, they were ready to share. Lou volunteered to begin the discussion. He took us back to 1940, when he had his own business. He described some of the pressures on him concerning economic conditions and a rash he developed on his leg then. His doctor referred him to a psychiatrist who was brand new at the hospital. In fact, it was the psychiatrist's first job. Lou's enthusiasm and feelings while describing this experience captured the attention of the group. They smiled and nodded agreement with his comments.

As he was about to describe his encounter, the door to the group room opened and the fifth couple, Frank and Jane, arrived late. Group members often arrive late for a first session, but group workers many times feel doubtful about what to do then. In this case, I had the new couple introduce themselves, and I asked the other couples to give their names as well. I then briefly summarized the contract, explaining that we had been hearing about some problems to help get a feel for the concerns that had brought the couples to this session. I then pointed out that the theme of helping people who had not been very helpful had come up. I said that we were focusing on this right now and that just before they had entered we had been with Lou in 1940. With that, I turned back to Lou to continue, and the group picked up where it had left off. Workers should recognize the entrance of the new group members and help them connect to the group, but taking a great deal of time to start again would be a mistake. As will become clear later in this group session, the lateness of these group members was their way of handling a new and frightening experience.

Lou continued the story of his first encounter with the young psychiatrist, indicating that the psychiatrist had tried to lead him indirectly to recognizing that he had a marital problem. As Lou put it, "I was talking about the economic conditions and the problems of the time, and he kept coming back to the wife and the kids, and the wife and the kids, and the wife and the kids until I said to him, 'Are you trying to tell me my problem is with my wife and my kids?'" Lou went on to say that when the psychiatrist indicated it was, he stood up, called him a charlatan, and quickly got out of the office as the enraged psychiatrist came out from behind the desk shaking his fist at him.

LOU: OK. I knew that my wife and my family were part of the problem, but I also knew that they were not at the core of the problem. They were a contributing factor because of the social and economic conditions. I went to this guy to get rid of this rash on my leg and not to have him tell me that my wife and my kids were giving me the problem. It took a while for the rash to go away, but eventually it did. That was item number one. I am going to skip a lot of the intervening incidents that had to do with families, and I will go to the one which we just experienced recently. We went to a psychiatrist in the community for two and one half years (and then with emphasis) *two and one half years!* I knew I had to go with her to give her some support plus I wanted to find out what made her tick. I couldn't understand her depression. I had been down in the dumps and felt blue, but I had never felt depressed as she seemed to feel. He asked her a lot of questions, asked me a lot of questions, tried to have us do some play acting and had us try and discuss the problems. "You're not communicating" was his term. I didn't know what he was talking about when he said we didn't communicate, so we tried to communicate. But nothing really came of it because we saw we weren't communicating.

As Lou related his experiences, he was describing several techniques that professionals had apparently used to try to help him and his wife deal with their problems. The central theme appeared to be that of a helping person who had decided what the problem was and tried to educate them as to its nature. Lou resented this approach and resisted it in most of the sessions. Yet part of him deep inside knew that there was a problem that he attempted to deal with in his own way. He described an incident when he had tape-recorded a conversation with his wife, listening to it later. His description of the aftermath of this recording contained the first overt expression of the sadness and pain the couple had experienced but were not ready to share. In this case, I believe Lou needed to share the anger and the frustration at the helping people who had not understood him before he was willing to share his hurt and pain.

LOU: We talked for about 15 minutes, and I realized when we played the tape back, that I was screaming at Rose. Now I never realized that I was screaming at her. But I heard my voice. (Lou clears his throat at this point and begins to choke up, obviously feeling emotions and trying to fight back his tears.) This is a little rough for me, can I have some water?

WORKER: (Getting a glass of water from the decanter) Sure you can, Lou, take your time.

LOU: It's kind of tough to get over the fact that I was screaming at her. Then I realized that when I was screaming at her, I was treating her like a kid. I took this tape to the psychiatrist, and he couldn't hear the screaming. He got nothing out of it.

WORKER: He didn't seem to understand how it felt to you to hear yourself screaming?

LOU: That's right. He didn't even hear me screaming. The other thing he tried to get us to do which I found really devastating is he tried to get us to reverse roles; she should be me and I should be her. OK, we tried it. But while we were doing it, I was thinking to myself: "Now, if that isn't stupid, I don't know what is." (Turning to me at this point) But you're a psychiatrist—you know what the score is. How can you reverse roles when I'm not feeling like she's feeling and she doesn't feel like I do? How can I communicate? Well, it was things like that that had been going on for two and one half years, and when we had finished, I was nowhere nearer being helped to be able to live with Rose than I was when we started. Now that's two and one half years! It isn't that we didn't try; both of us used to discuss this. Rose went back to the doctor, but I said I wouldn't go because I found I was just getting more frustrated.

At this point, there was some discussion on the part of group members about the use of the tape recorder. Rick thought it was a good idea and wondered if Lou had tried it again. Lou said he had not. The conversation returned to his feelings of frustration and his sense of not having been helped.

LOU: I felt stupid. The psychiatrist kept telling me something, and no matter how hard I tried, I simply couldn't understand.

WORKER: You also seem to be saying, not only couldn't you understand him, but he didn't seem to understand you.

LOU: Well, yes. Peculiarly enough, that thought had not occurred to me. I felt, well you are a professional (facing the worker at this point), so what you're doing, you're doing on purpose. You know what you're supposed to be doing. And whether you understand me or not is immaterial. That's not what the game is. It's my responsibility to understand what you, if you are the psychiatrist, are saying. (There was anger in his voice.)

WORKER: If you're asking us (referring to the other coworkers) in this group, that's not the way I see it. I think that if we can be of any help to you or the other group members, the help will be in our listening and in our trying to understand exactly how you see it. The gimmicks and the things that seem to get tried on you is not my idea of how we can help. You'll have to wait to see if I mean that.

LOU: Yeah, we'll see.

WORKER: I think you folks have a powerful lot of help to give each other. And essentially, what I will try and do is to help you do that. And I'll share my own ideas along the way. But I have no answers or simple solutions.

LOU: Then, well, OK. (General silence in the group as the members appear to be taking in the meaning of the words.)

COWORKER: I'd like to know, Lou, as we go along, how you see things. So, if you're feeling stupid or whatever, you'll let us know.

WORKER: It might be because we've said something dumb (some subdued laughter in the group).

Although I had described the group as a mutual-aid group in the opening statement, only at this point did the members really began to have a sense of how the group might work. Also, they actually "heard" the clarification of the group worker's role contained in this exchange. As an internal group leader, Lou could articulate the fears and concerns that members felt about the potential power invested in the group worker's role. If the group leader is feeling insecure, as most beginners do, then she or he might see Lou as a "deviant member" challenging the leader's authority. In reality, he provided an opportunity for an initial clarification of who we were as group leaders and what we did. Skills of accepting and understanding his feelings and his frustrations, and of helping to connect his past experiences to the present moment, were crucial in this session. The feeling in the group was that we had moved past the first step in building our relationship. The authority theme would come up again; however, one could sense that an important start had been made. Following this exchange, the group members could move into work on their contract with more energy, involvement, and intermember interaction.

The Work Continues

The 2-hour session allowed the group to move past problem swapping and clarification of purpose and worker role into beginning efforts to define the primary work. Interestingly, Frank and Jane, the couple who had arrived late, provided an opportunity to do this. Frank began to share, with some elaborative assistance from the group worker, a problem that they were experiencing in relation to his wife's teenage sons who were living with them. It was an interesting example of a group member raising a problem tentatively, moving quickly back and forth between the implications of the difficulty for the couple and for his relationship to the children. He spoke of the sexual difficulty they had, attributing most of it to a medical problem he was having treated and also to the lack of privacy in their home. The bedroom door was never locked, and the children would wander in without notice. As Frank was sharing this concern, he phrased it in terms of his problem with his stepsons, but one could hear throughout the discussion hints of the implications for his relationship to his wife. Each time the worker would acknowledge, even gently, the implication for the relationship, Frank would back off slightly, and both he and Jane would quickly reassure the group, emphasizing the positive nature of their communications.

As we have seen, group members often use the early sessions to offer near problems in a way that presents them as issues and at the same time defends them from discussion. This move reflects the members' ambivalence about dealing with real concerns (see Part II), as well as their testing of the group to see if it is safe to share. The group members worry about sharing in front of not only the worker and the other members, but also their partners. Each of the couples has developed a "culture" in their marriage that has included certain norms, behaviors, taboo areas, rules for interaction, and so on. The group will in many ways be a place for them to learn how to change that culture, or at least those parts of it that are not conducive to their marriage. With so many factors to consider, group members often come close to a concern while watching to see how the partner, the other members, and the workers will react. Timing is important in a first session, and it would therefore be a mistake for a group worker to attack defenses at a point when the group member greatly needs them.

As Frank began to describe his efforts to deal with the children and privacy, I suggested that they might use this as an example of one of the ways in which the group members might help each other:

Worker: (Speaking to the group) Perhaps we can use this as an example of how we can be helpful. Frank can describe the conversation he had with his son, and the rest of the group members might respond by suggesting how they would have reacted if they had been the son. We could do some thinking with Frank about how he might handle this kind of an issue.

The group members agreed, and Frank went into some details of a conversation in which he sarcastically implied to the son that they needed some privacy. After several group members supported his right to privacy, the coworker pointed out that it would be difficult to take his comments seriously because he always seemed to be joking as he described things and never seemed as if he could really get angry. This triggered a response from his wife, Jane.

JANE: Aha! That's it exactly. Frank has trouble getting angry. Ever since he has been a kid, he has been afraid to be direct and angry with people. I keep telling him, why don't you let yourself get angry and blow off steam? He says that he feels that it is just not the thing to do. You just don't do it. I do it all the time. I didn't use to, but now I do, and I get angry at least a couple of times a day.

FRANK: You know the kids are scared of you because you get angry so much.

WORKER: (Noticing that Sally appears to want to say something) Go ahead, Sally, get in.

SALLY: (Laughing as she speaks to Frank) You have got to meet my Len! (The whole group, including Frank, erupts in a great roar of laughter.) You sound like two of the same kind, and you're hard to live with.

WORKER: Frank, what made it hard for you to speak seriously to your son right then?

FRANK: I don't know. Well, you know the image of a stepfather like in the fairy-tale books, he is like a monster. I've got a nice thing starting to build with these boys, and I don't want to ruin it.

WORKER: You are afraid they would get angry if you were direct and honest.

JANE: (Laughing, but with a touch of anger) It's all up in your head.

WORKER: You know, Jane, I think Frank really is worried about that.

FRANK: I do worry about that. I really do.

In response to the worker's next question, "What are you afraid might happen?" Frank went on to describe the cold relationship the children had with Jane's former husband. Then he shared his fears of being unable to prevent the continuation of the same coldness and the problems that he envisioned in that relationship.

FRANK: It was because I didn't want to hurt that relationship that I more or less symbolized what I really meant.

WORKER: You kind of hinted at what you felt rather than saying it directly.

FRANK: Well, it's like you are in a washroom and you see a fellow peeing on the floor. You would probably say, "Hey, you missed, fella." (Group members roar with laughter at his story.)

Frank went on to describe, much to his wife's surprise, a very direct conversation in which he explained the problem to the son. Frank's point was that since that time, the son had been much more understanding about not interrupting. At this point in the group session, Lou, who had been listening intently, moved in and took responsibility for the group process. In a striking illustration of internal leadership at an early stage in the group development, Lou moved directly from the general discussion of anger and indirect communication to the implications for each couple. The worker had noticed during the discussion that on several occasions Lou had attempted to whisper to his wife, Rose, to ask her a question, but she had refused to respond, and remaining impassive and expressionless. Lou now used the group and this theme to deal with his concern—a concern common to all members. I believe that he was able to make this direct intervention and assume some leadership responsibility in the group because the way had been cleared through our earlier discussion of the role of the worker. This was an example of Lou accepting the worker's invitation for the members to begin to own their group.

WORKER: (Noting Lou's indirect communication of his desire to get into the discussion) Were you going to say something, Lou?

LOU: Something has come up here which I would like each couple in turn to answer if they can. (Turning to John, he asks his name, which John gives him.) I would like each couple to add to this in turn if they can. John, do you get really mad at Louise? I mean really mad, peed off? Do you yell at her, do you tell her off?

JOHN: Not really.

LOU: Why not?

JOHN: That's my style, that's the way I have been all my life.

LOU: Louise, how about you?

LOUISE: I'll probably hold back until as long as possible and then usually end up to where I'm in tears, or slam cupboards or dishes, or give John a cold shoulder rather than coming right out and saying that I'm angry. (As Louise is speaking, Lou is nodding and saying yes.)

LOU: Why? By the way, I am referring to Rose and myself right now when I'm asking this question and I want to hear from everyone.

JOHN: It happens sometimes, but it is really rare that we actually yell at each other. (Louise shakes her head, agreeing.)

LOU: Are you afraid to get angry, either one of you?

JOHN: I don't think I'm afraid. I don't have a problem yelling at other people. It's kind of strange. I don't know why.

LOU: How about you, Frank and Jane?

Jane and Frank both discussed her getting angry regularly, blowing her top all the time. She indicated that it worried her. Frank said he had trouble getting angry directly at Jane and gave an example of her not sharing her load of chores (they are both working), and he shared that he had been getting angry at that, because it was setting a bad example for the kids, but that he had not told her. He paused when he said that, and then said, "I guess I hadn't said that to you until tonight." As the conversation went on, the other workers and I were monitoring the members, making sure they were involved and paying attention. Occasionally one of us would comment on some of the feelings associated with the comments.

LOU: (Directly to Jane) You have no aversions about getting mad, I mean spontaneously mad?

JANE: What other way is there to get mad?

LOU: You don't build anything up and then have it boil over?

JANE: Not anymore, not now.

After a pause, I turned to Lou and said, "Stay with it." Lou responded, "Fine, because something is happening here that happens to us," (pointing to his silent wife, Rose) "and I would like to hear from everyone in the group on this." At that point he asked Fran, who had declined to speak thus far, if she got mad.

FRAN: I hold it for a little while, and then I start and I pick, and I can't stop at the issue. Often I can't even determine what the issue is at the time. Since I can't figure out what it is, I go through the whole gamut to make sure I get to the right one. And—maybe I should let Rick speak for himself—my opinion is that he's quiet. He listens to all of this without a comment back. That really drives me out of my mind. I can't stand the silence. If only he would yell! Even if I'm wrong, then I know I'm wrong. But like I said, I go over the whole ballpark because I know I may hit the right one, since the right one is in there somewhere. There's not much of a reaction, because Rick is the quiet type. He doesn't like to argue or fight. And the quieter he seems to get, the angrier I get. I have to push even harder. It's just recently, the last couple of months, that we've started to fight physically. We've been married for seven years, and this is just coming out now. Well, I didn't think that Rick had a breaking point and that he could get that mad. And I wasn't even aware that I could get that mad, but I can. I'm the pusher, I'm the one—the things that I could say could definitely curl your hair.

RICK: She basically said it all for me.

FRAN: And that's usual, too.

LOU: (Smiling in a supportive way) Your hair looks pretty straight to me, Rick.

RICK: (Sighing) It has been a long day. Yes, I am the quiet type, and I have a very long fuse, but once it gets to the end, look out. I've done some stupid things in my time, and they usually end up costing me. I guess I just reach my breaking point and take the frustration out somewhere. If it happens that Fran is taking hers out on me, I try and cool it as long as I can, but then I can only take so much of that, and we end up going at each other. That's about it.

LOU: Let me ask you a question, Rick. When Fran is at you like she does, is it that you don't want to or are you afraid of hurting her feelings so that she'll come back at you again and this thing will snowball, or is it that you have a reluctance and you feel you'll let her get it off her chest and then things will calm down again? Which of these is it?

RICK: I guess I'm just hoping that she'll get it off her chest and things will calm down again. But it doesn't work that way.

WORKER: (Turning to Lou) If I can just ask Rick this before you go on, Lou—what's going on inside of your guts when Fran is pushing that way? What do you feel?

RICK: (Takes a big sigh before he speaks) Well, I guess I'm trying to just block everything out of my mind. That's the reason I become quiet, even go to the point of reading the newspaper and just completely try to wipe it out.

WORKER: Because it hurts?

RICK: Right.

Lou continued, turning to Sally, who also described how she saw herself in Fran because her husband, Len, is like Rick, the quiet type. She described several similar examples, ending by saying, "I don't think I have ever found his boiling point. Heaven help me if I ever do."

WORKER: That must be as hard as having found it.

SALLY: Yes, I guess it is. The problem is that you hoard the hurts and when you get a chance, zap, you give them right back. The sad part is that I really don't think Len has a mean bone in his body.

There was a long silence after this as the group waited in anticipation. The next speaker was Rose, Lou's wife, who had not said a word nor changed her expression during the entire session. She had been watching and listening intently. Because of her silence, her comments at this point had a stunning impact on the group members as well as the group worker:

ROSE: Well, I think there is a common thread running through with everyone and part of it is anger, and there may be some recriminations amongst the couples here. Some people have learned to live with it, but obviously, those of us here have not. And no matter how long you're married, it's still something you don't know how to handle. I found that I got very angry here.

WORKER: You mean here tonight?

ROSE: Yes, but I wasn't going to interrupt my husband to tell him that I didn't want him to say that or I didn't like what he was saying. So, I'm back to zero, not just one. I can pack my bags and go back to the hospital. (At this comment, her husband, Lou, flinches almost as if in pain and looked toward the worker.) And I don't feel comfortable talking about it.

WORKER: It's hard even now, isn't it?

ROSE: Yes, but I made up my mind I was at the point where I would pack my bags or talk. (Rose was referring to returning to the inpatient ward of the Center.)

WORKER: I'm glad you talked.

LOU: (His face brightening) Well, I have been thinking that that was about the only way I could get Rose to talk and to burst open.

ROSE: Sure, well, I knew that's what was going on.

LOU: She wasn't going to say anything to me. I asked her during the group if she was mad, and she said she was. I asked if she would say something, and she said no.

ROSE: Right, I said no.

LOU: Plus the fact that what goes on is that all our lives both of us have always been afraid of hurting each other.

ROSE: So, we kept quiet. Or else one spoke and said too much. I always felt that Lou had spoken lots more than I did. Now, I had an opportunity to do a lot of speaking at the hospital for five weeks, and certainly I found it helped me quite a bit. I told myself and the people there that I was going to try and remember to use everything they taught me. And there's really no way. Because different things come up and, say, they're not in the book that I went by.

WORKER: I guess you have to write your own book, then.

ROSE: That's right. I'm not very quick on my feet, and I don't think my mind operates very quickly either. But how to deal with anger seems to be everyone's particular problem. (There is a pause in the group as Rose's words sink in.)

WORKER: It's close to the end of our session, and I wonder if what we haven't done is identify a common theme and issue that we might want to look at in more depth next week. Perhaps you could be prepared to share some of the incidents and difficulties, because I think if you can bring some of those arguments from the outside into here, where it is a little safer, and where there are people around to help, maybe it's possible to learn to do what Rose did just now without hurting. Perhaps it is possible to say what you are really thinking and what you're feeling without having to store up the hurts. My own feeling is that any real, intimate relationship has to have both some loving and some fighting. That comes with the territory. But it's a hard thing to do. We simply haven't learned how to do it. So maybe this could be a safe area to test it out. Does that make any sense to the rest of you? (Group members nod.) Maybe we could pick up on this next week as something that we're interested in. How do you find a way of saying what you're really thinking and feeling toward each other without wiping each other out?

JANE: Is there a way to do that?

WORKER: I think so, but why don't we test that out here in the group? If there isn't, though, then I think we're in trouble, because I don't think you could really care for each other if you can't also get angry at each other. Does that make some sense to the whole group? (Once again, there is some nodding in agreement.) What we could do is different couples could bring some examples. Maybe you'll have a hard time during the week that's tough to handle. Well, we could go over that with you here in the group and see if we can find a way of helping you identify what you were really feeling and also be able to say it directly and clearly in a way that keeps communication open. I think this is the way it would work. Even if one couple raises a specific example, the rest of us could learn in helping them with that example. So, you would get something out of each week's session even if you weren't talking about your own marriages.

With a clear contract and some work in the beginning of the session that helped create the safe conditions within the group, members felt free to begin to risk themselves. The group moved directly to one of the core issues in marital relationships. What is striking is the way the members themselves directed the emergence of this theme. Each group is different, reflecting the strengths and experiences as well as the weaknesses of its members. Lou brought a sense of urgency and a willingness to risk himself to the group that helped them not only tackle the issue of authority directly and constructively but also helped them to move past their early defenses into the common concerns they had about their relationships with each other. Although the particular way in which this group worked during its first session is unique, the level of its work or the speed with which it began is not unusual. It reflected the sense of urgency of the group members, the clarity of group purpose, and the workers' role. The members were willing to attack the issue of authority directly, and the workers consistently tried to articulate the feelings expressed by the group members, even being slightly ahead of them. Given these core conditions, the impetus of the group members carried them toward productive work.

Ending and Transition

Now that the session was nearly over and the group had agreed on a theme for additional work, the ending and transition part of this session continued with an opportunity for evaluative comments. The workers wished in the first session to encourage members to talk about the way the group was working.

WORKER: We have five minutes left. This was our first session. I would like you to take a few minutes to share with each other and with us what your reactions are. What are your feelings and your thoughts? How has this session hit you? What will you say to each other on your way home in the car about this evening's session? It's important that you say it now.

ROSE: Well, I have the feeling that the first thing out the door, Lou is going to ask me what it is he said that made me angry. I can't define it right now. I'd have to pull it out of my head.

LOUISE: That's tough. That's really tough trying to figure out what it is that makes you angry. I feel that way, too. When I was an inpatient and someone showed me that I was angry at a resident and why I was angry, well that was fine; I was able to do a little bit of yelling and get it off my chest. But it's not always easy to put my finger on what it is I'm feeling.

WORKER: Maybe that's what we can do here—help you figure out what those feelings are. (Turning to Lou) What's your reaction? I'm really interested in your reaction because I have a feeling that you came in here thinking about all of the people in the past who haven't been helpful. Where do we stand so far?

LOU: So far I feel that we're beginning to break a little new ground. Actually, the most important thing that happened to me tonight was Rose getting mad.

WORKER: Is it easier to handle it when you know where she stands?

LOU: No, not really. I don't know where she stands. I knew she was mad; I asked her to tell me what she's mad about, but she said no. The reason I am feeling good about this is that she has just gone through five weeks as an inpatient, and I can assure you (voice cracking) I've just gone through the same five weeks.

WORKER: I think these things change step by small step and perhaps tonight made a beginning. Perhaps if you aren't too harsh with yourself and demand too much, you have a chance of doing it. I am glad it hit you that way. How about the others, what will be your reactions tonight?

FRANK: Whew!

JANE: (Laughing) I think we were so apprehensive about what would happen here tonight it wasn't funny.

WORKER: What were you afraid of?

JANE: Well, I guess it was the fear of the unknown, and yet when we got here, we immediately started to sense that here are people who are concerned, who care, and this came right to the fore.

LOU: Larry, I'd like to make a comment here. Our youngest son is 36 and one of the things he complained about to us was that "you never taught me how to argue with my wife." I wondered where in the world did he get the idea that it was necessary to argue with each other. As time went on, I realized that we used to argue and keep things on the inside. My son today is having problems, and he even called me last night on the very same subject. The important thing he said was, "You haven't taught us how to argue." Oh, yes not only that but, "You haven't taught us how to argue and to win the argument." (The group roared with laughter.)

Other members of the group were given a chance to comment. Frank pointed out that he and Jane were late partly because they were ambivalent about coming. He had been telling my coworker all week that he was not sure whether he really belonged here. As he described his conversations, he laughed along with the other members of the group. They all acknowledged that coming to the first session had been frightening. Frank went on to say that what impressed him was the people in the group; they all seemed to be a really "super bunch," and that helped a lot. Lou commented that it was reassuring to find out that he was not alone and that others had the same feelings.

After some additional positive comments, I pointed out that it would also be important to share their negative reactions or questions; these were tough to share but were also important. Sally indicated her concern about whether or not the group would really help, if anything would really change. She was also worried about her husband, Len, having missed the first meeting. We talked about this, and I asked the group to strategize how we might bring Len into the second meeting quickly, because he would be feeling a bit like an outsider. This helped indicate to the group members that they all had a responsibility to make the group work well. After they made some suggestions for myself, Sally, and the group, I told Sally that there were no promises, no sure answers or easy solutions. Marriage is hard work, as she knew, but perhaps through the group we might be able to offer some support and help with their difficult tasks. She nodded in agreement.

Fran and Rick responded that they had felt a bit shy and found it difficult to talk in the group. John and Louise jumped in and reassured them, saying that they thought they had participated quite a bit. I pointed out that they had risked some very difficult subjects in the discussion with the group and gave them credit for that. Rick said that after a week or two he would probably find getting in easier; I told him to take his time and that he would get in as he felt comfortable.

As the evaluation seemed to be coming to an end, I pointed out that there were three rules we would follow in the group. I explained that members were expected to come each week and that it was OK to come even if your partner could not make it because of illness or some other reason. I said that they should treat what they shared with each other as confidential so that they could all feel that the other couples in the group would not be talking about them to outsiders. I also asked that if they wanted to drop out of the group at any time before the 23 sessions we had planned were over, they would agree to come back and discuss it with the group before quitting. All agreed that these seemed to be reasonable rules.

I then complimented them on what I thought was an excellent start. I told them that I could understand how nervous they must have felt at the beginning, because I felt a little of that nervousness, too, but that I thought they had launched some important work, and that boded well for our future. The session ended at this point, but people did not leave immediately; instead, they milled around talking to other members and the workers. Then, slowly, the group members left the room.

This has been a detailed description of the first session of one kind of group. You may already be thinking about some of the differences in the groups you have led. For example, these were generally articulate group members. They had volunteered to come to the group session and were not there under duress. The group leaders carried no additional functional responsibilities in relation to the members (such as a child welfare protective function). Of course, groups differ according to the setting, the members, the purpose, and so forth. Some of these are illustrated in the next section with brief excerpts from first sessions of groups from different contexts. Nonetheless, the basic dynamics and skills involved in effective beginnings with groups cut across these differences. You will find in the examples that when these dynamics are respected, they more often than not lead to an effective start. When ignored, however, they haunt both the group leader and the group members. First sessions are important because they lay a foundation for the difficult tasks to follow. If handled well, they can provide a fund of positive feeling as well as a clear framework, both of which will influence the remaining sessions.

One final note concerns a comment made by more than one social work student after watching the videotape of this session. Students are struck by Lou taking the initiative in asking the couples about anger in their relationships. The video images reveal my facial expression, which clearly indicates my delight at his moving into a leadership role. At one point I asked Lou if it was all right for me to interrupt him and ask a member a question. The surprised students ask, "Why did you let Lou take over your group?" My response is that it was not my group. The group belonged to the members, and the fact that they accepted my invitation to take over in the first session was a very positive sign and indicated the strength of the group members. This exchange often triggers an important discussion of the fear of an inexperienced group leader of losing control of the group. It takes some experience and growing confidence for the group leader to realize that leading groups effectively depends on the process of letting go.

Variations on First Group Sessions

In the previous section we explored common dynamics and skills related to first group meetings. These were illustrated using a first session of a group for married couples. However, not all groups are composed of articulate adults or of clients attending voluntarily. In this section we consider the most important variant elements that may affect the worker's strategy. These can be broken down into the following five categories: the age and relative articulateness of the members, the authority of the worker, the specific concerns of the clients, the setting of the encounter, and the impact of time. Each of these variations will be illustrated with one example of a first session. You can also refer to additional process recordings for Chapter 10, which are listed at the end of the chapter and available on the text's companion website.

Working With Children and Adolescents

The problem of lack of clarity of purpose or embarrassment about making a direct statement of purpose, discussed in Part II, is even more common with group work than individual work. The presence of more than one client may increase the reluctance of the worker to be direct. In the examples that follow, you will note a correlation between directness and honesty in the contracting and an effective start to the group.

Foster Adolescents in a Child Welfare Setting In this first extract, note the worker's reliance on safe and generalized topics in her opening statement to a group of foster adolescents in a child welfare agency:

> I opened the discussion by telling all the members that what was said in these groups would remain confidential. Neither workers nor foster parents would ever know what was being discussed. In addition, I pointed out that the same sort of commitment would be required on their part. I then mentioned the kinds of things we could discuss; for example, the trouble they have making their allowances stretch and whether or not the clothing allowance was sufficient. There followed a great period of silence, at which point I suggested that if they could think of nothing else, perhaps they would like to talk about the lack of conversation (which seemed to be a little too far advanced for the group to handle).

Nothing in the worker's statement recognized that they were all foster children. The examples she used could have been drawn from any discussion group for teenagers, and yet they all knew that they were foster children and that this group was sponsored by a child welfare agency. The worker omitted any comment about her role in the proceedings. The silence probably reflected their confusion about the group's purpose and their reluctance to begin. The worker's comment about the silence could reflect her own anxiety about their lack of immediate enthusiasm. In the rest of this session, the discussion was marked by wide shifts in subject matter, with youngsters talking about related topics (such as trouble with foster parents) and totally unrelated ones (such as TV shows).

Setting Limits: An Adolescent Acting-Out Boys' Group Ambiguity in contracting is common in work with children's groups. A good example is the "activity group" in a school setting, for children who are having difficulty with schoolwork or peers. A common problem with such groups results from having borrowed a traditional view of group work from the original group settings, which were leisure-time agencies, settlement houses, community centers, and the like. In this view, while members attended programs for what seemed like recreational purposes, the group leader actually had a hidden agenda related to agency purposes. In the school setting, the group worker might contract with the school administration to lead "clubs" that were designed for "teaching the youngsters how to get along better with each other and how to manage their own activities." A worker would argue that this would help the children get along better in school. The worker would view the group as a medium to "change the group members' patterns of behavior." The assumption is that a transfer of training will occur, and the learning from the group experience will make the children better students. A further assumption is that the worker can influence the group members indirectly by using the group activity as a medium for the "real purpose." The validity of both assumptions is questionable.

I have written elsewhere about the ways in which group members can use activities (singing, games, crafts, and so on) as important tools in their work (Shulman, 1971). There are many routes whereby group members can provide mutual aid for one another; certainly, it would be a mistake to view words as the only significant medium of exchange between people. The argument here challenges the view that program activity is the worker's tool for "changing" group members. For instance, the worker may withhold the real purpose of the group, leaving the members unclear as to the reason for the activity. When the youngsters look around during the first session, however, they know who the other children are and that they are the "losers," the "bad kids," or the "dummies" in the school. Because the contracting is not straightforward and honest, they become more anxious, often acting out their anxiety in disruptive behavior. The worker may assume that this behavior is intended to "test" authority or is an example of why the members have been referred in the first place. Early sessions may involve a great deal of limit setting by the worker, resulting in a battle of wills between the leader and the group. An alternative pattern is that the youngsters may involve themselves quickly in the group activities, which they might say are "a lot more fun than school." The worker would then find it harder to deal with school problems directly. Because the worker promised the teachers and the principal that the group would "change" the children's school behavior, the worker may be in trouble with the school staff when this does not happen and may then have to defend the rationale for the group against attacks by staff who view the group activities as "rewards for the kids' bad behavior."

In the example that follows, the worker makes an effort to clarify the real purpose with a group of 12- and 13-year-old sixth-graders described by the school staff as disruptive and noncooperative. The members respond to the worker's offer in two ways: First, they verbally describe their unhappiness with school as the worker encourages them to elaborate in this problem-swapping part of the contracting; second, they act out their anxiety through behavior that simultaneously shows the worker (the process) why they have been referred (the content). It is a new group worker's nightmare come true as she struggles to deal with the members' verbal and physical attacks on one another. In this excerpt, we see the worker integrating two roles. First, she sets limits on behavior in order to protect the individual members and the existence of the group itself. Second, she reaches for the meaning of the group members' behavior and points out the process-content integration.

> All five children know each other and are in classes together. Four are white, one Hispanic, and all come from troubled families. Juan has been physically abused by his estranged father. Greg has an older brother who is very violent and has terrorized this particular junior high school. James lives with his aunt, not his living parents. Jason (absent from the first meeting) has been sexually abused by his father. Collin's parents have separated. Three of these kids have had core evaluations and have been slotted for special education classes that have not started yet because of hiring difficulties within the school.

WORKER: I think that some of you could be nervous about being here. I want to try to reassure you and remind you that you are not in trouble, you have not done anything wrong, and this group is not detention or punishment. (James interjects.)

JAMES: We think it's great to get out of study period. (The others concur.)

WORKER: I hope this group becomes more than a way to get out of study period. The guidance director, Mr. Sher, and your teachers, Mr. Zacks and Ms. Trimble, are concerned because they want you to get more out of school and they feel you all can do much better. They thought I might be able to help you talk about some of the things that might be bothering you about school. You guys will be responsible for bringing up problems and solving them. My job will be to make sure we stay on the subject. Together, maybe we can think of ways to make things better for all of you at school, so let's get started. What is it like to be in sixth grade and in a brand new school for six weeks? (Greg raised his hand after I said the word *like*.) Greg, thank you for waiting until I finished, but it is not necessary for any of you to raise your hands in order to speak. I will ask that one person speak at a time and people should really listen to each other.

GREG: School sucks! (As Greg finishes, the others chime in.)

COLLIN: Yeah! School sucks! (Both Greg and Collin are trying to see whether I will react to the vulgarity. I do not react.)

JUAN: It's so boring.

JAMES: It's not as boring as elementary school.

JUAN: That is true; at least you are not stuck in the same room all day.

WORKER: In what ways is school boring?

> All the members begin talking at the same time, attempting to provide me with vignettes as to their own or present company's antics, making sure to hurl insults at each other; i.e., Greg stood on his chair and began to boisterously accuse Juan of never doing his homework. Juan snapped back that Greg was retarded and could not sit still. I told Greg to sit down in his chair and Juan not to name call. Collin asked permission to go to the bathroom (but didn't really need to go and did not ask again during the meeting). Then James spoke to me, stating that sometimes he finds schoolwork boring because he does not understand it. As I was focused on James and about to respond to him, Greg pulled the chair out from under Collin in such a way that Collin landed on his coccyx and was in severe pain.

WORKER: (Shouting) That's it! I want everybody to sit down and be quiet for a minute! (I gave Collin a brief neurological exam. I used to be an Emergency Medical Technician. Collin was OK. As his pain lessened, I helped him into his chair, and I sat back down.) I am sorry I yelled at you guys, but I felt things were getting out of hand. I got angry because I felt you guys were hurting each other with words, and, Greg, I know you did not want to hurt Collin, but you've all got to stick to our original agreement—no physical abuse. I think you guys were trying to hurt one another to avoid talking about what is hurting you inside about school. I wonder if this isn't what happens in class when things get uncomfortable.

The worker had to shout in order to get the group members' attention. In retrospect, given the reasons for referral for this group, acting out could be expected. Having a coleader might have helped the group leader feel more comfortable. The limit-setting intervention is familiar to the group members; they have experienced it in most of their classes. What may be different is the way in which she apologized for getting angry and then explained the limit as coming from concern about the members and her desire to provide a safe place in the group. The limit emerged from the reality of the group experience and was not expressed, as they may have often heard it, as an arbitrary imposition of authority (such as "In my class I will not tolerate this kind of behavior!"). Also, the worker did not fall into the trap of using this incident as an opportunity to preach or teach about "proper" behavior, as she had so unsuccessfully tried earlier ("Greg, thank you for waiting until I'd finished . . ."). If these children could work in this manner, they would not be in the group. Instead, she honestly expressed her own feelings, reinforced the element of the working agreement against physical abuse, and started to identify for the boys their maladaptive pattern of reacting. It will take some time until they learn to manage their feelings without using flight or fight to avoid their pain. Some may not be able to do it and may have to leave the group. However, with her first reactions, she let them know that this group (and she) will be different.

Impact of Authority: Involuntary Groups

The authority of the worker is always an issue in the first session. In some settings it can take on increased importance when the agency, and therefore the worker, carries functional responsibilities that may profoundly affect the client. Examples of workers with these additional functions include parole officers, child welfare workers in abuse situations, welfare workers dealing with income assistance, and adoptive workers who make judgments about who can or cannot receive a child. Fears of sanctions heighten normal concerns about the authority of the worker, and these fears can create a powerful obstacle that may block effective work. As with other obstacles, if the worker can reveal and explore them with the group members, then the power of the obstacle often declines.

A **mandatory client** group is one in which the members are required for some external reason to attend. For example, it may be a condition for getting their driving license returned, staying out of jail, keeping their children, or having their spouse return home. The common element is that group membership is involuntary; the members have not requested the service. They usually start the group presenting either passive resistance (through silence, apathy, creating an illusion of work, and so forth) or active resistance (through anger, confrontation, open denial of the problem). For the novice group worker, working with an involuntary group can increase the normal anxiety associated with new groups in the first session. The problems of engaging a reluctant client are similar to those raised in Parts II and III; however, in the group modality, the difference is characterized by the following statement of a young worker: "There are so many of them and only one of me!" Most new workers are so pleased at any conversation at all that they are perfectly willing to accept an illusion of work—a conversation in which the group members are "conning" the worker, each other, and even themselves.

The problem is that with the kinds of issues usually associated with involuntary groups, such as addiction, family violence, and sexual abuse, the denial itself is a problem. The requirement by the external authority that the group members must attend "or else" is a crucial part of the helping process and the only way to reach many of these clients. As long as the boss, spouse, agency, or court allows the client to continue to get away with behavior that is oppressive and dangerous to themselves and others, they will not seek help. Demanding that they face the problem is the beginning of the helping process. The tendency on the part of the client to minimize the problem lies at the core of the issue: They might say, for instance, "I only drink on weekends," "I only hit her with my open hand," "How can I raise my kids properly if I don't punish them to teach them right from wrong?" "The Bible says that to spare the rod is to spoil the child." One cannot begin to work effectively with such clients until their denial is dealt with. In one study, acceptance of a problem strongly and positively influenced client motivation, which in turn had a positive impact on the client's ability to use help (Shulman, 1991). Ability to use help influenced the working relationship with the social worker, as well as other outcome measures.

Stages of Change Model Some of the more recent conceptualizations about the nature of change and the change process can be helpful when one is working with involuntary clients, in that they try to reframe denial in a manner more amenable to intervention. The model developed by Prochaska and DiClemente (1982) describes the stages of change for people who are involved in addictive behavior. Their model is incorporated into a practice theory called *motivational interviewing*, in which the helping professional adapts her or his intervention to match the client's readiness for change (W. R. Miller & Rollnick, 1991). This model views clients as being at different stages of readiness for change and suggests that resistance is often the result of a counselor using the wrong strategy with respect to the client's stage of change. As DiClemente and colleagues suggest,

> A therapist can be understood as a midwife to the process of change, which has its own unique course in each case. The role for the therapist is to assist the individual, couple, or family in negotiating this process as efficiently and effectively as possible. In fact, the therapist can be a help or a hindrance to the process. . . . Skillful therapists will best facilitate change if they understand the process of change and learn how to activate or instigate the unfolding of the process. (DiClemente, Prochaska, Fairhurst, & Velicer, 1991, p. 191)

This stages-of-change model (DiClemente et al., 1991) suggests that clients can be in one of five stages:

1. ***Pre-contemplation: Resistance and the "Four R's."*** Individuals in pre-contemplation about a problem behavior such as smoking are not even thinking about changing that behavior. In fact, they may not see the behavior as a problem, or at least they do not believe it is as problematic as external observers see it. . . . There are many reasons to be in pre-contemplation. These can best be summarized as the "four R's": reluctance, rebellion, resignation, and rationalization. (p. 192)

2. *Contemplation: A Risk-Reward Analysis.* Contemplation is often a very paradoxical stage of change. The fact that the client is willing to consider the problem and the possibility of change offers hope for the change. However, the fact that ambivalence can make contemplation a chronic condition can be extremely frustrating. Contemplation is the stage when clients are quite open to information and decisional balance considerations. (pp. 194–195)

3. *Determination: Commitment to Action.* Deciding to take appropriate steps to stop a problem behavior or to initiate a positive behavior is the hallmark of the determination stage. Most individuals in this stage will make a serious attempt at change in the near future, and many have made an attempt to modify their behavior in the recent past. (p. 197)

4. *Action: Implementing the Plan.* What do people in action need from a therapist? They have made a plan and have begun to implement it by the time they come to the session. Often, making a therapy appointment has coincided with other change activity. Clients in the action stage often use therapy to make a public commitment to action; to get some external confirmation of the plan; to seek support; to gain greater self-efficacy; and finally to create artificial, external monitors of their activity. (pp. 198–199)

5. *Maintenance, Relapse, and Recycling.* The action stage normally takes three to six months to complete. This time frame is supported in our research on addictive behaviors, but may vary with the type of problem. Since change requires a new pattern of behavior over time, it takes a while to establish the new pattern. However, the real test of change for most problem behaviors, especially the addictive behaviors, is long-term sustained change over several years. This last stage of successful change is called "maintenance." . . . Relapse, however, is always possible in both the action and maintenance stages. (pp. 199–200)

By recognizing the difficulty associated with the change cycle, and by acknowledging relapse as part of the cycle, this approach allows the client to identify what she or he has learned from the relapse and to "recycle" into the stages to begin the action phase again, ideally this time in a stronger position to effect a longer or permanent "maintenance" of the change. Note that members of any group can each be in their own stage of change—from precontemplation to recycling. In the case of involuntary groups, many of the members may be in the precontemplative stage, not yet acknowledging the existence of a problem or the need to change. One way to view the requirement to participate in an involuntary group is that it may serve as the stimulus to help move a client from the precontemplative stage into the contemplative stage or further. While clients may not accept the idea that they have a substance abuse problem, for example, they can see that the use of the substance has led them to a conflict with the legal system, their boss, child welfare, their spouse or partner, and so on. One of the advantages of group practice is that a client in one stage of change may be motivated, by listening to a client in a later stage, to consider moving toward the action stage.

Most new group leaders are preoccupied with the potential negative impact of group members on each other and often miss the real strengths of mutual-aid groups with these populations. Once the worker deals openly with the authority issues in the first session, the group members may be the ones who most effectively identify each other's stage of change or confront denial. Further, by recognizing the involuntary nature of the group and encouraging a discussion of its impact on the potential for group effectiveness, the worker may be able to minimize this obstacle. In reality, while members may be forced to attend, they cannot be forced to participate in a significant way or to make real changes. The group leader's open recognition of this fact in a first session one may help to lower the barriers.

Male Batterers For example, in a first session with men who batter, Trimble (2005) included in his opening statement the following comment:

> I am sure it is possible to follow all of these rules and not change, not open up to facing yourself or the other men here. You can probably get through this group and really not change. That's up to you. The judge may order you to be here or your wife may be saying she won't come back unless you get help. And as I have just said, we require your anger diary and regular attendance in order for you to stay here, but no one can reach into your mind and heart and order a change. That's where you have complete control. (p. 360)

This honest recognition by the worker that change is in the control of the client helps to set the stage for the work to be done. The task of the group leader is try to find the faint lines of connection between the real, felt needs of the involuntary client and the potential services offered by the group. To do this, she or he must be ready to confront the illusion of work.

Driving While Intoxicated (DWI) This example comes from a mandatory substance abuse group for men who have committed a crime. It illustrates the worker's changing recognition of the meaning of denial, his recognition of his contribution to the resistance of the client, and his growing skill in involving the group members. In this case, the worker confronted the members early in the group, in an angry manner, failing to also provide the support the members need to face the problem.

According to the stages-of-change model, this form of confrontation of clients in the pre-contemplative stage, all exhibiting symptoms of the "four R's" described earlier (reluctance, rebellion, rationalization, and resignation), may stiffen their resistance. W. R. Miller and Rollnick describe it as the "confrontation-denial trap" (1991, p. 66). Essentially, as the group leader insists on the presence of a problem and the need for change, the client will argue the opposite—that there is no problem—until the interaction becomes an escalating battle. Another trap in early sessions is the "expert" trap, in which the group leader appears to have all the answers and tries to "fix" the client. A third and common one is the "labeling" trap, where the worker attempts to pressure the client to accept the socially unacceptable label of "alcoholic." Finally, the authors describe the "premature-focus" trap, where the counselor attempts to home in on the substance abuse problem when the client needs first to deal with broader issues (pp. 66–69).

The confrontation-denial trap in particular is illustrated in a third session of a mandatory group for drug users and alcoholics convicted of a crime. This is also an example of how contracting can take place over time and may not be completed in a first session.

August 28 (Third Session)

It was at this particular session where I was becoming very frustrated. I failed to interpret their resistance and came on too strong. In this group there was a lot of resistance and denial. John stated, "I went out over the weekend and got drunk." I tried to confront this and I felt like I was hitting a stone wall. He did not see this as a problem, and some of the other group members supported this type of behavior. I confronted those that continued to use but kept on stating that they did not have a problem, and they had a right to use.

I felt myself getting mad at the group, and they clearly sensed this. John asked, "Why are you picking on me?" Gary stated, "You don't have a right to tell us what to do." Gary was telling me that I cannot control their lives. Outside of the group they can do what they want. This made them more resistant, and one individual seemed to get a little angry with me. Steve, who is a marijuana addict and admits to that problem, has stopped using but continues to drink. I confront him on this, and he stated, "I don't have a drinking problem, so why is it a problem if I drink?" The tone throughout the session was my confronting and their denying. I really felt that I missed tuning in with their feelings about loss of control. For the next year or so the court will be in control of their lives. At the end of the group, I felt exhausted. I really never came to realize it until after I presented my case to the staff and our clinical supervisor.

Armed with the advice of supervisor and colleagues, the worker decided to stop pushing the clients during the next session and to relinquish control of the group. This led to a more comfortable meeting for the group leader and more active involvement in discussion by group members. However, the discussion was an illusion of work. A more helpful response during the first or second session would have been for the worker to explore with the members what makes it hard for them to face the problem. In addition, a focus by the worker on the negative consequences of the behavior may miss the important positives associated with the behavior that the client would have to give up. In referring to clients in the contemplative stage, W. R. Miller and Rollnick (1991) suggest using early sessions to explore "both sides of the coin," for example, by asking, "Tell me about your use of cocaine. What do you like about it? And what is the other side? What are your worries about using it?" (p. 72). This approach involves support integrated with confrontation and an effort to avoid the confrontation-denial trap.

September 18 (Fifth Session)

In group tonight, I had two new members beginning. I decided to have all the members speak about their drug and alcohol use, both past and present. Having the two new members was a benefit. This was one of the best groups in a while. The two new members were both sober. One stated, "I am an addict and I need to stay drug-free." This was helpful for other members to hear, because for them it seems to become more real. As I went around, some of the other members were now able to say that they may have a problem. A couple of the older members have also been sober for the last couple of weeks. In this group, people seemed to be more open. I still am confronting them on their denial, but not in a direct way. One tactic I have used is to ask all the members to stop using for a month, just to see how it feels for them. The ones still using refused but were willing to compromise. They agreed to cut their use in half. I told them that I felt that was OK. To me this seemed like a good intervention.

September 25 (Sixth Session)

The focus in this group session was on the difficulties of getting off of drugs. The members spoke about how some drugs are very difficult to get off of, particularly cocaine. There are two members, Bob and John, who continue to use. An interesting thing happened: A couple of the group members confronted them. This felt good, because for a change I did not have to do the confronting. It is now where I am beginning to feel that some of the denial is beginning to break down. The walls are slowly beginning to crack. I have to admit that part of the reason is because of the new members, who have brought in a positive attitude. There has been less silence in the group over the last couple of sessions.

Current Status of the Problem

I feel that this group is now beginning to head in a more positive direction. My role now in this group is to try and keep it heading in that direction. I feel that one thing I have learned is that it is unproductive to confront in a negative way. It only gets me and the other group members frustrated. Another ongoing problem is trying to keep this group feeling safe for the members. Since it is an open-ended group, there are new members coming in every ten weeks or so. At times this is helpful, but other times it seems like the group digresses. In the last few weeks, having a couple of new members begin was very productive for the group.

One thing I hope to do is to keep this group continuing to look at their own drinking or drug use in a more honest way. I need to let them decide when they are ready to get sober and not try to force it on them. I need to realize that the most I might be able to do is to educate them and at least give them respect and understanding about their addictions. It will be important for me to understand that at this time and space they are not ready to stop, and the reality is they may need to get into more trouble before they are willing to come to the realization that they are addicts and have to take more responsibility for their actions.

If this worker could go back and redo the first session using his current understanding his opening might have been quite different. For example, in another first session for men convicted of driving while intoxicated, when the worker sees men pointedly folding and putting away the schedule of topics for discussion, she directly confronts their reluctance to be present. When one of the men (an internal leader) says he does not want anyone calling him an alcoholic, instead of falling into the trap of the power struggle described in the earlier example, the worker writes, "Don't Want" on a flip chart and below it writes, "To be called an alcoholic." She then asks, "What else don't you want?" A second member says he does not want to be made to feel guilty. She writes that down as well. As the list grows, it becomes clear that by exploring the resistance rather than fighting it, the worker and the group members have actually developed a list of topics for the group. "Am I an alcoholic?" "What are the triggers that lead to my drinking?" "What are the things I have done with myself, my family, my job that I now feel guilty about?" When she summarizes the list at the end of the session and suggests these are the exact issues they can explore, she has demonstrated her understanding of the pre-contemplative stage and the way in which initial resistance (the process) may be understood as the beginning of work on the content.

All new workers face the struggle to synthesize support and demand, particularly with populations in denial (or the pre-contemplative stage). This skill comes with experience. The first step requires that the worker look closely at his or her own feelings and begin to manage them effectively. This frees the worker to deal with resistance by using the affective energy that comes from caring for the client. In the example of work with men who batter, described earlier, Trimble (2005) illustrates this synthesis by responding in the following way to a new group member's refusal to disclose the specifics of the violence committed toward his wife:

> I know it's hard to face it, to realize you hurt someone you love. Many men feel guilty and don't want to talk. But you can't change a problem that you try and forget. The basic goal here is to help you stop being violent. To do that, we start by asking you to tell exactly what you did when you were violent with your wife. (pp. 364–365)

The examples in this section and the additional process recordings on the text's companion website illustrate how the worker's authority is a crucial issue in first sessions of a group. It will remain an issue throughout the life of the group (see Chapter 11). However, the impact of authority is heightened in the early sessions before the development of a working relationship, which can cause authority to be a major obstacle to group development. Openly recognizing and clarifying the issue of authority diminishes its power to obstruct.

Working With Specific Client Problems

Some groups require attention to a particular problem. The specific concern facing the members of the group needs to be stated clearly and without embarrassment in the worker's opening statement. Providing examples can serve as "handles" for the group members. In the following example and those on the text's companion web page, we see how important this directness and specificity is to successful contracting.

Parents of Children With Cerebral Palsy In the next example, a worker begins a group for parents of children with cerebral palsy.

> Everybody had already introduced themselves, so I began by saying I wanted to give them an idea of what the group was about and then find out what they thought. I said that bringing up a teenager can be difficult, but when the teenager has cerebral palsy, a whole new set of difficulties and problems arises. In this group we are bringing parents together who are in a similar situation to discuss these problems. Hopefully, this will enable you to go back to your children with some new ideas of ways of coping with them. I also said that when I was talking to parents on the phone, they had mentioned several areas that were important to them right now. For example, what about starting high school? At this point Mrs. Boehm jumped in and said, "You know, that's exactly what I've been thinking about." She went on to describe her ambivalence about whether or not to send Stevie to a regular high school (he's 12). She talked about her desire for him to be with normal children, but she didn't really know if he'd be able to do it—it was a hard decision. She talked about this for quite a while. Finally, I said that the whole idea of the future for her son seemed to be an important thing to her now. She said, yes, it just began to be important in the last 6 months or so when she realized that he was getting older.

Women With MS: Crying in the First Session This group consisted of women, in their twenties to forties, all white and middle-class, who had recently been diagnosed as having the progressively disabling disease of multiple sclerosis (MS). This is the first session in which the women focused on the shock of the recent diagnosis and side effects. The group leader began with a request for introductions and a sharing of information about the illness. As is often the case, the sharing moved deeply into the work before the leader could make an opening statement. In retrospect, a brief statement about purpose and role prior to the introductions would have been help-ful. As one member moved quickly and emotionally into the work, the group leader responded with support.

This was the first group meeting. As members arrived, those who had previously been in a group exchanged greetings with the leader. The newer people sat down quietly. Members were asked to introduce themselves and to share infor-mation on their illness. Specifically, members were asked to inform others when they were diagnosed, of the current status of their condition, and what they hoped to get out of being in the group. We went round in a circle. It was Cathy's turn. She appeared somewhat startled that it was her turn.

Cathy was asked to introduce herself. The group's attention focused on her as she tearfully began talking about herself. She related how she had been diag-nosed with MS a few months ago and that she had been confused since then. "It must have been a very upsetting time for you; could you tell us more about it?" She related further how she had begun developing symptoms and after seeing doctors was diagnosed by a doctor who told her in a definitive way that she had MS. "It sounds like you heard about your illness in a very abrupt way and without any preparation or understanding of the implications it could have on your life."

Cathy went on to talk about her frustration with the illness. She described how her family and friends did not seem to understand what she was going through. "It would seem that the illness has not only been difficult for you, but also for others who are close to you." Cathy responded by saying that people did not know what to say to her nor did she know how much to tell them. "That is an understandable reaction when you first discover that you have MS." Cathy said that she felt very alone. There was silence. She went on to talk about how she could not remember things and would say incorrect words for what she meant to say. "That must be very frightening. You have brought up one of the side effects of this illness. In this group you will find that others may have had similar experiences, and it may be helpful to find out how they have coped."

Jane pulled from her purse a sticker notepad and declared that she used these everywhere to help her remember. Others agreed that these pads are very useful. I said, "You have made an important step in coming here tonight and sharing your feelings with the group."

At times throughout this exchange, Cathy was crying. When a group member cries during a session, the others may feel uncomfortable and embarrassed. Some models of practice argue that the group leader should control such expressions of emotion in a first session, so that they will not frighten other members. Unfortu-nately, this approach sends the wrong message to the members. They perceive the workers as being uncomfortable with the emotions, which reinforces the norms lead-ing to an illusion of work. Rather than controlling the expression of emotion by ignoring it, changing the subject, moving to other members, and so on, the worker needs to reassure the member and the group that the expression of strong feelings is natural and appropriate. In understanding and accepting these feelings, the worker demonstrates a way of working that will help the group members create a new culture in which all the emotions of sadness, anger, joy, and so forth can be freely expressed.

When a group has begun with a particularly strong first session, in terms of emo-tional expression and quickly getting to core issues, the worker needs to use some time at the end of the session to discuss the members' reactions. At times, members will feel embarrassed after having expressed strong feelings or ideas that they think are theirs alone. Some attention to this issue often results in other group members reassuring the exposed members that they are not alone. For example, in the MS group, the worker could have said near the end of the session,

> I would like to take a few minutes to talk about your reactions to this first session. You all shared some strong feelings this evening about what you are going through—particularly you, Cathy. In my experience, sometimes people feel uncomfortable when they share so much or have cried at a first meeting. They wonder what the other group members are thinking and feeling. Could we talk about it for a moment?

Inevitably, some members will come to the support of the individual who cried and reassure him or her that they shared in the emotions. Some members may raise their concerns about how they are going to feel if so much emotion is shared at the meetings. This provides the worker and the group an early opportunity to discuss the impact of emotions on their lives and on the group itself. Whatever the outcome of the discussion, it is usually better to have it at the session than to have the individual (Cathy) or the other client (the group) worrying about these issues on their own.

Impact of the Setting

The setting for the group meeting will affect the group itself. One cannot simply invite the members into a meeting room, close the door, and pretend the system surrounding the group is not there. For example, in residential settings such as group homes, hospitals, or prisons, the members bring their common environmental experiences into each session. A suicide attempt on a psychiatric hospital ward will affect the content and process of the ward meeting that follows. Convicts in a group session will have to overcome the culture in the prison that makes being honest and vulnerable extremely risky. In their first sessions, members of a foster parent group may want to complain about agency policies and social workers, rather than focus on parenting. In many ways, the setting of service will affect the nature of the group contract.

Chapter 15 explores in detail the dynamics and skills involved in helping group members with the task of negotiating their environment. In this section we focus on contracting and beginning issues in groups where relating to the environment is central to the work.

In the following illustration, a social worker in a hospital contracts with a patient ward group to discuss their illness and hospitalization. He views the hospital as a complex system that patients must negotiate, and he sees the group as a vehicle for helping them do that.

> I introduced myself to the patients and asked them to go around and introduce themselves, which they did. I asked whether they had been told anything about this group. They hadn't. I told them we get together to discuss what it means to be a patient in the hospital, how it feels being in a strange place away from family and friends. I said that often patients found it difficult getting used to a hospital experience, and sometimes it helped to talk with other patients. Often they have the same feelings of anxiety, fear, and uncertainty; we get together as a group so that we can freely talk about hospital experiences and feelings around

being a patient. I mentioned that they will probably notice that I take notes from time to time, the reason being so that I can look back on the session to see where I could have been more helpful to them.

Mrs. Jones began talking about the doctors and how they change, just after you get used to one doctor. I said that it must be a frustrating and anxious time when the doctors change. She agreed. Mrs. Beatty said that this is her first hospital experience and it was upsetting. Mrs. Carter said that she's used to hospitals and she felt she adapted well. Mrs. Victor said that the system didn't bother her. I asked Mrs. Beatty why she felt so upset about the hospital. She said it was strange and she felt all alone. If it hadn't been for Mrs. Carter "adopting" her, she would never have stayed after the first hour. I remarked that it must have been terribly frightening, this being her first time here and her not knowing the ropes. She agreed.

Mrs. Carter said that the hospital system didn't bother her, but she's scared they won't find out what's wrong with her. She was very sick at home, and she hopes they'll be able to do something. I said that it's a natural feeling to worry about one's illness, particularly when the diagnosis is not known. At this point, an orderly came to take Mrs. Jones to X-ray.

Mrs. Carter said that when you're not told what's happening, you feel bad. I asked in what way she felt bad. She answered that all of a sudden you're told to go through a difficult test or examination, about which you know nothing, and you feel horrible. I remarked that you need time to adjust to the idea of a test and prepare yourself for it. She agreed. I asked whether the others had similar experiences. Mrs. Beatty said one day a doctor came in for a heart examination. She was very upset because nobody had told her anything about it and she was thinking she must have had a heart condition; otherwise, why would she have to have this examination? The nurse explained that this is routine and that every patient who is on the ward gets cardiac and respiration examinations while they're here, and it certainly does not mean that there is anything wrong with her. I asked Mrs. Beatty how she felt now, knowing that it's a routine examination. She said, much easier; she would have felt less upset had she known this before.

In addition to helping the patients adjust to the difficult situation and clarify their concerns, the worker can use this group as a vehicle for change within the hospital. Serious illness often makes patients feel out of control over their lives. When a system appears to treat them as objects, their feelings of helplessness and impotency increase. These feelings can affect their use of the medical services (as in following the treatment plan), their satisfaction with services, and their ability to hear, understand, and remember what is said in conversations with medical personnel (Shulman & Buchan, 1982). Involving staff in the group sessions can help bridge the gap between the providers and consumers of service. In Part V, I explore how a worker can use patient feedback to affect the way in which the system relates to the client. This is the mediating function applied to the second client, the system. As will become evident, before workers can empower their clients, they must feel empowered themselves.

Impact of Time

Time can significantly affect the worker's activities in the first session. For example, some groups meet for a single session and must incorporate the beginning, work, and ending/transition phases in that time frame. In this section, we discuss the variations in a first session of a *short-term group*—one that is designed to meet for only a single or a few sessions.

In the first session of my married couples' group, described earlier, I could use the entire session for contracting and setting the stage for work, because we had many sessions to follow. Knowing this affected the work of the group workers and members alike. For example, I did not feel the need to confront defenses; instead, I could concentrate on providing a clear framework and as much support as possible. The group members could take their time, as well, starting with near problems designed to test the waters until they felt safe.

This contrasts with a group I led for single parents, which illustrates the differences in a first session when time is limited. The entire group experience needed to be contained in three 3-hour sessions, held over one evening and a day. Community professionals in a small, rural town felt the need for a mutual-aid group for single parents, so I was invited to fly into town to spend one evening and one day. Local helping professionals also attended the group, with two purposes in mind. First, they could provide ongoing services to the group members after the sessions were over. I felt it was important that resources be readily available to pick up with clients on issues that might be raised through the group meetings. Second, they could observe my group leadership so that they might be better equipped to start mutual-aid groups of their own. The group was advertised as open to the public, and many community professionals suggested it to their clients. I met the 15 group members who attended the night of the first session. In this section, I focus on the implications for the first session only.

Before the group meeting, I had tuned in to the possible themes of concern and had prepared an opening statement that I hoped would focus us quickly on their most central concerns. I also tuned in to two difficulties. As an "expert" from out of town, who would not be around long, I imagined that getting started with such a new group, in a small town where people tended to know about each other, would be challenging. Also, I saw the difficulty in opening up issues in a short-term context. I decided I needed to move quickly from the problem-swapping stage into work on specific issues, because we did not have the luxury of a long contracting phase. In addition, I felt we needed to demonstrate quickly how helpful the group could be, if members were to risk sharing. Finally, I tuned in to my own hesitations about risking in a first session and prepared to raise the issue directly with the group whenever I sensed defensiveness or the illusion of work. The following is an excerpt from my recording of the session dictated immediately following the meeting.

> I explained the purpose of the group as providing an opportunity for single parents to discuss with each other some of the special problems they faced because they were alone. I explained that my role was not as an expert with answers for them, but rather, I would try to help them to talk and to listen to each other, and to provide help to each other from their own experiences. In addition, I would throw in any ideas I had that might be helpful. I then offered a few examples of possible concerns around dealing with friends and relatives after the split in the relationship, problems in relating to the ex-spouse, the financial strains, and problems that often accompanied being a single parent and the difficulties presented by the children. There was much head nodding as I spoke. I finished by describing briefly the phases that parents and children commonly go through after a separation (denial, anger, mourning, and finally, coming to terms with it). I then invited the participants to share their own

experiences and suggested that these could form an agenda for our work that evening and the next day.

There was a brief silence, and then Irene asked how long it took to go through the phases. I asked her why she was asking, and she said it was 3 years since her separation and she doesn't think she has passed through all of them yet. The group members laughed in acknowledgment of the meaning of the comment. I said I thought there must have been a great deal of pain and sadness, at the time of the split and since then, for it to still hurt after 3 years. I asked Irene if she could speak some more and she continued, in a more serious tone, by describing her ongoing depression. She described days in which she feels she is finally getting over things and picking herself up, followed by days when she feels she is right back to square one. Others in the group agreed and shared their own experiences as I encouraged them to respond to Irene's comments. I told them it might help just to know that they were "in the same boat" with their feelings.

I then asked if the group members could be more specific about what made it difficult. This resulted in a number of areas raised by members, which I kept track of in my written notes. They included most of the problems I had raised in my opening statement. There was much emotionally laden discussion of the first area, problems with friends and family, with a great deal of anger expressed toward others who "didn't understand" and related to them in ways that hurt.

Dick, a young man in his mid-twenties, spoke with great agitation about his wife, who had left him with their 6-month-old baby only 6 weeks before. The group seemed to focus on Dick, who expressed a very strong sense of urgency and was clearly still in a state of shock and crisis. I had earlier noted that Dick was the first to arrive that evening and, during the premeeting chatter, he had told the person next to him all of the crises he had gone through just to get there that night. I pointed out to the group that it seemed that Dick was feeling this concern about friends and relatives rather strongly, and in fact he had had a great deal of difficulty even getting here tonight. I asked if they would like to focus on problems with friends and relatives first, using Dick's example to get us started. They all agreed it would be helpful, including Dick.

My effort to move us more quickly into the work began with my contracting statement and continued when I responded to Irene's joking comment about "not getting through the phases yet" by reaching for the underlying hurt and bitterness. If we were to move quickly in the group, I felt I had to send an early message that I was ready to deal with the difficult feelings as soon as they were. The group responded by immediately moving into the painful feelings as well as the anger. Feeling the need to get into substantive work early in this first session, I moved to obtain group consensus on an initial theme of concern and to bring Dick's urgency to the members' attention. Thus, we moved into the work phase less than an hour after my opening statement. In the continuation of the first session description that follows, Dick's resistance to taking personal responsibility for his problems emerges. I responded with a demand for work, pointing out that we had little time in which to work.

After Dick described the details of his separation and his current living situation with the 6-month-old child, he went on to describe the problems. He emphasized the difficulty of living in a small town, and in his particular case, being in a personal service occupation that put him in daily contact with many town residents. He said, "Sure, I feel lousy, depressed, and alone. But some days, I feel I'm getting over things a bit, feeling a little bit up, and everywhere I go people constantly stop me to tell me how terrible things are. If I didn't feel lousy before I went out, I sure do by the time I get home."

Dick added a further complication, in that the baby had a serious case of colic and was crying all the time. He told the group that everyone was always criticizing how he handled the baby, and even his mother was telling him he wasn't competent and should move back home with her. He continued by saying he was so depressed by this that he had taken to not talking to anyone anymore, avoiding his friends, staying home alone at night, and going out of his mind. Others in the group shared similar versions of this experience. I said to Dick, "And that's the dilemma, isn't it? Just at the time you really need help the most, you feel you have to cut yourself off from it to maintain your sense of personal integrity and sanity. You would like some help, because the going is rough, but you're not sure you want to have to depend on all of these people, and you're not sure you like the costs involved." Dick nodded, and the other group members agreed.

After providing recognition and support for these feelings, I tried to move the group into examining how they handled their conversations with friends and relatives, as a way of dealing with these feelings. I encountered a good deal of resistance to this idea, with Dick balking each time I tried to get him to look at how he might have handled a conversation differently. He evaded this by jumping quickly to other comments or examples, or by expressions that seemed to say, "If you only knew my mother/friends, you would realize it is hopeless." When Rose, a member of the group in her early fifties, confronted him from the perspective of his mother—she had children close to him in age—he rejected her comments.

I pointed out what was happening. I said, "It seems to me that when I or a group member suggests that you (Dick) look at your part in the proceedings, you won't take in what we are saying." I said I only had a day and a half with the group, so I really couldn't pussyfoot around with them. I wondered if it was tough for Dick, and all of them, to take responsibility for their part in their problems. Dick smiled and admitted that it was hard. He already felt lousy enough. Others joined in on how easy it was to blame everyone else and how hard it was to accept any blame themselves. I agreed that it was tough, but I didn't think I would be of any help to them if I just sat here for a day and a half agreeing about how tough things were for them. The group members laughed, and a number said they didn't want that.

At this point, Doris, one of the three workers participating in the group, surprised us all by saying that she had intended to listen and not talk during the session, but that listening to Dick's problem made her want to share hers. She said she had come to the group as an observer; however, she was pregnant and unmarried and therefore was about to become a single parent. She thought she was having the same problem in communicating with her mother as Dick was having with his. It was a classic example of a conflict between a mother who is hurt and embarrassed and a daughter who feels rejected at a critical moment in her life. At my suggestion, Rose offered to role-play the mother as Doris tried to find a new way to talk to her mother. The group was supportive, but at the same time, following my example, they also became quite confronting with each other, in a healthy way.

Dick listened and participated in the work on Doris's problem and, as is often the case, was able to learn something about his own situation as he watched someone else struggling with the same concerns. When I asked him later if he had taken something from it, he said it had helped him a lot to see how he was holding back his real feelings from friends and his own mother. I pointed out to all of the group members what a shock their situation was to their friends and close relatives and how, at first contact, they could not respond in a way which met their needs. I said, "This does not mean they don't love you. It just means that they have feelings and aren't always able to express them. Your mixed messages also make it difficult."

Cerrise, another worker/observer in the group, joined the discussion at this point and described how she had felt when close friends had split up her marriage. She realized now that it had taken her a couple of months to get over being so angry at them for ending the marriage, because she loved them both. She hadn't been able to reach out to them to support them, but she was lucky, because they had not given up on her and she had been able to work it out. Dick said that hearing that helped a lot. That was what was probably going on with some of his friends.

Carrie, who was both an unmarried parent and a worker in the community, described her own experiences with her mother when she split up. She shared how she had involved her mother in the process, had let her know her feelings, and that she wanted her mother's love and support but felt she had to handle the problems herself. Dick listened closely and said that this was probably what he had not been able to do. We did some role-play on how Dick could handle the conversation with his mother—how he could articulate his real feelings. The group was supportive and helpful.

When I asked the group how they felt about this discussion thus far, Doris said it was helpful because I kept stressing the positive aspect, the reaching out and caring between people. Most of them were so upset they could only see the negatives. The discussion turned to how much they needed others to talk to about what they were going through. As the session neared the end, in typical "doorknob" fashion Dick revealed that a close male friend of his, in a similar situation with a young child, had told him he was considering committing suicide. He went on to tell us, with tears in his eyes, that the friend had just killed himself. I said, "It must have hit you very hard when that happened, and you must have wondered if you could have done something more to help." Dick agreed that was so, and the group members offered him support.

After some time, I asked Dick if he was worried about his own situation, since he had many of the same feelings as his friend. He said he was worried, but that he thought he would be strong enough to keep going, to have a goal in life, to make it for his child. I told him he had shown a lot of strength just coming to the group and working so hard on his problem. Carrie said that he was not alone, and that he could call her if he needed someone to talk to—as a friend or as a worker. Rose pointed out that there was a single-parent social group at the church, and Dick said he had not realized that. Others in the group also offered support. I asked Dick how he felt now, and he said, "I feel a lot better. I realize, now, that I'm not so alone." Irene, who had opened the discussion by saying she had not yet gone through all of the phases, summarized the evening's work when she said, "I guess we are all struggling to find ways of saying to friends and close relatives, 'Please love me now, I need you.'" The discussion ended, and we agreed to pick up again in the morning.

This example has illustrated how a group can move quickly into the middle phase of practice if the worker makes a demand for work. We shall return to this group example in Chapter 11 to explore the middle and ending phase work that followed this opening session.

Recontracting

After watching the videotape of the couples' group described earlier, many students feel intimidated. As they often put it, "My first session didn't go that way!" I reassure them that neither did my early efforts. Even if the new group worker has done excellent preparatory work, is clear about the working contract, and has role-played an opening statement with a supervisor, unexpected events and problems can occur. Retrospective analysis often reveals that the worker left something out or the actual opening statement did not resemble the carefully constructed and rehearsed version. New group workers are understandably nervous when leading their first groups and should not be too hard on themselves. They also need to realize that they usually have an opportunity to recontract with a group if they do not get it right the first time. **Recontracting** is the process in which the worker reopens the issues of contracting by providing a clearer statement of purpose or exploring the group members' resistance or lack of connection to the service. Even if they are able to begin exactly as planned, group members may not understand or even hear the opening statement. Contracting in an ongoing group always takes place over several sessions.

Another common problem may be encountered when workers join an already functioning group: They may have to recontract in terms of their role as leader and the purpose of the group. Joining an ongoing group as a coleader and discovering that the contracting was never done or has been done badly can also be disconcerting. One student put it this way: "This sounds great in class, but I don't think the psychiatrist running our group has ever read your book!" In some circumstances, the ongoing group leaders have adopted a group practice model that operates under assumptions that differ from the interactional, mutual aid model put forward here. I reassure students that there are many frameworks for helping and that this circumstance would provide them with an opportunity to see another model in action. Also, elements of the interactional model can often be integrated easily into other frameworks.

In some groups, there simply is no model at all. Groups can be disorganized and unfocused, with members and the group leaders unclear about the purpose. Group sessions can resemble individual counseling in a group, with each member being helped by the group leader in turn. In this case, it becomes the social worker's job to try to influence the process with coleaders and members to recontract for a more effective group.

In the example that follows, we look at recontracting in the context of one's own group. Then we explore further the concerns arising from contracting with an ongoing group.

Recontracting With One's Own Group

In the detailed example that follows, a worker with an open-ended group in a shelter for battered women begins a first session with a mixed message about the contract. In her opening statement she briefly mentions several powerful themes related to the abuse and oppression that have brought these women to the shelter. In her structuring of the first session, however, she moves immediately to her agenda of providing information on independent-living skills. Rather than structuring time for problem swapping, which would have allowed the women some control over the agenda, the worker makes the decision for them. If one applies the oppression psychology outlined in Chapter 1, encouraging these women to take control of their own group could be seen as an important step toward independent living.

Several group members signal that they are at a different place in their needs related to this group. While independent-living skills, job opportunities, and so on all matter to these women, at this moment their sense of urgency may be more connected to their abuse and their living situations. The worker continues to control the first session, providing a sermon about the importance of community support. Later, her understanding and skills evolve over the next few sessions as she recontracts with the women.

Session 1

As I was setting the room up for the group session, one resident of the shelter arrived. She helped me arrange chairs and, as other residents arrived, she introduced me to them. I had planned to go around the room so that each woman could tell me her name, her length of stay at the house, and the number of children in her family, but I decided against it since we had already been introduced. Now I feel that I still should have asked them for a little more information about themselves. I did tell the women a few things about myself and then I stated the purpose of the group. I said, "The purpose of this group is to provide you with some helpful information that you can use once you leave the house. The group will also provide you with an opportunity to talk about feelings, experiences, and concerns that you might have about the different topics we'll be discussing. Tonight's topic is independent living skills." I went on to say, "Some of you are here because of abuse either by a boyfriend or a husband. You may find tonight that you have some feelings in common with each other. Some of you may be here for reasons other than abuse, and you may have your own set of circumstances that you'll want to share. My role is to help you to talk and to listen to each other. So I hope that we can all learn tonight not only from the material I have brought but also from the comments that we share with one another."

I began by giving the women information about two job-training programs. One woman, Linda, talked about a job-training program that she had attended and how she had landed a job afterward. Two other women talked about the skills they had, one in accounting, the other in word processing and stenography. Four out of the seven women were interested. The other three women showed no interest at all. I didn't ask them why they seemed uninterested. I feel that I should have confronted them.

From there we moved on to the subject of community support. I stated that many people think asking for help is a sign of weakness. People, in many cases, think it's important to handle problems on their own. I said I disagreed with this type of thinking. I said people who think this way are oftentimes worse off because individuals aren't always equipped to handle situations that come up on their own. I said that people who look to their community for support could be better off in many ways. I then asked the women if they had any ideas or suggestions on where to find community support when they leave the house. No one had any suggestions off the bat, so I mentioned places such as churches, local community action programs, etc.

Although the worker wrote, "We moved on to the subject," she should have written, "I moved on"—clearly, the members did not move with her. In the next excerpt, an internal leader emerges to move the women to a discussion of the "here and now" of their experiences in the house and the pain of the abuse they carry with them.

One woman said she was very glad to be at the house. She said she came into the shelter wondering what the other women would be like and found out that many of the women were just like her. She said, "It feels good to be with people who have the same problem." She said that when she lived with her husband, he would be on her mind all day long. She would worry about what he would be like when he came home. Before she came to the house, she would stay with her parents when her husband became abusive. Eventually, her parents would talk her into going back with her husband. She said, "Here at the house, you get support. You're told he has a problem, not you." She said she was very glad to hear that. I said, "So it sounds as if you're relieved to be here." She said, "Yes."

Another woman said she used to wonder what her husband would find wrong when he came home. She also said he wouldn't allow her to talk with friends. I said, "You probably feel good that you don't have that pressure over you now." She agreed. In addition, she said she planned to attend Al-Anon meetings for support once she left the house.

In the next excerpt, one of the members sends a signal to the worker that the session is not meeting her needs. The worker's written comment about "reaction formation" indicates that she noted the negative feedback and reacted with internal anger and an external smile. The worker's early anxiety about doing a good job makes it hard for her to hear negative feedback. The group members' anxiety about their dependency on the shelter may make sharing such feedback difficult. The discussion finally turns to money and issues of economic oppression that are closely tied to a major source of anxiety experienced by these women—economic survival. The worker does not understand the meaning of the flight behavior and thinks that she will need to do a better job at setting out the rules—a step that would cut off the expression of feeling rather than dealing with it.

One woman who had left the group for 15 minutes came back and said, "What did I miss out on?" Angela, one of the uninterested women, said, "Oh, you only missed out on some boring information." I should have asked her why she found the information so boring. Instead, I just smiled at her (reaction formation?). Then Janice, a night staff person, joined the group. Everything was fine until she started talking with the woman next to her. They continued to talk between themselves for about 5 minutes. I didn't know how to handle this situation.

When we started to talk about the area of financial management and I mentioned budgeting, one woman said, "What do I want to know about budgeting? I don't have any money to budget." Then she said that actually she did want to know about budgeting. She felt that someone should have sat down with her at the welfare office and shown her how to get the most for her money. Angela said she was always worried about having enough money to make ends meet, and she didn't see what good a budget would do. Angela has four children, one of whom is handicapped. The group began to talk about how she could get help for the handicapped child with cerebral palsy. The women suggested that she or her social worker call a cerebral palsy foundation. I turned to Angela and said, "You must get very discouraged at times." She agreed.

As the discussion continued about financial management, the discussion became somewhat chaotic. People were talking at once, cutting each other off. The women were skipping from topic to topic. I finally asked them to please talk one at a time. For the most part three women were doing all the talking. I could see that the other women were not paying attention. Next week I'd like to lay down some ground rules for discussion and emphasize the fact that everyone has important comments to make and we should take the time to listen to one another.

With hindsight, the worker might have been able to address the second client, the group, by acknowledging that the discussion was not hitting home for all of them. She could have identified the flight behavior as an understandable expression of the anxiety associated with the economic oppression and humiliation of being on welfare. These women had to demonstrate remarkable courage to overcome the economic restraints that our society places on them when they consider fleeing an abusive home. Inadequate financial supports function as a societal "shackle" helping to keep women chained to oppressive family situations. The worker might have responded to the group with the same empathy she had demonstrated moments before when she said to Angela, "You must get discouraged at times."

Next, the worker is surprised when a shelter staff person intervenes with the offer of going to church the next Sunday. This staff member may have responded to the group members' anxious flight with what she felt might help.

Suddenly, Janice, the staff person, asked if anyone wanted to go to church the following Sunday. This question was somewhat disruptive because we were talking about managing money at this point. She may have been responding to our discussion earlier about finding community support. It's difficult to say. The discussion became focused again when Linda asked for information about apartment hunting. One woman said that transportation was a big problem. Everyone chimed in on this. One woman said they should write a letter to the governor asking him to supply a car for the shelter. The women got excited at this point. I agreed that it sounded like a good idea, and I asked who would be in charge of writing the letter. Pam volunteered. Janice, the staff person, said they could talk about the letter the next day at the house meeting.

I told them that we had discussed a number of important issues. I said I hoped they would be thinking about questions and ideas for next week's session on single parenting, and said I would see them next Wednesday night.

For the second session, the worker again planned an agenda without the involvement of the women. Even the best plans can go awry, however, and the worker had problems with a film projector. The worker's hidden agenda was selling to the mothers the importance of providing emotional support to their children, but the women needed support for themselves to strengthen them for their children. The "deviant" member of the group the previous week, Angela, who had said that the group was boring, sent another signal the second week through her nonverbal behavior of sitting outside of the group. The worker was still too insecure to reach for it. The response of the other women, to bring Angela into the group, may have represented their understanding of her role and importance. This time, the worker reached for Angela's individual needs by providing some concrete help. Although this was an effort at relationship building and an expression of individual caring, it did not deal with Angela's message on behalf of the group-as-a-whole.

Session 2

I started the group by asking the women if they had any questions about the material I had handed out the previous week. No questions. I told them, as I had the previous week, that tonight's topic would focus on parenting. I said that I had planned to show a 15-minute film called *Special Times,* but the projector I had rented didn't work correctly. Since I had watched the film twice, I said I would go over the main points of the film and we could have a discussion focusing on these points. I said, "Before we get started, let's go around the room so that each of you can tell me how many children you have, their names and ages." After the women told me about their families, I asked Angela to move in closer because she was outside the circle of the group. She said she was fine where she was. Two of the women got up, went over and picked up the love seat that Angela was sitting on, and moved her closer to the rest of the group. Everyone, including Angela, had a good laugh.

At this point, I mentioned to Angela (the woman who, last week, had said the group was boring) that I had called the Cerebral Palsy Foundation. "They gave me a few referrals that might be helpful to you." I said that I could make another call for more information or I could give her the number to call. I said, "You can think about it and let me know at the end of group whether you want to call or if you'd like me to call." Angela talked for 5 minutes about the problems she was having finding services for her handicapped son. Everyone in the group listened.

When Angela finished, the focus on parenting began. I told them the movie's main point is that a parent should set aside a special time—1 or 2 hours every week—to spend with her child. The parent and child should plan ahead for this time. Additionally, the parent should ask the child what he or she wants to do. The child should decide. Angela said, "My son would say, 'Ma, take me to Zayre's and buy me something.'" Everyone laughed. I said that there had been a scene in the movie where a mother initially felt uncomfortable with this special time. The son said he wanted to browse through the sports department at the store. They spent an hour looking at sports equipment (not necessarily buying anything). The time they spent together was enjoyable for both of them.

Linda said, "One day I brought my child to the store. I put her on the swing set in the children's department. She had a great time. While she was on the swing, I went to the sewing department and bought some material." I said, "Well, you know, there is a scene in the film where a mother and daughter are at a park. The mother is reading a book while the child is playing on the slide. The narrator says, 'Let's do this scene over.' When the scene is shown again, the mother and child are sliding on the slide together. The narrator says, 'The important thing to remember is that you do things together during this special time. Change your role from parent to that of a close friend.'"

Linda said she didn't remember her mother ever getting on a slide with her; however, she said she got the point. She said, "You don't care if the kid's face is dirty and you're not on their back saying don't do this and don't do that." I said, "You can see how important this special time is especially since most of you, as single parents, are the ones mainly responsible for disciplining your children. It's good for both you and your child to get a break from this role." Cindy said, "Yes, I'm always disciplining the children. Then when they go with their father, they're like angels." At first, she couldn't understand it. Then Kathy, the counselor, said, "Did you ever stop and think that maybe they're afraid he won't come back to see them if they don't act very good?" Cindy said she had never thought of that. She said now she sits her children down and says, "You have to listen to me. I'm your mother. I know what's best for you." These talks are helping her relationship with her children.

I told Cindy that I had read a little about single parenting. One writer had mentioned that sometimes the child will act very good with the parent who is not living in the household in hopes that the parents will get back together. The children think that somehow they can be responsible for the parents getting back together. She said, "You know, one time when Julie was only two, Matt and I happened to be with her one day together. We were walking and she was between Matt and me. We were both holding Julie's hands. Julie started swinging our hands back and forth. Then, she took our hands and brought them together." Cindy said, "I couldn't believe that at that age she knew that things weren't right between us and she wanted us back together."

I said that what Cindy had just mentioned brought us to another major point of the film. The narrator says that children should be encouraged to talk openly about their feelings. Cindy picked up on this point and said she agreed one hundred percent. She said when the children ask her questions she tries her best to answer them. "They ask me if I still love Daddy. I tell them that I do love Daddy, but in a different way. I tell them that it's not good for Daddy and me to live together." She said that her children listen to her. Linda said that she agreed with Cindy. She said that she's trying to explain to her daughter the changes that have taken place since they've come to the house. "My daughter doesn't know where she is or what's going on. She's clinging to me like a leech all of a sudden. I don't understand it." I asked Linda when she came to the house. She said 1 week ago. I said, "When parents split up, oftentimes the child is afraid that the parent the child is living with will also leave. Your daughter may be very afraid that you're going to leave her."

The next major point that the film made is that special time can take away the worries that parent and child have. I said, "I think all of you worry more than the average person because of abusive situations that you've been in. That's why special time is very important for you and your child. You can both put your worries aside." Cindy said, "The other day I took my two daughters to the beach. They were looking at snails, examining them closely." Pam broke in and said, "If that was my son, Jason, he wouldn't have looked at the snails, he would have eaten them." Everyone laughed. Cindy continued, "My daughters didn't fight, they didn't make a lot of noise. It was wonderful." I asked her how she felt. She replied, "I felt very relaxed." Pam jumped in to say, "One of the first days here at the house, I was playing with a couple of the kids. We started wrestling; we were laughing and playing for about an hour. We had so much fun. I felt great for the rest of the day. When I put Jason to bed at night when I'm relaxed, he falls asleep right away. I rock him and he falls asleep. If I'm aggravated or tense, I'll put him to bed and he won't fall asleep. He knows that something is wrong."

Linda said she feels that she is yelling at her child 24 hours a day. "My daughter does things that she never did before we came here." She said the other day her daughter was walking by Pam's son, Jason, and she slapped him on the face. Linda said she felt terrible about this. Pam said, "Don't worry about it. How do you think I feel? My son (who is big for his age) goes around trying to hug everyone. He's so big he knocks the kids over and they begin to cry. I feel the same way you do." I said, "Just the fact that you're expressing how you feel about your children's behavior makes it easier for you to understand one another." The women began to talk about how they discipline their children.

After a few minutes, I said, "Can we come back to Linda for a few minutes? I think she's very concerned about the changes she sees in her child since she came to the house." Linda said, "I wish I knew I was doing the right thing coming here with my daughter. I wish there was some research that said, 'It's better to leave your husband when the child is such and such an age'—then I could feel better. I don't want to be yelling at my child all day long." Vicki said, "But, Linda, every situation is very different from the next. It's not easy to say that for everyone who leaves her husband, the children should be a certain age. It takes time for a child to adjust to a new situation and a new environment." Angela said, "Look, as long as the kids aren't killing each other, I leave them alone. If one kid takes another kid's toy, at first they cry. But two minutes later they're playing with another toy." I was getting ready to ask Linda if she thought she should be home with her husband. But I didn't have to say anything. She said, "Well, I guess my only other choice is to go back home and have my child see my husband beat me up." I said, "Yes, that's right."

I wrapped up the discussion about the film by naming different activities that they might want to consider for special time. Then, I asked them how they thought the discussion went. Everyone thought it was a great discussion. They said they never have an opportunity during the week to get together to talk. At this point, Cindy started to talk about one of the children and the funny things he says and does. We sat and laughed for about 10 minutes. I felt very pleased that everyone seemed so relaxed—much more relaxed than last week. As everyone got up to leave, Cindy said, "This was a good discussion, even though you were only able to get a few words in." Linda said, "Yes, you might not think so, but you're really helping us." I thanked her and said I was glad that I could be of help to them.

The closing comment by Cindy, about the worker only being able to "get a few words in," reflects her sense of the worker's viewing her role as teaching. In many ways, these women used the film as a starting point and took the discussion to their own issues related to their stress and its impact on their children. As the worker felt more comfortable and started to refrain from giving advice, the members took over and the power of mutual aid became apparent.

In the third session, marked by changes in the group composition, the worker still began with an agenda; however, this time, she acknowledged that it was up to the group members to decide what they wished to discuss. The resulting conversation moved the group well into the middle phase.

The worker's fourth session presented a completely new group of six women. This gave the worker an opportunity to start again. The worker's continued growth is evident when we compare this session with the first, held only 3 weeks before.

Session 4

This week's group session included six new women. Because of the new group composition, I told the women some information about myself and then asked them to tell me their names, how many children they have, and how long they've been at the shelter. Then, I stated the purpose of the group session. I said, "This group will give you an opportunity to talk and to listen to one another. This is what's called a mutual-aid group. All of you here are experiencing some difficulty in your lives because of abusive relationships. This is not an easy time for you. In fact, it's a time of crisis. Because you've experienced similar difficulties, this group session will give you a chance to help each other. As you listen to each other, share some of your problems and feelings, I think you'll learn a great deal from each other.

"In order to get the group discussion started, I'd like you to do some problem swapping—share with each other some problems and difficulties you've experienced in your abusive relationships. If you want to, you can share some of the things you'd like to see differently in your lives now. By problem swapping, we'll find out what your major concerns are, and then the discussion can focus on these issues. There's no sense in having a discussion if it's not about issues that you're concerned with." I said, "Who would like to start?" Joyce said, "My problem right now is that I don't have any money, and the last time I tried to apply for welfare, they told me I wasn't eligible." The women talked about this for a few minutes and tried to offer Joyce suggestions about receiving welfare. Next, Linda said that her life was very disorganized. At this point, she doesn't know where she's going.

This example illustrates how the working contract with a group can evolve over time and how the group process can educate a worker to deepen his or her understanding of group dynamics, group skills, and the themes of importance to the clients. Now we turn to the dynamics of recontracting when a worker joins an ongoing group.

Joining an Ongoing Group

As we just saw, when workers start a new group, contracting issues are complex. They grow even more complex when a worker joins an ongoing group that may have been operating for some time without a clear working agreement or with an agreement that has not led to effective mutual aid. In this situation, the new group leader has to deal not only with the members of the group but also with the ongoing leaders, who have an investment in the current status. Students often raise this as a perplexing problem when they report sitting in on group discussions as coleaders and observing clearly the problems associated with poor contracting, coleader conflict over the contract, or simply a lack of understanding of the mutual-aid process. Tension develops as the students learn about alternative models and helpful examples while feeling that, as "mere students," they cannot or should not intervene and effect change. In a situation such as the one in the following example, their stress increases when the team leader is also of another discipline—in this case, a psychologist—which introduces issues of status and power.

This example simply represents a special case of the general problem in which the service offered in the setting does not meet the needs of the clients. As such, the definition of the social work function presented in this book—mediating the individual-social engagement—places this problem on the student's agenda for **systems work:** the set of activities in which social workers attempt to influence the systems and systems people important to their clients. Systems work was introduced in Parts II and III. It was discussed again in the chapter on group formation, where we saw how important it was to include all staff in establishing a new group. The issue will be addressed in detail in Part V of this book.

In the example that follows, two students attempted to be involved in the group formation process, with little success. Staff in the setting—a psychiatric hospital—had developed ideas about the limitations of the patient population. Under continued pressure by the students, a group was started, but its purpose and structure reflected the culture of the system. Although this is not an example of joining a group in progress, the principles are close enough for our purposes in this section. The record of service describes the effort over time as one of the social work students analyzes her own early efforts to influence her colleagues and develops interesting strategies for change that minimize defensive and territorial responses.

RECORD OF SERVICE

Client Description and Time Frame

This is an open-ended, support and stabilization group for chronic mentally ill patients on an inpatient unit of a large psychiatric hospital. The age range of the members is 33 to 64 years. The group is predominantly male (currently eight males, three females), all white, with various ethnicities. The period of time covered in the record is from January 18 to April 26.

Description of the Problem

The major problem this group faced from the beginning was a lack of agreement on the group's purpose, goals, and structure by the treatment team putting the group together. This resulted from uncertainty and disagreement as to what would be the most appropriate group format on the part of some members of the treatment team. The problem was reflective of and exacerbated by a hospital culture that was very hierarchical and did not easily tolerate discussion or disagreement among team members of various professions. Also, since specific alternative recommendations for group purpose, structure, and so on were coming from social work students, I believe the resistance to change was also a function of the challenge to the team culture. We were making our own recommendations, rather than just following the team leader's guidance. This restrictive hierarchical culture is an issue that is faced by both clients and staff in this setting, so resolution of the problem at the group level meant confronting the culture on the treatment team level as well.

How the Problem Came to the Attention of the Worker(s)

This problem was noticeable in my first semester at the placement, when development of a group kept being delayed—sometimes because there was "no one available" to co-lead the group, sometimes because we "just didn't get to that item" on the agenda of our weekly team meetings, and sometimes for no stated reason at all. Another student and I were both trying to begin groups, and it became increasingly clear that there was a resistance to beginning this process that was not being admitted or dealt with. In addition, once the groups did get a start date, there was continued reluctance to plan for them, to discuss what type of groups they would be, to discuss group composition, or to engage other staff from the dorm in the process of setting them up. The psychologist, Dr. Brown, expressed frequent concerns about our trying to do too much, or not being realistic in our expectations for the group, and cautioned frequently that "people with schizophrenia are different and the books don't tell you all of it."

Summary of the Work

I attempted to get clarification on the proposed purpose whenever a new group was recommended. Throughout the first semester, whenever possibilities for groups were mentioned, I expressed enthusiasm for getting started and asked about purpose, structure, and composition. It often seemed that a major purpose for the development of many group ideas was the fact that another student and I both needed to have a group experience at our placement, and our supervisor was trying to ensure that this happened. Specific concerns about group purpose and structure, therefore, often seemed to be secondary in our conversations to the possibility of getting a group at all. For example:

> SUPERVISOR: We may have a group for you. I was talking with Edward (the team leader, Dr. Brown) about a family group that you and Evelyn (a social worker on the team) could run.
> WORKER: Great! What kind of family group would it be?
> SUPERVISOR: Well, we're not too sure about the specifics yet, but it would be to help people deal with their families. Maybe we'd have a little party and have them serve refreshments to their families at the end.
> WORKER: So, would it be family members and patients?
> SUPERVISOR: Well, it's hard to get families in. It might just be for the patients to talk about problems with the families. But we don't know if it's going to happen yet. We have to check Evelyn's schedule to see if she'll be available to do it with you.

As noted above, purpose and structure were my concern, but my supervisor's interest was more in just getting a group started, and my questions about purpose and structure seemed to feel like pressure to her, or perhaps just irrelevant to the major concern, which was getting a group.

Once the group was decided on, I repeatedly brought up issues of group purpose and structure in group supervision meetings and in meetings with my coleader, initially just by asking for clarification, but later also by making recommendations. I asked about purpose and structure when the group was first decided on, and was told not to worry about it, that we'd be lucky just to get the members to stay in the room. I was also told that my coleader (the team leader) would be there and I should just follow his lead. When I pressed further for information, my supervisor tried to make it irrelevant:

> WORKER: Well, I can do that (follow his lead), but I think it's important to know what we're trying to accomplish so I can be more effective in helping to guide the group.
> SUPERVISOR: You probably won't get much of a chance anyway, in the beginning. They (the group members) are going to look to Dr. Brown mostly in the beginning.

When I continued to press at another time for group purpose, just before we were to begin our first group, Dr. Brown finally asked what I would suggest:

> WORKER: Well, we could say something like, "This is a place where people can learn how to support each other and how to get along better."
> DR. BROWN: Hmm. I think that might be too frightening for them to hear. Schizo-phrenics have a hard time with relating to others, and they may just get

scared if we try to tell them they have to talk to each other. I don't think we really need to tell them anything. We can just make it very general.

WORKER: Like what?

DR. BROWN: Well, we could say there's just so much to talk about and we don't get enough chance to talk that much, so this is a chance for us to be with them.

I did as he recommended at that point but continued to bring up the topic in future group supervision meetings.

By this point in the process the student was expressing, in class, increased feelings of frustration and anger. She decided to use this record of service to focus on her work with the system, recognizing that influencing her coleaders' and supervisors' perceptions about the group would require at least as much thought and skill as her work in the group did. This represented an important shift in her thinking from complaining about the existence of the problem to recognizing her functional responsibility to try to influence the system. At first, she still had difficulty tuning in to the concerns and feelings of her coleaders. The important change in her work, however, was her focus on taking some responsibility for her part in the interaction, which she can control.

I did eventually get some general answers about my coleader's (and by extension the hospital's) purpose, but I failed to tune in adequately to the team leader's place in the agency and its implications for what he could feel free to do. In the example above, Dr. Brown gave evidence of an important concern: the psychological feelings of safety of the clients. In the following excerpt, Dr. Brown notes other concerns:

DR. BROWN: I think you'll find that they don't react the way you're expecting them to. If we push them too far, I'm not sure what they'll do.

WORKER: Right. I wouldn't want to push them too far. But I think they may be able to handle some attention on relationships, and then we can see what happens and back off if someone is getting too upset.

By trying to convince him to do it my way, I failed to really give attention to his concerns or to explore what he thought might happen so that we might come up with some way to avoid it that really worked and that felt right to both of us. Since I wasn't really respecting his concern or trusting that it was a valid one, I was dismissing its importance and missing an opportunity to really tune in, to reach for the negatives, and to show empathy for the needs of the organization as well as of the clients. If I had this part to do over again, I would have asked for more information about his concerns, acknowledged them, and then tried to work with him to solve the anticipated problems. In fact, I did get to do it over again in a later session and did better at tuning in at that time:

WORKER: I thought it was great how they were able to challenge each other and really interact with each other.

DR. BROWN: Yeah, but I was concerned. Fred seemed to be getting upset at what was going on.

WORKER: Does he have any history of having problems when he gets anxious like that?

DR. BROWN: Yeah, actually he was at XXX (a forensic psychiatric unit) a number of years ago for attacking somebody with a knife.

WORKER: Well, no wonder you're so concerned! I didn't know about that.

DR. BROWN: Yeah, it was a few years ago, but you never know with some of these people.

Worker: We have never really talked about what we would do if someone became violent in the group. I've had some training in nonviolent self-defense, but what is the procedure on this unit?

We were then able to talk about procedures and about other concerns about what could happen in the group. Again, I think I could have paid a little more attention to Dr. Brown's concerns by asking, "Do you think something like that might happen during group?" rather than by talking about procedures right away, but it did seem at least to acknowledge the importance of his concerns in a way I hadn't done before.

The tuning-in and empathic responses to colleagues must be genuine. Perhaps because of training that has often led professionals to respond with a pseudoempathy (speaking the words without feeling the feelings), an acute sensitivity to being "social worked," in the worst sense of the term, will result in a negative response. In this example, as the student examined and managed her own feelings better, her capacity for genuine empathy increased. In the next excerpts, the student describes a strategy she has developed for influencing the team leader. Instead of confronting him with his "deficiencies," she invites him to join her in her own analysis of her work. She does this through the sharing of her process recordings, which include her written self-analysis of her practice.

After the first session, I began to share my thoughts on what I would like to be doing in the group with my coleader via process recordings. I began writing weekly a description of what happened in group, the main themes I saw, my overall impression, and my plans for follow-up, and I gave a copy of this to my coleader each week. I hoped that if I shared my thoughts with him in a written format, he might be better able to take in my ideas without having to respond to them right away. I also felt that I could show in more depth in these recordings the scope of what I envisioned for the group, and that by giving me a chance to show him the things I would have liked to say, even when I wasn't yet able to say them, he might come to trust my judgment more. An example of what I shared with him follows, from the ninth group session:

Description: Helen started talking about her family and how her children and grandchildren kept her young. She also spoke about her job at the library and specific things she did there. I said it sounded like she really loved her job, and she agreed. She spoke more about this, addressing most of this to me, and I felt uncomfortable that the rest of the group was not being included, so I responded to her several times but then didn't pursue it further, hoping that others would be able to jump in then.

Reaction/Analysis: Not a great strategy, I see now! Perhaps I could have said how I felt and brought it to the group more, or said I thought it was interesting what Helen was talking about and wondered how other members were feeling as they heard Helen talk about her job, or asked her if she wanted anything from the group.

The second example, which is from an earlier session, shows my thoughts about my working relationship with my coleader, as well as some ideas on group structure. I hoped that by sharing some of my own transference issues with him, I might reduce any threat he might be feeling from me and engage him more easily in working through our differences to work together more effectively.

Description: Dr. Brown described why Fred was not on the unit today. There was no response to this, so I went on, saying, "We went over some ground rules last week, and I'd like to just review them quickly again today. The first is no smoking, which has already been mentioned. The second is that it's OK to leave if you have to go to the bathroom, but then we expect you to come back. Um, what else? Oh yes, we talked about confidentiality, that what we talk about here stays here, and that we won't talk about people who aren't here."

Reaction/Analysis: We had agreed to review the rules at the beginning of each of the first few group sessions at least, but we hadn't decided who would do which of these tasks. I felt Dr. Brown was giving me some space, so I went ahead and started. I noticed part way through that I wanted to share the task with my coleader, but we hadn't discussed it, so I wasn't sure if he'd jump in or not. I was glad when he did. I was also concerned about the confidentiality rule because, although we had discussed it in supervision group last week, I hadn't discussed it specifically with Dr. Brown. I guess the question arises as to whether or not I believe he can take care of himself in a situation like that. Clearly there's some transference here of me seeing him as a dad who would quietly disapprove but never talk about it directly. I guess we should talk about whether we can feel free to disagree or at least clarify things in front of the group (I hope so), and I need to trust Dr. Brown to discuss any differences that may come up openly with me, whether in group or later, and I need to trust myself that I can stand it if he disagrees with me sometimes.

This strategy seemed to work well. When I saw Dr. Brown after he had read my notes on the session, he said he had enjoyed reading it and looked forward to getting more. We then spoke more about the group and our plans for the next session. Although we rarely talked about the specific content of the process recordings, it seemed that giving Dr. Brown the recordings did help him get to know me better and trust me more, and gradually we did come to work together much better. I believe these recordings had a major impact on our relationship developing as well as it did.

I pointed out evidence of successful client interaction whenever I could to my coleader to support the notion of mutual aid. After one session in which a lot of participation happened, I mentioned in the "overall impression" section of my weekly recording my positive views of the ability the group shows to do mutual aid:

"This was a very exciting session! Lots of participation, including real, relevant concerns about what the group will be like. There was also a lot of evidence of people supporting each other (Ben trying to support Martha, Robert supporting Gene), and willingness of members to discuss and challenge (Ben, Martha, Jack, and Hilary on poverty; Martha and Jack on why people don't come; Robert on difficulty following conversation). Overall, it's much more participatory and interactive than I had imagined it would be. I see a lot of potential for this group!"

In our meetings as well, I consistently pointed out the positive evidence I saw of the effectiveness of the group, and Dr. Brown would usually acknowledge the evidence and acknowledge that he hadn't paid so much attention to that. I started to listen better to my coleader and became better able to hear his concerns and really take them in. We then became better able to work together to come up with strategies for working in group that achieved both our goals.

I continued to press for a more mutual-aid focus and more empowerment of group members to help each other and take control of the group. As my coleader and I continued to talk about purpose and structure, he gradually became more willing for me to try to promote interaction and a mutual-aid focus, and often agreed to suggestions

I made for ways to let group members decide how to run the group (regarding how to handle members who leave, for example). In fact, in the 10th session, Dr. Brown joined me in helping people talk to each other and in beginning to encourage members to take some control over their group (This time, when a new member showed up at group, instead of Dr. Brown telling the group he could stay, as he had done in previous sessions, he asked the group if it was OK if the visiting patient stayed!).

As my coleader and I started to agree more on the goals, purpose, and structure of the group, I brought up to the group the changes in how we were using the group, often using the introduction of new members as an opportunity to restate, review, and clarify any changes in those aspects of the group. For example, in session 14, after asking a new member to introduce himself, and having others introduce themselves to him, I continued as follows:

> WORKER: Michael, I know you've been to the Tuesday community meeting. I'd like to tell you a little about this group because it's different from the Tuesday meeting. In this group, we talk about all different kinds of things, but it's a smaller group, and people talk to each other more and try to help each other here. Sometimes someone will talk about a problem and others will try to help them figure out how they can make things better, or sometimes people will just talk about how they feel about something and they might find out that other people feel the same way.
>
> MICHAEL: Oh, like a support group?
>
> WORKER: Yes, have you been in groups like this before?

Finally, when problems came up for individuals in the group, I encouraged a mutual-aid focus. A pivotal session was one in which Gene, a patient whom I see individually, stated that he was going to leave the hospital in 3 days to get his own room. Although I was concerned about the inadvisability of this move, my coleader and I focused on the meaning to the group.

> WORKER: That's an important thing to be announcing here. I wonder how other people feel about your leaving.
>
> GENE: Well, I just wanted to tell you and Dr. Brown.
>
> WORKER: Well, we can talk more about it later. But, since you're here now, I wonder if you wanted to say good-bye to people in this group.

Other members then began to give Gene feedback, some supporting his move and initiative, some expressing concerns for him. And, instead of his being isolated by making this dramatic statement, as he had been in the past for similar statements, the group members were able to engage with him this time and help him think about his decision in a more realistic and fuller way.

Current Status of the Problem

Where It Stands Now

Tremendous progress has been made in getting the team leader to accept some different possibilities for goals and formats for use with these patients. Through much discussion, he has been able to accept the possibility of their interacting with each other in a safe and empowering way and, even more significantly, has begun to look at the system practices that work against the patients' being able to function independently in any areas. He has begun seeing possibilities that he didn't see before for them to have more independence in the group, and he is showing interest in continuing to encourage that kind of independence. The structure of the group has been pretty well set by now, although the goals and purpose still need to be more clearly stated to group members and to the entire treatment team. There is a lot of work yet to be done, but a lot has been accomplished toward creating more empowering and effective goals and structure.

Strategies for Intervention

- Use the remaining group supervision sessions to review with all involved group staff (myself, my coleader, the two coleaders of the other similar group on the ward, and my supervisor, who will be replacing me as coleader of this group) the progress of the group to date—what worked, what didn't, and so on—and discuss ideas for any changes that are needed now or in developing future groups.
- Write up a summary report of my impressions and analysis of the group to date, along with the recommendations below and any identified at the meeting above. Present this to my coleader and my supervisor.
- Continue to point out positive results of the mutual-aid focus in group supervision meetings, team meetings, and planning sessions with my coleader.
- Help group members use mutual aid to deal with my termination (and ask my coleader to do this as well).
- As I sum up my work with the group, point out how group members have been able to use mutual aid to help each other, and express hope that they will continue to do so.

This example has not only illustrated a recontracting process over time, it has demonstrated the importance of the two-client idea, with the agency or setting as the second client. The attitude toward group work practice in the setting reflected the general attitude toward work with psychiatric patients. The student social worker helped individual members of the group; however, her most important social work impact was on the system. Rather than just remaining distressed and angry about the deficiencies of the system, she began to see addressing these problems as central to her role as a social worker. The effects of her impact on the system would be felt long after she had left her placement. She had also learned that in order to empower clients, social workers (and other staff) must first deal with their own disempowerment.

Coleadership in Groups

The previous example brings us to the question of coleadership. Whenever the general subject of coleaders is raised by workers, I inquire if they have had experience working with another staff member in a group. Almost invariably they have, and the experience was usually a bad one. The list of problems includes disagreement on the basic approach to the group, subtle battles over control of group sessions, and disagreement during the group session over specific interventions— particularly those introduced by a coworker that seem to cut off a line of work one feels is productive. Underlying all of these problems is a lack of honest communication between coworkers both within and outside the group sessions. Workers often feel embarrassed to confront their coworkers outside the session and believe it would be unprofessional to disagree during the session. This stance is similar to the parental syndrome of "not arguing in front of the children." Coworkers usually face an unreasonable expectation that they must appear to agree at all times. This lack of honesty usually reflects the insecurity of both workers and often leads to defensiveness and the illusion of cooperative work.

Coleadership can be helpful in a group. Because a group is complex, assistance by another worker in implementing the helping function can be a welcome aid. In my couples' group, one coworker was female and brought perspectives to the work that were strikingly different from mine. For example, she reacted with a different mind-set to issues raised in the group related to women.

Several factors enabled us to work well together. First, we shared a similar approach to the helping process. While our theoretical frameworks differed and we used different conceptual models for understanding client behavior and dynamics, we shared similar attitudes toward clients and a commitment to mutual aid and the importance of reaching for client strength. Within this common framework, our different conceptual models served to enrich our work with the group.

Second, we set aside time to discuss the group. We met before the start of the first group session to strategize and also met before the start of each session to tune in, using the previous session as well as any additional knowledge gained from individual contacts with couples. We also set aside time after each session to discuss the group. In this case, the discussions took place with a group of students training at the school of social work who had viewed the group sessions on a video monitor. We made every effort to encourage honest communication about the sessions and our reactions to each other's input. This was not simple; because I was the senior group worker, coworkers found it difficult to challenge me. As our relationship grew and trust developed, direct communication increased. Finally, we agreed that we could disagree in the group. In many ways, the coworker and I would be a model of a male-female relationship in action. Supporting honesty and willingness to confront while maintaining professional "courtesy" toward each other in the group would make a mockery of our effort. Observing that coleaders could disagree, even argue, and still respect and care for each other can be a powerful object lesson for group members.

Group members can pick up subtle cues of tension between leaders, no matter how hard workers try to hide them. This came to light in the midyear evaluation of this couples' group. A third coworker in this group was a former student of mine, and although he had participated in the sessions up until that point, the presence of the other coworker and his feelings about working with a former teacher had inhibited him. We had discussed this in the sessions with the student observers, who had been quick to pick up his hesitancy. In the midyear evaluation session of the couples' group, I inquired how the group members felt we could improve our work during the second half of the year. Rose turned to my coworker and said, "I hope you don't take what I'm going to say personally. I think you have a lot to give to this group, and I would like to hear more from you. I don't think you should let Larry (the senior worker) frighten you just because he is more experienced." He responded, "You know, Rose, I've been worried about my participation, too. It is hard for me to get in as often as I want to, and I'm going to work on it."

As a final comment on coleadership, I would say that two beginning group leaders would find working together difficult, if not impossible. Their own anxieties are so great that they often become more of a problem for each other than a help. Working with a more experienced worker provides learners with an opportunity to test their wings without taking full responsibility for the outcome. When mutual trust and sharing develop between coworkers, the workers can be an important source of support for each other. The feelings of warmth and caring that develop among members and between the group worker and members must also exist between the coleaders as they tackle the complex task of working with groups. Of course, they need to keep the problems of coleadership, only partially elaborated in this brief discussion, in mind.

Now that we have explored the beginnings of group work, the following chapters will attempt to answer the question of what to do after the first session. They also examine the core dynamics of groups at work and explore the specific functions and skills of the group worker.

Chapter Summary

The core skills of contracting in first sessions, introduced in Parts II and III, apply to the group work context. These skills include clarifying purpose, clarifying the group leader's role, reaching for client feedback, and dealing with the authority theme.

The age and relative articulateness of the members, the authority of the worker, the specific concerns of the clients, and the impact of the setting and time each affect first sessions and in part determine the way workers handle contracting. Each worker brings a unique personal style to the beginning as well.

Recognition that contracting does not always go well the first time, or that it may take several sessions for the group to deal with all the issues, is central to the idea of recontracting—the process in which the worker raises contracting issues with an ongoing group. The worker must employ strategies and skills for working with coleaders and the system, regarding the system as the second client.

Related Online Content and Activities

Visit *The Skills of Helping* Book Companion Website at www.socialwork.wadsworth .com/Shulman06/ for learning tools such as glossary terms, InfoTrac College Edition keywords, links to related websites, and chapter practice quizzes.

The website for this chapter also features additional notes from the author and additional process recordings:

- Acting-Out Adolescents in a Training Workshop: Recontracting and Clarifying Group Purpose
- Foster Parents: The Late-Arriving Members
- Older Foster Teens Transitioning to Independence: The Impact of Lack of Contracting
- Outpatient Psychiatric Group: Initial Resistance
- Parenting Group for Mandated Members Who Have Abused or Are at Risk for Abuse
- Pregnant Teens in a Shelter: The Power of Clear Contracting
- Teen Boys in a Residential Setting: Empowerment for Change
- Ten-Year-Old Girls in a School Setting
- Twelve-Year-Old Boys in Trouble in a School Setting: The Impact of Clear Contracting

CHAPTER ELEVEN

The Work Phase in the Group

CHAPTER OUTLINE

Sessional Contracting
    in the Group

The Work Phase in a Group
    Session

Sessional Endings
    and Transitions

In this chapter, we focus on the interaction between the individual and the group and on the way in which the group worker assists this interaction during the work phase. Using time as an organizing principle, we first examine the contracting phase of group sessions, emphasizing how the worker at the beginning helps individuals present their concerns to the group and simultaneously helps the group members respond. Next, we look at the middle phase of a session, illustrating the dynamics of mutual aid and the way in which group members can help each other and themselves at the same time. Finally, our discussion of the sessional ending/transition phase stresses the importance of resolution and transition to next steps or next meetings.

Recorded material from a range of settings will illustrate each of these phases and the requisite skills. Although this chapter focuses on the individual-group interaction, note that both clients—the individual and the group—require further examination. In the next chapter, we analyze the individual's role in a group and also concentrate on the group-as-a-whole.

Beginning group workers, particularly those who have worked with individuals, often raise the following problem: In an attempt to deal with an individual's concern, they find themselves doing **casework in the group.** This is a common pattern in which the group leader provides individual counseling to a client within a group setting. This contrasts with an effort to mobilize mutual aid for the client by involving the other members. Suppose, for example, a member raises an issue at the start of a session and the worker responds with appropriate elaborative and empathic skills. The group member expands the concern, and the worker tries to help deal with the problem while the other group members listen. When this problem has been explored, the worker then begins with another client as the others patiently await their turn.

After the meeting, the worker worries about having done casework in front of an audience. In reaction to this feeling of uneasiness, the worker decides not to be trapped this way during the next session, but then makes a different kind of mistake. In an attempt to focus on only the "group" aspect of the work, the worker refuses to respond with elaborating skills when an individual opens the session with a direct or indirect offering of a concern. For example, one member of a parent group might say, "It's really hard to raise teenagers these days, what with all the changing values." The worker quickly responds by inquiring if other members of the group find this to be true. One by one they comment on the general difficulty of raising teenagers. The discussion soon becomes overly general and superficial, and meanwhile the first group member is anxiously waiting to air a specific concern about a fight with her daughter the evening before.

When trying to deal with individual concerns, workers may find themselves doing casework in the group, and when trying to pay attention to the group, workers may find themselves leading an overly generalized discussion. Both maladaptive patterns reflect the worker's difficulty in conceptualizing the group as a system for mutual aid and in understanding the often subtle connections between individual concerns and the general work of the group. Schwartz's notion of the two clients, discussed earlier, can help to resolve the apparent dilemma. He suggests that the worker simultaneously must pay attention to two clients, the individual and the group, and that the field of action is the interaction between the two. Thus, instead of choosing between the "one" or the "many," the worker's function involves mediating the engagement between these two clients. This is a special case of the general helping function for social work.

The worker's tasks in addressing these two clients are examined in this chapter against the backdrop of time—the contracting (beginning), work (middle), and ending/transition phases that characterize each group session.

Sessional Contracting in the Group

In Chapter 2 we examined some of the barriers to open communication in the helping situation. These included ambivalence toward taking help, because of the resultant feelings of dependency; societal taboos against discussion of certain topics, such as sex; the client's painful feelings associated with particular issues; and the context of the helping setting, such as the impact of the helping person's authority. These blocks often cause a client to use an indirect form of communication when sharing a problem or concern. For example, clients might hint at a concern (state a specific problem in a very general way), act it out (begin a session by being angry at the worker or other group members, using the anger to cover up the pain), employ metaphor or allegory as a means of presenting an issue (by telling a seemingly unrelated story, for instance), use art or other mediums (a child might draw a picture of an abusive parent), or send the message nonverbally (by perhaps sitting quietly with a pained expression or sitting apart from the group with an angry expression). The indirectness of these communications may cause the group members and the worker to miss important cues in the early part of the session. Alternatively, a member might raise a concern but hide the depth of feeling associated with it, thereby turning off the other group members. The worker's function is to assist the group in interpreting individual members' indirect communications.

Reaching for Individual Communication in the Group

Because of the problems involved in individual-group communication, the worker should in the early stages of each meeting concentrate on helping individual members present their concerns to the group. The beginning of each group session should be seen as a tentative, slow process of feeling out the group, endeavoring to determine which member or members are attempting to capture the group's attention for their own issues, and exploring how these issues may represent a theme of concern for the group. In a like manner, the group itself may be approaching a major theme of concern for that week, and the individual offerings may thus present specific examples of the central concern of the group.

Whether the concern originates with the member or expresses the feelings of many, the worker should focus on answering the question, "What are they (the group members) working on in this session?" For workers to rush in with their own agenda simply because the first productions of the group members are unclear would be a mistake. Likewise, workers should not believe that simply because the group had agreed to deal with a specific issue or an individual's concern at the end of the previous meeting, it will be the issue for the current session. Even if the discussion picks up exactly where the members had agreed it would, the worker should monitor the conversation in the early part of the session with an ear either for confirmation of the theme or hints that members are just going through the motions. In structured groups where an agenda for each session may be preplanned and a topic assigned for discussion, the group leader must still remain alert to the possibility that another or a related issue is emerging and must at least be recognized.

Two skills serve workers in this regard. **Monitoring the individual** involves observing individual group members, remaining alert to verbal and nonverbal clues signaled by each individual. This is an acquired skill and therefore requires practice. When this skill is integrated, a group leader can simultaneously monitor the group and each individual. **Monitoring the group** involves observing the second client—the group members—by watching for verbal and nonverbal clues as to their reactions while a member is speaking.

As they are monitoring the individual and the group, workers should remain aware that even though the conversation may not seem directed toward the group's purpose, it is always purposeful. For clarity of exposition, I shall focus here on examples in which the worker directs the early discussion toward a specific theme of concern. In a later chapter we shall explore examples where the purpose of the early conversation is to raise an issue concerning the working of the group or the leader. In both cases, workers should ask themselves early on, "How does this conversation connect to our work?" or "What is troubling this particular member?" By doing so, they stand a better chance of helping the individual relate a concern to the group.

An illustration from the couples' group described in Chapter 10 can demonstrate this process as well as the importance of sessional tuning in. The session was the 18th. At the previous one, Louise, who was then present without her husband, John, had revealed that he had a drinking problem. There was general agreement to pursue this concern with John present the next week. In my tuning-in session with coleaders prior to the start of the 18th session, I had learned that Fran and Rick had had a particularly difficult week and had threatened separation during their individual counseling session. Rick had questioned returning to the group. This couple previously had made substantial progress in the group and in a related sexual therapy group program. However, they had hit a critical point and were regressing. Over the course of the sessions, I had observed that Fran tended to express her own concerns and fears indirectly as she responded to other couples in the group, and Rick tended to physically retreat.

Having accomplished the preparatory work, the coleaders and I strategized to reach for Fran's indirect cues if they were evident, and we prepared to help the group discuss priorities for this session. The session began with some hints from the group about the ending process, a topic to which I had planned to respond directly. After I acknowledged the group's sadness, as well as my own, about ending, and the members briefly discussed their feelings, there was a silence that was broken by John:

JOHN: I know about your discussion about my drinking last week, since I met with Larry (the worker) and he filled me in. If you have any questions, let me have them.

At this point there was some relaxation of tension, and group members offered supportive comments for John for having raised this difficult concern. I noticed that Fran and Rick had turned their chairs so that they faced apart from each other. Rick was staring into space with a bland expression. Fran turned to face John.

FRAN: I want you to know, John, that I think it's great that you have come here prepared to talk about this problem. It takes a lot of courage on your part. It would have been a lot easier if you simply stayed away or refused to discuss it. That would have been the coward's way out.

WORKER: Fran, I wonder if that's what you think Rick is doing right now in relation to you. His chair is turned away from you and you seem to be upset with each other.

FRAN: (After a period of silence) I don't understand how you do this, how you read my mind this way. It must be a form of magic. (Pause) But you're right, we had a really bad fight this week, and we're not over it. Rick didn't want to come this week, and he won't talk to me about it. (Fran shows signs of becoming upset emotionally.)

WORKER: How do you see it, Rick?

After Rick's confirmation of the seriousness of the situation, both he and Fran stated that they were concerned because this was supposed to be the week for John and Louise. I raised the issue with the whole group and they decided to stay with Rick and Fran because of the degree of urgency in their situation. John and Louise felt they could wait another week. The session turned out to be an important turning point for Rick and Fran, as well as one that yielded important insights for the other couples into their own relationships.

There was no magic in picking up Fran's cues; tuning in and the identification of a pattern over time had helped, as had recognizing the often indirect nature of members' initial efforts to raise themes of concern. In another example from the same group, the problem of identifying the issue was compounded because the member, Lou, did not clearly understand the nature of the concern and presented it indirectly as a part of an angry attack on the group leaders. In the previous session, the group had viewed a videotaped segment of a meeting when one of the couples had blown up at each other. Although the couple had given their consent, Lou was upset that this painful exchange had been replayed in the group. He began with an angry attack on helping professionals, denouncing "the way they played games with people's lives." He was extremely upset at the way workers encouraged the expression of bitter feelings between couples, feeling that this tore them apart emotionally. He argued that this was not necessary. I reached for the specific meaning of his opening comments.

WORKER: Lou, I think you're talking about us and last week's session—when we watched the tape. (I had missed this session because of an accident but had reviewed the videotape. The session had been led by my coleaders.)

LOU: Of course I am! I've never been more upset. I tore my guts watching what you people put them through.

Lou went on to attack the helping professions in general as well as us in particular. The coleaders responded by attempting to explain what they had done. We were generally made to feel defensive and incompetent. Group members will often make the workers feel exactly the way the members themselves feel. When they are unaware of or unable to express their own pain and the hurt under their anger, they sometimes project it onto the leaders or other members. Bion (1961) describes this process as "projective identification," in which the client communicates his feelings by stimulating the same feelings in the worker. The difficulty for the worker is that there is always some element of truth in the attack, which is usually aimed at an area in which the worker feels less than confident. In this situation we stayed with the issue raised by Lou.

WORKER: Lou, you're angry with us and also feeling that we really hurt Len and Sally last week. Obviously we missed how hard it hit you to see their pain. Why don't you ask them how they felt?

LOU: Well, am I right? Wasn't that terrible for you to go through?

LEN: It wasn't easy, and it hurt, but I think it helped to get it out in the open. It also helped to have all of you care about us and feel the pain with us.

LOU: But there must be some way to do this without having to tear your guts out. (Lou seemed a bit taken aback by Len's comments, which were echoed by his wife.)

WORKER: When you attacked us, Lou, I have to admit it hit me hard. A part of me doesn't want to get at the anger and pain that you all feel, and yet anther part of me feels it's the way back to a stronger relationship. I have to admit you shook me.

ROSE: (Lou's wife) I think you have to understand this has been a hard week for us.

WORKER: How come?

ROSE: We just got word that Lesley, our granddaughter who lives in London, is splitting up with her husband.

Lou and Rose have spoken before in the group about their children and the pain it has caused them to see each of them experience difficulties in their own marriages.

Lou has been particularly angry with helping professionals who have helped neither him nor his family members. This was the first grandchild to experience marital problems, and it signified to Lou and Rose the continuation of the family's instability into another generation. Under much of the anger lay their pain as well as their defensiveness and doubt, to which Rose responded by clarifying Lou's signal.

WORKER: It must have hit you very hard, Lou, having the first grandchild experience marital problems.

LOU: (Seemingly deflated, the anger gone, slumped in his chair, speaking with a tone of resignation and bitterness) After 45 years, you learn you have to live with these things. It's just another notch that you have to add to all to the other hurts.

The discussion continued with Lou and Rose describing their feelings of helplessness as they watched their family disintegrating, as well as their desire to show the children that it did not have to be that way. The group members commiserated as they described how they also felt impotent in affecting the lives of their children and their grandchildren.

In the first illustration with Fran and in the second with Lou, the individual was reaching out to the group indirectly through her or his opening comments. With Fran the concern was presented in the guise of a response to a group member, while with Lou it appeared as an attack on the leaders. In both cases, the communication had two meanings. The first was the actual statement of fact, while the second was a disguised call for help. Unless workers are tuned in, are listening hard for potential offerings from group members, and are clear about their own function in the group, they can easily miss the early, indirect productions of group members. Of course, the member will often present a concern more directly, thus making it easier for the group to hear. And sometimes an issue may emerge at a later point in the meeting.

The following example involves a group for 10- and 11-year-old children who had lost a close family member. They were referred to the group because of behavior problems in school and elsewhere that signaled their inability to cope with death. The group members called themselves the "Lost and Found Group," because they had lost someone close but had found each other (Vastola, Nierenberg, & Graham, 1994). The authors describe how Mark, at the start of a group session following one in which members had begun to open up and discuss their losses, sends a mixed message using paper and pen. He repeatedly writes "Bob," the name of his grandfather who had recently died.

CARL: Mark, your grandfather died?

MARK: I don't want any damn body talking about my grandfather or I'll kick their butt.

LEADER: You sound pretty angry.

MARK: I'm not angry. I just don't want anybody talking about my grandfather.

LEADER: It's very difficult.

MARK: It's not difficult. I just don't want anybody saying that he died. (His anger is escalating.)

GLORIA: Nobody wants to talk about nobody dying.

DICK: Yes, we don't want to talk about that.

LEADER: How come?

GLORIA: That's why he (Mark) is running around. You can't force him if he doesn't want to.

LEADER: Are you saying that perhaps that's what makes you run around—so you won't have to talk about something upsetting?

MARK: Nope.

LEADER: Maybe you feel it's too hard to talk about.

MARK: No, it's not hard for me to talk about anything . . . but that reminds you, and you could be dreaming.

CARL: Yup, you dream for about a week when you talk about your mother, then it takes about five days to try to get over it, but it comes back again and it stops and it comes back again. . . . Nightmares, I hate. I hate talking about my mother. (p. 87)

Through his behavior, Mark demonstrated his difficulty in dealing with the loss. The group members moved to his defense, because this was their problem as well. The group leader's persistence sent a message to Mark (and the group) that she would not back off from this difficult issue. As she explored Mark's resistance by acknowledging the difficulty and asking what made it hard to talk about his loss, the members began to open up.

This worker was prepared to deal with the taboo subject of death and grieving—a very painful topic when children are involved. By responding to the behavior only and attempting to set limits and stop Mark from running around the room, the worker would actually have been signaling her own resistance to the discussion. The fight over the behavior would have allowed both Mark and the worker to avoid the pain. This is why social workers need to have access to support for themselves as they attempt to deal with these powerful issues (Shulman, 1991).

The final example of behavior as communication comes from the beginning of a session of an ongoing, open-ended group for friends, lovers, and relatives who were grieving the loss of someone from AIDS. A woman who had just lost her son was attending her first meeting. The meeting started with **check-in**, in which each member briefly shared what had happened to him or her during the preceding week. The new member began with an extremely rapid nonstop monologue about how busy she had been keeping herself since her son died. She described a daily, hectic round of activity, showing little emotion other than the hint of an underlying anxiety. She had clearly been in flight from her loss during the week and was indirectly communicating this flight by her opening conversation. It was as if she were saying, "Do you want to see how I am coping? Watch me!" The leader responded by cutting her off, after a while, pointing out that they needed to hear from all of the members as a part of the check-in. Later analysis by the leader revealed that he had sensed her anxiety and simply had not been able to deal with it. Had he been able to be honest about his feelings at the moment, he would have shared how he experienced her presentation— being uncertain about how to help, feeling her sense of overwhelming loss, and wondering about proceeding with the check-in. Any or all of these comments might have opened the door for further discussion and expression of emotion.

The group members joined in the collusion, in a flight process of their own. They were at a different stage in their grieving, and this new member's behavior may have reawakened feelings they would have preferred to have left behind. This example also reveals some of the problems associated with rituals such as check-in, which can take on a life of their own when adhered to dogmatically. Instead of providing an opportunity to deal with individual members' concerns, they can become a way to avoid deepening the work. In retrospect, the leader could have acknowledged the indirect communications of the member and raised, with the group, whether they wanted to respond right away or continue check-in. Either way, acknowledging the feelings underlying the individual's acting out of her pain would have laid the groundwork for dealing with her loss and the feelings evoked in the second client, the group.

This first section has focused on helping the individual reach out to the group. In many cases, particularly when the feelings expressed reflect those held by the group members, the worker's second client—the group—paradoxically appears to turn away from the individual. In the next section, we discuss the meaning of this dynamic.

Reaching for the Group Response to the Individual

It is easy to see how a worker can become identified with a particular client's feelings as a theme of concern is raised. If strong emotions are expressed, the worker may feel supportive and protective. Not surprisingly, if the other group members do not appear to respond to the individual, workers will often feel upset and angry. The worker is shocked and surprised to observe group members apparently not listening, to see their eyes glazing over as they appear to be lost in their own thoughts, or to witness a sudden change in subject or a direct rebuff to the client who has bared innermost feelings. At moments such as these, the worker's clarity of function and the notion of two clients can be the most critical. Instead of getting angry, the worker should view the group members' response as a signal, not that they are uninterested in what is being said, but that the theme may be powerfully affecting them.

The mediation function calls for the worker to search for the common ground between the individual and the group at the point where they seem most cut off from each other. This clear sense of function directs the worker simultaneously to empathize with the members' feelings underlying their apparent resistance and to express empathy with the individual client. The group leader must be with both clients at the same time.

The following example is from a day treatment outpatients' group for adult clients with a chronic mental illness. The group's focus was family issues. In this fifth session, a member raised her depression on the fifth anniversary of the brutal death of her child. The group members responded with silence, and the worker intervened to support the second client:

> At the beginning of our meeting, after group introductions and as people settled into their seats, Joan began speaking. She looked straight ahead of herself, eyes downcast most of the time, and occasionally made eye contact with me (one of the coleaders) or looked furtively around the group as she spoke.
>
> Joan said, "Well, I just want to tell everybody that the fifth anniversary of my daughter's death (the daughter was raped and murdered) is coming up this week and it's bothering me a lot. It always has bothered me. I try to deal with it OK, but I just don't always know how. I get to thinking about it, and the more I think, the more I'm afraid that I'm gonna lose it or do something against myself. I've tried to come to terms with it, but it's always hard when it comes around to when I lost her. So anyway, I've made arrangements to use the 24-hour bed (an emergency bed in the center) 'cause I'm too afraid when I get to feeling like this."
>
> There was complete and utter silence in the group. I remained silent for a few moments as well. As I looked around the group, the members too were looking straight ahead or acting uncomfortable and as if they didn't know what

to say. I said, "Wow, that's some pretty heavy issue that you're bringing up. It seems like it is hitting people pretty hard." The group was still silent, and I paused, although, just as Elizabeth was about to say something, my coleader said, "I'm wondering what people in the group are thinking or feeling about what Joan has just said, and if it's difficult to respond to it." There was a little more silence, and Joan went on, "Maybe I shouldn't have brought it up. Everybody here already knows that this is a problem for me. It's just that I felt so close to her. She was the one whose birth I remember. She was the one, instead of whisking her away and doing what they have to do right after they're born, they put her on me and I felt so much closer to her than the others. I remember it so much better. But maybe I just shouldn't bring it up here."

I waited a little and looked around the group once more and then said, "You're talking about a pretty big loss, here, and especially with it being your daughter, it's very appropriate to bring it to this group. Everyone has had some losses with people close to them; maybe some of them don't seem as earth-shattering as others, but we all know the experience of loss in our families, one way or another."

Then Elizabeth, who had been about to speak earlier, said, "Whew. That's just it. Thinking about your daughter and the 24-hour bed; that's pretty serious." Wendy spoke up, saying, "Yeah, that's scary. I mean I've been thinking about my accident (she had been in a car accident a few days before and has a long-standing fear that she may kill herself in a car) and thinking about losing my sons in the divorce like I did. It really troubles me." I said, "So, we're not only looking at family losses, but also at what we do to deal with them and look for ways to cope with them and feel safe."

With the worker's help, the group revealed that their silence did not reflect lack of feeling or concern for Joan. In fact, it was the opposite, as Joan's feelings about her loss triggered many of their own. Joan was reassured that the group was the place to bring these issues, and knowing she was not alone helped her.

As I have described the sessional contracting phase of a group meeting, many of the dynamics and skills discussed in Parts II and III of this book have reappeared. The worker's sessional tuning in, sessional contracting, elaborating, empathic, and demand-for-work skills are as important in helping the individual present concerns in the group session as they were in individual work. Such skills form the common core of practice skill. The worker's function is also the same, because the work centers on helping the client negotiate important systems in life. The differences in group work, compared with individual work, derive from the presence of one of these important systems—the group—and the need for the worker to pay attention to its responses. The core skills play a central role in implementing this aspect of the worker's function as well.

Reaching for the Work When Obstacles Threaten

In the analysis of work with individuals, we explored the connections between the process (way of working) and the content. For example, we identified the flow of affect between the worker and client—the authority theme—as a potential obstacle to work as well as a source of energy for change. Workers need to pay attention to these feelings—to acknowledge them before the work can proceed. This same issue was highlighted in our analysis of first group sessions, where I pointed out the importance of discussing the worker-group relationship. In the group context, workers must also deal with the interchange that takes place among the members—what Schwartz refers to as the **intimacy theme**. In the next sections, we look at authority and intimacy in the context of sessional contracting. For example, it may be important to discuss the process between members as a way of freeing individuals to trust the group enough to offer concerns in painful and sensitive areas. (We discuss both of these issues more fully in the next chapter.)

Teenager in a Residential Center, Raising a Difficult Subject In the example that follows, a youngster in a group for boys at a residential center wants to discuss a difficult issue but is hesitant about revealing himself to the group. By pausing and encouraging the group to discuss briefly the intimacy theme, the worker frees the member to continue.

> I began the meeting by asking if there was anything that anybody wanted to ask or say before we got started. Mike said, "Well, I have some things, but I am not sure that I want to talk about all of it." I said that Mike wanted to get at what was bothering him but he wasn't going to be able to do it right away. Perhaps he needed to test the group a bit to see if he could trust them? He said, "I don't know if I can always trust people." Terry came in here and said, "This is our group here, and we can say what we want to. What goes on in here does not go outside to others, isn't that right? If we have something that we want to talk about, something really personal, we won't let it out of our own group, right?" Terry got verbal approval from all the boys in the group. I also felt that Terry was demonstrating the basis of our contract. I said that I agreed with what Terry had said. To clarify the point further, I said that I saw our purpose as being able to talk about some of the feelings that we have around being here in the Boys' Center and that out of this might come family problems, work problems, and the problems of "what is going to become of me"—for example, am I really worth anything? Steve elaborated this aspect by referring to his willingness to share his feelings with the group.

The next move by the worker was important. After acknowledging the problem and restating the contract, the worker returned to Mike and his specific issue. This demonstrates the importance of not getting lost in a discussion of process. As will be illustrated later, there are times when a group needs to discuss obstacles and to explore them in depth; however, in most cases the recognition of the obstacle suffices. Workers can be "seduced" into expanding the discussion of the obstacle unnecessarily, thus subverting the contract of the group, even though the members themselves seem to want to talk about their work as a group rather than other concerns. In this case, however, this worker properly returned to the member, Mike.

> After this brief return to the contracting, I asked Mike if he thought he might feel like sharing some of the things he had said at the start of the meeting that were bothering him. He said that he thought that he could talk about part of it. John said that he thought that he knew what was bothering Mike. I let this hang. I wanted to see if Mike would respond to John or if the others would respond to either John or Mike to help us work on what Mike had come up with. Terry reiterated what he had said earlier: "What is said in the group is for the group." John said, "I think that it is about your family, isn't it, Mike? " Mike said, "Yes, that's part of it." I asked John what he meant by Mike's family. John said, "Well, Mike doesn't have any parents, and we are all the time talking about

troubles with our family, or we always have someplace to go if we make a weekend." Mike said, "Yeah, that's part of it. Like I make a weekend and I stay here."

Another way in which process and content are synthesized was described earlier in the discussion of resistance. For example, the client may appear to hold back from entering a difficult area of work, and the worker senses the client's reluctance to proceed. Such resistance is viewed as central to the work and a possible sign that the client is verging on an important area. In such cases, workers should suggest the need to explore the resistance. In much the same way, a group may resist by launching a tacit conspiracy to avoid painful areas. This is often the reason the members of a group hold back in the early stages of a group meeting. Once again, the worker's task involves bringing the obstacle out in the open in order to free the group members from its power.

Mothers of Children Diagnosed with Hyperactivity The following example concerns work with mothers of children who have been diagnosed as hyperactive. The early themes had centered on the parents' anger toward school officials, teachers, neighbors, and other children, all of whom did not understand. The parents also acknowledged their own anger at their children. The worker empathized by saying, "It is terribly frustrating for you. You want to be able to let your anger out, but you feel that if you do so, it will make things worse." After a few comments, the conversation became general again.

> I told the group members that they seemed to be talking in generalities again. Martha said it seemed they didn't want to talk about painful things. I agreed that this appeared to be hard. Every time they got on a painful subject they took off toward something safer. I wondered if the last session had been very painful for them. Martha said that it was a hard session, they had come very close, and she had a lot to think about over the weekend. Lilly said that she felt wound up over the last session, so much so that she had had trouble sleeping at night. I asked her to tell us what made it so upsetting for her. She said that she had felt so helpless when they had been talking about the school boards and the lack of help for children like her own. Doreen said it really wasn't so helpless. She had talked to a principal and had found out some new information.

Note that when the worker asked the group what made it so upsetting, the answer brought the group back to its work. This is a simple, effective, and usually underused technique for exploring and moving past resistance. When a client says, "I don't want to talk about that!" the worker often simply needs to reply, "What would make it hard to talk about that?" As clients talk about what makes talking about it hard, they usually find themselves talking about it. In the current example, later in the same session, the worker picked up on the acknowledgment of the members' anger toward their children and the difficulty of talking about that anger, with similar results. Workers find exploring resistance easier if they do not view it as a commentary on their lack of skill.

One final connection between process and task has to do with the power of specific examples in the work of the group. We saw earlier how moving from the general to the specific—an elaboration skill—could also powerfully affect the deepening of work with individuals. This skill is even more essential in work with groups. Because of its numbers, a group can sustain a general discussion about problems for quite a long time. The problem, mentioned earlier, of responding to a member's general comment by asking all the other group members if they too feel that way, and then forgetting to return to the original member, is one of the most common problems in the sessional contracting phase of group work.

Mothers of Sixth-Grade Underachieving Boys   In the following example, the group is for mothers of sixth-grade boys who were underachieving in school. The purpose was to discuss how they could more effectively help their youngsters with their schoolwork. After the members had engaged in a general discussion of their feelings when faced with their children's resistance to homework, their own memories of failure at school, their identification with their children's feelings, and their recognition that they sometimes push their children because of their own need for success, the worker recognized the need for more specificity in the work. She began by focusing the members toward this end, then made a demand for work.

> I said that I thought it would be useful if they described what actually happens at home concerning the issue of homework—how they handle getting the kids started on and completing assignments—and then discuss the pros and cons of the various ways of handling this.
>
> I told them that they had come up with some good ideas during the past meetings and that if they could apply these to their own children, they might begin to resolve some of the difficulties they had been describing. I said that it seems to me that they already have found some alternate ways of dealing with their children related to schoolwork and homework, and it is just a matter of seeing where they can be applied in their own particular situations. I asked that each describe as fully as possible what goes on in their home concerning getting the children started on the homework and also to describe the means they may use to get them to complete it.

The members needed help at this point to get into the details of their experiences, for only in analysis of the specific details can the worker and the group provide the required help.

To summarize, in this section we have seen how individuals reach out, often indirectly, to raise their concerns with the group. We have also explored the group's ambivalent responses. In analyzing the worker's function in mediating this engagement and the importance of paying attention to the process in the group, we have concentrated on problem areas such as members' reluctance to trust the group, the resistance that sets in when the work gets difficult, and the problems arising from helping in general terms, rather than specifically. In the next section, we focus on the mutual-aid process in the middle stages of sessions, examining how individuals and the group are helped and outlining the tasks of the worker in this process.

The Work Phase in a Group Session

In Chapter 8 we discussed many mutual-aid processes, including sharing data, the dialectical process, exploring taboo areas, the "all-in-the-same-boat" phenomenon, mutual support, mutual demand, individual problem-solving, rehearsal, and the "strength-in-numbers" dynamic. In this section we look at some of these processes as revealed in recordings from work phase sessions of groups. The first set of excerpts illustrates how general themes of concern are presented and discussed over a period of time, emphasizing how individuals use the general discussion for help with their specific concerns. The second set of excerpts shows how individual problem-solving can influence the general concerns held by group members.

Note that work in a group is not neat and orderly—with general themes or specific problems presented at the start of the meeting, worked on in the middle segment, and then neatly resolved toward the end. In reality, themes and problems may emerge only partially in early sessions and then reemerge later in new forms as group members become more comfortable with each other and with the worker. For example, in the early sessions of an unmarried mothers' group, most of the conversation involved sharing the hurt and bitterness the young women felt over the reactions of the child's father, their own parents, friends, and others. Only as trust developed within the group and their feelings were accepted and understood could the members began to consider doing something about their relationships with significant others.

Change takes time, and group members need to explore their thoughts and feelings at a pace appropriate for them. Difficult issues may take weeks or months of "working through" before the group member is ready to face a problem in a new way. The worker needs to offer support during this process and at the same time stay a half step ahead of the client, thus presenting a consistent yet gentle demand for work. The sections that follow illustrate the process of helping group members work on themes over time and the process of facilitating problem-solving mutual aid. The latter also shows how workers confront members to take personal responsibility.

Helping the Group Work Over Time

Helping a group work over time involves a series of beginnings, middles, and endings. We therefore need to examine several sessions in order to gain a full understanding of the way help is given over time. The next example, of Puerto Rican pregnant teens living at home, illustrates this point.

The members of the group to be discussed are 14- to 16-year-old American girls of Puerto Rican descent. The transition through puberty and emerging sexuality is a central developmental theme facing adolescents at this age. While this may be a universal, life-cycle theme, it emerges in different ways within different ethnic groups. Devore and Schlesinger (1996) describe this stage for the Puerto Rican female child as follows:

> As the Puerto Rican female child learns the female role by imitating her mother, she receives much affirmation from the entire family. Gradually she takes on more female responsibility in caring for young siblings—the babies—but there is no talk of sex. She gains knowledge from friends with similar meager experience and from overheard conversations of adults. (pp. 69–70)

The lack of appropriate sexual information, or the inability to make use of this information, led to pregnancies for the group members in our example. The members found themselves facing adult responsibilities, but they still had the bodies, hearts, minds, and developmental needs of children. They found it easier to express their anger at their boyfriends, who emerged relatively unscathed from the experience, than to share their pain honestly. Within their ethnic group, Puerto Rican girls are often taught to adhere to the concept of "marianismo, referring to the importance of motherhood and of deferring to men in their culture" (Devore & Schlesinger, 1996, p. 229). The responsibility of caring for the family's babies is illustrated as one member must bring her 4-year-old brother to the meetings. Her anger at the impending changes in her life and the way in which they were already affecting her choices were acted out toward the child. Here we look at the first month of meetings.

RECORD OF SERVICE

Description of the Problem

This group of young, pregnant women of Puerto Rican descent have had no difficulty verbalizing their anger at their boyfriends, parents, and friends. They are expressive of their feelings of victimization. The challenge for this worker is helping them move beyond their anger and feel their pain and sadness. It is my hypothesis that only be after experiencing their grief as well as their anger will they be able to move out of the victim role, recognize their part in the negative aspects of their relationships, and find solutions for action to make the changes they desire in their lives.

How the Problem Came to the Attention of the Worker(s)

During the first few sessions of this group, an underlying current of angrily trashing men was established. In particular, they tended to focus this anger on their boyfriends. Beatriz emerged as the leader of this pattern, though the others eagerly joined in. In the second group session (10/9), Valerie brought her 4-year-old younger brother, whom she was looking after that day. During the course of the session, even though it was obvious that Valerie was very depressed and upset about something, she resisted looking at her own feelings and exhibited great anger at Dennis. At one point she exploded, striking him. After I asked her what she was feeling, she admitted she was having a bad day and looked like she wanted to cry. However, she almost immediately regained her composure and put up her tough defensiveness again. At this point Yardy defended Valerie's behavior toward Dennis, saying it was just discipline. Not much later in this same session, Valerie actually stood up and said the she was sorry, but she needed to leave immediately.

In session three (10/16), in response to finding out that her boyfriend had been cheating on her, Beatriz exhibited no pain but said instead that she couldn't wait until after her baby is born, so that she can "show him some."

Before proceeding, it is important to raise the issue of the striking of the 4-year-old child. Valerie acted out her issues by hitting her brother. The worker had been shocked and upset at the behavior but had withheld her response for fear of cutting off the beginning relationship. This was a mistake, because the worker needed to consider the protection of the child. In addition, Valerie may have been saying to the worker and the group, "This is going to be what it is like for me with my own baby." She may also have been raising issues about how she was raised as a child. If the worker could have responded honestly, using this as an opportunity to deal with the topic of confidentiality, it would have been helpful. It might also have opened up the issue of how these children having children were using flight and fight to run from their pain. Valerie would give the worker another opportunity at a later session.

Summary of the Work

October 2 (First Session)

I attempted to open up the conversation to explore a range of emotions. Early on in the first session, Beatriz expressed anger and the desire to break up with her boyfriend. I asked her what it would feel like to break up with him. She replied that it would be easy and that she didn't care about him. When I suggested that, as well as creating those types of feelings, mightn't it also be somewhat painful and difficult, she replied firmly that it wouldn't be at all, as she didn't really care about him. (They have been dating for 2 years.) This told me a lot about Beatriz. I saw right away how tough and hardened she was and how difficult it is for her to admit her vulnerabilities. This was an important signal early on that painful feelings would not be easily accessed in this group.

I pointed out the commonality and intensity of the feelings in the group. I said, "Are you angry, Beatriz? You sound like it." She replied with an enthusiastic "Yes!" Then I said, "In fact, it sounds like something you are all feeling is very angry—am I right?" Once again, there was a round of enthusiastic agreement. It seemed helpful to put into words the emotion that was present in the room. They all seemed to experience some relief in having it named and noticing that they were all feeling the same. At the time I did not realize how this one emotion would dominate the group, and how by openly noticing the anger now, it would help me later to be able to point out how other emotions were so blatantly missing from the group culture.

Valerie shared some very rejecting behavior by her mother since she had become pregnant. I asked how this made her feel. She said that it made her feel very alone and like she didn't have a mother. Valerie took the lead at that point as the person who was the most willing to share deeply about painful feelings. She created an opening for Yardy to share about some of the rejecting behavior of her mother.

October 9 (Second Session)

I ignored strong signals that Valerie was giving me and stuck to concrete questions. Valerie arrived with her younger brother and within the first few minutes threatened to hit him. Just before this, she said that she had broken up with her boyfriend that week. I ignored her behavior toward her brother and asked her another question about her situation with her boyfriend. My thinking was that if she could talk about her boyfriend, it would relieve some of the pressure and her attitude toward her brother would shift. However, I was wrong. She did not answer my question and instead yelled at her brother again. Then she sat with her eyes down. I asked Yardy a question. In fact, I think I was shocked and immobilized at her aggressive behavior and the possibility of abuse happening in the group itself. I was reluctant to make her upset or step in and set limits around her treatment of her brother.

I attempted to open up a space for Valerie to share her painful feelings. As Valerie grew tenser and tenser during the session, I noticed out loud how tense she seemed and told her in a gentle voice that I was wondering what was going on with her. She told us that she had a toothache that had been bothering her for 3 days. She also said that she was supposed to have started high school that day (under a special midyear promotion program) but that she hadn't been able to because she had to look after her younger brother. Seconds later she leapt from her chair and hit Dennis.

I didn't know what to do and was frozen in my chair. The group stopped dead while I was in shock and trying to figure out what to do. I was torn between acting parental and setting limits around abuse in the group and helping her reach for her feelings.

I shared my feelings and attempted to help Valerie reach for her pain. I said that I felt very tense when she hit Dennis and I was wondering what was going on for her just beneath the surface. Valerie was not able to talk about her pain. I think if I had a second chance, I would have acknowledged out loud all the different, difficult things that were going on for Valerie that gave her a reason to be upset, i.e., her toothache, missing her first day of high school, being pregnant, and the fight with her boyfriend. I would have attempted to articulate for her the underlying pain, saying something like, "All of these things have happened and I imagine you may be feeling very alone right now, like there is no one there to support you. And yet you are expected to look after somebody else. I imagine that might be very difficult." I also would have arranged for Dennis to either leave the room and have someone else look after him or have him come closer to me, giving him a coloring book or something to do near me, and I would have taken over looking after him for a while.

I attempted to define a group norm that would be different from the norm in their homes. Valerie said that when she felt like this she didn't like herself and she just preferred not to say anything at all. I then said that, as the group continued, I hoped that it would become more and more a place where people felt that they could say anything on their minds and express whatever mood they are in. I told her that I wouldn't judge her for being sad or angry or depressed or whatever mood she was in on any particular day. This kind of expressed permission may be something the group needs to hear often at the start, since I imagine it contradicts the situation at home. It may also address their reluctance to express themselves fully that may evolve from their mothers' unavailability to all their feelings (transference).

Although the worker was more direct about the abuse of the child, she did not take it the next step and clearly indicate that as a mandated reporter she would need to let the child welfare authorities know if she feels a child is at risk. I believe the young woman had been letting the worker know that she cannot control herself, because of her anger at having to take care of Dennis. This was also an important signal of the kind of problems they will all have when they have children of their own while still trying to grow up and be a teen. The process and content integration is clear.

October 16 (Third Session)
I intellectualized and jumped in, cutting off the group process. We were talking about hitting people and whether it was OK to do that. I suggested that perhaps it was never a good idea, and I asked them why they thought I said that. Yardy said that it didn't work—it wasn't effective. Beatriz said that she thought it made things worse. Yardy said it was better to talk things through. When Beatriz said that didn't always work, I jumped in and said that I hadn't said it would be easy, and that hitting always created bad feelings. Beatriz replied that men deserve it sometimes and then went on to complain about men, something she frequently does. I notice that I jumped in, wanting to be right, and I stopped allowing the group to explore the issue themselves. This whole session was very different from the last one. For one thing, Valerie wasn't there (she was at the dentist), and a new member had joined the group. This week I kept the group more intellectual, posing questions and asking the girls to think about things from different perspectives. I know there is part of me that is put off by Beatriz's constant raving against men. I know that I am looking for a way into her deeper self, and I haven't found that way yet. This is probably why it is bothering me so much.

October 23 (Fourth Session)
I try to call Valerie during the week to touch base with her. Interestingly enough, her phone number has been changed and is now unlisted. I have no idea whether or not she will come. Sure enough, she does not show. One of the other members also cannot come, because of an appointment at the hospital. There are only two

members present, and it is an educational group, with one of the nurses coming in to talk about fetal development and birthing. It is a good group; the girls are excited to be learning these things—new to both of them. There is little chance, however, to open up deeper feelings. There is a lot of giggling and squeamish faces as they look at the pictures and try to imagine themselves pushing out a baby.

October 30 (Fifth Session)

During the week, Carmen gives birth to a baby girl. I make plans for us to go to the hospital to visit her. I have written a letter to Valerie, telling her we will be celebrating both her and Yardy's birthday at the next meeting and I hope she can make it. Sure enough, she comes early to the group and is in the waiting room! I am very glad to see her. It turns out that she had come to last week's session. She had gotten a ride with her boyfriend, and they had had a fight in the car, and they ended up driving back to her house. This taught me that the circumstances in these girls' lives are complex and play a larger role in their getting to group than I had thought.

I let Valerie know that she was missed. I told Valerie how disappointed the group was that she didn't come the week before. Beatriz agreed and said that the group wasn't as good without her. By doing this I emphasized that she was important and that her open display of strong emotions 2 weeks before had not created negative reactions in the group or from me as leader. By fully welcoming her back, I set a group norm that it is OK to display strong feelings and/or not be able, for whatever reason, to attend group for a few weeks and you will still be accepted for who you are and remain part of the group.

Although the trip to the hospital [to visit Carmen and her baby] did not allow for an in-depth talk in which we were able to have a conversation about painful feelings and the group's tendency to avoid them (a conversation I know we will need to have at some point), I felt it was essential to set a culture of being there for each other at those critical and special moments just before, during, and after giving birth. As each girl picked up Carmen's baby and held her, they expressed a lot of feelings about being pregnant themselves. They were able to see the eventual end result of their pregnancy and ask Carmen lots of questions about her experience. As we were leaving, Yardy asked Carmen, "Are you still going to be able to be part of the group?" and Carmen responded, "Of course, I'll bring my daughter!" I knew, in that moment, that they had become a group. I knew this because the girls named it and gave it a life.

Current Status of the Problem

Where It Stands Now

Although I do not feel that we have cracked the shell of defensiveness and entered a new arena of free expression of painful feelings, I believe that this will happen in the next stage of the group. It has taken these first five meetings for the group feeling to gel. There is now a bond established, created in part by the return of Valerie to the group after we had all given her up as possibly lost, as well as Carmen's commitment to be a member of the group after having given birth. Given the fact that it is a small miracle that these girls get themselves to each group meeting, given the complexity of the circumstances in their lives, I think we have done well. I know I underestimated all the factors that would make it difficult for them to get to group, especially before it became clear to them what was in it for them. I also think I underestimated the influence of culture in their ease with anger and the unfamiliarity with expressing their pain, particularly in front of others.

On the other hand, the stage we are at could be considered normal for a group that has only had five sessions. It takes this long to establish a group bond and a culture of safety in which deeper sharing can take place.

Strategies for Intervention

- For the next two to three meetings, we will not go out anywhere, but stay in and "talk." This is so we can get down to the next level of work.

- The next time someone in the group points to painful feelings but indirectly expresses them through other channels, I will confront the group with their pattern of avoiding painful emotions and ask them why they think they do this.

- I will support the "emotional leader" of the group (which thus far appears to be Valerie) in any risk taking she does in sharing painful or difficult emotions.

- I will tell them that I think it is helpful and important for them to share their pain with one another.

- I'll ask them to look and see how the norm of falling back on anger and blaming appears in their families and, in particular, with their mothers and have them look and see how that has been helpful and unhelpful.

- I will model unconditional acceptance of their feelings when they do share them in the group, creating a culture of acceptance.

Focusing the Group on Problem-Solving Mutual Aid

Mutual aid is also offered in relation to specific concerns raised by an individual member. As group members help an individual to look closely at a particular problem and find a new way of dealing with it, they are helping themselves to deal with similar issues in their own lives. Thus, mutual aid can also start with a specific issue and move to a general concern.

This process will now be illustrated using excerpts from a group offered in a family agency. The five women and two men in the group were separated, divorced, or widowed. All of them had experienced heavy depression and difficulties in their interpersonal relationships. The group contract was to discuss these concerns and to find some solutions. The session began with a young woman, Sheila, asking for help. The first response from group members was to offer consolation. The worker asked for elaboration while offering empathic support.

Sheila suddenly broke in and in a choked voice said, "I am feeling so down tonight." Bob quickly responded, "You, too?" Sheila continued that she had called Don in Montreal; he had been busy and had not wanted to talk to her. I said, "You sound very hurt." Tears filled her eyes, and Sheila said, "Yes, I am. I blew up and acted like a baby and now I have to apologize when he comes down on Saturday." Roberta and Bob rushed in to support Sheila saying they would be hurt, too, if they called someone and he was too busy to listen. Libby nodded but said nothing. I asked Sheila why she had called and why she blew up. She softly and sadly replied that she had called Don because she was lonely. Evelyn questioned if she had told Don this. Sheila hadn't. Bob asked why. Sheila smiled and said, "That wasn't the only reason I telephoned. I sometimes call to check up and see if he is really working." Roberta said, "You can't dwell on the fact that he had an affair, and Joan is going to have his baby."

Sheila began to talk about Don and Joan and the baby. I suggested, after listening a few minutes, that it seemed to me that Sheila's relationship with Don right now was important, rather than again talking about what had happened in the past. I asked the others in the group, "What do you think?"

The worker refused to allow Sheila to discuss ground that had already been covered in the group. Instead, she made a demand for work by focusing Sheila on the here-and-now details of her discussion with Don. A major step in such work involves asking the group members to take some responsibility for their part in their problems. Our defenses often cause us to explain our problems by projecting the blame onto others in our lives or justifying the present difficulty by describing past reasons. In this case, the worker focused the client and the group on the immediate situation in the belief that this was the only way to help. The client's responses elaborated on the specifics of the concern.

Sheila did not wait for a response and replied directly to me, "I feel so tense. I don't know what to talk to Don about. I don't want it to be like it was before we separated." I said, "You sound scared to death." Sheila became very sad and nodded. Evelyn added, "I have felt the same way with Jacques. I was his shadow. When he left and moved in with a girlfriend, I thought I could not exist on my own. I have learned to do so. Sheila, you talk as if you had no life of your own." Libby continued, "Do you always do what Don wants?"

Sheila then revealed the reason she was angry on the telephone with Don. She had earlier thought of going on a trip to England on her own and had wanted Don to say no. He had not, and when financially she had been unable to make the trip, she called Don expecting him to be very happy that she was staying. He was busy and did not say much. Sheila then accused him of not caring and hung up crying.

As the details emerged, so did a fuller picture of the problem. The worker recognized a common problem in intimate relationships—one partner feels that the other should "divine" what she is feeling and wants to hear, but when this does not happen, the first partner feels hurt. This is a specific example of a general problem: that risking ourselves by sharing real thoughts, feelings, and needs directly with those who are important to us is hard to do. As a group member began to provide feedback to Sheila on her part in the proceedings, she cut him off, and the worker moved quickly to point this out:

Bob started to say that Sheila had put Don on the spot, when Sheila interrupted and continued talking. I stopped her and said to the group, "Did you notice what just happened?" Everyone except Sheila and Bob smiled but said nothing. I said to Sheila, "Bob was trying to say something to you when you cut him off." She cut in to say anxiously, "Did I? I'm sorry, Bob." Bob quietly said, "My God, I didn't even notice. It has happened to me so often I guess I just expected to be cut off." She picked this up and said Don and Bob were alike and that Don let her get away with talking too much and cutting him off. Roberta commented, "Don seems hard to get close to," and there followed a few more comments on how Don seemed unapproachable.

The worker then challenged Sheila's view of the event and asked her to take responsibility for creating part of the problem. Because the worker had already built a positive working relationship with the group, Sheila could accept the confrontation and examine her own actions. As the group worked on the details of this specific example, it is easy to see how they were also working on their own variations on the theme.

I then went back to Sheila's telephone call and asked Sheila why she had called Don at work when he was likely to be busy, rather than calling him at home. She stumbled around and didn't answer the question. I kept pressing her with the same question and then asked the group if they had any ideas on this. Bob said, "I don't know what you are getting at." I said, "Let me check this out with all of you. My feeling is that Sheila called Don when she knew he would be likely to be busy and set it up so that he would probably be annoyed with her. Once again, she got very hurt." Evelyn added, "You did that with Don around the trip. Had he told you not to go to England, you would have been angry. If he told you to go, you would have said he did not care. I did the same thing with Jacques, and I never knew what I wanted. I was the little girl who asked her father's permission for everything."

Sheila said, "I guess I set things up so that I am the sad little girl and everyone feels sorry for me, just like I am trying to do tonight. How do I stop?" Bob said, "How do we stop hating ourselves—that is what it comes down to." Sheila continued thoughtfully, "You know I took the job at the airline so that Don and I could travel, and he really doesn't like traveling. I also bought him a bicycle to go cycling, but then found out he hates it." I said, "It sounds like you assume things about Don but somehow never check them out with him—how come?" There was a short silence, and I continued, "Is it because when, as Bob said, we hate ourselves, we are too scared to say what we feel or want?"

Sheila talked about how horrible and stupid she feels she is, and the group members gave her much support. They also reminded her of the one area where she feels she has accomplished something—teaching piano. She brightened and talked of her love of music and how she enjoyed teaching.

Roberta then remarked on how much everyone needs to be told they do some things well. She recounted an incident at work where she had been praised and how pleased she was. The others in the group, except Libby, agreed. She said it depended on whether or not you believed it. Sheila agreed and stated it was hard for her to accept praise. Evelyn went back to Sheila's relationship with Don, saying Sheila had given indications that she knew the marriage was breaking up, although she had said Don's decision to separate was a complete surprise. Sheila said she partly knew but did not want to admit it to herself. She had been withholding sexually, although they had had good sexual relations prior to marriage. I asked if she often gets angry at Don, and Sheila replied angrily, "I get furious at him, but I end up being bitchy, which I don't like. I am also scared he will leave." As the end of the group session was approaching, the members began making some suggestions around dealing with Don on the weekend. She should be a little more independent, say what she is feeling and not always what she thinks she should say.

As the group members work on a specific problem, workers should share any of their own thoughts and ideas that could help place the problem in a new perspective. To do this, they must draw on their own life experience; the information they have gathered by working with people, either individually or in groups, who have had similar concerns; and the professional literature. For example, in this brief excerpt, group members were learning something about taking responsibility for one's own actions, the difficulties involved in interpersonal communications, and specific interactional skills that might promote more effective interpersonal relationships. These agenda items were set in the context of their own experiences as they explored their often mixed feelings about themselves and others. Workers often serve to provide data that have been unavailable to the client and that may provide help with the problem or issue of the moment. In working with a couples' group, for example, the leader could draw on communications theory, ideas about "fair fighting" in marriage, developmental life theory, game model theory, gestalt, and the like. As workers deepen their own life experiences, as they use group experiences to learn more about the complexities of life, and as they review the literature, they can enrich their contributions to the group members' struggle.

Sessional Endings and Transitions

In Chapter 4 we discussed sessional endings and transitions, pointing out that each session requires a resolution phase. We saw that summarizing, generalizing, identifying next steps, rehearsal, and exploring "doorknob" comments were helpful skills for the worker at this stage. Each of these skills from work with individuals applies to the group session as well.

In the illustration that follows, a worker helped mothers with children diagnosed as hyperactive move toward more realistic next steps in their work as a mutual-aid group. In making this demand for work, the worker endorsed the power of resilience, suggesting that no matter how hopeless the situation may seem, the group could begin by taking steps on their own behalf.

There was a lot of exchanging of problem situations, with everyone coming out with her problems for the week. There seemed to be some urgency to share their problems, to get some understanding and moral support from the other members. Through their stories, themes emerged: an inconsistency in handling their children's behavior (lack of working together with husband), the tendency to be overprotective, and their hesitancy in trusting their children. The issue of "nobody understanding" was again brought up, and I recognized their need to have someone understand just what it was that they were going through. Betty said that her son was never invited to play at the neighbors' houses, because he was a known disturber. Others had the same experiences with neighbors who didn't want their hyperactive son and daughter around. I expressed the hurt they were feeling over this, to which they agreed.

After further discussion about the impact of their children on others (teachers, neighbors, children), they moved to a discussion of how their children's behavior affected them. Rose said that she ends up constantly nagging; she hates herself for it, but she can't stop. Her son infuriates her so much. Others agreed that they were the biggest naggers in the world. I asked what brought the nagging on. The consensus was that the kids kept at them until they were constantly worn down and they gave in to them. Also if they wanted the children to do something, they had to nag, because the children wouldn't listen. I said that the children really knew them, how they reacted, and also exactly what to do in order to get their own way. They agreed but said that they couldn't change—they couldn't keep up with the badgering that these children could give out.

The group members expressed two divergent ideas: On the one hand, they "couldn't change," and on the other, they could not "keep up with the badgering."

They quickly moved to a discussion of medications as a source of hope for change. The worker pointed out that their hope in this solution was mixed with their recognition that the drugs were addictive and that they could not provide an answer in the long run. This is an example of a process in groups that Bion (1961) calls *pairing,* in which the discussion of the group members appears to raise the hope that some event or person in the future will solve the problem.

For these group members, drugs provided this hope but also gave them an opportunity to avoid discussing what they could do to deal with the problem. In a way, it represented a "primitive" group response: attempting to deal with the pain of a problem by not facing it. As the session moved to a close, the worker sensed the heaviness and depression caused by the group's sense of hopelessness. She had empathized with these feelings but now needed to make a demand for work on the members, asking them to explore what they could do about the problem. When the members raised another hope for a solution in the form of an outside expert who would help, the worker pointed out their real feelings that no "outsider" could help and that they needed to find the help within themselves. In this way, the worker helped them resolve a difficult and painful discussion by conveying her belief in their strength and her sense of the concrete next steps open to them.

> There was further discussion around the children's poor social behavior and the mothers' own worry about how these children will succeed as adults. What will become of them? Will they fit in and find a place for themselves in society? I was feeling the heaviness of the group and pointed out what a tremendous burden it was for them. Our time was up, and I made an attempt to end the meeting, but they continued the discussion. I recognized both their urgency to solve the problem and their need to talk with each other and get support from each other. Marilyn said that it was good; she came away feeling so much more relieved at being able to talk about how she felt, and she certainly was gaining some new insight into herself.
>
> Discussion diverted to the problem with the children and how they were to deal with it. I asked what they wanted to do. Edna suggested they ask a behavior modification therapist to help them work out solutions. Others thought it was a good idea. I said that was a possibility, but I wondered if in wanting to get an "expert" involved, they were searching for someone to solve their problems for them. They agreed. I asked if they thought all these experts could do this. They said that it hadn't happened yet. I wondered if we could use the group for the purpose it was set up, to help each other problem-solve. I suggested that next week we concentrate on particular problems and work together to see what solutions we could come up with. They seemed delighted with this and decided that they should write down a problem that happened during the week and bring it in. Then we could look at a number of problems. Consensus was reached as to our next week's agenda, and the meeting ended.

This illustration of one form of sessional ending and transition work brings to a close our description of the work phase in a mutual-aid group. Having seen the general model of the individual-group interaction, we can now examine the elements in depth and explore some variations on the theme. In the next chapter, we examine the individual's role in the group, concentrating on how members are informally assigned to play functional roles such as scapegoat, deviant, and internal leader. We also explore the needs of the group-as-a-whole and the way in which the group leader can help the group work on its central tasks.

Chapter Summary

The sessional skills for helping individuals also apply to the group setting. In the beginning stages of a session, group workers need to work with the individual and the group as they reach out to each other. During the work phase, mutual aid deals with general themes of concern explored over time as well as specific problems of individuals. Such concerns require the worker to make demands for work and show the members how to take responsibility for their part in problems. Groups can move from the general to the specific and from the specific to the general. Finally, as meetings draw to an end, successful helping involves striving for resolution.

Related Online Content and Activities

 Visit *The Skills of Helping* Book Companion Website at www.socialwork.wadsworth .com/Shulman06/ for learning tools such as glossary terms, InfoTrac College Edition keywords, links to related websites, and chapter practice quizzes.

The website for this chapter also features additional notes from the author and additional process recordings:

- African American Public Welfare Clients: Dealing With Issues of Authority and Racism
- Alternative Public Day School: Parents of Children With Emotional and Behavioral Difficulties
- Parole Group for Ex-Convicts: Dealing With Issues of Authority and Internalized Negative Self-Image
- Preadoption Group: Authority and the Illusion of Work
- Preadoption Group: Clarifying Purpose and Acknowledging Concerns
- Preadoption Group: Dealing With Friends and Relatives
- Welfare Mothers' Group: Mediating Between the Client Group and the Agency

Working With the Individual and the Group

CHAPTER OUTLINE

The Concept of Role
    in a Dynamic System

The Scapegoat

The Deviant Member

The Gatekeeper

The Defensive Member

The Quiet Member

The Monopolizer

The Group as an Organism

Developmental Tasks
    for the Group

The interactionist model presents the notion of two clients: the individual and the group. In this chapter an artificial separation of these two clients is employed to deepen your understanding of each in interaction with the other. First we focus on the individual within the group, discussing how clients bring their personalities to bear in their group interactions. The concept of role is used to help describe how individual personality is translated into group interaction. Many common patterns of individual-group relationships are described and illustrated; for example, we look at scapegoats, deviant members, gatekeepers, and monopolizers. As these individuals are isolated for closer analysis, you will see that understanding individual clients without considering them in the context of their group interaction is often impossible.

In the latter half of this chapter we examine the concept of the group-as-a-whole. This is the entity created when more than one client is involved at a time. I introduce an organismic model and illustrate some of the worker's tasks when he or she must intervene to help in the growth of the second client, the group.

The Concept of Role in a Dynamic System

Two ideas central to the discussion of the individual in a group are role and dynamic system. Ackerman (1958) describes the ways in which the term **role** has been used and proposes his own definition:

> Sociology, social psychology, and anthropology approach the problems of role through the use of special concepts and techniques. They apply the term in two distinct ways, meaning either the "role" of the person in a specific, transient, social position or the characteristic "role" of the individual in society as determined by his social class status. Working in the psychodynamic frame of reference, I shall use the term to represent an adaptational unit of personality in action. "Social role" is here conceived as synonymous with the operations of the "social self" or social identity of the person in the context of a defined life situation. (p. 53)

Ackerman suggests that the individual has both a private "inner self" and a social "outer self" that emphasizes externally oriented aspects of his or her personality. I shall use this idea of social role in the following way. When clients begin a group, they present their outer self as their way of adapting to the pressures and demands of the group context. Their pattern of action represents their social role. Ackerman argues that incongruity between the reality of the inner self and the outer self that is presented in a group can cause tension there. In many ways, the task of the group worker involves helping individuals find the freedom to express their inner selves in the group. The central idea is that each member brings to the group an established pattern of translating a unique personality into social action.

When considering oppressed and vulnerable groups, we can integrate Ackerman's notions about role with the oppression psychology concepts described in Chapter 1. The outer self of survivors of oppression represents their adaptive behavior to the defined situation of oppression. We can understand the incongruity between this outer self, which they present in social situations, and their inner self as one of the defense mechanisms employed in an effort to cope. This resulting incongruity is a form of alienation from self-identity, as described by Fanon (Bulhan, 1985). The effort in the mutual-aid group is to help members use the group to integrate their inner and outer selves and to find more-adaptive mechanisms of coping with oppression, including personal and social action. The small group is a microcosm of the larger society. If we consider the impact of oppression, our understanding of the role played by a survivor of oppression within a group context deepens.

Keeping in mind the concept of individual roles, we can view the group as a dynamic system, (see Chapter 5) in which the movements of each part (member) are partially affected by the movements of the other parts (the other members). This view is rooted in the work of Kurt Lewin (1935, 1951), who is often considered the founder of group dynamics. Thus, members bring their outer self into this dynamic system, then adapt to this system through their social roles. All group members engage in this process of adaptation. The model presented thus far provides a general description of the individual-social interaction in group. For our purposes, however,

I shall concentrate on specific social roles emerging over time and requiring special attention by the group worker.

Patterned social roles are most easily illustrated using an example from a formal, organized group, such as a tenants' association. To function effectively, the association usually identifies specific tasks that group members must assume and then assigns these jobs by some form of division of labor. For example, the association may need a chairperson, a secretary, a treasurer, and a program coordinator. The essential idea is that group roles are functionally necessary and are required for productive work. In taking on any of these roles, specific members will bring their own sense of social role to bear. For example, depending on their experience, their background, their skills, and their sense of social role, various members would implement the role of chairperson differently. Because the group is a dynamic system, the group and its individual members will also somewhat affect the chairperson's implementation of this role. The actions of the chairperson are best described as the product of the interaction among the individual's sense of social role, the role of chairperson as defined by the group, and the particular dynamics of the group and its members.

The roles just described are formal. Every group also creates less formal roles to help in its work, even though these might never be openly acknowledged. For example, in a group led by a worker who leads the discussion as an external leader, one or more internal leaders may emerge as if they had been formally elected. The individuals who assume internal leadership in a group often bring a concept of social role that includes this function. By responding positively to them, group members encourage the internal leaders' assumption of this important role.

Other, less constructive functional roles can emerge in a group; these reflect maladaptation rather than healthy development. For example, scapegoats are often selected by the group because they have the personal characteristic that members most dislike or fear in themselves. Thus, a group of young teenage boys who are worried about sexual identity may select as the group scapegoat the teen who seems least "macho" or least sure of himself. The members, of course, do not hold an election for such roles. It is not as if the group members held an informal meeting in the coffee shop, prior to the group session, and asked for volunteers to be the group scapegoats, internal leaders, deviant members, and so on. If the group has a need for these roles, however, they will go through a subtle, informal process to select members to fill them. The dysfunctional aspect of employing a scapegoat is that it often leads the group to avoid facing their own concerns and feelings by projecting them onto the scapegoat.

Similarly, individuals do not raise their hands and volunteer to act as scapegoats, pointing out that they have successfully played the scapegoat role in their families and social groups for most of their lives. The scapegoat in the group usually subtly volunteers for this role, because it is consistent with that individual's concept of his or her social role. Adapting to groups by playing this social role is as dysfunctional for the individual scapegoat as it is for the group as a whole. Once again, the idea of the group as a dynamic system helps us to understand the process of scapegoating in a dynamic way. (The next section explores the role of scapegoat in greater detail.)

In the sections that follow, we look at informal roles developed in groups, such as scapegoats, deviant members, monopolizers, and gatekeepers. (See the book's website for discussion and examples of other roles in the group.) In each case, the discussion focuses on analyzing the dynamics as they reflect the individual's social role within the group. In addition, we examine the skills of the group worker as he or she implements the individualizing part of the work.

The Scapegoat

The discussion of individual roles in the group begins with the scapegoat because it is both one of the most common and one of the most distressing problems in work with groups. The **scapegoat** is a member attacked, verbally or physically, by other members. These members are usually projecting onto the scapegoat their own negative feelings about themselves. The scapegoat role is often interactive in nature, with the scapegoat fulfilling a functional role in the group. Whether it is overt scapegoating in groups of children and adolescents or the more subtle type in adult groups, the impact on the group and the worker can be profound. As we explore this particular role in detail, I shall introduce several important concepts regarding social role in the group and the function of the group worker. These central ideas will reemerge as we examine other roles. This discussion can then serve as a general model for analyzing individual roles in the group.

First, we must consider the history of the term *scapegoat*. Douglas (1995) attributes the origin of the term to the 15th-century biblical scholar and translator Tyndale. Tyndale's translation of sections of Leviticus referred to an ancient ritual among the Hebrews practiced on the Day of Atonement. Two live goats were brought to the altar of the tabernacle. One was killed as a sacrifice. The second goat, after the high priest transferred his own sins and the sins of the people onto it, was taken to the wilderness and allowed to escape. Douglas suggests, "If Tyndale had read into the Hebrew idea that the goat was 'suffered to escape,' then his coining of the word 'scapegoat' becomes much clearer" (p. 8). Douglas describes the scapegoat ritual as

> essentially a process of purification, which means in essence that its practitioners felt that they were contaminated by the transgressions of their daily lives and that the ritual of scapegoating was one that would disperse that contamination and reinstate them as clean in their own eyes and, more importantly, in the eyes of their god. (p. 14)

Whole populations, such as African Americans, Jews, and homosexuals, have experienced extreme forms of scapegoating as part of the systematic oppression described in Chapter 1. These have included the projecting of negative stereotypes as an underlying justification for slavery as well as more current forms of economic and social oppression; anti-Semitism and the Holocaust in which millions of Jews (as well as many homosexuals, gypsies, and others) were systematically killed; and gay-bashing activities in which gays and lesbians are physically attacked on the street or serve as the butt of homophobic jokes.

Bell and Vogel (1960) have described the dynamics of this phenomenon in the family group, emphasizing the functional role played by the scapegoat in maintaining equilibrium in the family by drawing all of the problems onto him- or herself. Many scapegoats in groups have been socialized into this social role by their family experiences and are ready to assume it in each new group they enter.

Scapegoating is also discussed by Garland and Kolodny (1965), who provide an interesting analysis of the forms of scapegoating prevalent in practice:

> No single phenomenon occasions more distress to the outside observer than the act of scapegoating. Frequently violent in its undertones, if not in actual form, it violates every ethical tenet to which our society officially subscribes. As part of that society, the group worker confronted with scapegoating in the midst of interaction often finds himself caught up in a welter of primitive feelings,

punitive and pitying, and assailed by morbid reflections on the unfairness of fate which leaves one weak and others strong. (p. 124)

Another article addresses the common mistake in practice of the worker moving into the interaction between the scapegoat and group in a way that preempts the opportunity for either the group or the individual to deal with the problem (Shulman, 1967). Most often, when the worker protects the scapegoat, the hostility merely takes more covert forms. Appeals to fairness or requests to give the member a chance do not seem to help, and the worker is usually left feeling frustrated, the scapegoat hurt, and the group members guilty.

A Scapegoating Example

As we think about scapegoating in the social work group, the concepts of social role and the group as a dynamic system provide us with clues to the meaning of this interaction. We cannot understand the behavior of the scapegoat simply as a manifestation of his or her "personality." Rather, it is a result of the interaction between the scapegoat's sense of social role and the group's functional needs. The relationship between the individual role and the group need becomes clear if the group loses its scapegoat—if, for example, the member leaves the residence or drops out of the group. As though operating on an unconscious command, the group immediately searches for a new candidate to take the scapegoat's place. One member is usually waiting to do so.

The example that follows illustrates the scapegoating process, some of the pitfalls the worker faces, and effective strategies for intervention. In this example, we see a new worker's interventions with a group of teenage girls for 2 months in a school setting. The worker was white and the girls were African American and Hispanic. The worker started by developing insights into the scapegoating process and tuning in to her own feelings. Her protective responses toward the scapegoat were subtle; she tried to deal with the problem indirectly because of her concern over the possibility of hurting the member who was scapegoated. Although she never directly confronted the process, she did deal with the concerns of the second client, the group, which led the group to have less need for a scapegoat.

RECORD OF SERVICE

Client Description and Time Frame

A seventh-grade girls' peer support group of 12- and 13-year-old adolescents (3 African American and 2 Hispanic girls) from a racially mixed, low-income part of the city. The time frame is from 12/5 through 2/6.

Description of the Problem

This group is projecting its dependency needs onto one individual, causing the group to remain in the beginning stage of development. This individual, Rachel, acts out these dependency needs for the group. Rachel does her own thing, not involving herself in any group activities, keeping to herself. Thus, the group temporarily remains in the power and control stage, as described by Garland, Jones, and Kolodny (1965)—a stage in which authority, permission, autonomy, and confidentiality are crucial issues for these adolescent girls. The group's investment in the role of the scapegoat both hinders and helps the development of the group as it pushes toward its next stage, intimacy.

How the Problem Came to the Attention of the Worker(s)

On January 23, I observed that Rachel sat away from the other members of the group and refused to join in the group activity (which was painting) and was unwilling to speak. This behavior brought a negative reaction from the group, and the other girls hypothesized about why she was acting as a loner. The group soon ignored this behavior when Lisa brought up a "hypothetical" situation in which she was involved. Lisa stated that she was tired of a girl whom she used to be friends with and now does not like anymore. Lisa asked the group for advice about what to do and how to tell this girl. At this point, I saw that the girl she was discussing was Rachel. When questioned by the other girls as to who this girl was, Lisa would not say. At this moment I was very unsure of my position as a worker and what I should do about the situation. My first instinct was to see this as an issue that needed to be dealt with by Rachel and Lisa only, but, in thinking about it further, I decided it was indeed a group problem, especially considering our group goal of improving peer relations. It became clear to me that this need for the role of a scapegoat was an issue for the entire group.

Summary of the Work

December 5 (First Session)

We were discussing the purpose of the group, and I asked them what they thought some of the rules should be. Most of the members jumped in and offered suggestions, many of them expressing concern about confidentiality and "secrets." Rachel and Kim sat on either side of me, neither of them saying anything, but they nodded when Lisa and Amy asked them what they thought of a rule or idea they suggested. I attempted to engage Rachel and Kim in conversation, and I gave the group permission to make their own rules. I asked them both what they thought we should do as a group if someone broke our rule of confidentiality. They both replied by looking confused and shrugging their shoulders. Rachel said, "I don't know—what do you mean?" Lisa immediately jumped in, asked Rachel if she was "deaf or what?" and gave her idea of a "punishment," causing Rachel to sink in her chair and look down at the floor.

I could sense what was going on, but did not know how to respond to it. Looking back, I can see these were all issues related to the theme of authority. I did not want to discourage anyone from saying what they wanted, and did not want to push anyone into talking if they did not want to. I was simply thrilled that anyone was saying anything, and that they were enthused about the group.

December 12 (Second Session)

Kim had a problem and I supported her bringing it to the group. Kim told the group that she had a problem and that she wanted to ask everyone what she should do about it. She had been involved in a fight earlier that week and now she had to go to court. She said that she was afraid that she would be sent to a school where "they are real strict and don't let you do nothing you want to do." She asked me what she could do about this and asked if I could help her by talking to the principal for her. I told her I was glad that she brought this to the group. I asked the group what they thought about the situation. Lisa stated that, if the situation happened to her, she wouldn't worry about it because she knew her mother would not get mad at her and would not care. I completely missed the boat on this statement! Kim was discussing the entire incident with Mary, and the group became interested in the details of the fight. I became interested in who did what to whom and who was responsible for what, trying to determine if Kim was indeed going to be punished severely by the court system.

Kim told the group that the reason she got into the fight was because someone in the school had spread the rumor that she was pregnant. She said that she had to let everyone know that she was not, and so she had no choice but to get into this fight with the person who started the rumor. The group agreed that she did have to fight this girl because, after all, she had no business saying such things and she ruined Kim's reputation. (I missed an important issue the group was raising and asked the group to work on the more obvious issue.) I asked the group about other things they could do to avoid fighting in such a situation, and did not focus in on the pregnancy issue which, in retrospect, I think was the real problem. Almost everyone in the group was actively involved in a discussion of who can and cannot be trusted in their class, and who the people are in the school that spread rumors. I missed the significance of Rachel not participating in the discussion. I realized toward the end of the group that Rachel did not participate actively in the conversation and, in fact, had sat next to me again. I also was able to recognize the fact that I was quite uncomfortable in addressing the issue.

At a later session, the worker realized that she had missed the central theme of concern for Kim. Although Kim raised her problem in terms of the fight and the discipline, this was actually a first offering of her deeper concern—the fact that she was pregnant. The issue did not resurface until the fifth session.

December 19 (Third Session)
I avoided an issue that I was having a difficult time dealing with. The fact that Christmas is often a sad time for many poor people was an issue that I was unable to confront in this session. It was the last day of school before Christmas vacation, and only four of the members were there. We had a Christmas party and spent most of the time talking about what they would be doing with their time off. When I asked them what they would be doing, Lisa said nothing, and that it would be boring. I allowed countertransference to take over and I felt very guilty that I was excited about my own vacation and Christmas. I tuned out as a result of this guilt. Mary seemed very quiet; I assumed that it was because Kim was not in school that day (they are best friends). Cindy said that she was going to stay home, watch TV, and sleep.

Rachel asked if we could "have group" even though they did not have school. (She was sitting next to me again and I was aware of her need to be close to me and have me recognize her presence.) I used this as an opportunity to tell them that I would be on vacation and that we would not meet until the second Monday that they would be back in January. I then stated that, if I was going to be around, I would love to get together with them, and that maybe we could do something on a Saturday to make up for lost time. Lisa stated that under no circumstances would she want to get out of bed during her vacation or on a Saturday. I did not verbalize the feelings of the group. Rachel asked me where I was going and why I couldn't come back early. Mary immediately jumped in and told her that I obviously had another life and had important things to do. Lisa said that I was lucky to be leaving "this dirty and boring city." Although my first instinct was to side with Rachel and protect her, I reminded the girls that this was their group to do what they wanted with and it was up to them if they wanted to meet on a Saturday. In retrospect, I realize that I missed the issue they were raising: the fact that Christmastime is not fun for them and that they recognize differences between me, a middle-class, white worker, and themselves.

January 23 (Fourth Session)

Before group started, Rachel came in and told me that Lisa had been acting unfriendly toward her and that this upset her a great deal, because they were supposed to be best friends. We discussed some ways that she could confront Lisa on this and the friendship in general. Rachel told me that she wanted to meet two periods a week instead of one. I encouraged her to bring this up in group.

When everyone arrived for the group, the girls all asked why Rachel got to get out of class early to come and talk to me. They appeared annoyed that Rachel may have received "special attention" but soon forgot this discussion when Lisa brought up a problem. I supported Lisa for coming to the group for advice, but missed an underlying issue. Lisa told me that she had a problem this week and asked if we could please talk about her this week. She went on to say that this was a hypothetical situation and that it did not involve anyone they knew. Lisa said that she has a friend who is always doing everything she does, is always wearing the same clothes she wears, says the same things she says, and even likes the same boys she likes. I sensed that Lisa was talking about Rachel, and I felt a strong urge to protect the individual being scapegoated.

The group members jumped in on this subject and stated how they all hate this behavior. Rachel sat in the corner of the room, watching the group and looking out of the window. I suggested that maybe this friend really likes Lisa a great deal and she wants to be like her. Kim jumped in and agreed with me and told Lisa that she should be complimented. I made a demand for work. I asked the group what they would do in this situation. I made the assumption that I was the only one who knew the entire picture and acted accordingly. Everyone was very involved in the pictures they were drawing and did not seem to feel like discussing the subject.

In retrospect, I see that the group knew exactly what was going on and that it was my own feelings of discomfort that allowed me to avoid the issue. I avoided the main issued being raised in an attempt to protect the scapegoat. Lisa insisted on getting my opinion on the subject, even though I threw it out to the group for answers. I picked up on a conversation that Kim and Mary were having, and began talking with Cindy about a teacher they disliked. Lisa put her problem back on the table for discussion. I was feeling very annoyed at her insistence and I told her that we had answered her question and that she could come and discuss it with me later if she wanted to. As the members left that day, Lisa pulled me aside and told be that this person was Rachel and that she did not want Rachel to know. I was able to support her as an individual group member and told her that I would be free to speak with her later that morning and gave her a pass to get out of class.

The pattern of scapegoating is not directly addressed. Rachel, the group members, and the worker all know it is going on. The worker's reluctance is rooted in her not wanting to hurt Rachel, yet the persistent pattern of scapegoating is more painful than any direct discussion might be. Workers are also often afraid to open up an issue such as this because they are not sure what will happen and where it will go. The worker's indirect efforts to deal with the problem match the group members' own use of indirect communications, thus frustrating the growth of the group. As the group culture becomes more positive, the group members are able to deal with some of their issues and lessen their need for a scapegoat.

January 30 (Fifth Session)

I supported Kim for bringing a problem to the group. Kim brought up a problem she was currently dealing with and asked the group for advice. She said that she has a friend who thought she was pregnant. Her friend's cousin told her to drink "this awful stuff" to get rid of the baby. She said her friend did not want the baby, but that her friend's boyfriend wanted it very badly. Now her friend does not know what to tell her boyfriend. I reached for the group's feelings. The group immediately confronted Kim and wanted to know if she was speaking about herself. Kim said it was a friend. I said that this must be very difficult and was a scary situation to be in. I verbalized the group's nonverbal behaviors. I acknowledged that there seemed to be a great deal of tension around the subject of pregnancy and that it was a difficult topic of discussion. Cindy said that her mother would kill her if she ever came home pregnant and that she felt sorry for this girl. I pointed out to the group that the problem was not only an individual issue, but also an issue for the group. The members appeared uneasy discussing the topic of pregnancy and even willing to change the subject and talk about something else.

The group tried to avoid the issue by concentrating on who in the school they thought could be pregnant. I made a demand for work. I stated to the group that a member had raised an important question and that it was an issue that demanded their attention. I asked the group what they would tell their boyfriends in a similar situation. Lisa stated that she would simply dump him and not tell him, since he must be crazy to think a 12-year-old should have a baby. Rachel stated that she did not have a boyfriend, and Mary said that she would tell him and hope he did not leave her. At this point, Kim broke in and told the group that it was her whom she was talking about. I said that everyone might be feeling a great deal of emotion and that it must have taken a great deal of courage and trust to come to the group with this issue. The members focused in on the situation, giving Kim advice, and reflecting the situation onto themselves, talking about what they would do in such a situation.

In this session the group did not appear to need the scapegoat; the conversation was intense, and everyone worked together on the issue at hand. I began to feel that the group was progressing, and I felt much more in tune with my own feelings about things that happened in the group. I was able to catch myself more quickly and did not feel such a strong urge to protect everyone.

February 6 (Sixth Session)

A girl, Sandy, was very interested in joining our group and, because she was a good friend of the other members, I considered it and brought it up in group. I encouraged the group to state their feelings. The group had very divided reactions. Kim said, "There is no way I'm going to stay in this group if Sandy comes here . . . it's either her or me!" I reminded the group that they are in control. I told them that this is their group and that they are the ones who make the rules, and that the decision about Sandy is up to them. Rachel said that she liked Sandy, but that she knew that Sandy already came to the Collaborative for individual counseling. "She already gets to come down all of the time, so why should she get to come when we are here?" I made a demand for work and asked for clarification. Rachel stated that it is not fair that some people get to come to talk one-on-one whenever they want, but that they themselves can come only one time a week for only one period. Mary said that she likes Sandy also, but that she has too many problems and would not fit in with our group.

I missed the racial issue that came up in Lisa's next statement because I was so wrapped in the issue at hand. Lisa (who is African American like Mary) said to her, "You dumb nigger, what you think this group is for, anyway?" I used the current issue to talk about how they may be feeling about the group. I told the girls that it is OK if they want to keep the group the way it is now, and that they all seemed to be happy with the way it has been going. I then suggested that many of them need a place to come and talk about their feelings and that they've found this to be a good place to do that. Rachel (sitting next to me) said that she was glad that they could keep me "all to themselves." Lisa said, "I don't think that's fair; we don't need to be here as much as Sandy does . . . I don't see why this is so important to you, Rachel."

I verbalized the feelings that appeared to be present. I said I think that you are all saying that you don't want Sandy in the group, because you all need this group for yourselves and that, because you like it so much, you would rather not let someone new in. We have a great group here and you are happy with who we have in the group now. It's not easy to show that you need something and like something. Sometimes when you are a teenager you need to be really independent and don't want to rely on anyone. That's OK to do; it means that you are growing up! But it's also OK to need to talk about these feelings and to need your friends. Lisa said that she could not wait to grow up so that she could move out of the house and be on her own. I focused on what she was saying. Mary said yeah, she didn't always like it at home either, so growing up and moving out as soon as possible was a good idea. I made a demand for work. I asked them what it was like for them at home and how it felt to want to leave.

As soon as a reason for scapegoating was identified, the group steered away from Rachel and did not seem to need to scapegoat her. Instead, they began discussing their home situations and saying to me indirectly that they did, indeed, need someone to talk to about growing up. They were able to begin to show me their individual dependency needs and not feel like they had to scapegoat Rachel for outwardly showing hers.

Current Status of the Problem

Where It Stands Now

The group has entered the intimacy stage and, although power and control remain essential issues in the group, they are not issues that dominate our entire group sessions. We are able to do "real work" and discuss issues that they want to talk about. Scapegoating still occurs at times, but I am able to recognize it and address it at some level. I have found that, when I call attention to the scapegoating, it is no longer an issue (at least at that time). Rachel has been integrated into the group more often and has not been in the role of the scapegoat in our last few sessions. The group is able to discuss issues that are of concern to them, such as boys, friendship, and the violence that they frequently see in their neighborhoods.

Other issues are still very difficult for them to talk about, such as racism, what it's like to be black or Hispanic in the city, and the fact that I am a middle-class, white worker in a group for minority girls. The theme of authority remains an issue for the group, as they have a difficult time understanding that they have control of this group. I need to work on letting them know this more often. It is when the members fully understand and accept the purpose of the group that they will no longer need the role of the scapegoat and will be able to move completely into the stage of intimacy.

Strategies for Intervention

- I will be aware of the group's occasional need for a scapegoat and will investigate the reasons behind such a need.
- I will verbalize and bring out in the open issues that are hidden and are under the surface.

- I will continue to make demands for work and challenge the group to explore their feelings on issues that are difficult for them to discuss.
- I will let the members know that the group and I are there for them and that it is OK to express dependency needs.
- I will try to make myself and the group available on an occasional Saturday and vacation day so that the members recognize that the group is also important to me.
- I will continue to address the power and control issues that the group has and will let them know that the group belongs to them.
- I will empower both the individual members and the group to feel comfortable with both their emerging feelings of independence and their dependency needs.
- I will challenge the group about their need for the role of a scapegoat and bring to the surface my feelings about what is happening.
- I will encourage Rachel's need to be dependent on me and the group, yet at the same time I will look for meaning in her need to take on this role.
- I will make quicker verbalizations of what I am observing, pointing my impressions out to the group.
- I will continue to make the group aware of the fact that I'll be leaving in May and will challenge them to discuss their feelings about this.

Note that this student-worker identifies race as an issue for the girls in their lives and an issue between the girls and herself. She even includes it in her assessment of where the problem stands; however, she identifies it as an issue that the members are having difficulty discussing. However, her list of strategies for intervention does not include any in this area. This is an agenda item for her professional growth. Her struggle in dealing with this crucial issue is not uncommon, and she will need support and supervision to recognize that her group members' difficulty in exploring the potentially explosive area of race reflects her own reluctance. When they are clear that she is ready, they will respond. This would be important to free her to attend to the meaning of the clues that emerge, including the African American member's use of the self-derogatory phrase "dumb nigger" to refer to the scapegoat.

By understanding the dynamics of scapegoating, the worker can more easily avoid the trap of siding with either the individual or the group. This natural response misses the essential message: that the group and the scapegoat are using the process as a means of raising a theme of concern. The process can best be understood as an attempt, albeit maladaptive, to offer a theme of concern. Because scapegoating may be the only way the group members know to deal with their thoughts and feelings, the worker should not get too upset with either the group or the scapegoat. The worker's task involves helping the group and the scapegoat to recognize their patterns and helping them find a new way of dealing with concerns common to both. By viewing both the individual and the group as clients in need, the worker can become better at understanding and empathizing with the feelings the two share.

Dealing With the Scapegoating Pattern

Work with the scapegoating pattern involves several steps. First, the worker observes the pattern over time. Second, the worker must understand his or her own feelings in the situation to avoid siding with or against the scapegoat. By using the tuning-in skill, the worker can attempt to search out the potential connections between the scapegoat and the group. If the worker is not clear about these, he or she can ask the group to reflect on the question. The next step involves pointing out the pattern to the group and the scapegoat. Thus, the worker asks the group to look at its way of working and to begin the struggle to find a more positive adaptive process.

When workers challenge this scapegoating process, they must not criticize either the group or the scapegoat for having developed this way of dealing with their underlying feelings. In fact, the capacity for empathy and understanding of how hard it is to face these feelings is the very thing that allows the worker to make this demand for work. This demand includes two tasks: asking the group to consider why they are scapegoating and asking the scapegoat to reflect on reasons for volunteering for the role. Discussion of this process is designed to free the members to explore further their underlying feelings. It would be a mistake to support ongoing discussions of the individual's life pattern of being a scapegoat or the group's analysis of its process. When the discussion is honest, invested with feeling, and touching all the members, then the group will no longer need a scapegoat. The discussion may help them moderate their harsh judgments of themselves that lead to the need for a scapegoat. In turn, the scapegoat may discover his or her feelings are not unique.

The Deviant Member

One of the most difficult clients for workers to deal with is the *deviant member*. In this discussion, the term is used broadly to describe a member whose behavior deviates from the general norm of the group. This deviation can range from extremely inappropriate and disconnected behavior (as in a participant who refuses to stop talking at the first meeting or a member who manifests psychotic behavior) to one whose actions deviate only mildly or sporadically (as in a member who stares out the window while the rest of the group is deeply involved in a discussion). In my practice, I have made two major assumptions about such behavior. First, deviant behavior is always a form of communication. The worker's problem lies in figuring out what the member is saying. This difficulty is compounded by the fact that workers often experience the deviance as directed toward themselves, thus activating powerful emotions in the workers. For example, workers may see acting-out behavior in a children's group as testing their authority. Second, deviant behavior in a group may be expressing a communication that has meaning for the group as a whole. That is, just as the group may use a scapegoat as a means of dealing with difficult feelings, a deviant member may be serving an important social role for other group members. This assumption is related to the view of the group as a dynamic system. In this section we explore these two assumptions.

Again, we can consider deviant behavior on a continuum ranging from extreme to slight. On the extreme end would be a client or group member who evinces bizarre behavior that is totally inappropriate for the group. This can happen on occasions when meetings are open to the community or screening of prospective members has not taken place. When this happens in a first session, the impact on the worker and the group is profound. As the member speaks, one can sense the group shrinking in embarrassment and at times in fear. The leader needs to take responsibility for gently but firmly asking the member to withhold comment or, in extreme cases, to leave the session. Group members are not prepared, in an early session, to deal with extreme deviance and therefore depend on the group worker to clarify the boundaries and to enforce the limits if needed.

Extreme Versus Mild Deviance

In one such example, a woman attending a foster parent recruitment session responded to the worker's opening contract statement and requests for group feedback by beginning a long, and essentially unrelated, tale of personal tragedy. When the worker tried repeatedly to clarify the contract or to discover how the woman's concerns might relate to the discussion, she met with no success. The woman refused to allow others to speak and went on in detail about her personal problems and her fears that people were after her—even that the room was bugged. The discomfort in the eyes of the group members was clear. The worker, herself uncomfortable, finally moved to control the situation.

WORKER: Mrs. Pane, it is obvious that you're having a tough time right now, but I simply can't let you continue to use this group meeting to discuss it. I'll have to ask you to leave, but I would be glad to talk with you further about your concerns at another time.

MRS. PANE: You f—ing workers are all alike. You don't give a s—t about us, you're no different from the rest. You took my kids away, and I want them back.

WORKER: I'm sorry, Mrs. Pane, I can't talk with you now about that. You will have to leave, and I can discuss this with you tomorrow.

Mrs. Pane finally left, and the worker turned to the group to acknowledge how upset she was feeling about what had just happened. The group members expressed their own feelings. After emotions had settled, the worker picked up the group members' reactions to Mrs. Pane as a parent of children in the care of the agency. This led to a discussion of parents, their feelings about placements, and contacts between natural parents and foster parents. The worker followed up the next day with Mrs. Pane and did get to see her. There was a long, sometimes rambling and disjointed conversation during which the worker consistently tried to reach Mrs. Pane and acknowledge her feelings. Mrs. Pane turned to the worker as she left and said, "I'm sorry for what I said last night. You know it's just that I'm so angry—I miss my kids so much." Mrs. Pane's behavior at the meeting was an extreme example of the use of deviant behavior to express deeply held feelings. The worker could not allow the session to be captured by Mrs. Pane and, using all of her courage, she protected the group's contract.

Most workers do not experience such extremes of deviant behavior. This example has been included because workers often fear that such an experience will happen to them and because it demonstrates how even bizarre behavior contains a message for the worker. On the other end of the continuum is an example drawn from another group for foster parents who already had children in their homes. The worker was well into the presentation of introductory material on the agency and fostering policies, when a member arrived. She was dressed elaborately, wore a big hat, and sauntered up to the front of the room. All eyes in the group followed her as she made a grand entrance. The worker was shaken by her entry but continued to speak. As the woman sat there, the worker noticed what appeared to be a scowl on her face and occasional grimaces in response to the worker's comments. The worker later described how she tended to "speak to this member" as the evening drew on. After the session, unable to contain herself because of the implied negative behavior, the worker inquired why the member seemed so antagonistic. The member, who had not said a word during the evening, was surprised by the worker's question. She explained that she was not angry at all, and that in fact, she was having a really hard time with her new foster child, because it was her first time fostering, and she was looking forward to getting help from these sessions.

Reaching for the Underlying Message of Deviant Behavior

It is striking how often group leaders are surprised to find relatively normal reactions and feelings underlying initial deviant behavior that they have taken as personal attacks. For example, a group member whose first comment is to challenge the need for the group itself or who responds defensively about his own need for help may seem deviant at first but not later, after the source of the behavior comes to light. All that is needed, at times, is to confront the group members directly and to ask about the meaning of the behavior. Two skills are involved: the ability to tolerate deviant behavior and the ability to reach for the underlying message. Consider the following example from a group for children having trouble in school. The meetings were held at the school in the afternoon, and John started acting up as he entered the meeting room. He picked a fight with Jim, knocked over the desk, and appeared ready to tackle the group worker next.

WORKER: John, what the hell is up? You have been roaring mad since you walked in here. (John remains silent, glaring with his fists clenched.) Did you just come from a fight with someone? Or was it Mr. Smith [the teacher]? Did you have an argument with him?

JOHN: (Still angry, but slightly more relaxed) He's always picking on me, the bastard.

WORKER: OK, now slow down and tell me what happened. Maybe we can help you on this one. That's what the group is all about.

The worker was able to reach for the meaning behind this behavior, instead of getting caught up in a "battle of wills" with John, because he understood his own function, was clear about the purpose of the group, and understood that children often raise their problems indirectly by acting out. The group member does not always immediately respond to the worker's efforts to reach past the behavior; however, he often understands the worker's meaning and will sometimes pick up the invitation later. Clarity of function is important, because if the worker is concentrating solely on his limit-setting function (as in stopping the fight), he may miss the other part of the work. The skill often involves setting the limit and reaching for the meaning of the behavior at exactly the same time.

Deviant Behavior as a Functional Role

As mentioned earlier, deviant behavior may in some way reflect the feelings of the group-as-a-whole. This notion stems from the idea of the group as a dynamic system, in that the movement of one member is somewhat affected by the movements of the others. The deviant member can be viewed as simply a member who, for various reasons, feels a particular concern or emotion more strongly than the others in the group do. This greater sense of urgency causes the deviant member to express the more widely held feeling, often in an indirect manner.

Schwartz (1961) refers to the function of the deviant member in the client group as follows:

> Such clients often play an important role in the group—expressing ideas that others may feel but be afraid to express, catalyzing issues more quickly, bringing out the negatives that need to be examined, etc. This helped us to see that such members should not immediately be thought of as "enemies" of the group, diverting it from its purposes, but as clients with needs of their own, and that these needs are often dramatic and exaggerated versions of those of the other group members. (p. 11)

It is critical, therefore, that the group leader not dismiss a deviant group member too quickly as simply acting out a personal problem. This would constitute the mistake of attempting to understand the movements of one member of a dynamic system (the group) apart from the movements of other members of the system. While this member may bring this particular social role to bear in all groups, one cannot understand him or her simply as a separate entity. The first hypothesis should always be that the member may be speaking for the group-as-a-whole. In the first session of the couples' group described in detail earlier, the member (Lou) who attacked "professionals" was carrying out the important task of dealing with the authority theme, an issue for the whole group.

The following examples demonstrate two specific ways in which deviant behavior operates functionally: in opening up a discussion of group function and in deepening the work already in progress.

Opening a Discussion of the Group's Functioning In the following excerpt, a member attacks the purpose of the group in a counseling session at a psychiatric hospital:

MR. WRIGHT: (Who has been quiet for most of the first two sessions, although he seemed to have a critical look on his face) I think this is really all a bunch of crap! How in the hell is it going to do us any good sitting around and talking like this?

MRS. SAMUELS: Well, you know, you really haven't had much to say. Maybe if you spoke up, it would be more worthwhile.

For most inexperienced workers, the force of the attack would be taken personally because the worker felt fully responsible for the success of the group. It would not be unusual for the worker to view Mr. Wright as negative, hostile, and resistant and to set out to challenge him or encourage the group members to "take him on." For example, "Mr. Wright doesn't seem to think the group is too helpful. Do the others feel that way, or do they feel the way Mrs. Samuels does?" If Mr. Wright's behavior is viewed in the context of the dynamic interaction, and if the worker sees him as a potential ally, he might instead help him to elaborate.

WORKER: I think it's important that we hear Mr. Wright out on this. If there are problems with the group, maybe we can work them out if we can talk about them. What's bothering you about the group?

MR. WRIGHT: Well, for one thing, I don't think we are leveling with each other. We're not really saying what's on our minds. Everybody is too busy trying to impress each other to be honest.

WORKER: You know, that often happens in the first few sessions of a new group. People are unsure of what to expect. How about it, have any of the others of you felt that way?

MR. PETERS: I didn't last week, but this week I thought the discussion was a bit superficial.

By treating the deviant member as an ally rather than as an enemy, the worker gave permission for the group to begin a frank discussion of how they were working. Others in the group felt the freedom to express their dissatisfaction, and as a result, the members began to take responsibility for making their group more effective. This kind of discussion is essential for all groups, but it is often considered impolite to be direct in such areas. Members feel they do not want to "hurt the worker's feelings." As the group proceeded, the worker found that Mr. Wright, rather than not wanting to work, had several pressing issues he wished to deal with. His sense of urgency had forced him to speak out. Often in a group, the member who seems most negative and angry is the one who wants to work the hardest. It is easy to understand, however, how the worker's feelings might make it hard to see Mr. Wright in a more positive way.

Deepening a Discussion Expressions of deviant positions in a group are often a lever for the group leader to deepen a discussion. For example, in one group on parenting skills, a major argument occurred when Mr. Thomas expressed the view that "all of this talk about worrying about the kids' feelings is nice for social workers but doesn't make sense for parents. Sometimes, the back of the hand is what they need." The other members pounced on Mr. Thomas, and a verbal battle royal ensued. Once again, for new workers who are not clear about their function, the expression of an idea that ran counter to their view of good parenting would arouse a strong reaction. The new worker would be particularly angered by the jibe about social workers and might set out to "educate" Mr. Thomas. Instead, this worker saw Mr. Thomas as expressing a feeling that in part was true for all the parents but was not considered "proper" in this group. The worker reached to support Mr. Thomas:

WORKER: You are all attacking Mr. Thomas's position quite strongly; however, I have a hunch there must be many times when all of you feel the same way. Am I right? (Silence.)
MR. FISK: There are times when the only feelings I'm interested in are the ones he has on his behind when I let him have one.

With the worker's help, Mr. Thomas gave permission for the parents to begin to discuss the reality of parenting, which includes anger, loss of temper, and frustration. The worker continued by asking Mr. Thomas why he felt he had to express this position so strongly.

WORKER: You know, Mr. Thomas, you come on so strong with this position, and yet you don't strike me as someone who doesn't care about how his kids feel. How come?
MR. THOMAS: (Quietly, looking down as he spoke) Feelings can hurt too much.
WORKER: What do you mean?
MR. THOMAS: It wasn't easy to talk with my kids when their mother died.
WORKER: (After a silence) You really know what that is like, don't you? (Mr. Thomas just nodded.)
MR. SIMCOE: I've never had to handle something that tough, but I know what you mean about it being hard to listen when your kids are pouring out the hurt.

In summary, the deviant member who challenges the authority of the leader provides negative feedback on the work of the group, raises a point of view contrary to the group's norm, or fights strongly and with emotion for a position may be playing an important functional role in the dynamic system of the group. The deviant member can be an ally for the worker if the worker can deal with personal feelings and then listen to the deviant member as a messenger from the group. In this last example, we can see how a deviant member can turn into an active participant over time.

The Internal Leader: Ally or Enemy?

Group workers who are unsure of their function often experience internal leaders as a threat to their own authority, even viewing them as deviant members. Actually, if the mutual-aid process is central to the work, workers know that the work is going well when an internal leader emerges. The mistake of viewing the internal leader as a deviant member is most evident in work with teenagers and children, when the internal leader challenges the authority of the worker.

The following excerpt is from a first meeting of a group I led during my first year of social work professional training. I share this example for several reasons. First, students need to realize that all workers start out with similar feelings, making most of the same mistakes. Many students who read examples of my more recent work with married couples, single parents, or people with AIDS do not know about the many mistakes I made, and still make, during my professional development. Second, this particular group—acting-out adolescents—can be one of the most painful and stressful groups to lead. I still vividly remember dreading the early sessions, which seemed like a perpetual battle of wills—a battle both the group and I were destined to lose. Third, it provides a good illustration of how the worker may at first see an internal leader as "the enemy" rather than as an ally. Finally, it is an example of a community center group in which activities are a central part of the work. These kinds of groups often make up the bulk of early group practice of social workers.

The group consisted of acting-out adolescents (13 and 14 years old) who were members of a community center club. I had been warned that they were a difficult group and that they had given other workers a tough time in the past. Although the group was set up so that the club members planned their own activities, the agency had structured the first night by planning a mass sports program in the gym. The first issue on the group members' minds was "What sort of worker will this be?" but my supervision had mistakenly led me to think that I must "demonstrate my authority in the first session and assert myself as leader," which in effect began the battle of wills.

> Only five boys had shown up by 7:45, so we spent the first 10 minutes talking about the club last year. At this point, Al showed up and completely changed the tone of our meeting. It seemed as if the first five boys had been waiting for the catalyst that had finally arrived. Al was bubbling over about the school football game he had played in that afternoon. It was their first win in 3 years. When I asked how it had gone, he described it abruptly. He then wanted to know what we were doing that night. When I explained the prearranged evening program he became very negative about it. "Rope jumping" (one of the competitive events) "is for girls," he replied. I told him boxers use rope jumping for training, and he replied, "I'm not a boxer, and I'm not a girl." Although the other boys had not been overly enthusiastic about the evening program when I had described it earlier, their tone changed sharply as they agreed with Al.

Lack of clarity of function and initial nervousness led me to defend the program and to see Al as competition. Contracting was unclear, and an important discussion about the role of the worker in relation to the group members was missed because of my own fears and misconceptions. As the meeting proceeded, I got myself deeper into trouble:

I tried to discuss at least next week's program with the guys. Girls from another club started pressing their faces against the window of the door, and before I could stop him, Al was racing to the attack. The contagion was immediate, and what had been a quiet group of boys were now following their leader. I jumped up and asked them to ignore the girls. Instead, they chose to ignore me. I went over to the door, closed it, and politely guided them back to the desk. This time, when they sat down, Al's feet were on the table (one of the wooden-finish types). Five more pairs immediately joined Al's (the testing was in full swing). I asked them to remove their feet, because they could damage the table. Joe and Ken responded, but the others didn't. I tried to maintain a light and firm stand. They slowly responded, stating that last year's leader let them keep their feet up that way. Another said there were a lot of things their leader let them do last year that I probably would not. I said that I would only allow them to do these things that were acceptable to the agency. One of the boys asked me what an agency was. I explained I meant the center (first week of field work and I was already overprofessional). It was time to hit the gym for the games (much to my relief).

It is clear that my sense of function, that of "taming the group," led me to miss important issues. Discussing the last leader's role would have been helpful. In addition, relationships with girls was an emerging and uncomfortable theme for this group, given their age. Al was the only club member to dance with girls later in the evening during the social part of the program. He asked about having a party with a girls' group, and I put off his request by saying, "We would need to plan this ahead of time." Al provided leadership in several areas, expressing the feelings and concerns of the group, but because I missed the importance of his role, a battle over "who owned the group" resulted.

Because I missed the signals, the indirect testing continued. Al led the members in throwing paper around the club room and leaning out of the windows, spitting on other center members as they left. I kept trying to set limits while not allowing myself to get angry (not thought to be professional). Finally, my instincts got the better of me.

I said I would like to say a few words before we finished. I was attempting to reestablish the limits I had set earlier, but my own feelings got the best of me. I explained that this evening was really difficult for me and that probably it was so for them too. I said that if we couldn't relax enough to discuss further programs, there probably wouldn't be any. At this point, I said something that surprised me as I said it. I said their behavior better improve, or they could find themselves a new leader. They replied by saying that compared with the group members who hadn't shown up this evening, they were well behaved. My reaction to this group was mild panic.

It is easy to understand my panic in this situation. My idea of being professional was to be able to "handle" the group without losing my temper. Actually, in these moments at the end of the meeting when I revealed my real feelings, I was starting to develop a working relationship with the group members. After a few more sessions of off-and-on-again testing, I moved to discuss the issue of the authority theme and to help the group members develop their own internal leadership and structure.

I told the boys that because I had been with them for 5 weeks, they might be interested in hearing what I thought about the group. They perked up at this.

Bert said, "You love us," and everyone laughed. I said that during this time I had been able to talk to each one of them individually and seemed to get along well. However, when we got together as a group, we couldn't seem to talk at all, right from the beginning. In spite of what they said, I thought that each one of them was concerned about stealing, acting wise all the time, and being disrespectful. Al said (very seriously this time) that it was different when they were in the group. I asked why that was so. Bert asked all the guys if they had stolen anything, and they all agreed that they had. After some discussion I told them I thought they were really afraid to say what they thought in the group. Bert said he wasn't afraid. I asked about the others. Al mockingly put up his fists and said, "I'm not afraid of anyone in the group." I laughed with the rest and said I thought it was easy to be brave with your fists but that it took a lot more courage to say something you thought the other guys would not like. I said it was their club, and although it was important to me, it was really more important to them. Joel made a wisecrack, but he was silenced by Ken, who said, "That's just the kind of thing he [the worker] was talking about."

As the discussion continued, the boys explained that they often didn't like my suggestions for activities, and I encouraged them to say so in the future, because it was their club. A surprising amount of feeling emerged about the kidding around in the group, much of it directed at one boy who acted out a great deal but was not present that night. They talked about how they could plan their own programs. The group members suggested that I could bring in ideas from other clubs and that they would then decide what they wanted. At this point, Al suggested they have a president. After some discussion about the respective positions, a president (Al), vice-president (Bert), and treasurer (Ken) were elected. A social committee was also formed to speak with the girls' club to discuss a party.

At this point in the meeting, I realized we were actively talking about something with no kidding around and no testing of me. I felt at ease for the first time. I commented to them about this. Al said, "We won't be able to do this all the time." I said I realized this and that there still would be a lot of kidding around. It would be OK as long as they could pull themselves together at times to get their work done. Al said that would be his job, and that I could help by telling them when they got out of hand. I agreed.

At the end of the process recording, I commented that "all of the boys gave me a warm good-bye" as I left the building. From this point on, much of the work shifted to helping the group members develop their own structure. For example, I met with Al before sessions, at his request, to help him plan the agenda and to discuss his problems in chairing the sessions.

These group sessions were a painful initial lesson on the need to clarify my function and recognize the group's internal leadership. I had experienced Al as the groups' deviant member, when in reality, he was their internal leader. I had told them it was their group but, following a different paradigm of practice, I believed it was really my group for implementing my "social work purposes." I encouraged them to plan activities when I already had the "appropriate" activities in mind. I experienced Al as my enemy, when in reality he was my main ally. Chapter 15 includes further illustrations of my work with this group, in which I describe what the group taught me about helping clients to negotiate the system—in this case the community center.

The Gatekeeper

The previous section pointed out that the deviant member is often the one who feels the strongest sense of urgency about a particular issue. In a sense, the deviant behavior is an effort to move the group toward real work. The internal leader often serves this function in a healthier, more direct way. A group can be ambivalent about work in the same way an individual can be, and members can take on the function of expressing that ambivalence for the group. This is sometimes seen in the form of a **gatekeeper** role, in which a member guards the "gates" through which the group must pass for the work to deepen. When the group discussion gets close to a difficult subject, the gatekeeper intervenes to divert the discussion.

In one group, for example, every time the discussion appeared to approach the issue of the worker's authority, one female member would light up a foul-smelling cigar or in some other way attract the group's ire. The group would rise to the bait, and the more difficult authority theme would be dropped. The worker pointed out the pattern, describing what he saw: "You know, it seems to me that every time you folks get close to taking me on, Pat lights up a cigar or says something that gets you onto her back. Am I right about this?" The group rejected the interpretation and turned on the leader with anger, thus beginning to deal with the authority theme. Later in the session, Pat commented that the worker's observation might be accurate, because she had always been fearful of seeing her parents fight and probably had done the same thing in childhood. It was not appropriate in this group to discuss the reasons for the pattern, either Pat's or the group's reasons, nor did the group members need to agree with the observation. The mere statement of the pattern offered the group an opportunity to face the worker directly, and Pat no longer needed to carry out this role.

People often use humor to protect the gates in difficult and painful areas. A group member, usually one who has learned to play this role in most areas of her or his life, will act out, crack a joke, make a face, and so forth in an effort to get the group members and the leader laughing and distracted. Note that humor can also be used to help advance the work of the group and does not always represent a means of gatekeeping. It helps, at times, to be able to laugh when facing painful work. Staff groups, for example, often use macabre humor to deal with their tensions. However, when this the only means of releasing tension, and the underlying feelings resulting from the stresses and traumas are not dealt with, such humor can cause worker burnout rather than preventing it. With the client group, the worker needs to observe the pattern over time and to note the results of the use of humor. If the humor consistently results in an illusion of work, then the gatekeeper function is a likely explanation.

In the following example of gatekeeping through humor, a worker in a residential setting picks up directly on the sexual innuendo involved in an apparently casual conversation in the lounge. The boys are young teens.

FRANK: (Watching a television show) Wow! Look at the build on that broad. Boy, I wish I could meet her after the show.

LOU: You wouldn't know what to do with her if you had her, you big jerk. Besides, your pecker isn't big enough. (At this comment there is general kidding around and teasing of a sexual nature.)

WORKER: You know, you guys kid around a lot about this sex business, but I bet you have a lot of questions on your mind about it—a lot of serious questions.

FRANK: What kind of questions?

WORKER: Well, I'm not sure about your questions, but I bet you are interested in what would make you attractive to women, sexually, and how you actually handle sexual relations as well as other relations with women. It's probably a tough area to talk about seriously.

LOU: My old man never talked to me about sex.

TERRY: (Who has a pattern of clowning in the group) Did you hear the story about the kid who asked his father where he came from? The father gave him a 15-minute sex talk, and then the kid said, "That's funny, and Jimmy comes from Chicago." (Some of the boys laughed and others groaned.) I got another good one . . .

WORKER: Hold it, Terry! There you go again. Every time we get to some serious discussions in tough areas, you start with the jokes. And the rest of you guys go right along with it. What's wrong? Is it tough to talk about sex without kidding around?

The boys returned to the conversation with several serious questions specifically related to sex, as well as others related to the whole question of intimacy with women. Terry sat quietly during the discussion and did not participate. The worker later talked alone with Terry about his discomfort in such discussions. The worker asked if it was related to some of his difficult sexual experiences. Terry's mother had been a prostitute, and he had been a male prostitute for a time when he was 12. He could not talk about this in front of the other boys, and the worker had respected this. In most cases the gatekeeper carries out this functional role because he feels the resistance aspect of the group's ambivalence a bit more strongly than the rest of the members do. In a sense he is the spokesman for this feeling, in the same way the internal leader or the deviant may speak for the opposite pole.

The Defensive Member

Defensiveness represents its own social role, although other social roles may involve it. The defensive member refuses to admit there is a problem, to accept responsibility for his or her part in a problem, or to take suggestions or help from the group after a problem has been raised. Group members often respond to a defensive member by attacking the defense and then eventually giving up and ignoring her or him.

Lewin (1951) described a model for change that can be applied to defensive members on several levels—individual, group, family, organizational. Stated simply, the individual personality in relation to its environment has developed a **quasi-stationary social equilibrium** in which some form of balance has been worked out. For the defensive member, denial has worked as a way of dealing with painful problems. The three steps for change involve "unfreezing" this equilibrium, moving into a phase of disequilibrium, and freezing at a new quasi-stationary equilibrium. The important point is that defenses have value to the individual, and to expect the unfreezing process to be easy misses the essence of the dynamics. The more serious the issue—the more deeply the individual feels a challenge to the sense of the core self—the more rigid the defense. Like resistance, a group member's defensiveness is a signal that the work is real. To begin the unfreezing process, the worker or group must challenge the individual. However, the individual will need all the support, understanding, and help possible to translate unfreezing into movement and then into a new level of quasi-equilibrium.

Workers often underestimate the difficulty of what they and group members are asking people to do when calling them to move past defensiveness and denial. The difficulty of this process needs to be respected. Only a delicate integration of support and demand can create the conditions in which the group member may feel free enough to let down the barriers.

A Defensive Father in a Parents' Group

In the example that follows, a father has described a conflict with his 18-year-old son that has resulted in the son's leaving home and the family's being in turmoil. As the situation plays out in some detail, other parents point out how the father has been stubborn and failed to listen to what his son is saying. They try to pin him down to alternative ways of relating, but to each he responds in a typical "yes, but . . ." pattern, not able to take in what they are saying. Finally, after a few minutes of this, the group grows silent. The worker intervenes by pointing out the obstacle.

WORKER: It seems to me that what has been going on here is that Ted has raised a problem, you have all been trying to offer some answers, but Ted has been saying, "Yes, but . . ." to each of your suggestions. You look like you are about to give up on him. Are you?

ALICE: We don't seem to be getting anywhere. No matter what anyone says, he has an answer.

WORKER: Ted, I think you must feel a bit backed into a corner by the group. You do seem to have a hard time taking in their ideas. How come?

TED: I don't think they can appreciate my problem. It's not the same as theirs. They all seem to be blaming me for the fight, and that's because they don't understand what it really is like.

WORKER: Maybe it would help if you could tell them how this struggle with your son makes you feel.

TED: I gave this kid so much, raised him since he was a baby, and now he treats his mother and me like we don't matter at all. I did the best I could—doesn't he understand that?

WORKER: I think it's tough when you feel you love your child the way you do and you still see him as your kid, but he seems to want to pull away. You still feel responsible for him but you also feel a bit impotent, can't seem to control him anymore. Can any of you appreciate what Ted is feeling right now?

The group members moved to support Ted in his feelings, with others recounting similar experiences and feelings. The focus had shifted for a moment to the common feelings between group members rather than the obstacle that seemed to frustrate them. The worker sensed that Ted needed to feel understood and not be judged harshly by the other parents, precisely because he tended to judge himself more harshly than any of them. Having established this support, the worker reached for the feelings underlying the resistance.

WORKER: Ted, if I were you, I think I would spend a lot of time wondering what went wrong in the relationship. I would be wondering how this could have happened when I had tried so hard—and if I could have done things differently. Is that true for you?

FRAN: (Ted's wife) He stays up nights these days, can't get to sleep because he is so upset.

TED: Sure, it's tough. You try your best, but you always wonder if you should have been around more, worked a little less, had some more time . . . you know?

WORKER: I guess that's what makes it hard for you to believe that anyone else can understand, and you feel so lousy about it yourself. Can the rest of you appreciate that it would be tough to listen if you were in Ted's shoes?

RAY: I think we are in Ted's shoes. When I see him getting stubborn in this group, I see myself and my own defensiveness.

The group discussion focused on how hard it was to take advice in the group, especially when they felt uncertain themselves. As the conversation shifted, the worker could sense Ted physically relaxing and listening. After a while, Ted asked the group to take another crack at his problem. He said, "This is really tough, but I don't want to lose the kid completely."

Often, defensive members need more time than a single session to feel safe enough to "move." Workers will often find that the member has thought deeply, after the meeting, about the way he reacted, so that readiness to change and unfreezing appear in a later session. This is the client's part in the procedure; once again, the worker can only take responsibility for establishing the best possible conditions for change—the rest is up to the client and depends on many factors. One of my studies found that clients' acceptance of a problem contributed to their motivation to change as well as their ability to use help (Shulman, 1991). For some clients, the stress of the issue was so great, or the issue so loaded, that they could not accept any help at that point. Although such situations are frustrating and often sad, they exist. Accepting this is one of the most important things a new worker can do. He or she must avoid taking responsibility for the client's part in the proceedings. Nonetheless, workers often feel guilty because of lack of clarity on this point and feelings of failure, and this guilt leads workers to feel angry at a defensive client for not cooperating. Note in our example that the anger from the other group members appeared to be a result of their seeing some of their own feelings and attitudes exaggerated in the defensiveness of the member. In fact, the more they pushed him, the more they heightened his defensiveness. The issue of the functional role of the defensive member is explored more fully in the next example.

Denial in a Living-With-Cancer Group

The following illustration explores the denial exhibited by cancer patients and family members in a group designed to help them cope with this life-threatening disease. We focus on the role of one defensive member, Al, who helps the group avoid the taboo subject of death. In addition, the members' different responses to the disease of cancer illustrate the impact of gender and ethnicity. The two men in the group, for example, respond by using increased work activity as part of a strong pattern of denial of their emotions about their wives' cancer. At one point, Al says, "You have to understand what it's like to be an engineer. Engineers are used to working with problems that can be resolved, and her cancer is a problem that I can't resolve."

Further, as a Hispanic mother and daughter describe their reactions and those of their husband and father with cancer, we can see a contrast with the white members of the group that reflects the influence of culture, as described by Schaefer and Pozzaglia (1986):

Unlike their uninhibited expression of grief and sadness, Hispanics try to control their anger. This, however, is not necessarily the case with white, middle-class families who are more comfortable in openly expressing their anger at the disease and their frustration with the hospital system. The Hispanic family's strong belief in God and His will is used to explain why the child is ill and minimizes their anger. (pp. 298–299)

The Hispanic father contemplates suicide rather than becoming a burden on his family; his reactions of shame to his diagnosis of cancer can be partly explained by *machismo:* "As macho, he is the head of the family, responsible for their protection and well-being, defender of their honor. His word is his contract" (Devore & Schlesinger, 1991, p. 81).

RECORD OF SERVICE

Client Description and Time Frame

A weekly support and education group for cancer patients and family members. It is a 6-week, time-limited, closed group. The setting is a large teaching hospital, and the group is offered free of charge through the social services department.

Age Range of Members: 30–78 years old. Ten group members are Caucasian American. Two members, a mother and daughter, are Latin American. There are ten women and two men in the group. There are five patients and seven family members.

Dates Covered in the Record: February 1 to March 8.

Description of the Problem

The problem is the group's avoidance of painful issues that would lead to a discussion of the taboo subject of death. The taboo needs to be breached so that the group may begin to redefine its norms to include direct discussion of the reality of cancer. Though there is reality-based discussion of living with cancer, there is resistance to discussing the reality of dying from cancer. An additional problem is our collusion as coleaders in the process of avoidance.

How the Problem Came to the Attention of the Worker(s)

As an observer of a previous 6-week cancer group, I was witness to and aware of the incredible courage and depth of hope displayed by two patients in the group. They and their struggle were an inspiration. As the group ended, I wondered if they had gotten what they needed from the group. I had a sense that they had never faced up to the harsh reality and finality of cancer as they had maybe hoped they would in the group. I felt they may have been cheated of an opportunity to confront the reality of the disease. Though raising the more painful issues seemed taboo, I suspect it is part of the reason the group members chose to attend the group. As a coleader of this new group, though aware of the issue of false hope, I found myself again caught up in the gifts of inspiration shared among members. In an attempt to refocus the group on more painful issues, I felt a resistance to their discussion and retreated from making interventions, thus colluding with group members in their hopefulness and avoiding discussion of the virtues (?) of cancer.

Summary of the Work

February 1

I overlooked the group's response to a member as an introduction of a major group issue: the desire to resolve the unreasonable. I kept my observation to myself. Rosina and her mother, Maria, talked quite a bit about their father and husband, who had lost interest in everything since his diagnosis of cancer. They talked about what he had been like before cancer and how he had changed. People were trying to be very helpful and supportive in giving advice to them. I wondered if the members responded this way because if you give advice and people accept it then you have helped and possibly resolved a problem—the very thing you cannot do with cancer.

I failed to reach for the feelings underlying the statement of hope. Faith, a daughter of a nonlocal patient, said her mother described cancer as the great liberator and she said that this part of the disease was contagious. Both she and her mother were becoming more assertive as well as expressive. She talked about friends who are there for her parents and how wonderful they are. I wondered (to myself) what about cancer was liberating.

I allowed the group to gloss over the pain and return to the hope. I succumbed to my own fear of discussion of death. Frances (a patient attending the group with her daughter, and the widow of a cancer victim) began to talk about her husband after Rosina said her father would rather have died of a heart attack than lived feeling like a burden to her and her mother. Frances said her husband felt the same way. He had lung cancer (here, she pointed to Sara, who has lung cancer) and was given a year to live. He died in 7 months. She said she was working when he was first diagnosed, but one day she came home and found him trying to commit suicide. She said, "We held each other and cried and I said 'We're going to fight this thing on my shirttails' . . . and we did . . . one day at a time." Sara, always an inspiration, said, "You need to fight, you need to find something to make every day count," and she began to talk to Rosina and Maria about ways they could help their father and husband make every day count. I wondered (to myself) if the return to advice giving was the group's response to the pain of Frances' disclosure about her own husband's painful and conflicted death.

February 15

I failed to recognize the underlying disappointment that there may be no satisfactory resolution and to note the pain masked by a hopeful discussion of drugs and experts. As in the two previous groups, Doris talked about her allergic reaction to the chemotherapy drugs. She focused on how much she had been "digging" for information, calling the manufacturer and even the inventor. She was discouraged to find out she was the only patient to have such a severe reaction to the drug, but she seemed to feel better by taking some action. Group members seemed to admire her initiative.

I missed the connection of an individual's themes to the purpose of the group. Al, Doris' husband, talked about what a hard week it had been for him. He had overslept that morning after working night and day for 3 weeks on a contract that was meant to be in the mail that day.

I missed the group's attempt to resolve the problem with more advice about drugs and experts. I was caught up in the hope of resolution. Faith asked Doris if the dosage of the drug might be diluted. Christine shared that her mother was participating in a drug study and gave Doris the name of the physician conducting it.

I thought about reaching for feelings, but I held back. Doris talked about having no pain and discomfort except for the rash on her legs. I wondered what it was like for her to have no pain and discomfort and still be sick with colon cancer.

I would have liked to support a group member's progress, but I remained silent. Faith read a poem from her mother. She began to cry as she read it. She reiterated her mother's description of cancer as a blessed, terrible happening. Faith said she had been crying daily for 10 weeks. She said in all that time she thinks it never quite sunk in that her mother has cancer and she said the word that she previously could not say. She said she was angry about it.

I attempted to generalize to the rest of the group. I said I wondered if anger was something they had all experienced. There were many nods. Maria asked Faith who she was angry at and why she was angry. Faith talked about how her mother had not taken care of herself, though she did not directly say she was angry at her mother. She said she did not know whether or not to blame God. Al said, "You can't blame the person with the disease and you can't blame God. It's nobody's fault, it just happens." Christine asked Maria if she was angry. Maria said, "No, never." She had never been angry at God or her husband. She talked about how wonderful their life had been and said she thought God needed to give them some pain and that whatever happened they would accept. Rosina said, "You haven't always felt this way. In the beginning you were really depressed and feeling badly when he was sick." Maria said, "That's true." Rosina said she even got sympathy pains. Maria said they don't talk that much about his cancer. They just hold hands and that's enough; they don't have to talk about cancer.

Al said he understood where she was coming from, but that you cannot sacrifice and change your life because of your husband's illness. He said, "I haven't. I go to work and do what I need to do and, of course, I've given up some things." "Not many," Doris said. "No, not many," he said, "You just have to go on with your life, otherwise you'll just get depressed. You just can't let yourself get depressed." I attempted to bring the reality of the disease into the room and connect his intellectual discussion with the emotions he was trying to avoid. I said, "I understand what you're saying about needing to have a life of your own, but what do you do with the feelings? You may not want to get depressed, but the disease is depressing." Al responded somewhat angrily, saying, "I only allow myself 15 minutes of depression a year. Any more than 15 minutes is too long."

I backed off in response to his response and remained silent. Al said he gets depressed around Christmas but always brings himself out of it. Grace (coleader) said his feelings around Doris's disease were coming out somehow and that it sounded like he was avoiding them by being away so much. He denied this and talked about how crucial it is that he put in the evening and weekend hours at work. Christine said, "With all due respect, I don't know about your relationship, and I think I'm talking to you so much because I'm thinking of my parent (her mother has colon cancer like Doris), but I think Doris is asking you to spend more time with her and be there more."

All group members got involved in this discussion, speaking for Doris to Al who, when people said they did not want to attack him, responded by saying this was nothing, he was used to handling this kind of argument at work all the time. He defended his need to be at work. Sara said, "But Doris needs you there too." I missed an opportunity to ask if Al may have been speaking for the whole group and allowed the discussion to return to a struggle between the group and Al.

February 22
I attempted to connect present group activity and previous content with the issue of avoidance. Al talked for a while about the pressures on him at work. He talked about having spent 35 years building his career. Sharon (Frances' daughter) said, "I'm sitting here listening to you, Al, and I'm not sure what went on last week (she and

her mother had been absent because of poor weather), but I can say that I see a lot of myself in how you're dealing with this." She talked about when her father had gotten sick. She was in Washington and her parents were in Pennsylvania. She talked about the sense of relief every time she got on the plane to go back to D.C. She did not want to and couldn't face her father's illness. She said when her mother called and said, "You'd better come," she even waited then to go to Pennsylvania. She said, "I know about career pressures. I work for an agency that regulates the type of company you work for and I know about those pressures. When my mother got sick, it was the same time that a promotion came up that I'd been working toward for years and I passed it up because I needed to be with my mother."

I failed to point out that Al's need to see himself as different was a common reaction to defend against a painful reality. Al said, "But there's a difference. You're at the beginning of your career—I'm in the last 10 years of it when my entire pension and retirement are determined." Sharon said, "None of us know if we're even going to be here tomorrow."

At that point, Sylvia and Sid came in with their daughter, Laura (not a member of the group). Grace briefed them on what was going on, and everyone quickly introduced themselves. Sid asked what they had missed last week, because they had also been absent. Al laughed as he said, "They all ganged up on me." He had already been through this with the other people who'd been absent the previous week. Sid said he was sorry he'd missed it. Al said, "So you could join in?" Sid said, "Who knows, maybe I would have joined in with you against everyone else." (These two were the only men in the group.) Frances asked Sylvia (the patient) how she was doing. She said her treatment had been going well, though she had been sleeping a lot. Laura said that she always sleeps a lot and said she even falls asleep at movies.

Then Doris and Al got into a discussion with them about how he loves movies and she hates to go to them. I said I wondered, as I thought Sharon had been saying to Al, if there was a tendency to avoid thinking, feeling, and talking about cancer—even in the group right now. I wondered if people found that they tended to or felt like avoiding it all. Frances said, "You avoid it and then don't know that you're doing it." Al said, "I'm not avoiding it, it's just my way of coping. You just can't think about it all the time."

I failed to clear a space for Al to be able to connect his feelings about his past losses with his current situation, by my tuning in to Doris's fear of that connection. Al said, "This isn't the first time I've been through it." "But it's not the same," Doris said. "But I was 10 when my father died of cancer," said Al. "You were just a child, it's not the same." "My mother died of leukemia," said Al. "But you weren't in the house, your brother and sister took care of her." Al said, "That's true." I neglected to share my thoughts about how he managed to distance himself from his mother's illness as he seems to be trying to do with Doris. Frances said, "It's different when you're living with the person than if you're away." I said it's different and it's the same. Al said, "No, it's definitely different when you're living with the person."

I mistook Sylvia's successful attempt to steer the conversation away from the topic of how difficult it is to live with a cancer patient as an inappropriate interjection into the conversation. Sylvia asked if anyone had seen the show *20/20* that week. Group members said they had not. Sylvia said it had been about chemotherapy drugs.

I responded to my own desire to avoid pain instead of tuning in to the probable pain of many of the group members. I allowed an eloquent expression of a painful experience to be perceived only as moving and inspiring. Frances asked Maria how her husband was doing. Maria and Rosina looked at each other and Rosina said it had been a discouraging week for them. Her father was no longer responding to the chemotherapy. Maria talked some but mostly cried as Rosina talked about a new lump her father had found behind his ear. Frances said that was the last thing he needed, to find that lump. She said her husband had gotten a great big tumor on his neck and couldn't stand it so she had to shave him. She spoke eloquently about her husband, her experience with him and his death.

I overlooked Frances's own need to confront her own cancer, which she only talked about in terms of beating. The group was engrossed. Al asked, "How do you do it?" Frances looked at him and said, "Sometimes you just hold each other and cry." She said again, "I told him to grab on to my shirttails and we'll make it though this thing." After a while her husband had said, "I'm not going to make it." She told the story of how he had died, in the hospital, not at home. I wondered how everyone felt. I imagined that everyone was moved by Frances's story but that they also related it to themselves or their own loved one. We missed the boat.

March 1
Grace mentioned that this was the fifth group and that we had one more left before the end. Doris said, "That's a bummer," and that was all that was said by her or anyone about the group ending. I failed to tune in and connect Al's feelings to Doris's illness. Al talked about what a tough couple of weeks it had been. He said it had been emotionally draining, and he attributed it mostly to work.

I attempted to confront the group's denial around its ending, but I was unable to connect their difficulty in confronting the group's end with how it related to cancer and the pain of having to say untimely good-byes. In the middle of the group, I said that Doris had said it was "a bummer" that the group was ending next week and I wondered how others were feeling about it. After an attempt to confront the denial, I copped out and colluded with it, allowing their discussion of how they could keep the group going. Sid asked if it could be extended. Doris said that it was a bummer and that she always felt better after the group. Then everyone talked about ideas for how it could continue rather than talking about what it was like that it was ending. I wished I had said, "But this group as it exists now is ending next week."

Grace said how the tone of the group seemed different tonight and wondered if it had anything to do with the two unexplained empty chairs. I missed the opportunity to comment on the very depressing reality and finality of cancer that group members were now unavoidably facing in the form of two glaringly empty chairs and to ask how it related to themselves. Rosina and her mother, Maria, were unexplainably absent after having spoken of their father and husband's turn for the worse the previous week. Frances, often the "cheerleader" and major source of group inspiration, said they were occupying her mind. The conversation for the next 10 minutes revolved around the group's concern for the missing members and their loved one.

March 6
I listened intently to information I wished had been shared earlier in the 6 weeks. I felt sad that I had not helped facilitate its earlier entrance into the group. At the end, Christine talked about what had gotten her to come to the group. She said she didn't know if people could tell what kind of person she was, but that she went on a cross-country bike trip alone and hiked and camped and was very independent. She's also organized and likes to keep things in order and be healthy. She said a few weeks after hearing her mother's diagnosis she had a terrible headache one night

and realized she hadn't eaten in 3 days. She said she made some cream of wheat but couldn't eat it. She looked around her apartment. There were clothes in every room and dirty dishes in the sink. She said she didn't know who was living in her apartment. She saw the flyer the next day and said, "I've got to get into that group."

I regretted that I had not trusted and acted on my instincts, which told me that this group was not dealing directly enough with the issue of death. Christine said the group had been keeping her in touch with the disease, but that she wasn't really facing that her mother could die from this. She said she talked to her boyfriend and he got so upset and said to her, "I can't believe you're in this group and you're not dealing with death." She said it as if she were the only one in the group who was not. I looked at Grace and thought that Christine said what I had been thinking throughout the 6 weeks of group. We had 5 minutes left of our final group. Sadly, this group did not confront death.

Current Status of the Problem

Where It Stands Now

This group ended, though they have made a commitment to informally continue their meetings. Possibly they will begin to confront their own avoidance, particularly if members begin to become sick. I am looking forward to the start of another 6-week group March 22. I hope to be more cognizant of the ways in which avoidance surfaces and be more assertive in noting and helping the group confront their avoidance without letting the discussion drop. I am also more acutely aware of how attractive it is to collude with the hope of group members as a defense against not only their fear death and dying but mine as well. I want to support their struggle to heal from the disease without cheating them of an opportunity to talk openly about the painful reality of cancer. Having taken a closer look at the issues of avoidance, I feel better prepared to facilitate that process.

Strategies for Intervention

- Be more active about listening for and speaking to the group's underlying messages as they relate to cancer.
- Point out a pattern of flight and be persistent in raising the issue.
- Believe that death is something that group members are thinking about, then raise the issue, breach the taboo, and bring it into the group for discussion.
- Communicate with my coleader about my need to confront the issue of avoidance.
- Notice my own discomfort with discussing taboo areas and share it with the group in an effort to help group members free up the energy that is bound up in their discomfort.
- Do not fall into the trap of believing that group members are doing my job for me by asking questions of each other.

The worker in this illustration has used the experience to deepen her understanding about her clients and herself. Typical of new workers, she overly criticizes her work, focusing on what she did not do while not crediting herself enough for what she accomplished. A little guilt is helpful for professional growth; however, workers should not undervalue their work along the way.

In exploring the worker's hesitancy about dealing with the subject of death, you may have noticed a piece missing—the support system for staff that is essential in such emotionally draining practice. Case-related stressors on staff can directly affect practice (Shulman, 1991). Davidson (1985) examined the impact of the special stresses affecting social workers who work with cancer patients and their families. He hypothesized that workers experience their work as stressful and lack adequate support to help them cope with the emotional impact of working with clients affected by a chronic and life-threatening illness. Pilsecker (1979) found that social workers, like other hospital staff, used strategies to deal with their painful emotions, including reduction of their direct involvement with patients. By recognizing, accepting, and trying to meet their own needs, social workers can better support their clients.

The Quiet Member

The **quiet member** is one who remains noticeably silent over a an extended period of time. In small groups the worker and the other group members notice after only a few sessions that someone has said very little or nothing at all. A quiet member can create problems for the group, because they do not know what thinking and feeling goes on behind the facade. Group members will tend to believe that the quiet member is sitting in judgment of them, does not share their problems, or feels that others in the group talk too much. Workers, too, often grow uncomfortable, feeling that a member who is not speaking may not be involved.

The silence of a member in a group is similar to the silence in an interview. It is a form of communication that, as we have seen, can be difficult to understand. For some group members, it simply means they are uncomfortable speaking in the group. This is one of the most common explanations. Others feel left out or uninvolved in the group because they feel their problems are different. Some sit in judgment of the group's activity (as was the case in one of the deviant member illustrations). In my experience, sitting in judgment is the least stated reason for silence but interestingly is the interpretation most often put on silence by the active group members and the worker, probably reflecting their own feelings. The two examples presented shortly will examine the quiet member who is afraid to speak, then the quiet member who is left out. First, let us see how the worker can help the group when they react to a quiet member.

Worker Strategies

Believing that all members need to speak equally is a mistake. Social roles developed by individuals include patterns that involve active participation through speech as well as active participation through listening. A member may get a great deal out of a discussion without directly participating. On the other hand, small groups carry a sense of mutual obligation: Members who risk themselves feel that others should do the same. In fact, the silent member often feels uncomfortable about "taking" and not "giving." In addition, many silent members have been so used to being quiet in groups for so long that they have not developed skills required for intervention. Some quiet members say that they are always too slow with their thoughts. The group moves too fast for them, and by the time they can get in, the idea has been stated and the group has moved on. Others say that after they have been quiet in a group for several sessions, they are afraid the group members will "fall out of their chairs if I open my mouth." So although all members should be able to move into a group at their own pace and although equal participation is not a goal, the quiet member often needs some assistance in participating in the group.

Workers sometimes try to deal with this problem either directly through confrontation or indirectly. Each tactic can backfire. For example, if a member has been quiet because of discomfort in speaking, a worker who suddenly turns and says, "I notice you haven't spoken yet in the group and wondered what was on your mind?" may find the member even further immobilized by embarrassment. This direct confrontation may be exactly what quiet members feared would happen.

Indirect means can be just as devastating. The worker has noticed a member not verbally participating in a discussion and turns and says, "What are your ideas about this question, Fran?" A member who is afraid of speaking often finds that any ideas she did have completely disappear in this moment of panic. The other indirect technique, of going around the room to get all opinions when it really is only the quiet person's opinion the worker seeks, may be experienced as manipulative and artificial by members.

The task, then, is to be direct and nonthreatening at the same time. My own strategy is based on the belief that people have a right to their defenses and their characteristic patterns of social interaction. As the worker, my job is to mediate the engagement between each member and the group, so I feel a responsibility to check with a quiet member and see how that engagement is going. If there is an obstacle between the member and the group, I can offer to help.

The Member Who Is Afraid to Speak

As we have seen, members sometimes are merely afraid to speak. They have likely always held back in groups. The following conversation took place after the second meeting of a group. Richard had been particularly silent in both meetings, although his eyes seemed to indicate he was involved.

WORKER: Do you have a second to chat before you go?

RICHARD: Sure, what's up?

WORKER: I noticed you haven't spoken in the group these two sessions, and I thought I would check to see how it was going with you. I know some people take longer than others to get involved, and that's OK. I just wanted to be sure there were no problems.

RICHARD: Well, you caught me.

WORKER: What do you mean?

RICHARD: I managed to get through all of my years in school without ever saying anything in class, and now it looks as if I've been caught.

WORKER: Is it hard for you to speak in a group?

RICHARD: I always feel unsure of what I'm going to say, and by the time I've figured it out, the group has gone past me. Sometimes, it's just hard to get in with everyone speaking at once.

WORKER: Look, I can tell from your eyes that you are actively involved in the discussion. However, after a while, you will probably feel uncomfortable not speaking, and then it will get harder and harder to talk.

RICHARD: That's the way it usually is for me.

WORKER: Not just you, you know. Lots of people feel that way. If you would like, I can help by watching for you and if I sense you want to get into the conversation by the look on your face, or your body, or if you give me the signal, I can reach for you and help you in. Would you like me to do that?

RICHARD: That sounds OK. If I give you a signal, you'll call on me?
WORKER: Exactly! I find that has helped people in the past.

At the next session, Richard avoided the worker's eyes for the first 15 minutes; he was probably afraid of giving a false signal. The discussion was heated and the worker kept glancing at Richard. After a while, the worker noticed Richard leaning forward a bit, with his eyebrows arched, looking at the worker. The worker simply said, "Come on in, Richard." The group paused, and Richard began to speak.

The Member Who Feels Left Out

Another type of quiet member is one who feels that his particular concerns and issues may not be of interest to the group or that his problems differ from those of the others. Such members do not share problems with the group members, and after a while they feel left out and the group members wonder what is happening.

In the following example, Mrs. Trenke, who had shared some difficult experiences with the group, stated that she felt let down when the group did not respond to her feelings. Mrs. Davidson, who had been quiet in the group, supported Mrs. Trenke's comment.

The worker said, "Maybe we could hear how Mrs. Trenke felt let down by the group?" Mrs. Trenke continued, "I felt that I was not a part of the group and that I was not going to get anything out of it." Mrs. Davidson cut in, "Yeah! We didn't listen to other people's troubles because we had enough of our own!" The worker turned to Mrs. Davidson and said, "Have you felt let down and left out of the group?" "No," said Mrs. Davidson, "I don't feel I have the same situation—they have husbands." (Mrs. Bennet reached out and touched Mrs. Davidson on the arm.) The worker asked Mrs. Davidson how she felt about not having a man. Mrs. Davidson replied, "Sad, depressed—I wonder if he could be as proud of the kids as I am?" She went on to say that maybe things would be different if her husband were still alive—maybe they could have made a go of it. The worker said he felt that Mrs. Davidson had been cut out of the group for some weeks. Mrs. Davidson agreed.

Mrs. Bennet said that was probably due to the fact that she had not been able to share with the group the concerns she had. All agreed. The worker cut in after a silence and said, "I felt the group would like to know what it is like, what it feels like to be alone. What do you need help with?" Mrs. Bennet cut in, "There you go on that feeling theory again." The worker asked if it worried Mrs. Bennet when we talked about feelings. "No," she said, "but is it important?" The worker said that it seemed important because everyone in this group was having trouble talking about and sharing feelings while at the same time they were interested in what others were feeling. "Do you see what we have done here? When we began to find out about Mrs. Davidson's feelings, someone suggested that we avoid it and we all agreed. Let's go back to Mrs. Davidson's feelings!"

Mrs. Davidson said, "I feel like an s-h-i-t (spelled out) at home with the kids." The worker cut in and said it was OK with him if she said *shit*—why did she feel that way? "It rips me right across here (indicating midsection) when they are fighting—I've had nothing but fighting all my life—first in my own home—then with my husband—now with my kids." "How do you see the fighting—what does it mean to you?" asked the worker. "I feel on my own, all alone." Mrs. Trenke cut in, "I know that feeling—I had it with my husband—we used to argue. . . . What can I do? Why is it always me?" The worker asked if Mrs. Davidson could share a specific problem with the group, and she did. It involved setting limits, then wavering on them and letting the kids have their own way.

The Monopolizer

The previous section on the quiet member brings up the opposite side of the issue: People who talk a great deal and are sometimes referred to as **monopolizers.** My observation is that people who talk a lot are often more of a problem for the worker than are quiet members. In first sessions in particular, group members are pleased to see someone pick up the discussion. A problem arises, however, when the person talking does not also listen to others, cuts them off, and creates a negative reaction in the group. The worker who sees this happening can raise the issue directly. Usually the discussion between the member and the group helps to ease the problem. If the group worker inquires why the member acts this way in the group, the individual will often reveal that talking is a way of covering up feelings, avoiding a problem, or expressing concern about actions in the group. The overly verbal member's words are often a way of handling the same feelings that the quiet member handles, but in a quite different manner.

The following brief excerpt illustrates how immobilized both the group leader and the other group members can feel when faced with a monopolizer. This member, Dawn, acted out her anxiety by responding to a doctor's presentation with an unstoppable stream of talk.

Agency Type: A hospital and rehabilitation center for children and adolescents.

Group Purpose: To educate the group members about their children's medical and therapeutic conditions, as well as to inform them of safety precautions for children who have had a traumatic brain injury.

Gender of Members: 3 men and 11 women (including worker).

Age Range: Mid-twenties to early forties.

As soon as Dr. Thomas began to explain that children who have experienced traumatic brain injuries tend to be impulsive, Dawn started to describe what had happened with her child to demonstrate that she agreed with the doctor. She went on and on for almost 10 minutes, and nobody intervened. Then, she started to talk about her other child, Lisa, and what had happened at home during the past weekend. I turned to Dawn and said, "Dawn, I know you have many things to say, but why don't we go back to Eileen's behavior?" Dawn replied, "I know. I know. But let me finish. This is related to Eileen, too." People in the room rolled their eyes, but I did not object. She spoke another 3 minutes or so and finished her story by saying, "So I told my children that school is always number one." I jumped in and said, "Good. Why don't we ask Melissa (the hospital tutor) about school?" People, including Dawn, laughed. When Melissa finished reporting about Eileen's school issue, I encouraged Dawn to ask Melissa questions. Then, I announced to the treatment team that we were running out of time so I would like to ask everyone to be short and precise. They nodded.

In retrospect, this first meeting focused almost entirely on the concerns of one member. Although the other group members signaled their displeasure by rolling their eyes, the group leader, perhaps feeling unclear about how to intervene, let Dawn continue unchecked. The leader would have been helpful to Dawn and the other members if she had intervened more directly and firmly. In a session such as this one, the monopolizer often feels embarrassed afterward for having dominated the conversation, and the other members wonder about the value of the group. In a first session, the group leader must take responsibility for providing structure. In doing so, the leader needs to be both direct and empathic, saying something like this:

> Hold on a second, Dawn. I know your child's injury and this discussion provokes a lot of feelings in you, and you probably feel you want as much help as you can get for your own child. But we need to allow room for everyone to ask their questions and make their comments, so I'll play traffic cop if it's OK with the rest of you.

If Dawn continued to test, such as by saying, as she did in the session, "Let me just finish," the worker would need to say something like "Nice try, but we need to give someone else a chance." Continued persistence would require some discussion of the significance of being so full of one's own feelings that very little room remains for anyone else's. There is also a good chance that Dawn has also just acted out the problem she has with friends and other family members—of overwhelming them with her issues and not being able to respond to theirs. Once again we see the integration of process and content.

If the worker handles such interventions directly, openly, without anger, and where possible with nonhumiliating humor, he or she will be reassuring the group that the worker will not let them subvert the purpose of the group or act out their anxiety. The problem is that such interventions go against societal norms, which encourage passively allowing the monopolizer to go on at length, intervening indirectly with little success, or intervening from anger as the group leader feels frustration at one member's dominating the group. In most cases the monopolizer wants the worker to set limits, because structure helps to bind anxiety and helps the member feel more in control over what must be a devastating situation. In this case, the other members reacted negatively to the monopolizer.

The Group as an Organism

As promised, we have explored the various roles individuals play in a group setting—the interplay of one member in a dynamic system. In the second half of this chapter, we take a more detailed look at the group as an entity much like an organism, with its own properties and dynamics, and then we explore a strategy for the worker's intervention in relation to it. Next, we trace the tasks of the group as it attempts to deal with the relationships of members to the worker (the authority theme), relationships among members (the intimacy theme), the group's culture for work, and the group's internal structure (communication patterns, roles, and so forth). A fifth task requires the group to relate to the environment—the setting that houses the group (the school, agency, institution). We address this task in Chapter 15, when we examine the role of the worker in helping the client (the group in this case) relate to other systems.

It is not easy to describe this second client called the group-as-a-whole. In part, the difficulty comes from the fact that we cannot actually see the properties that describe a group. When we watch a group in action, we see a collection of individuals. Compare this to a solid object, such as a chair. When we are asked to describe its properties, visual references such as materials (plastic, wood, chrome), parts (back, seat, legs), shape, size, and so on immediately come to mind. With a group, describing the properties is more difficult. For example, **cohesion** in a group can be defined as a bond among members—a sense of identification with one another and with the group-as-a-whole. An observer cannot see "cohesion," but if we observe a group for a time, we can see all of the members acting as if the group were cohesive. Other properties of groups include shared norms of proper behavior and taboo subjects. We cannot see a norm or a taboo, but we can see a pattern of behavior from which we can infer that a norm or taboo exists. Our discussion will focus on the unique properties that help to define the group.

Practitioners who wish to better understand group dynamics can draw on a large body of group theory and research. As we discuss these dynamics, we shall use theoretical models and research results to develop an integrated model of group practice. I have selected two classic theoretical models and one relatively new framework for discussion in relation to the group tasks: developmental (Bennis & Shepard, 1956), structural (Bion, 1961), and self-in-relation (Fedele, 1994; Schiller, 1993). Each of these theories offers ideas relevant to all of the group tasks.

Before we discuss developmental tasks, we need to explore the very idea of a group. When attempting to describe something as complex as a group, using a model is helpful. A **model** is a concrete, symbolic representation of an abstract phenomenon. To develop a model for describing a group, we must find an appropriate metaphor. Two common metaphors are the machine and the organism. In the mechanistic model, the observer describes processes such as "input," "through put," and "output" to describe the group. Many theorists interested in human social systems have adopted the **organismic model** as the most appropriate. The choice of an organism rather than a machine as a model reflects the organism's capacity for *growth* and *emergent behavior*. These terms describe a process in which a system transcends itself and creates something new that is more than just the simple sum of its parts.

To apply this idea to the group, we need to identify what is created when a group of people and a worker are brought together that goes beyond the sum of each member's contribution. What properties exist that are unique descriptions of the group, rather than descriptions of the individual members? An example of such a property is the creation of a sense of common purpose shared by all the members of the group. This common purpose is a catalyst for the development of a tie that binds the members together. **Group culture** is a second example. As the group process begins, activities in the group are governed by a group culture made up of several factors including accepted **norms of behavior.** In a first session, the group culture generally reflects the culture of the larger society from which the members have been drawn. As sessions continue, this culture can change, allowing new norms to emerge and govern the activities of the members. Thus, common interests and group culture are two examples of properties of the group that transcend the simple sum of its parts, the individual members.

A third example is the group's relationship with its environment. As the group is influenced by its environment—for example, the agency, school, or hospital—or the worker as a representative of the agency, it must develop adaptive behaviors to maintain itself. This pattern of adaptive behavior is yet another example of a property of the group.

To summarize, we cannot actually see a group as an entity. That is why a model, such as the organism, is helpful. What we can see, however, are the activities of a group of people who appear to be influenced by this entity called the group. For example, when group purpose is clear, we can explain the members' actions as contributions in pursuit of that purpose. Again, group pressures, group expectations, and the members' sense of belonging all influence the members' behavior. The fact that a member's behavior changes as a result of believing in the existence of the group makes the group real. In the balance of this chapter, we shall refer to the group as an entity, employing the organism as a metaphor, and focus on the group's developmental tasks.

Developmental Tasks for the Group

Two major group tasks have already been discussed without having been specifically described as such. These illustrate how a group can have tasks that differ from the specific tasks of each member. In the chapter on group beginnings we addressed what could be called the group's formation tasks. The group needed to develop a working contract reflecting the individual members' needs as well as the service stake of the sponsoring agency. In addition, a group consensus needed to be developed. This consensus reflected the common concerns shared by members as well as agreement as to where the work might start. Reaching consensus on the work is a task unique to work with multiple clients (group, family, couples, and so on), because individual clients simply begin where they wish, with no need to reach a consensus with other clients. The group's formation tasks also include initial clarification of mutual obligations and expectations. The effectiveness of the group depends on how well it accomplishes these formation tasks. The skills of the worker in helping the group to work on these formation tasks are described as contracting skills.

A second critical group task involves meeting individual members' needs. For the group to survive, it must have individual members. Members feel a sense of belonging and develop a stake in the work of the group when they can perceive that their own related needs are being met. If these needs cease to be met, then members will simply drop out of the group, either by not attending or by not participating. In the chapter on the work phase of the group, we saw how easily the group can miss the offered concerns of a member or turn away from these concerns when they hit the group members too hard. In still other examples, individual members did not immediately see the relation between the work of the group and their own sense of urgency. In the first part of this chapter, we saw how members can play functional roles in the group, some of which cut them off from being able to use the group to meet their own needs. In each of these cases, workers attempted to help the members use the group more effectively, helped the group reach out and offer mutual aid more effectively, or both simultaneously. All these efforts were directed toward helping the group with its task of meeting individual members' needs.

Thus, in order to grow and survive, a group must address the tasks of formation and meeting individual members' needs. Other sets of tasks linked to the developmental work of the group are those in which the group works on its relationship to the worker (the authority theme) and relationships among members (the intimacy theme). Schwartz (1971) describes these two critical tasks as follows:

> In the culture of the group two main themes come to characterize the members' ways of working together: one, quite familiar to the caseworker, is the theme of authority in which the members are occupied with their relationship to the helping person and the ways in which this relationship is instrumental to their purpose; the other, more strange and threatening to the caseworker, is the theme of intimacy, in which the members are concerned with their internal relationships and the problems of mutual aid. It is the interplay of these factors—external authority and mutual interdependence—that provides much of the driving force of the group experience. (p. 9)

The group's ability to deal with concerns related to authority and intimacy is closely connected to the development of a *working culture:* common interests and group norms of behavior. Finally, the group needs to develop a structure for work that will enable it to carry out its tasks effectively. For example, responsibilities may have to be shared through a division of labor, and roles may need to be assigned formally or informally.

These four major task areas—the relationship to the worker, the relationship between members, the development of a working culture, and the development of a structure for work—will be introduced in the balance this chapter. Obviously, these tasks overlap a great deal, in that work on one area often includes work on the others. Although somewhat artificial, the division is helpful. Recall that discussion of these tasks will draw on elements of group theory from three major models, focusing on constructs that seem relevant. For example, Bennis and Shepard (1956) address the themes of intimacy and authority in their model of group development, and several of their key concepts are useful in explaining group process. Their observations, however, are based on their work with laboratory training groups (T-groups), in which graduate students studied group dynamics using their own experiences as a group. As a result, some ideas in their theory may be group-specific and therefore not apply to groups of the type discussed in this book. Our analysis will illustrate how a practitioner can use what he or she likes from a good theory without adopting it whole.

Dealing With the Relationship to the Worker

In the early phase of the group development, the group needs to sort out its relationship to the worker. Much of the group's beginning energy will be devoted to this theme. An early question concerns issues of control. Like work with individuals, group work includes the dynamics of transference and countertransference. Members bring their stereotypes or fantasies about group leaders to the first meeting, and these generate a fear of a powerful authority person "doing something" to them. Thus, in my description of the first session of the couples' group in Chapter 10, the member named Lou raised the authority issue by sharing his negative experiences with workers in the helping field. Open discussion of the implications of this issue for the workers present helped the group members relax and become more actively involved in the session. However, such an open discussion does not resolve the question, in that feelings and questions concerning the relationship to the worker always remain. What the group and the worker do achieve is the ability to address this issue openly as it emerges. The comfort of the group may increase, but the theme remains. In the second session of the couples' group, the members were watching to see if I would carry out the role I had described in the first session. Once again, Lou signaled the members' concern about this issue:

> One couple was presenting a problem that they were having that involved the husband's grown children from another marriage. I noticed each spouse was telling the group things about the other, rather than speaking directly to each other. I interrupted Frank and suggested he speak directly to his wife. After a noticeable hesitation, he began to speak to her, but he soon returned to speaking to me. I interrupted him again. Once again, he seemed slightly thrown by my action.
>
> As this was going on, I noticed that Lou was looking distressed, staring at the floor, and covering his mouth with his hand. After watching this for a time, I reached for the message. "Lou, you look like you have something to say." He responded, "No, that's all right. I can wait 'til later." I said, "I have the feeling it's important, and I think it has something to do with me." I had been feeling uncomfortable but unaware why. Lou said. "Well, if you want to hear it now, OK. Every time you interrupt Frank that way, I think he loses his train of thought. And this business of telling him to speak to Jane is just like the stuff I described last week." I was surprised by what he said, and I remained quiet while I took it in.
>
> Frank said, "You know, he's right. You do throw my line of thought every time you interrupt that way." I said, "I guess I ended up doing exactly the kind of thing I said last week I would try not to do. I have not explained to you, Frank, why I think it might help to talk directly with your wife rather than to me. I guess you must feel my comments, because you don't really understand why I'm suggesting this, as sort of pushing you around." Frank said "Well, a bit." Lou said, "That's exactly what I mean." I responded, "I won't be perfect, Lou. I will also make mistakes. That's why it's so important that you call me on it, the way you just did. Only why wait until I ask?" Lou said, "It's not easy to call you; you're the leader." I said, "I think I can appreciate that, only you can see how it would speed things up if you did."

This second week's discussion was even more important than the first, because the members had a chance to see me confronted with a mistake and not only acknowledging it but also encouraging Lou to be even more direct. The point made was that they did have rights and that they should not let my authority get in the way. At this point you may be thinking that reaching for or encouraging such negative feedback would be difficult for a beginning group leader. Ironically, the worker needs this kind of honesty from group members most when she or he is least confident and prepared to hear it. Beginning group workers should expect to miss these signals in sessions, but as their confidence grows, they should start to reach for the negatives later in the same session or in the session that follows.

The authority theme appeared many other times in similar discussions, for example, about the agenda for our work. When I appeared to return to an area of work without checking on the group's interest, members would participate in an obvious illusion of work. When I challenged the illusion, we could discuss why it was harder for them simply to let me know when they thought I was leading them away from their concerns. Issues of control also emerged in connection with responsibility for the effectiveness of the work. In this example, one couple had spent an unusually long time discussing an issue without getting to the point. I could see the reactions in the group and inquired as to what was going on.

> Fran responded by saying it was getting boring and she was waiting for me to do something. Because this was a middle-phase session, I found myself angry that everyone was waiting for me. I said, "How come you are waiting for me to do something? This is your group, you know, and I think you could take this responsibility, too."

The resulting discussion revealed that members felt it was risky to take each other on, and so they left it to me. We were able to sort out for a time that members, too, needed to take responsibility for the group's effectiveness.

These excerpts help to illustrate the two sides to the members' feelings: On the one hand, they were afraid of the worker and the worker's authority; on the other, they wanted the worker to take responsibility for the group. Bennis and Shepard (1956) attribute these two sets of feelings to two types of personalities in the group: the **dependent member** and the **counterdependent member**. They believe that the dependency invokes great uncertainty for members and that the first major phase of group development, the **dependence phase**, involves work on this question. They describe three subphases within this first phase. In the first subphase, **dependence-flight**, the group is led by the dependent leaders, who seek to involve the worker more actively in control of the group. In the second subphase, **counterdependence-flight**, the counterdependent leaders move in to attempt to take over the group. The group often shows much anger toward the worker in this phase. Two subgroups develop—one arguing for structure, the other arguing against it.

In the third subphase, **resolution-catharsis**, members who are **unconflicted**— independent and relatively untroubled by authority issues—assume group leadership. According to Bennis and Shepard (1956), this "overthrow" of the worker leads to each member taking responsibility for the group: The worker is no longer seen as "magical," and the power struggles are replaced by work on shared goals. The groups studied by the authors were marked by group leaders who were extremely passive in the beginning, which, in my view, increased anxiety about the authority theme. While many of the specifics of the model are restricted to the particular groups observed, we can apply to all groups the general outline of this struggle over dependency.

Issues of control are just one aspect of the general theme of relationship to the worker. A second area concerns the worker's place as an outsider to the group. This comes up particularly in groups where the worker has not had life experiences central to the group members' themes of concern. For instance, in a group for parents of children who have been diagnosed as hyperactive, the question arises of whether the worker who has no children can understand them and their problems. This is a variation on the similar question raised in the discussion of the beginning phase in work with individuals. The following excerpt illustrates this aspect of the authority theme struggle in the group context:

> Discussion got back again to causes of hyperactivity. Ann, who had thought it was hereditary, explained that her husband thought that he had been hyperactive as a

child, except that nobody gave him the title. Marilyn said that her husband had also said that he had been like her son and had felt that her son would grow out of it. The group picked up on this idea and seemed to like the possibility. I was asked by Betty what I thought. I said I didn't know the answer, but that from what I did know, not enough research has been done. The group began throwing questions at me, related to general conditions, medications, and I couldn't answer them. I admitted that I knew very little about hyperactivity. I was certainly nowhere near being the experts that they were.

Someone asked if I had children. I said that I didn't. Beatrice wondered what work I had done with hyperactive children and extended this to children with other problems. I answered as honestly as I could. She wondered whether I was overwhelmed by their feelings. I replied that she and others present were really concerned about how I felt toward them, and whether I really understood what it felt like to be the mother of a hyperactive child. She agreed. I added that last week when I had said I was feeling overwhelmed I was really getting into what it felt like to have such a child. It was pointed out to me that I was the only one in the group who didn't have a hyperactive child, that I was really the outsider. Beatrice offered to lend me her son for a weekend, so that I could really see what it was like. Everyone laughed. (I think they were delighted at this.) I said that they were telling me that it was important that I understand what it's like, and I wondered whether I was coming across as not understanding. They didn't think so. I said that the more they talked, the better the feeling I got about what they were going through. Toward the end of this there was a lot of subgroup talking going on, and I waited (thankful for the break).

The third area of the authority theme has to do with the group's reaction to the worker as a person who makes demands. For the group to be effective, the worker must do more than contract clearly and be empathic. The group will often come up against obstacles, many of which are related to the group members' ambivalence about discussion of painful areas. As the worker makes demands, group members will inevitably generate negative feelings. If the worker is doing a good job, group members will sometimes get angry at the worker for refusing to let them off the hook. Of course, clients also have positive feelings associated with the fact that the worker is empathetic and cares enough about the group to make these demands. The angry feelings, however, need to be expressed; otherwise they can go under the surface and emerge in unconscious expressions such as general apathy. As we have seen, the worker must feel comfortable in the role to be willing to deal with this negative feedback. In the same group of parents of hyperactive children, the worker picked up the signals of this reaction and reached directly for it:

Millie began talking about her son's learning disability. After a little while I cut in and asked the group what was happening here, to the conversation and to the members. (My feeling was that they were way off the track again.) Marilyn said that they had gotten off the subject again; they were supposed to be discussing how they felt and their attitudes. I added that indeed this was what was happening; it seemed that they were unable to keep on talking about themselves. Millie and Marilyn thought that it was probably because it was hard to accept the fact that they get angry. I started to say something in response to this, and I noticed that Claudette kind of sighed and made a face. I pointed this out to her and suggested that perhaps she didn't want to discuss some of the things I thought they should. She nodded.

I told the group that perhaps this was a good time to talk about how they felt about my forcing them to look at themselves, to keep on the subject, and to talk about what they didn't want to talk about. I said that they must have some feelings about me; perhaps every time I open up my mouth and point this out to them and try to refocus them, they say to themselves, "Why the hell doesn't she get off our backs and let us talk about something easy?"

Beatrice said that she had the feeling that was true, every time I brought them back to talking about how they felt, she could feel people moving back in their chairs, as if they were looking for a place to hide, and then they would hide by talking about school, teachers, and so on. She said that her own behavior has changed considerably with these sessions, and although it has been hard, she's been able to see herself a little more clearly. But not everyone in the group has moved at the same pace; some people are really changing their attitudes because they are willing to risk and look at themselves, but others still hide behind the facade. I said that I agreed. Often I felt how terribly hard it was for them to face things, and I kept pushing them at it. Sometimes I pushed them hard, like two sessions ago. And then other times I felt it was too hard, and like last week, I hardly said anything and really let them talk about anything and everything. I don't think that is being helpful to them if I let them do that, even though I can feel their hurt so much, and my own gut reaction is "I should let you alone; it hurts too much to look at yourselves." People nodded in agreement.

A fourth issue here is the need for the group to come to grips with the reality of the worker's limitations. Members hope that the worker, or some other expert, will be able to solve their problems. This is, in part, a result of the emerging dependency of the group. When the group members realize the worker has no solutions, then their own work really begins. However, this realization is painful for the members and often for the workers as well. At the end of one particularly painful and depressing discussion in the same parents' group, when the members recognized that the drugs and the professionals were not going to "make the problem go away," a member appealed to the worker to cheer them up:

We were way over our time, and I started to sum up some of the feelings that came out today. I said that they had really been saying all along how helpless they felt that they couldn't do anything to help the children, and how hopeless they were feeling that there wasn't a solution for them. Marilyn said to me that that's how they felt, depressed and helpless. She said that I always came up with something at the end to make them feel better. I had better come up with something really good today, because they needed it. I said that I was feeling the same way, thinking to myself, "What can I say that's going to take the depression and hurt away?" I told her that I didn't have a magic formula, that I wished that I could suggest something. I knew how much she and all of them wished that I could help them with a solution. Rose said that they were feeling depressed, but they shouldn't blame themselves. I said that perhaps part of the depression was related to the fact that they themselves hadn't been able to help their children more, and they felt terrible about it. She seemed to be so terribly depressed, more than ever before. I know because that's exactly how I felt.

There was not too much discussion on the way out, as I didn't to know what to say to them (usually we joke around a bit). Marilyn said to me I let her down, I didn't come up with my little blurb to pep them up. I said that she was feeling very depressed and she looked to me to say something to make things easier. I said that she wanted a solution, and I didn't have one. She said to me that perhaps I had, and I was holding back. I said to her that she was very disappointed in me that I hadn't been able to make things easier. I wished that I did have the magic solution that they all wanted so desperately, but I didn't have one. After this, the members left.

A final aspect of the authority theme requires the group to deal with their reactions to the worker as a caring and giving person. The group members watch as the worker relates to them and to the others in the group. They can see the pain in the worker's face if he or she feels the hurt deeply; after a while, they can sense the genuineness of the empathy. This side of the worker provokes powerful responses in the group, and a mutual flow of positive affect results. An interesting discussion in my couples' group illustrates the importance of this aspect of the authority theme, as well as the group's awareness of this issue. In the session before the Christmas break (the eighth), one member arrived late and distraught. She sat down in the empty chair to my right, and for the first time in the group she shared a frightening problem she was facing. Until then, the member had appeared to be "without problems," because her husband was, in her mind, the identified patient. I comforted her while she told her story, and I tried to help her verbally and nonverbally—touching the back of her hand, communicating my empathic responses to her feelings. The group also reached out with support. In the second part of the session, after the immediate issue had been somewhat resolved and the member was in better shape, we carried out a midpoint evaluation of the group. In discussing the way we worked as a group, one of the members raised the authority theme.

Fran said, "I knew that this was Jane's night to get help the minute she walked in the door." (Jane was the member who had been crying.) When I inquired how she knew, she said, "Because she sat in the crying chair." She went on to point out that all of the people who had cried in sessions, 4 of the 10 group members, had all sat down in that chair at the beginning of the session. In fact, some had sat apart from their spouses for the first time in the group. Other members nodded in recognition of the accuracy of Fran's observation. I inquired if they had any thoughts about why that was so. Rose said, "Because that's the chair next to you, and we sit there to get some support when the going gets rough." I responded, "Could you talk a bit about what it is about me that causes you to sit there or feel I can support you? This is important as part of our evaluation, but also, it can tell us something about what it is you might want from each other."

The request for specifics was designed to encourage discussion of the members' feelings about the worker reaching out to them with caring. In addition, as is often the case, the process in the group can serve to assist group members in understanding their own relationships more clearly. The record continues:

Louise said, "It's because we can feel free to say anything to you, and you won't judge us. We can tell you our feelings." Rose continued, "And we know you really feel our hurt. It's not phony—you really care." Lou said, "It's safe next to you. We can share our innermost feelings and know that you won't let us get hurt." As I listened to the members, I felt myself deeply moved by the affect in their voices, and I shared that with them. "You know, it means a great deal to me to have you feel that way—that you can sense my feelings for you. I have grown to care about you quite a bit. It's surprising to me, sometimes, just how hard things in this group hit me—just how important you really have become."

The authority theme is a two-way street, and the worker will have as much feeling toward the members as they have toward the worker. The countertransference dynamics, described in Chapter 4, need to be made a part of the discussion. The honest feelings of the worker, freely expressed, are often the key to aiding the group as it comes to grips with its relationship to the worker.

In summary, some aspects of the authority theme to be dealt with during the life of the group include the worker's control, responsibility, and status as an outsider and the group's reactions to the worker's demands, limitations, and caring. Although the phases in which a group deals with issues are never neat and orderly, a pattern emerges: As the issues of authority are dealt with, the group becomes more ready to turn to its second major developmental task, the relationships among members (the intimacy theme).

Dealing With the Relationship Among Members

Once again, Bennis and Shepard's (1956) theory can provide helpful insights. In addition to concerns about dependency, a second major area of internal uncertainty for group members relates to *interdependence*. This has to do with questions of intimacy—that is, the group members' concerns about how close they wish to get to one another. In Bennis and Shepard's model, the group moves from the first phase, concerned with dependence and marked by a preoccupation with authority relations, to the **interdependence phase,** characterized by issues of peer group relationships. The two sets of member personalities that emerge in relation to this issue are the *overpersonal* and *counterpersonal* group members. These parallel the dependent and the counterdependent personalities of the first phase. Once again, three subphases are identified: the **enchantment-flight** subphase, in which good feelings abound and efforts are directed toward healing wounds; the **disenchantment-flight** subphase, in which the counterpersonals take over from the overpersonals in reaction to the growing intimacy; and finally, the **consensual validation** subphase, in which the unconflicted members once again provide the leadership needed for the group to move to a new level of work characterized by honest communication among members.

While the specifics of the Bennis and Shepard model relate most directly to the dynamics of T-groups (training groups), ambivalence toward honest communications among members can be observed in most groups. After dealing with the authority theme, the group often moves through a phase marked by positive feelings among members, as the enchantment-flight subphase suggests. As the work deepens and members move beyond simply supporting each other and begin to confront each other, more negative feelings and reactions arise. As members begin to rub up against each other in their work, these feelings are quite natural and should be an expected part of the process. However, group members have learned from their experiences in other situations (family, groups, classes) that talking directly about negative reactions to the behavior of others is not polite. This conditioning is part of the worker's experience as well. Often, then, the worker and the group get angry at members but nonetheless withhold their reactions.

Without direct feedback from the group, individual members find it difficult to understand their impact on the group, to learn from that understanding, and to develop new ways of coping. The worker's task is to draw these interpersonal obstacles to the attention of the members and to help the group develop the ability to discuss them. Workers often fear "opening up" discussion of the angry feelings they sense in the group, because they are concerned that things will "get out of hand," they will be overwhelmed, individuals will be hurt, and the life of the group will be threatened. Actually, the greatest threat to the life of the group is overpoliteness and the resulting illusion of work. Expression of anger can free the caring and other positive feelings that are also part of the group's intimacy.

Of course, the worker needs to take care that the contract of the group does not get subverted. Sometimes the discussion becomes centered on intermember relationships, thereby losing sight of the original reason the group was formed. This is one of my major criticisms of the type of groups (T-groups) studied by Bennis and Shepard. They have no other external group purpose other than to analyze the interactions among members. They are usually described as educational groups wherein members can learn about group dynamics and their own interpersonal behaviors. A second possibility to which the worker must be alert is that the member involved may attempt to use the group to deal with a personal pattern of behaving in groups, another attempt at subversion of group purpose.

College Student Counseling Group and the Intimacy Theme In the following illustration from a counseling group for college students experiencing difficulty in adjusting to their first year on campus, one member developed a pattern of relating in which she consistently cut off other members, did not really listen to them, and attempted to raise her own questions and concerns directly with the worker. The worker sensed she was relating only to him. The other group members showed elevating nonverbal signals of anger at her behavior that she did not perceive. The record starts after a particularly striking example of this behavior.

> I noticed the group members had physically turned away as Louise was talking. Their faces spoke loudly of their negative reaction. I decided to raise the issue: "There is something happening right now that seems to happen a lot in this group. Louise is asking a lot of questions, cutting some people off as she does, and I sense that the rest of you aren't too happy about that. Am I right?" There was silence for a moment, and Louise, for the first time, was looking directly at the other group members. I said, "I know this isn't easy to talk about, but I feel if we can't be honest with each other about how we are working together, we don't stand a chance of being an effective group. And I think Louise would want to know if this was true. Am I right about that, Louise?" She answered, "I didn't realize I was doing this. Is it true?" Francine responded, "Frankly, Louise, I have been sitting here getting angrier and angrier at you by the minute. You really don't seem to listen to anyone else in the group."

The worker opened the door by pointing out the pattern in the group and breaking the taboo against direct acknowledgment of an interpersonal problem. This freed members to explore this sensitive area.

> After Francine's words there was a moment of silence, and then Louise began to cry, saying, "You know, I seem to be doing this in all areas of my life. All of my friends are angry at me, my boyfriend won't speak to me, and now I've done it again. What's wrong with me?" The group seemed stunned by her expression of feeling.

Because this was the first real discussion of an interpersonal issue in the group, the worker needed to clarify the boundary of the discussion, using the contract as his guide. The group felt guilty, and Louise felt overwhelmed. The worker acknowledged both of these feelings:

> "I guess you all must feel quite concerned over how strongly this is hitting Louise?" Members nodded their heads, but no one spoke. I continued, "Louise, I'm afraid this has hit you really hard. I should make it clear that we won't be able to talk about the other areas in your life that you are finding tough right now—that wouldn't be appropriate in this group. I'd be glad to talk to you after the group, however, and maybe, if you want, we could explore other avenues of help. For right now, could you stick to what is happening in this group? How come you seem to be so eager to ask all the questions, and why do you seem so cut off from the group?" Louise was thoughtful for a moment and then said to the group, "I guess it's just that I'm feeling really concerned about what's going on here at school and I'm trying to get some help as quickly as possible. I want to make sure I get as much from Sid [the worker] as I can." I paused and looked to the group. Francine responded, "You know, that's probably why I got so mad at you, because I'm the same way, and I'm sitting here feeling the same feelings—I want to get as much help as I can as well." Louise: "Well, at least you were straight with me, and I appreciate that. It's much worse when you can sense something is wrong, but people won't level with you."

After the exchange between Louise and Francine, the group seemed to relax. Louise's readiness to accept negative feedback without defensiveness had an impact on the group. In other circumstances, members may feel more vulnerable and would need all the help the worker could give in terms of support. When Louise was able to express the underlying feelings she experienced, other group members were able to identify with her, and this freed their affect and concern. Louise could sense their concern for her, making it easier for her to feel more a part of the group rather than relating only to the worker. The worker proceeded to underline the importance of honest communication among members and then guarded against preoccupation with process, by reaching for the implicit work hinted at in the exchange.

> "I think it was really tough just now, for Louise and the rest of you. However, if the group is going to be helpful, I think we are going to have to learn how to be honest with each other. As Louise pointed out, it can be tougher not to hear sometimes. I think it is also important that we not lose the threads of our work as we go along. I noticed that both Louise and Francine mentioned their urgency about getting help with their problems right now. Could we pick up by being a bit more specific about what those problems are?"

Francine accepted the invitation by expressing a concern she was having about a specific course. From that point on, Louise was more attentive to the group and appeared a good deal more relaxed. The few times she interrupted, she good-naturedly caught herself and apologized. The worker spoke to her after the session and arranged an appointment for personal counseling. Members from that point on also appeared more involved and energetic in the discussion.

A group needs to develop a climate of trust that will allow members to lower their defenses. A powerful barrier to trust can be raised and maintained by what members leave unsaid. Group members can sense both positive and negative reactions by other members. The effect of these reactions increases when they remain beneath the surface. On the other hand, open expression of these feelings can free members, who feel more confident when they know where they stand with the group.

Workers usually experience intermember issues as particularly difficult. As they develop group experience, they become proficient at reaching for issues related to the authority theme; however, they take longer to risk dealing with the intimacy theme. So powerful are the taboos and so strong is their fear of hurting, and being hurt in reaction, that they will try many indirect routes before finally risking honesty. The reluctance may be partly rooted in workers' feelings that they are responsible for "handling" anything that comes from reaching for intermember negatives. As this excerpt has illustrated, a group that has developed even a small fund of positive feelings is better equipped for handling its own problems. They need the worker's intervention to act as a catalyst, giving them permission and supporting them as they enter the formerly taboo area.

Intimacy and the Relational Model Another theoretical model (mentioned in Chapter 1) that helps us to understand the intimacy theme is the relational model. It has emerged from the work done at the Stone Center in Wellesley, Massachusetts, which is dedicated to studying the unique issues in the development of women and methods for working effectively with them. The center has built on the early work of Jean Baker Miller, whose publication entitled *Toward a New Psychology of Women* (Miller 1987; Miller & Stiver, 1991) laid the groundwork for the relational model.

Much of the evolving work in this area can be found in publications and a series of working papers from the Stone Center. Recall that this framework is often classified under the general rubric of self-in-relation theory. In one example of a group work elaboration of this model, Fedele (1994) draws on three central constructs repeatedly found in relational theory: *paradox* (an apparent contradiction that contains a truth); *connection* ("a joining in relationship between people who experience each other's presence in a full way and who accommodate both the correspondence and contrasts between them"); and *resonance* ("a resounding; an echoing; the capacity to respond that, in its most sophisticated form, is empathy") (p. 7).

Referring to therapy, Fedele (1994) identifies several paradoxes: "Vulnerability leads to growth; pain can be experienced in safety; talking about disconnection leads to connection; and conflict between people can be best tolerated in their connection" (p. 8). She also identifies the paradox between "transferential" and "real" relationships in therapy as well as the "importance of establishing a mutual, empathic relationship within the context of the unequal therapist-client relationship" (p. 8) as additional primary paradoxes in therapy. She says,

> These dilemmas are dramatically apparent in group psychotherapy. The therapists and group members collaborate to create an emotional relational space which allows the members to recapture more and more of their experience in their own awareness and in the group. The feelings of the past can be tolerated in this new relational space. It allows us to reframe the experience of pain within the context of safety. The difficulty of creating an environment that allows vulnerability in a group format involves the complexity of creating safety for all participants. (p. 8)

In applying this theory to group therapy, she identifies the "basic paradox" of a simultaneous yearning for connection accompanied by efforts to maintain disconnection as a form of protection from being hurt—a need generated from earlier painful experiences. The paradox of "similarity and diversity" describes a tension between connection around universal feelings and fears of isolation because of difference. She points out that "the mutuality of empathy allows all participants to feel understood and accepted. The leader, creating a safe relational context, fosters connectedness within that safety by working to enlarge the empathy for difference" (1994, p. 9). Another related paradox is the fact that the very process of sharing disconnection can lead to new connection. For example, "When members phone the leader to report anger or dissatisfaction with the group, the leader can encourage them to share this experience in the group. Often, if one feels the disconnection, it is very likely that one or more of the other members experience similar feelings and resonate with the feelings of dissatisfaction" (p. 10). Thus, when members share the sense of disconnection, these feelings can lead to connection. Finally, the paradox of "conflict in connection" describes the importance of managing conflict and keeping anger within the context of safety and acceptance of divergent realities. As she points out, "One way to view anger is to see it as a reaction to the experience of disconnection in the face of intense yearning for connection" (p. 11).

In describing the second major construct of relational theory, the idea of "connection," Fedele (1994) says,

> The primary task of the leader and the group members is to facilitate a feeling of connection. In a relational model of group work, the leader is careful to understand each interaction, each dynamic in the group as a means for maintaining connection or as a strategy to remain out of connection. As in interpersonal therapy groups, the leader encourages the members to be aware of their availability in the here-and-now relationship of the group by understanding and empathizing with their experiences of the past. But it is the yearning for connection, rather than an innate need for separation or individuation, that fuels their development both in the here-and-now and in the past. (p. 11)

Finally, the third major concept, "resonance," asserts that the "power of experiencing pain within a healing connection stems from the ability of an individual to resonate with another" (Fedele, 1994, p. 14) She suggests that resonance manifests itself in group work in two ways:

> The first is the ability of one member to simply resonate with another's experience in the group and experience some vicarious relief because of that resonance. The member need not discuss the issue in the group, but the experience moves her that much closer to knowing and sharing her own truth without necessarily responding or articulating it. Another way resonance manifests itself in a group involves the ability of members to resonate with each other's issues and thereby recall or reconnect with their own issues. This is an important element of group process in all groups but is dramatically obvious in groups with women who have trauma histories. Often, when one woman talks about painful material, other women dissociate. It is a very powerful aspect of group work that, if acknowledged, can help women move into connection. It can also cause problems if women become overwhelmed or flooded. The leader needs to modulate this resonance by helping each member develop skills to manage and contain intense feelings. (p. 14)

Many of the constructs of this theory, particularly its group work implications, fit well with the interactional framework presented in this book. For example, a former colleague of mine, Linda Schiller (1993), was able to use the self-in-relation framework to rethink a classic theory of group development known as the Boston model (Garland et al., 1965), adapting it to a feminist perspective.

In the example that follows, from a support group for women with cancer, we can use the relational model to explain the patterns of interaction over time. We can see examples of paradoxes, connections, and resonance in each session of the work.

RECORD OF SERVICE

Client Description and Time Frame

Members: Four 45- to 58-year-old white women from different ethnic and socioeconomic backgrounds. All have been diagnosed with breast cancer and either are in the midst of treatment or have just finished. The group was created in response to inquiries made by each of the members to the outpatient oncology clinic in the hospital. All members are voluntary.

Dates Covered in Record: 11/14 to 12/5.

Group Task: Individual need satisfaction.

Description of the Problem

The task of this group is for members to reach out to one another in order to find support around painful issues in dealing with their cancer diagnoses. One member in particular seems to be expressing the pain and anger for the group. The problem that I began to recognize was that this member was carrying a great deal of emotion about her cancer diagnosis. She demonstrated her emotion through anger and distrust projected onto group members and the medical staff in general. I suspect that all members shared similar feelings to some extent but were unable to recognize them as related to their illness. My coleader and I found ourselves faced with two problems: (1) we needed to find appropriate ways to address the emotions expressed by the angry member, or what appeared to be the deviant member, in order to get at the underlying message, and (2) we needed to help the group as a whole find the freedom to express and address their painful feelings rather than allowing this individual member to bear the responsibility.

How the Problem Came to the Attention of the Worker(s)

Through conversation and telling of individual stories, it seemed apparent from the beginning of the group that this particular woman was distrustful of people in general. I had originally suspected that she was someone who generally had not found people trustworthy throughout her life. After the second session, I began to wonder if this quality was not somehow related to her recent cancer diagnosis as well. She called my coleader and expressed a desire to quit the group because her "ways of dealing with her illness were diametrically opposed to the other members' ways." At this time she also mentioned the name of one member specifically. Although she continued coming, it was apparent that she was carrying anger with her, especially toward the member she had named. She would roll her eyes or mutter something under her breath whenever this woman spoke. The other members did not acknowledge this, nor did the woman to whom the behavior was addressed.

Summary of the Work

Session 1

For the first session, although I was very anxious about its newness, I was truly excited about the nature of this group, as the women attending had taken the initiative to request its formation. I felt that it was going to be an exciting and rich experience for all of us. My coleader and I began the group by introducing ourselves and then having each of the four members introduce themselves. I then went over confidentiality issues as well as the rules and the purpose of the group: This was a support group for women with breast cancer. It was created because of their requests in the oncology clinic, and I hoped that it would become a safe place for each of them to share their experiences and feelings around their illness as well as a place in which they could learn from one another. My coleader then stated that she, too, hoped to make this a safe place for the women to share their stories, and then she invited each one to talk about her experiences.

Each member told her story, offering an account of what she had been through. I noticed that none of the women expressed their stories with much emotion, only offering descriptive accounts of their experiences. However, one woman, Joan, did stand out in her account. She expressed distrust in the medical system and said that so far she had not found any of the doctors or nurses helpful. "I do my own research and reading. I can't count on them to give me the answers. They're in and out in a flash." Another woman, Judy, added that she had had a similar experience in the past and ended up switching doctors. Joan snapped at Judy, making an excuse for not being able to switch doctors, and said, "I just deal with it." I made a mental note of this exchange and gave some thought to Joan's account of her experiences as well as her stating that change was not possible. I, at this time, thought that she seemed to be a person who did not trust others, probably because of her own life experiences. I did not make a connection between her feelings about the medical staff and her cancer at this time, nor did I think much about why her reaction to Judy was so strong. In retrospect, I would guess that Joan was offering the group some insight into how she was feeling in the group and about her cancer.

Once each woman had shared with the group, my coleader asked if any of them had been in groups in the past. Only one woman had been in a prior group, and she talked about how each member in that group had died. The room was silent. Instead of letting the silence stay and then addressing its meaning, I asked the woman what it felt like to be starting another group. She commented that it was a little scary and added, "But we have to keep going on. We have no other choice." I then asked the other members what it felt like to hear her talk about the other group. They all commented about how it must have been an awful experience for her. My coleader pushed, "Does it make you start to think about your own mortality?" A couple of members said that they had not really given it much thought, and Joan said that it did make her think about it but that was all. Instead of pursuing this, both my coleader and I let the conversation drift back to the members' telling Barbara how it must have been hard to be part of that group. Again, Joan had given us an opportunity to recognize her as really wanting to do the work in the group. First, she brought up the anger and then acknowledged thinking about death. Both are very real issues for all the members in this group. We failed to pick up on her desire to work.

Because of time constraints, we ended the meeting. My coleader offered a summary of what she felt she had heard as being common among the women's experiences as they had portrayed them to the group, and she used this as a way to reiterate the goal of finding support from each other within the group. Death and anger were not mentioned. We both thanked them for coming to the group.

Session 2

This session began with all members arriving on time. We asked each member to give a brief check-in so that everyone could get an idea of how the others are doing. Joan was the last one to check in, and she brought up the fact that her daughter was going through chemotherapy at the time and that she herself was presently taking care of a depressed friend. This opened up a discussion for all the women to find something in common. It turned out that each of them was caring for elderly parents; thus, all these women were acting as caretakers while dealing with their illnesses. I asked, "What's it like to not only have to worry about your own health and ability to live from day to day, but have to worry about taking care of someone else as well?" Barbara said, "You gotta do what you gotta do." Everyone agreed. Judy then began to change the subject and talk about how when she's not caring for her mother she is working on a proposal that addresses research around tobacco- and cancer-related issues. She wanted to know if any of the other women would be interested in helping her out. Barbara and Gayle inquired about it, while Joan sat quietly, appearing to be somewhat annoyed. Neither my coleader nor I said anything. I did not realize at the time that this was Judy's way of avoiding the work of addressing painful feelings, the group's way of going along with it, and Joan's silent plea to do the work.

The women continued to talk about their own efforts in keeping busy, and then Joan chimed in, "I haven't been able to go back to work because of the amount of chemotherapy I receive. I have enough trouble trying to take care of everyone else and myself." Judy responded by stating that she knew how she felt because she wished she had more time to work on her proposal. She then went into how long a proposal takes to draft. Joan rolled her eyes. The other members seemed to fall into Judy's trap again. My coleader said, "I've noticed that the group sort of shifts a focus off issues that seem to bring up some painful emotions for each of you. Have you noticed that, Sandra? Has anyone else noticed that?" Gayle asked what she meant. She explained, without using names, that whenever the group got close to having to share how experiences or "realities" were affecting them, they seemed to shift to talking about less emotional topics. She then said, "I wonder why this happens." Here we began to point out the pattern that the group was establishing in addressing painful issues. What we failed to do was to recognize and to use Joan's experience in the group as a way to name the painful feelings that the members were avoiding discussing. Gayle stated that she hadn't noticed this. Judy and Barbara stated that they had not noticed either. Each of them was sort of smiling an embarrassed smile. Joan would not look at the group members; she just let out a very heavy sigh that caused everyone to look at her. No one said anything. Once again, we had missed an opportunity and had failed to answer what seemed like Joan's plea for work. We let the group sit for a little while and think.

Barbara commented on how quiet it had gotten. This broke the silence, and the other members began to admit that they "might" have been avoiding painful issues. Joan still sat quietly. I remarked that she had been very quiet for a while and that our time was running out. I wondered if she wanted to share anything with the group. She said no. My coleader said that she imagined her silence meant something. She said, very angrily, that it was sometimes easier to "just not talk." The group then began to inquire and stated that the reason they were together was to help one another and that if they could help her they wanted to. Joan just shook her head and said that she was fine. We, again, avoided bringing up the anger that was present. Maybe we (my coleader and I) did not want to deal with it?

The group then began to talk about some side effects of their chemotherapy. Judy was the only one in the group without hair. She expressed feeling fine about not having it: "It will grow back." Others talked about hair thinning and other side effects that they had read about. Joan joined in the conversation minimally. We still ignored the possible significance of her deviation from the group norm.

The group ended, and that afternoon my coleader got a call from Joan saying that she felt her way of dealing with things was very different from the group's, especially Judy's, and that she felt as though she wanted to quit coming. After talking it through with my coleader, Joan decided to return to the group for at least one more time. When my coleader and I discussed this, I did not see that Joan's phone call was probably a plea, again, for us to help her work with the group on addressing the pain she was feeling. We simply chalked it up to her not getting along with one of the members and feeling as though she was just not getting the kind of support that she needed from the group. My coleader expressed to her that the group was as much hers as anyone else's and that she hoped she would bring her concerns up to the group during the next session. In retrospect, what I think we were missing was that Joan was representing the ambivalence of the group to face painful issues. In addition, we failed to really note what Judy represented to her, and possibly other members. Judy is the only one who has completed chemotherapy and/or radiation, she is the intellectualizer (or initiator of flight), her baldness is a reminder of what might happen to others in the group, and she is getting back into her work and other parts of her life that she has put on hold, unlike the other members who are still faced with much uncertainty.

Session 3

The group opened again by checking in with each member. Joan appeared somewhat more cheerful than I had expected. Barbara brought up feeling worn out about caring for her mother and herself. This opened up a discussion around how they each were giving support to other people. Directing the question to any member, I asked, "Who gives you support?" Judy began to talk about how her friends used to provide her with transportation and/or come over with meals when she was sick from treatment. Each of the other women shared their "support" stories as well. I finally stated that the kind of support that they had all just talked about was support around concrete needs: food, rides, and so on. I then asked who gave them emotional support. The room got silent. Judy began to intellectualize. Joan rolled her eyes and shook her head. I pointed out that they were "doing it again," referring to their established pattern of avoiding painful issues.

Everyone but Joan smiled embarrassedly. I said to them that everyone was smiling but Joan, and I wondered what they were really feeling. They were silent. I said that I imagined it was hard for each of them to be here and to talk about their illness, especially while they are still in treatment. Here I failed to acknowledge or name the ambivalence and did not make its connection to Joan's desire to quit the group. Judy offered a reminder that she was finished with her treatment. My coleader took this opportunity to ask the group what it was like for them to still be in treatment and to have a member present who was through with it. Joan remained quiet. Gayle got tearful and began to pour out that she was "scared shitless" of what might happen to her hair, of how sick she might become and of how there's no real guarantee the chemo would work. I stated that I had just seen more emotion pour out of her than I had seen before. I named what I saw: "You seem like you're feeling sad and scared and angry all at once." She had tears rolling down her cheeks. I looked at Joan, who was tearful. My coleader asked the group, "What do you do with all of these feelings every day?" Joan made a sound of irritation. My coleader asked her what that sound meant. Joan just shook her head. My coleader stated that Gayle's outpouring of emotion was understandable and that she thought it must be hard for her to carry those feelings around. I then took the opportunity to narrow the focus to the anger, because it seemed to be an emotion shared at that moment by more than one member (both Gayle and Joan). At this time, I ended up taking advantage of an opportune moment to address Joan's anger without making her feel alone with it. When I mentioned that it must be hard to deal with the anger and asked how they managed it, Joan started right in about how angry she was at the hospital and about her depressed friend. The discussion continued until Gayle said that she just wished that she could get back to where she was before she got sick. Through this discussion the group was able to talk about their anger, an emotion that all of them admitted to feeling. They acknowledged that it "might" be about their "unlucky" confrontation with cancer, but no one would give a definitive "yes" on that.

As the group ended that day, there was a sense of peace in the room. At this time I was not sure what we had accomplished. But on reviewing my notes from this session it appeared that much work was done in breaking through the obstacles that the literature speaks to. By reaching for the underlying feelings and the meanings of the nonverbal messages, we were able to open up some painful areas that the group obviously felt ambivalent about sharing. We were also able to take the individual's issue (the anger) and bring it out as a common feeling among all the group members, rather than leaving it in one person's possession. One thing that was not addressed, though, was Joan's anger directed at Judy. I think the leaders were too afraid to touch this.

Session 4
The group started as usual with check-ins. The members shared some events that had taken place that week regarding new drugs that two of them were put on. A discussion opened up around side effects again, and this led Joan into discussing her anger about her visit with her doctor that week, as he had been "in and out in a matter of minutes." The group started to ask her questions about why she could not switch doctors if she was so unhappy. I noticed that Joan's response was somewhat different from how she had responded the first time the group had confronted her regarding switching doctors. She was less hostile, and her anger did not seem to be directed at the members. She was able to discuss with them the possibility of switching but came to the conclusion that she would rather still do her own research than switch doctors midtreatment. At this point, Barbara said to Joan, "You seem so angry at the doctors. I wish that your experience with them wasn't so dreadful. It makes it much easier if you feel like you are in good hands." The group began to discuss this thought, and Joan sat back and listened. She did not appear angry, just deep in thought. My coleader asked her what was going through her mind. Joan said, "I just feel like my life is in their hands. They have all the power, the cancer has the power, the drugs have the power, I have none."

For the first time, the group started to really talk about feeling helpless to their cancer diagnoses. After we had recognized and called attention to Joan's nonverbal messages, the group was able to benefit once again from Joan's ability to bring a common issue to the forefront. In addition, the members were beginning to feel comfortable in bringing up the issues themselves. This was evident when Barbara commented to Joan about her anger. No one other than the leaders had pointed this out before.

Current Status of the Problem

Where It Stands Now

At the time that these excerpts were compiled, it was apparent that the group had begun to address painful issues with one another. The leaders' push to address one member's obvious feelings of pain allowed these issues to emerge. The group also began to point out one another's nonverbal reactions, thus opening up deeper levels of discussion and understanding. Although the issues were constantly put in our (the leaders') faces, it took Joan several tries to finally reach us. The group continues to need prodding and reminders that they are "doing it again." Joan continues to display anger, but the group has begun to talk to her directly about this. However, the fact that her anger is often directed at Judy has never been brought up. My coleader and I have begun to discuss our hypotheses about Joan's anger being directed toward Judy. So far, however, neither of us has brought this observation to the forefront, nor has any of the group members. What is clear, still, is that Joan seems to carry the group's internal struggles. What I hope is that the group will somehow find a way to share that responsibility, and Joan will no longer be responsible for vocalizing their needs. Not only will the group benefit from this, but this will help to decrease the alienation that I suspect Joan has felt as her "deviant" way of dealing with issues has set her apart from the group.

Specific Next Steps

- I will continue to zero in on nonverbal messages and bring them to the attention of the group.

- I will continue to encourage group members to discuss painful issues and to point out the obstacles that are created to avoid this work.

- I will continue to collaborate about and review sessions regularly with my coleader so that we can gain greater insight from each other regarding group process.

- I will continue to search for connections between an individual's behaviors and those of the group in order to help the members become more aware of internal struggles.

- I hope to create an educational session for members to have their questions answered by a physician in order to address feelings of disempowerment and helplessness.

- I will continue to work on my group skills and to actively engage in seeking materials to increase my awareness about specific group tasks and problems.

The descriptions of the difficulties group members face in dealing with two major developmental tasks, the relationship with the worker and the relationship among members, refer to a yet more general task, the development of a culture for work. In the following section, we explore the question of group culture in more detail.

Developing a Culture for Work

The term *group culture* has been used thus far in its anthropological/sociological sense, with a particular emphasis on group norms, taboos, and roles. Earlier in this chapter we addressed the concept of role in some detail, so we focus here on norms and taboos. Hare (1962) has defined group norms as

> rules of behavior, proper ways of acting, which have been accepted as legitimate by members of a group. Norms specify the kinds of behavior that are expected of group members. These rules or standards of behavior to which members are expected to conform are for the most part derived from the goals which a group has set for itself. Given a set of goals, norms define the kind of behavior which is necessary for or consistent with the realization of those goals. (p. 24)

Taboos are commonly associated with primitive tribes who developed sacred prohibitions making certain people or acts untouchable or unmentionable. As we have seen, the term *taboo* in modern cultures refers to social prohibitions related to conventions or traditions. Norms and taboos are closely related; for example, one group norm may be the tradition of making a particular subject taboo. As groups are formed, each member brings to the microsociety of the group a strongly developed set of norms of behavior and shared identification of taboo areas. The early culture of the group therefore reflects the members' outside culture. As Hare points out, the norms of a group should be consistent with those necessary for realization of its goals. The problem, however, is that the norms of our society and the taboos commonly observed often create obstacles to productive work in the group. A major group task then involves developing a new set of norms and thereby freeing group members to deal with formerly taboo subjects.

We have already been dealing with the problem of helping group members develop their culture for work. For example, authority and dependency are generally taboo subjects in our culture; we do not talk freely about our feelings regarding either. Group experiences in classrooms over many years have taught us not to challenge authority and yet alerted us to the dangers involved if we admit feelings of dependency on a person in authority in front of a peer group. The discussions of the authority and intimacy themes in the first part of this chapter described the worker's efforts to help the group discuss these taboo areas and to develop a new set of more productive norms. The effort is directed neither at changing societal norms nor exorcising taboos. There are sound reasons for norms of behavior, and many taboos have appropriate places in our lives. The work focuses instead on building a new culture within the group, but only insofar as it is needed for effective group functioning. Transfers of this experience beyond the group may or may not be relevant or appropriate.

For example, members in a couples' group had to deal with taboos against open discussion of sex, an area critical to the work of the group. The frankness of the group discussion freed the couples to develop more open communications with each other outside the sessions. This change in the culture of their marriages was important for them to develop and was therefore an appropriate transfer of learning. On the other hand, if the couples used their newfound freedom to discuss issues of sexual functioning at neighborhood cocktail parties, they might quickly discover the power of peer-group pressure (or perhaps be invited to more parties).

To illustrate the worker's function of helping the group work on its important tasks, we shall examine five efforts of workers to develop a group culture. Then we examine the impact of ethnicity on group culture. This section uses the group theory outlined by Bion (1961) to illustrate again the way in which practitioners can draw on the literature to build their own models of group functioning.

Parents of Hyperactive Children: Accepting Difficult Feelings The first illustration is of a worker's efforts to help a group of parents of hyperactive children share their painful and angry feelings about their children's problems. This is the same group cited earlier to illustrate the need for group members to deal with feelings that result from demands for work.

RECORD OF SERVICE

Client Description and Time Frame

This is a group for parents of children with a hyperactivity diagnosis. It is a gender-mixed group. All of the members are white. The setting is an outpatient clinic at a general hospital. The time frame is five weekly sessions.

Description of the Problem

Members found it very difficult to talk about their own feelings about their hyperactive children. Instead, they continually focused on what other people—such as teachers, neighbors, husbands, and relatives—felt about the children. Despite their reluctance to focus on their feelings, they occasionally gave me clues that this was their underlying concern, and as this was also part of the contract, I felt we had to explore their feelings and work on them.

How the Problem Came to the Attention of the Worker(s)

During the first few meetings, the members continued to talk about how important this group was for them, as it gave them a chance to get together to discuss their problems related to their hyperactive children and get support from each other. The feeling was that no one, not even their husbands or wives, understood what they were going through and how they felt. Any time they would begin talking about their own feelings, they resorted back to discussing medications, school, etc.—in other words, a safe topic. Yet the need to talk about how they felt was always raised by members in different ways. This pattern began in session two, when one member raised the question of hyperactivity due to emotional deprivation at an early age—the group superficially touched on it but dropped the subject, resorting back to something safe. As their pattern of flight became more obvious to me, I could help them understand what they were doing, and thus help them deal with their feelings.

Bion (1961) can help explain such difficulties with emotions, a characteristic common to groups. His work was based on observations of psychotherapy groups, led by himself, in which he played the relatively passive role of interpreting the members' behaviors. Once again, as with the earlier theory, some elements of his model are group-specific, while other aspects lend themselves nicely to generalizing. A central idea in Bion's work is the **work group**. This consists of the mental activity related to a group's task. When the work group is operating, one can see group members translating their thoughts and feelings into actions that are adaptive to reality. As Bion describes it, the work group represents a "sophisticated" level of group operation. Most groups begin with a more "primitive" culture in which they resist dealing with painful emotions. Group development is therefore the struggle between the group's primitive instincts to avoid the pain of growth and its need to become more sophisticated and deal with feelings. The primitive culture of the group's early stages mirrors the primitive culture in our larger society, where the direct and open expression of feelings is avoided.

In the example of the parents' group, the worker described how the problem came to her attention, pointing out how the more painful subjects were dropped as the group took flight into a discussion of more superficial issues. This conforms to one of Bion's key ideas—the existence of basic assumption groups. He believes that the work group can be obstructed, diverted, and sometimes assisted by group members experiencing powerful emotional drives. His term **basic assumption group** refers to the idea that group members appear to be acting as if their behavior were motivated by a shared basic assumption about the purpose of the group—an assumption other than the expressed group goal.

One of the three basic assumption groups he identifies is the **flight-fight group**. In a primitive group, when the work group gets close to painful feelings, the members will unite in an instantaneous, unconscious process to form the flight-fight group, acting from the basic assumption that the group goal is to avoid the pain associated with the work group processes through flight (that is, an immediate change of subject away from the painful area) or fight (that is, an argument developing in the group that moves from the emotional level to an intellectual one). This process in the group context parallels the ambivalence noted in work with individuals when resistance is expressed through an abrupt change of subjects. Bion's strategy for dealing with this problem is to call the group's attention to the behavior in an effort to educate the group so that it can function on a more sophisticated level.

As we return to the worker's record of service on this problem, we see that her early efforts were directed at systematically encouraging the expression of feelings and acknowledging these with her own feelings in an effort to build a working relationship. As the pattern developed, the worker drew on this working relationship to point out the pattern of avoidance and to make a demand for work.

Summary of the Work

Session 3

I listened to what the members were saying, and I encouraged them to talk about their feelings toward their hyperactive children. Marilyn told us that since she had begun coming to the sessions, she noticed that she had changed her attitude in relation to her hyperactive son, and now he was responding more positively toward her. She had always thought of him in terms of being a normal child, and it had frustrated her that he was unable to react as normal children do. In fact, she had set up expectations for him that he couldn't meet. I encouraged her to continue talking about her feelings toward him. She said that she supposed she really couldn't accept the fact that he was hyperactive, and then after coming to the meeting she began to accept this. I asked how she felt now. She felt better, but the hurt was there.

By the fifth session, the group had come close to discussing some of the more difficult underlying feelings; however, each time they had come up, they had used the flight mechanism to avoid the pain. Some of the feelings experienced by these parents ran so counter to what they expected themselves to feel that they had great difficulty in admitting the feelings to others and at times even to themselves. The worker had developed a fund of trust during the first sessions through her efforts to understand the meaning of the experience for the members. In the following excerpt, she draws on that fund and makes a demand for work by pointing out the members' pattern of flight. Even as she does this, she tries to express her empathy with the difficulty the group experiences in meeting this demand.

Session 5

The group sometimes picked up on their feelings, and I tried to put a demand for work on them; that is, to stick with the subject and to really talk about their feelings. I pointed out their underlying anger and did not allow them to take flight. Betty started talking about George and the school again, and the others became very supportive, offering concrete help. She expressed anger at the school but also talked about George and how he didn't fit in—he couldn't read and cope with the courses, and he didn't care. I detected that some of her anger was directed toward him, and I asked how she felt toward him at this point. She said that she pitied him. I wondered if she wasn't also feeling somewhat angry at him for causing her so many problems and irritating her so much. I said that there were times when George made her very angry. Mildred agreed that she has reacted negatively, too.

The worker's synthesis of empathy and demand helped the group modify its culture and create a new norm in which they would not be judged harshly for their feelings, even those they felt were unreasonable. As they expressed feelings of anger toward their children, the group moved to a new level of trust and openness. With the worker's help, they described moments when they felt like "killing" their child, and, under her gentle prodding, they explored how they experienced having an "imperfect child" as a reflection on themselves as bad parents. This attitude, in turn, affected the children's sense of acceptance by their parents, which sometimes led to further acting out. Understanding and accepting these feelings was a first step toward breaking this vicious cycle. The worker's comments at the end of the session acknowledged the important change in the discussion:

I recognized how hard it was to talk about their feelings, and how much pain they felt. I credited them for their work and tried to create feeling among them that I understood. Denise had been talking about her own feelings about her son, and she seemingly had her feelings well under control. She had said that she was very sensitive and had trouble talking about it. I said that perhaps she was saying that she, too, had feelings that the others had mentioned, but she found them very hard to discuss. The others said that it was hard to talk about their concerns, to admit that these children weren't the same as the others, that you wanted to be proud of them but couldn't. I agreed that it was hard—they were living the situation 24 hours a day, and they had feelings about these children. . . .

The members discussed how much they were criticized by their relatives and were very upset. I said that people just did not know what it was like to be a mother of a child like this, and also they did not feel the pain and frustration that the parents felt. I waited, and there was silence. I noticed that our time was long ago up, and I said that they had done some very hard work. It was not easy to talk as they had today, to share the feelings of depression and hostility toward their children and to admit that they had wanted to kill them at times. I wondered how they felt now. Marilyn said that she couldn't understand everything I tried to get them to do, but I made her think and try new things, and also I made her look at things differently. I said that it wasn't easy for them to do this, I knew that, and I often felt their pain.

We have already seen in an earlier excerpt how the worker needed to help this group articulate its anger in response to her demands for work. Bion might describe those exchanges as examples of the flight pattern of reaction in the flight-fight group. Another basic assumption group, as described by Bion, is the **dependent group**, in which the group appears to be meeting in order to be sustained by the leader. This is another form of avoidance of the work group and was illustrated in the earlier excerpt by the group wanting the leader to "cheer them up." The third and final assumption group in Bion's theory is called the **pairing group**. Here the group, often through a conversation between two members, avoids the pain of the work by discussing some future great event. The event can be the discovery of a new drug or procedure that will cure the person who is ill. Another example would be the arrival of some person or organization that will solve the problem. The discussion in this group of "new drugs" or "outside experts" who would provide a solution to their problems is an example of the pairing group in action. Now let us see the rest of the record of service.

Current Status of the Problem

Where It Stands Now

The group is beginning to work on their feelings, although not all members are equally willing to take a good look at themselves. They are starting to share with each other the pain, guilt, and anger they have toward their hyperactive children. Also, they're sharing feelings of helplessness—of wanting to be the perfect parent but knowing that they're not—and their desire to find ways to deal with their children better.

Strategies for Intervention

- Keep the focus, and continue making the demand for work. Continue making this a work group and not a fight-flight group.
- Use the deviant member's behavior to point out their own underlying feelings.
- Continue to recognize their feelings and credit them for their work. In crediting, make them aware of their progress, as a means of encouragement.
- Credit the internal leaders for taking over leadership and focusing the group on the work.
- Help the group work on solutions to their feelings and problems. The group needs this if they are to lose their feelings of helplessness—they want to learn how they can function better as parents and help their hyperactive children.
- Help the group move into the ending and transition stage.

Married Couples: Legitimizing the Expression of Anger In a second example of helping a group change its norms to develop a culture more conducive to work, a worker in a different married couples' group notices the group members' reluctance to get involved when couples share very personal and angry feelings. She brings this to their attention.

By the sixth session (following Christmas vacation, during which the group had adjourned for 2 weeks), most of the group's work seemed to involve each couple presenting problems that had been decided on by both partners and within limits felt by both to be fairly comfortable. If there was intracouple disagreement and challenge, such conflict seemed to be on safe topics—e.g., related to problems of the others in the group or, if pertaining to their own marriage, then almost always at the level of the more reluctant spouse. Don, at the fifth session, challenged Liz directly. Liz responded to his charge that she was "always covering up the truth" by a return challenge, asking him why he had married her—daring him to share with the group the real reason, her pregnancy.

When he tried to evade her by deliberately misinterpreting her question, she stuck with it and said she had always suspected that he had felt an obligation to marry and had never really loved her. The group seemed reluctant at first to step into this interchange—they seemed to be giving the couple a chance to "unsay" what had been said. I pointed out the difference between their reaction to this problem and others they had picked up on unhesitatingly, and I asked if they agreed that there was a difference. A few members did, and I asked why they thought they hadn't wanted to get involved. Most felt it was "extremely intimate," and that made the difference. I agreed that it was and that I felt it really took guts to bring up something intimate. I said that problems were not often brought up, because they were so personal and that we were so used to keeping anything personal as private as possible. The group talked about family and friends and "how far" one could go in these relationships and how this group was different from "out there." Something clicked for Reisa, because without even checking it out with Jack, she told the group that she and Jack had been forced to marry because she had been pregnant, too. They talked about her family's reaction and how this had affected their marriage and their feelings about their first child.

Married Couples: Dealing With Sexual Taboos I described earlier how the skill of helping individual clients to discuss subjects in taboo areas was important to the work. The social nature of taboos magnifies their impact in the group setting. Many of the taboos have their early roots in the first primary groups, such as the family, and thus can represent a powerful obstacle to group work. Sometimes the worker simply needs to call the group's attention to the obstacle, but in the case of some of the stronger taboos, such as sex, the group may need more help.

In the couples' group described in Chapter 10, sexual concerns between members were hinted at toward the end of an early session. I pointed this out to the group and suggested that we pick up on this at our next session. The group agreed enthusiastically. I did not expect it to be that easy; because of the strength of the taboo in this area, simply calling the group's attention to the subject probably would be insufficient. At the start of the next session, the members immediately began to discuss an unrelated area. I called their attention to the existence of the taboo. I asked the group members to explore the obstacle that made it hard for them to discuss sexual subjects. As they discussed what made it hard to talk about sexuality, they were talking about sexuality:

> I said, "At the end of last week we agreed to get into the whole sexual area, and yet we seem to be avoiding it this week. I have a hunch that this is a hard area to discuss in the group. Am I right?" There was a look of relief on their faces, and Lou responded, "Yes, I noticed that as well. You know, this is not easy to talk about in public. We're not used to it." I wanted the group to explore what it was about this area that made it hard. "Maybe it would help if we spent some time on what it is about this area, in particular, that makes it tough to discuss. That might make everyone feel a bit more comfortable."

Fran responded, "When I was a kid, I got a clear message that this wasn't to be spoken about with my parents. The only thing said to me was that I should watch out because boys had only one thing on their mind—the problem was, I wasn't sure what that thing was." Group members were nodding and smiling at this. Lou said, "How many of you had your parents talk to you about sex?" The group exchanged stories of how sex was first raised with them. In all cases it had been done indirectly, if at all, and with some embarrassment. Those with older children described their own determination to do things differently, but somehow, their actual efforts to talk to their children were still marked by discomfort. At one point, Frank described his concerns as a teenager: "You know, from the talk I heard from the other guys, I thought everyone in the neighborhood was getting sex except me. It made me feel something was really wrong with me—and I made sure not to let on that I was really concerned about this." The conversation continued with the group noting that they had been raised in different generations, and that while some things were different in terms of attitudes toward sex, other things, particularly the taboos, were the same. I could sense a general relaxing as the discussion proceeded, and members discovered that there were many similarities in their experiences. I said, "It's easy to see how these experiences would make it difficult for you to talk freely in this group; however, if we can't get at this critical area, we will be blocked in our work."

By encouraging discussion of the taboo and the reasons for its power, I was helping the members enter this area. It was important that I did not blame or criticize them for their difficulty in getting started, but at the same time I needed to make a demand to move past the taboo.

"I can imagine that this difficulty in talking about sex must carry over in your marriages as well. I believe that if you can discuss some of the problems you are having here in the group, we might be able to help you talk more freely to each other—and that might be the beginning of a change." Rick responded, "We can never talk to each other about this without ending up in a fight." I asked Rick if he could expand on this. "We have this problem of me wanting more sex than Fran—sometimes we can go for months without sex, and I'm not sure I can take this anymore." Fran responded, "A relationship is more than just sex, you know, and I just can't turn it on or off because you happen to feel like having sex."

The rest of the evening was spent on Fran and Rick's relationship. The group was supportive to both as the couple's early conversation centered on who was to blame: Fran for her "frigidity" or Rick for his "premature ejaculation." During the next few sessions, the group kept discussing the sexual area as members explored the intricate patterns of action and reaction they had developed that led them to blame each other rather than take responsibility for their own feelings about sex. Once the taboo had been breached, and group members found that they were not punished, it lost some of its power and the discussion became more personal. Note that the process and the task are intermixed. As the group members discuss their difficulty in speaking about sex (the process), they are actually beginning to work on their concerns about sex (the task).

The final two brief excerpts in this section focus on helping young people deal with violence in their families. In these excerpts, the workers attempt to help group members share with each other the pain and posttraumatic stress that has become a part of everyday life for many of our most vulnerable children. In the first example, the worker helps the group discuss violence in their homes directed toward their mothers. In her analysis the worker shows how the violence also affects her feelings and actions. In the second example, the worker and the group try to help an older teen in a juvenile delinquency detention center deal with the result of his having accidentally shot and killed his best friend. As with the first example, we clearly see how hard it is for the workers to stay with the pain expressed by the group member. In the second example, one worker reaches for the member's underlying feelings while the other moves away from them, focusing instead on questions of responsibility. Both examples underline the importance of support for helping professionals so that they can manage their own feelings while helping clients manage theirs.

Inner-City Elementary School: The Impact of Violence in the Family

Purpose: Discussion group (with special attention to violent school behavior).

Gender/Age of Members: Female; age range: 9 to 10 years.

Cultural, Racial, or Ethnic Identification of Members: Two are African American and the third is African American and Hispanic.

Session 2

I asked if anyone had something they wanted to talk about today. Both Shaquandra's and Asia's hands shot up. I told them to decide who goes first. They pointed at each other and said, "You go first." Maria said nothing. It went back and forth for a few minutes with, "You," "No, you," "No, you," when finally Shaquandra said, "Oh, I will." She launched into a long, detailed account of how her stepfather tried to kill her mother. He was hiding in the room and she tried to get a gun but she could not get it because he pushed her down. She was talking very rapidly and staring blankly. She made no direct eye contact with anyone.

Finally, she paused, taking a deep breath. I said, "Wow, that's a lot of information all at once—sounds scary." She said, "Yeah." I asked her how that felt to her. She said, "It feels bad. I'm scared of him, but he's going to jail." Asia quickly chimed in, "Yeah, it feels bad." Then she launched into a similar story about an uncle who tried to kill her mother, but Asia hit him. "He's going to jail too, but I'm scared if he gets out he'll try to kill my mother again." I asked how it felt to hit him. She said it felt good. I said, "Wow, you girls have a lot to deal with. It must be hard for you. Did you know that sometimes when kids have a lot going on at home, they sometimes have unhappy times at school?"

Analysis

The major thing I would want to do if I had a chance would be to encourage a fuller development of statements the girls made. Because of my inexperience, and its having been only the second group meeting, I was feeling my way and did not explore as much as I would now. At the time, there was nothing coming from the group that could explain my last intervention statement. I think it meant I was scared, so I threw in a safe (for me) training manual statement! The Student Support Program at the school prepared a manual with suggested wording of statements for working with the kids. "Did you know that when kids are unhappy at home, they often have problems at school?" is a vintage example, which I used verbatim. In retrospect, I would still want to tie the school behavior together with the home problems at some point, but I would not feel so compelled to run away from the violence issues. I have a much better comfort level with tougher issues now.

Residential Center for Young Men in the Criminal Justice System

Purpose: To provide education and support to male juvenile delinquents with histories of anger and violence control problems.

Gender/Age of Members: Male; age range: 14–18.

Cultural, Racial, or Ethnic Identification of Members: Caucasian, African American, Native American, Hispanic, Cape Verdian.

Session 33

Jon (coleader) reminded Bill of family group when his mother was so angry with his apathy and resistance to treatment that she threatened to "leave her kids and get on with her life." There was silence in the room as Bill stared at the floor. In a soft voice, I said, "Bill, I was wondering about last week in family group—what was it like to hear your mom talk about stepping over the spot where Jim died?" Bill looked up at me as a group member asked, "Where did you shoot him? It was in your house?" Bill's gaze returned to the floor and he replied, "Yeah, it was in my living room. . . . My mom had new carpeting put in and stuff, but it's that spot, we know where it is."

I asked, "Had you considered what she continues to go through on a daily basis, or was that the first time you had heard she is stepping over it to close the drapes every night?" He raised his voice and responded, "I don't know, it made me mad to hear that she wants to sell the house or burn it or something! That made me mad." I replied, "She has a lot of memories there that she faces each day." There was silence. Then Bill said, "I used to sit on that spot on the floor and think about Jim." I said, "You have memories too, Bill?" He shared the moment of Jim's death on his living room floor. "I held on to him so tight . . . they pulled me off . . . the paramedics, they had to hold me so they could take him away . . . I just want him back." Bill began to sob uncontrollably. Jon encouraged Bill to feel the pain because that would be the only way it would go away. The group supported Bill with "Let it go, Bill," and "It's OK, guy, we're here for you." Jon then said, "You killed your best friend, Bill. You were out of control. You killed him and you cannot afford to forget that." The group remained silent.

The Impact of Ethnicity on Group Culture As the previous examples show, the worker faces many issues in establishing group culture. One such issue that deserves special attention is ethnicity.

One of my most important learning experiences occurred when I served as a consultant for the Hong Kong government department of social services. I provided short-term training workshops for social service professionals on how to organize and lead mutual-aid groups for clients. Although I had tried to get ready by reading about ethnic-sensitive practice and tuning in, nothing quite prepared me for the emotional impact and challenge to my adaptive skills I would face. I quickly understood that the process in the training groups would parallel what these social workers would face as they attempted to lead their client groups. Also, I realized that my task would be difficult: I would probably learn at least as much as I taught. The staff of the Hong Kong Social Service Department helped me in my efforts.

My first important insight was that fundamentals of human and group behavior are universal across cultures, but we can trace the roots of these norms, taboos, rules of behavior, and so on to quite different sources; thus, the intensity of their impact and the way they emerge vary among cultures. For example, I had prepared for the fact that the authority theme would be central in this group, as it is in all groups, in the beginning phase of work. With the Hong Kong groups, however, I was the "Professor," to be accorded status and deference in a manner that persisted for the life of the group. One group member pointed out to me that Chinese tradition bestows great prestige and authority on the group leader. This echoes the father in the Chinese family. As a person of knowledge, the group leader is entitled to respect and obedience from the group members who come to learn from him or her. Respect involves more than just ordinary politeness; it also involves agreement with the leader's view or at least abstention from open expression of disagreement. To disagree with a leader is to challenge his or her social role and hence harm his or her prestige. The leader would be seen as losing face. These values toward authority and others that stress harmony and order in all personal relationships can be traced to the three major streams of thought in Chinese history: Taoism, Buddhism, and Confucianism.

A second major insight was that principles of good practice also applied across cultures, but respecting and working with ethnic and cultural differences required me to make adaptations. For example, rather than opening each training group session with problem swapping and discussion, I prepared a brief and expected presentation. However, I did not abandon my requests for active discussion and involvement; I just delayed the demand, because I needed to respond to their expectations of me. I also respected their early resistance to disagreeing with me; however, I pointed out my awareness of their reluctance and my hope that, during our work together, we might find a way for them to provide feedback. Here is an excerpt from my notes from one of the early groups:

> I am very pleased that I will have an opportunity to share my ideas about leading mutual-aid groups with you. However, I have a problem with which I will need your assistance. These ideas were developed in my work with groups in a Western culture. I believe many will be useful for your groups as well, some will need to be adapted to respect your Chinese culture, and others may not fit at all. I understand and appreciate that your respect for me as a professor and your thoughtfulness will make you hesitant to disagree or suggest different ideas. It is my hope, however, that as we get to know each other, you will see that I very much value your ideas and will find your opinions helpful. I am prepared to teach what I know about group leadership, but I am also hoping to be a student as well.

There was no response to this offer, but I believe it was heard and understood. After the session, one group member, who had been educated at Berkeley University, where the cultural expectations governing the interchange between faculty and students differed somewhat from tradition, approached me privately to reassure me that it would take some time before I could expect a response and that I should not be discouraged.

I continued to try to find ways to encourage the group members to participate and provide feedback within their own cultural tradition. For example, when our groups had reached the point where they felt safe enough to share some of their difficult experiences leading groups, and we had reached a point in the analysis of an example where the skill of reaching for feelings or making a demand for work was appropriate, I would comment as follows:

> If I were faced with this problem in a group I was leading back home, I would probably say the following at this point: (I would then share my specific intervention). Can you help me to see how we could modify this so that we can accomplish the same end but do it in a way that would be comfortable for your culture and your groups?

This often generated an excellent discussion in which the workshop members artfully found their own ways of making the same intervention. Because my request was presented in a cooperative, rather than confrontational, manner, workshop members appeared to feel free to respond without fearing that they would be offending their group leader. An important additional benefit here was that I was modeling the same respect for culture in the workshop group that they would need to demonstrate in their own client groups.

One final tradition was observed with each of the groups I led: I was taken out to a celebratory luncheon banquet following the last session. This is one ethnic cultural practice I made no effort to modify; in fact, I would like to import it into my Western classes. This personal example has been provided to introduce the idea of respect for ethnic and racial variations in understanding and supporting the development of an effective group culture.

Developing a Structure for Work

As a group develops, it needs to work on the task of building a **structure for work:** the formal and informal rules, roles, communication patterns, rituals, and procedures developed by the group members to facilitate the work of the group. Regarding rules, some are established by the agency or host setting and are not in the control of the group members. At times, the group leader may try to help a group change a rule when conflict persists (see Part V). In other cases, the rules emerge from the members themselves.

In the following example, one member of an outpatient group for recovering addicts raises the issue of bringing her baby to the group sessions. Underlying the issue of structure are several other concerns for this client as well as questions for the workers about the need for additional agency support for the group.

The setting is an outpatient alcohol and drug clinic in a hospital. This is a group for young recovering addicts. The purpose of the group is for the members to learn from and support each other as they cope with a sober lifestyle. Two men and two women are at the first meeting, and up to four more members could be added. The members range in age from 19 to 27 years. The two women are black; one of the men is black and the other is white. The coleaders are white, and one is a counselor at the clinic.

> We had just finished going over the group rules and the group members were quiet. Beth (my coleader) asked the group if they wanted to add any more rules. There was a brief silence, and then Amanda said (to Beth), "You know what I would like to have for a rule." Beth nodded and said that maybe Amanda could explain what she meant to the group. Amanda turned back to the group and said that she had a 3-month-old baby. The social service department had the baby now, but she hoped to get the baby back soon. She was not

sure that she could find someone she trusted to watch the baby while she came to group. This was her first child, and she had been separated from her for so long that she didn't want to leave her. She said that while she was in group she would worry about the baby and that she had asked Beth in the pregroup interview if it might be OK for her to bring the baby along, but that we (Beth and I) had told her that she couldn't bring the baby. Amanda looked at Beth.

Beth said that traditionally the clinic hasn't had very many female clients and that this issue hadn't come up before at the clinic, so she hadn't given Amanda an answer right away but had talked to me and to the other staff members; she said that she and I had thought that it could be disruptive and distracting to have a baby in the group. Amanda, still speaking to Beth, said that probably the baby would just sleep most of the time. Beth said that the problem was that the baby wouldn't be 3 months for very long. Beth said that maybe Jen (another member) had some thoughts about the issue. Amanda turned to Jen. Jen smiled and said that she could remember when her daughter and her son were babies and that she had never wanted to leave them. She said that it's hard to leave your baby, but if there's a baby in the room, it's hard to ignore it even if it is asleep, because babies are so cute you always want to pick them up or play with them or touch them, so having a baby in the group could be disruptive.

Amanda appeared to take this comment in thoughtfully, and then she turned to Leo and Herb and said, "What do you think?" There was a brief silence and then Leo said that he didn't personally have children, but that he had a real soft spot for children and old people. He said from what he could tell it was going to be hard for Amanda to leave her baby, and he could see why. He said it seemed like Amanda was between a rock and a hard place, because if she brought the baby, it might distract her and the rest of the group, and if she didn't bring the baby, it might also distract her because she would be thinking about her baby and worrying about her. He said that it was important for Amanda to take time to focus on her own recovery, and bringing the baby to the group could get in the way of that as well as being distracting.

Amanda seemed satisfied with this and turned to Herb, who said that he basically agreed with Leo. Herb said that he liked kids a lot, but that he thought that a baby probably would be distracting and that it would be good for Amanda to take the group time to focus on herself. Amanda said that she could understand where everyone was coming from, but she still felt like she didn't want to leave her baby, but she'd do the best she could to get a babysitter. Leo suggested that maybe Amanda shouldn't get too worked up just yet, because it would be a few more weeks before she got the baby back and maybe a solution would turn up between now and then. He finished off by saying, "Easy does it," prompting Herb and Jen to follow quickly with two more AA slogans and everyone, including Amanda, wound up laughing. Then there was a brief silence.

I agreed with Leo and said that it was good this issue had come up because it might be the first time it had come up in the clinic, but it almost certainly wouldn't be the last time. I said that I thought it showed a gap in the clinic's services and it was something Beth and I could explore a little more and see if we could find a solution for. The members nodded, and Beth mentioned that there was a babysitting service in the hospital during the day, but that there clearly was a gap in the availability of services at night. Amanda said that she had not known about the daytime service and it made her mad to know it wasn't offered at night. She said she thought that probably a lot more women would come to the clinic if there was someone here to watch their kids. The other group members agreed. Beth said that maybe something could be worked out such as cooperative babysitting, and she asked me if I would bring that up at the staff meeting on Monday morning, because she isn't there on Mondays. I said I would be sure to, and I'd let them know what happened.

The discussion of the rule often raises many issues for the client, for example in this case Amanda's concern about caring for her baby and not losing it to the child welfare agency again. The worker remains responsible for enforcing the agency policy on the issue of Amanda bringing her baby to the group. In this case, the worker involves other group members in addressing the rule and its impact on Amanda and the group. Most important, the worker's sense of the mediating role between client and system leads her to begin immediately to identify potential systems work on the issue of providing child care resources so that members can attend the group without being concerned about neglecting their children. In exploring the other issue that may be being raised indirectly by the member—that is, her concerns about the demands on her life that emerge from her parenting responsibility—the worker provides an example of how process and content can be integrated. By bringing the baby to the group, the client may be indirectly saying, "Look how hard it is for me to take care of my own life and the baby at the same time." The worker might also want to explore this as a theme of concern for Amanda and for other members as well.

Chapter Summary

In this chapter, we have examined common examples of individual roles in the group, exploring the worker's helping role in relation to them. The concept of social role helps to explain patterned reactions by scapegoats, deviants, and gatekeepers, as well as defensive, quiet, and monopolizing members. In each case, the worker can best serve the group by understanding the individual member in terms of the dynamics of the group.

The worker's second client, the group-as-a-whole, is much like an organism: The sum of its parts is greater than the whole, and it goes through a developmental process. Early tasks include problems of formation and the satisfaction of individual members' needs. Problems of dealing with the worker as a symbol of authority (the authority theme) must be faced, as well as the difficulties involved in peer-group relationships (the intimacy theme). The worker also must attend the culture of the group so that it can develop norms consistent with the achievement of the group's goals. Taboos that block the group's progress must be challenged and overcome if the discussion is to be meaningful. A formal or informal structure must also be developed. This structure includes formal or informal rules, roles, communication patterns, rituals, and procedures developed by the group members. Effective work in the group develops a sense of cohesion, which in turn strengthens future work.

Related Online Content and Activities

 Visit *The Skills of Helping* Book Companion Website at www.socialwork.wadsworth .com/Shulman06/ for learning tools such as glossary terms, InfoTrac College Edition keywords, links to related websites, and chapter practice quizzes.

The website for this chapter also features additional notes from the author and additional process recordings:

- Boys in a Residential Center
- Boys in a Residential Treatment Center: Identifying With the Scapegoat
- Canadian Pregnant Teens in a Maternity Home: Development of Themes Over Time
- Developing a Group Structure Over Time: Teen Psychiatric Group
- Geriatric Reminiscence Group
- Homosexual Veterans with AIDS—Dealing With the Effects of Oppression
- Male Batterers: Moving From a General Problem to a Specific Concern
- Men's Counseling Group
- Men's Group: A Member Reaches Out to the Quiet Member
- Pregnant Teens in a Shelter: Mediating the Scapegoat—Group Interaction
- Teen Boys in a Residential Treatment Center: Raising a Difficult Family Issue and Dealing With the Group as the Second Client
- Teen Residential Group: Acting-Out Behavior as a Means of Communication
- Veterans With HIV/AIDS: Powerful Feelings and Powerful Fears
- Veterans' Outpatient Clinic: Management of Chronic Pain and Posttraumatic Stress

CHAPTER THIRTEEN

Endings and Transitions With Groups

CHAPTER OUTLINE

Ending and Transition Phase
  Summary
Group Illustrations
A Termination Session:
  The Worker Leaving
  the Group

The dynamics and skills involved in the ending and transition phase for individuals were discussed in detail in Chapter 5. All of these processes apply equally to work with groups. After offering a brief review, this chapter illustrates the variations that come with group work. The chapter concludes with a full description of an ending group session that demonstrates the unique aspects of endings in groups.

- Is a worker good-bye / feedback important in every group?

- Is anyone familiar of the written feedback discussed on p.463? Who uses this? What does it say? Can it be detrimental to a mbr's progress?

Ending and Transition Phase Summary

The ending stages of work with individuals, described in detail in Chapter 5, are also apparent in group sessions. First, there is the **denial of the ending**, in which group members appear to ignore the imminent end of the group. This is followed by **anger over the ending**, which emerges in direct and indirect forms and is often directed at the worker. The **mourning period** is usually characterized by apathy and a general tone of sadness in the group. Next, we have **trying the ending on for size**, in which the group members operate independently of the worker or spend a great deal of time talking about new groups or new workers. The *farewell-party syndrome* is seen when group members appear to protect the group by avoiding its negative aspects. It is not at all unusual for group members to suggest an actual farewell party in an attempt to avoid the pain of the ending.

Like the ending phases, worker strategies for dealing with endings in group work are similar to those described in work with individual clients. The worker should bring the ending to the group members' attention early, thereby allowing the ending process to be established. The stages should be pointed out as the group experiences them, with the worker reaching for the indirect cues and articulating the processes taking place: denial, anger, mourning, and so on. Because the group ending has meaning for the worker as well, he or she should bring personal feelings and recollections to the group. Discussion of the ending feelings should be encouraged, with the worker participating fully in the exchange of both positive and negative reactions. The worker should also help the group be specific as they evaluate their work together. For example, when a member says, "It was a great group!" the worker should ask, "What was it about the group that made it great?" Finally, the worker should reach past the farewell-party syndrome to encourage members to share negative feedback.

Because members have different reactions to endings, the group worker should encourage the expression and acceptance of differing views. The worker must also pay attention to the transitional aspect of the ending phase. For example, if members are continuing with other workers, how can they begin the relationship in a positive manner? If members have finished their work, what have they learned, and how can they use their learning in their new experiences? If they have found the group helpful, how can they find similar sources of support in their life situations? In this way, the worker can ensure that the ending discussion deals with substantive matters as well as the process of ending. In some situations, help can also take the form of a physical transition (such as a visit to a new school or institution). Finally, the worker should search for the subtle connections between the process of the ending and the substantive work of the contract. For example, endings for a group of unmarried mothers may coincide with separation from their children; foster teenagers who have provided mutual aid to each other may have learned something about giving and taking help from their peer group. These and other connections can help to enrich the ending discussion. The next section illustrates these dynamics and skills drawn from the group context.

Group Illustrations

The ending phase of work offers a powerful opportunity to deepen the work by integrating process and content. The losses involved in ending a group often provoke issues of intimacy and loss in other areas of the client's life. By constantly searching for the connections, however faint, between the dynamics of the ending process and the substantive work of the particular group, the worker can help the members use the ending as an important learning experience.

In the example that follows, a worker opens up the discussion of her leaving with a group of people who have multiple sclerosis (the group will be continuing). The announcement of the impending ending initiates a powerful conversation about intimacy and loss related to the illness. Note that the worker brings the group members back to their own endings in the here-and-now of the group experience.

Patients With Multiple Sclerosis

WORKER: As you know, I only meet with you one more time after today. You all will continue to meet until June. What are your thoughts about the group ending in a couple of months?

BOB: I am not looking forward to the summer because of the hot weather . . . it makes my MS flare up.

ALBERT: I know . . . I always feel tired and run down when it gets too hot. And then the group breaks up and I don't have anyone to really talk to about my MS. I used to look forward to the summer, but now I almost dread it.

BOB: I'm going to miss everyone too. I don't have anyone to talk to either. My wife is great, but she doesn't really understand what I am feeling.

WORKER: Do you guys keep in touch even when the group is not meeting during the summer months?

ALBERT: Not really . . .

FRED: I often talk to Rob from the other group pretty regularly.

BOB: Albert, you live not too far from me. We should get together once in a while this summer. Or at least talk on the phone.

ALBERT: I like that idea . . . I do want to stay in touch.

JAMES: (Who had been quiet up to this point) I used to dance and run track . . . and now I can't anymore. People look at me like I'm weird.

BOB: I always liked to dance too.

WORKER: James, you said people look at you weird. What do you mean by that? How does that make you feel?

JAMES: I get mad because I am not weird. I am just in a wheelchair. They don't know what I used to be able to do. All they see is what I look like on the outside.

WORKER: You're right. Strangers do not know who you are or what you are like, as we do. They don't know you as a person, and it isn't fair that they should judge you by your appearance or being in a wheelchair.

FRED: That's the trouble—no one can see the MS. They can't see the pain we feel in our legs, or the burning we have in our joints.

ALBERT: (He is one of the members whose MS is not as extreme. He still walks.) People don't even know anything is wrong with me because I am not in a wheelchair. But I still experience the MS symptoms. When they flare up, I get tired and sometimes walk off-balance, like I am drunk or something.

WORKER: It must be hard for you, Albert, because people cannot see your illness, and may not understand when you try to explain your physical symptoms.

ALBERT: Yeah, that happens a lot. When people find out I have MS, they don't believe me, because I am not in a wheelchair and they automatically associate MS with being in a wheelchair.

FRED: I went through that a lot when I was first diagnosed. I fought going into this wheelchair for as long as I could. I was lucky to be able to work until I was 60. But a short time after I retired, I had to get the chair.

JAMES: Yeah . . . when I first got those symptoms, the MPs on base used to stop me to ask if I was drunk because I staggered so much. That's when I first realized something was wrong. And then it just kept getting worse until I wound up in this wheelchair.

WORKER: You guys have lost important things associated with your identity because of this disease. Many of you had to quit working before you wanted . . . some of you lost important relationships.

JAMES: That's what I miss . . . having a girlfriend. (He pauses.)

WORKER: (After it looks like he won't continue on his own) Tell us more, James.

JAMES: I just miss the company. I don't care about the sex. I just wish I had the companionship. Someone to talk to, who will do things with me. I love my son and my parents, but I wish I had someone more my age to be with. (James is a young guy, in his early thirties and, in addition to being confined to a wheelchair, he has speech difficulties and shaking in his arms and neck. In retrospect, I wish I had explored more about how the change in his appearance and increasing disability affects his romantic possibilities. He has an 8-year-old son, but I don't know what his relationship with the mother was or if she left him when he became disabled. I'm sure this is something all the men have had to face—changes in their manhood, and how society views a disabled man.)

FRED: I know, James. Companionship is important.

BOB: There are a lot of symptoms of MS that people don't see and we don't talk about. Like our bladder and bowel problems. It's very degrading and embarrassing not to be able to control them all the time. (The others all voiced their agreement.)

WORKER: I know you were interested a few weeks ago in having Dr. C. (urologist) come to speak to you about these problems. Did she ever come?

ALBERT: Not yet.

WORKER: I will talk to the RN again and try to schedule her as a speaker in the future. (I bowed out of a sensitive and embarrassing subject here as well. I probably should have explored their feelings more around this subject, too.)

WORKER: I want to talk some more about our ending. I know I've been mentioning it the last couple of times we've met. It's really hard when people come and go from your life.

ALBERT: Yeah, it is. It seems like we just started with you and now you are leaving already.

WORKER: I want you to know that it is hard for me too. I am in a field where I will have to say good-bye many times to people whom I have grown to care about. But I believe that when I leave here, I will take a part of you all and internalize it, especially your courage. I have learned a lot from all of you about what it is like to live with MS, and how hard it is to deal with all the symptoms. But mostly I have seen how courageous and positive you are in light of all you have been through, and that encourages me. I believe I will be able to help other people in your position because of what you have taught me about dealing with a chronic disease like multiple sclerosis, and I thank you for this group and this experience.

Bob: I know you are going to do well. You are a kind person, and genuine and caring. I think I speak for everyone when I say we've enjoyed having you here. (The others nodded and voiced their agreement.)

Worker: Thank you. That's nice to hear. I've really enjoyed being a part of this group and getting to know all of you. (The time was up and we finished by saying good-bye and talking about meeting again in 2 weeks.)

As the ending approaches, there is always unfinished business between the group and the worker that needs to be explored. In the next example, we see the variation on the theme with children's groups.

Children's Group in an Elementary School

Sometimes the expression of anger can emerge indirectly as acting out. This is particularly true of endings in children's groups, as the members seem to revert to the behaviors exhibited in the beginning sessions. In the following illustration, a student worker returned after a 2-week absence from her group of grade-school children who had been meeting with her weekly because of trouble in school. The group had only 2 weeks left before its last meeting. The worker reached for the cues of the anger expressed in the children's behavior.

The children were sitting in the middle of the room in a circle waiting for me. This was different from usual. There was a big table at the back of the room, and we usually sat around it. The boys started cheering and clapping when I came in. I said hello and told them that I was glad to see them too. I had missed them, and it was good to be back. They asked me a lot of questions about where I had been, what I had done, and so on, and I had to give them a rather detailed description of my vacation. After a while of this joking around, I said that it had been a long time since I had seen them last, and I asked what was new.

They started talking about Chang, the Chinese boy in the class whom they hated, and how they had beaten him up. While I was trying to get the story straight about what had happened, a couple of the kids started becoming rowdy and rude, cutting each other off more than usual and cutting me off, too. I was surprised because, although they had the habit of interrupting each other and me as well, they had never been so belligerent. George continued telling me about the fight he had had with Chang, and how he had given him a bloody nose and sent him to the hospital for stitches. (I later found out the stitches part of the story was exaggerated.) Warren, Bobby, and a couple of others joined in and they all proudly described in detail the way they had beaten Chang up. I wanted to remark on this and finally had to tell them to hold it, I wanted to say something. They quieted down a bit, and I finally was able to say what I had wanted—that I couldn't get over how excited and proud they were about what they did to Chang, and I asked them why they did it.

They totally ignored my question and continued in depth about the fight. I waited for a while and tried again to say something, but they were so noisy, I couldn't finish my sentence. There was a lot of horsing around, and they continued extolling the merits of beating Chang up. I tried to speak but kept getting cut off. I let them continue for a couple of minutes and kept quiet. Finally I was able to ask them what was happening. I said that I got the feeling they were mad at me because they wouldn't let me speak. Jimmy nodded yes. Costa said, "We've wasted time, we've spent enough time talking about Chang, we only have a half hour left and then next week and that's all." I said that I thought maybe they were angry at me because I went away for 2 weeks, and maybe the group didn't go so well while I was away. They nodded yes. I said maybe also they were angry because the group was ending next week. John said he didn't want the group to end.

The worker astutely picked up the ending stage being acted out both in the children's behavior in the school and the process in the group. She chose to focus on the underlying meaning for the group and reached for the anger toward her. In retrospect, because the children were also describing an incident of a racist physical attack, the worker needed to at least acknowledge her distress over the idea that a child was "hated," potentially because he was Asian. While she might have needed to wait until later to go into this in more detail, she should not have let the discussion continue without her comment. Children need adult models, with whom they identify, to make clear a value system that their own homes or communities might not express. The skill involves the worker "lending a vision" by sharing her own views without falling into the trap of preaching or teaching and missing the underlying anger over the ending.

George asked why it had to end, was I leaving the school? I said no, I'd be in the school until the end of May, but did they remember that in the first session we had all agreed that we'd have 6 to 10 sessions and then it would end? They agreed. Costa said, "We'll miss you. I know we fool around a lot, but we'll really get down to talk about something properly." I said that I guessed that they were sad the group was ending, and they thought that it was ending because I was punishing them for being noisy and rowdy. They nodded. I said that this wasn't so; it was ending because I had other things that I had to do in the school. But, I said, the group was not supposed to end—it was supposed to continue with their teacher leading it, as we had all agreed. There was a lot of complaining about their teacher and what had happened when I wasn't there, how she had made them do health instead of having a discussion.

I said that they were saying that the group wasn't the same when I wasn't there, and I got them to elaborate on how the two sessions had been during my absence. The boys felt that it was terrible. Jimmy complained that next week would be their last session, so they had better make the most of it. I said that in part they were angry with me because I was saying that I could no longer come in after next week, and maybe they were feeling let down and deserted. They quietly nodded. I said that I could understand how they felt; I was also sad that I would no longer be able to come in on Tuesday mornings, because I really enjoyed working with them, but I would still be in the school for a while and they could come to see me alone if they wanted to, and I would come in from time to time to see them. One of the boys asked if I would come to their next party, and I said that I would love to. I added that besides talking about me and them, I knew that they were angry at Mrs. Morris, and I wondered if we could talk about that and see if we could work something out.

Mrs. Morris was a classroom teacher who had offered to continue the group. The worker focused on the transition question, realizing that she might be able to help the group members continue their work after she was gone. A discussion of the group sessions while she was away revealed that the children had been upset at her absence. They had not given Mrs. Morris a chance. They had acted out, causing her to abandon the group meeting and turn to a general health discussion. The worker strategized with the boys about how they could handle things differently with Mrs. Morris. She also offered to meet with Mrs. Morris to assist in the transition.

In addition to unfinished business with the worker, groups face unfinished business among members during the last sessions. These issues, particularly the negative feelings, often emerge only toward the end of the group. Workers tend to pass over these issues in order to end the group on a high note. However, the worker who trusts in the group will encourage exploration of the negative feelings as well as the positive ones, as illustrated in the next example.

Male Batterers' Group

In the next illustration, the worker encouraged group members to share negative reactions to the helping efforts. The worker asked the group, "How can I be more helpful to groups in the future?" The group was composed of men who had been violent with their wives or the women they had lived with. The members responded to the worker's first question by referring to a coworker, who was not present. Note how the worker brought the discussion back to himself.

WORKER: What I want to ask you is what do you think I could have done better? What did I do that I shouldn't have done? I would like some feedback about me in relationship to the group and what's been going on here.

CHARLES: I always felt like he [the coworker] was giving me the "third degree," but at the same time it brought out answers that probably wouldn't have come out any other time. I didn't feel like he was pushing, but at the same time he asked penetrating questions. And you had a choice, you could either lie about them or you could just fade out and go around them—or tell the truth; most of the time instead of hiding it I would answer his questions and I think I got a lot more said that way than talking on my own.

WORKER: Do you think I could have asked more questions?

CHARLES: Yeah, you could have, but . . . I don't like criticizing.

ALAN: I don't see where you could have asked that many more questions. I think you've done well at bringing things out. It always takes somebody to start it . . . and I think you've tried to get it going.

CHARLES: Yeah.

ALAN: I think it has slipped quite a few times, but I don't think that is necessarily your responsibility; I think that's the group's responsibility.

CHARLES: Yeah. For some reason we did seem to digress quite often, I felt. But I think it's my responsibility just as much as it is yours. Alan thought maybe we could have talked about some things more.

WORKER: How do you mean "slipped?" Do you mean we got off the topic?

CHARLES: Yeah,

BEN: We used to bullshit a lot!

ALAN: But I feel that's really good because you have to be comfortable with the people you're talking with, therefore you have to bullshit sometimes. You have to get off the subject in order to get back on to it because we always manage to get back onto the topics. I think it's good to get off the subject—it's a rest . . .

BEN: I'm just questioning how much we do, that's all.

ALAN: Yeah, well, we did quite a bit . . . but I think we got things done.

CHARLES: But we always noticed it, eh? If it got carried too far, one of the group would say something about it, but I think it helped in a way because it made things more relaxed. We weren't always discussing somebody's hang-up or anything.

WORKER: I won't say that I don't mind being criticized because I do—(laughter) OK! But at the same time, I recognize that . . . Larry [Shulman], the consultant in this outfit, says, "We make mistakes, we learn from those and then we make more sophisticated mistakes"—that kind of thing. I need that kind of input, not only for me as an individual, but for other guys who are going to be leading these groups.

CHARLES: Well, I think you're OK then—you haven't reached the sophisticated stage yet.

WORKER: You mean I'm just making the gross mistakes?! (Laughter.)

CHARLES: No, you're just making the everyday, ordinary ones.

WORKER: Like what?

CHARLES: I don't know, I haven't noticed you making any mistakes.

WORKER: What would you like to see me doing differently?

BEN: Going back to what I said earlier this evening about becoming more aware of how pervasive (maybe) this anger is, how it manifests itself in different ways, and one way is just kind of a sense of being uptight. And it seems to me that the only way I'm gonna change is that I first have to become somehow aware. I mean, I don't know how you ask questions to help another person become aware, but I think that's the kind of question that is helpful and maybe you could have asked more of those. Now, specifically, I can't say because I don't have a firm grasp on that. Do you (turning to John) have any idea of what I am talking about?

JOHN: Yes. Maybe we are putting too much responsibility on the worker? I don't think so. If I could do everything myself, I wouldn't be here in a group.

WORKER: I agree with that.

BEN: And I'm not sophisticated enough, I guess, to have penetrating questions . . . or to draw out . . . to help me become aware, I guess that takes . . . first of all that you have the knowledge or something and being able to see more than I can—or at least have an idea, so that you can ask the questions that will help me rather than telling me, but help me become aware of what, you know, uh . . . Because I'm just seeing now that I don't think I'm very aware of all the waves in my life—and I don't know why, but I think it's important that I gain that knowledge for myself. I'm not sure how to go about it. Because I don't think that my being is just going to change in the sense of my violence toward women—not just toward women; I think it has to change in other areas, it will carry over. (Pause.)

WORKER: (Speaking to Alan) I was really moved when you talked about your feeling of being set up and you were obviously very upset talking about it. Maybe I could have reached a bit more, I don't know, helped you get in touch with . . .

ALAN: Yeah, I think that you might have and I probably showed it too, because I was uptight that night, I was getting into it—I think maybe you should have pushed me a little more. It was a very touchy subject for me, because it's a helpless . . . I never really had a totally helpless feeling in my entire life; I've always been able to do something about it, but this is one thing that I can do nothing about; every time I try it gets worse, and the frustration that comes from that really gets me. I get hit by this almost every day . . . the feeling that I can do nothing.

By making a demand for work, the worker demonstrated that he really wanted the feedback, and the members responded. Of course, the worker had to have enough confidence in himself to invite the negative responses and to stay with them when the members tested him to see if he really meant it. In addition to making the ending discussion honest and receiving important professional feedback, the worker demonstrated a view of manhood that said it was all right to make mistakes and to accept criticism. This was critical for this group because of their tendency to avoid owning up to their own mistakes and taking responsibility for their abusive behavior.

Adult Survivors of Childhood Sexual Abuse

As the previous examples illustrated, the ending and transition phase of a group takes place over time. The stages are noticeable over the last three or four sessions for an ongoing group, beginning with the worker's reminder that the group is coming to an end. The next example provides excerpts from the last six sessions of a group for adult survivors of childhood sexual abuse.

The members of this group all experienced oppression on many levels. They were all sexually exploited as children, most often by people whom they knew and should have been able to trust. As women, they continued to experience oppression in relation to their gender. Some of the members were Hispanic and faced racism, which when combined with sexism strongly affected their lives. Finally, some were lesbians or bisexual, which also placed them in a group that commonly experiences prejudice and oppression. Thus, all of the group members carried a great deal of pain and internalization of their oppression.

As the group members moved into their ending and transition phase, and they reviewed and evaluated their work together, note their courage, their love for each other, and their social worker's conviction about their inherent strength not only to survive oppression but to overcome it and fight it. In many ways, the work of the group followed the three developmental stages described in Chapter 1, in which oppressed people attempt to free themselves from the oppressor within and the oppressor without.

RECORD OF SERVICE

Client Description and Time Frame

This 24-week group for adult survivors of child sexual victimization is a combination of support and stabilization and growth and education models. It is offered by a community rape crisis center and is led by two coworkers. The time frame of the meetings is August 28 to October 16.

The seven members range in age from 22 to 28. All members are women from working-class or middle-class backgrounds. Two members are Hispanic, and the rest are white or from various other ethnic groups. Two women are lesbians, one is bisexual, and four are heterosexual.

Description of the Problem

As the group begins its ending stage, members are reluctant to face the pain and loss of the impending termination and the potential effect of this transition on their lives. As survivors of sexual abuse, many of the women feel acute fear and discomfort when confronted with strong feelings. They have described families of origin in which the development and ending of relationships has been poorly modeled and they have learned to keep silent about their feelings and fears. The tasks of the workers will be to help build a group culture in which the taboo subjects of endings and losses can be explored, freeing the members to grapple with the tasks of termination. We must help the group establish a norm that supports intimacy and risk but also profoundly respects each member's need for safety and self-protection.

How the Problem Came to the Attention of the Worker(s)

As my coworker Jane and I prepared for termination, we tuned in to the potential problems of this stage, using both general knowledge of survivors' issues and our knowledge of the work and struggles of this particular group as a guide. Since the first sessions, safety had been vital to meaningful and productive work in the group. Members had worked hard to recognize when they felt unsafe or at risk and had learned to take steps to protect themselves. Because bonding and connection had been central to the group's creation of a safe and trusting culture, we hypothesized that the group might begin to feel unsafe as members began to separate. We believed that the group might need to create a different "safe culture" that could tolerate the coming ending. On August 28, we learned about the group's norms for saying good-bye and about subjects and feelings, related to endings, that were forbidden. Members responded with silence when asked direct questions about what the group's end meant to them and informed us that they usually run away from and ignore endings.

Summary of the Work

August 28

I tried to reach for the pain behind a group member's description of self-hurting behavior. Linda was describing how she felt compelled to binge on salted and high-cholesterol foods lately and how it was very dangerous for her high blood pressure. I observed that in the past she had done this when she was having really strong feelings and asked how she was feeling these days when she seemed compelled to binge. She began to cry and said, "There's just so much pain, so much loss." She described her fear of losing her whole family if she confronted her mother (the perpetrator of her sexual abuse), the death of a cousin who had been missing and whose body had been found, the anniversary of a rape in which she had nearly been killed at age 18, her loss of me as her individual therapist, and the impending loss of the group, the first people who had ever believed in and supported her. In the face of this she said that she was really isolating herself and wanting to eat.

I felt guilty for "abandoning her" at this difficult time and felt an impulse to fix things for her. I decided this was a signal that I should involve the group rather than respond as her individual therapist. I tried to enlist the support of the group to combat her isolation. I said, "Linda, it sounds like you're feeling overwhelmed by all this pain, and at the very time you could use some support, you're all alone. Is there any way the group can help you right now?" She responded that she isolates most when she's most in pain but that the group could help by reaching out to her, that she needs to be with people when she feels this way. Some group members responded with expressions of support and offers to talk on the phone or be with her. People shared how hard it was to see her pain but how important it was that she share it.

I used Linda's expression of loss to raise the issue of termination again for the group. I said that Linda had shared feeling really sad about the group and I wondered how others in the group were feeling about the end approaching. There was silence. I waited, thinking they might need time to respond. Jane, the coleader, asked group members how they usually say good-bye. Group members responded: "I just take off, usually." "Hey, I don't say good-bye, I say see you later." "I never say good-bye, I just disappear." "I try to pretend nothing's changed." Jane said that she felt it was important for members to understand how they usually cope with good-byes so that they can make choices this time about how they want to handle this ending. Issues of trust, intimacy, and loss had been important in the group's work, and we could do vital work in these areas during our final weeks. Time was up, and I said that we would be spending more time next week talking about the approaching end of the group and how people wanted to work on it.

September 11
I reframed a member's inability to reach a stated group goal and attempted to unite ending process with content. A major goal for Martha had been to spend time in the group telling the story of her abuse, but each time she had planned to do it she had felt unable to go through with it. She had felt flooded with fear and pain. The group had processed why it was so difficult and suggested different ways she could prepare and cope with this "disclosure," but to no avail. This time, what came up was that she felt unable to risk and be vulnerable in the group when it was so close to ending and she could be rejected and abandoned by the group members. She said that it no longer felt safe in the group. I said that perhaps what she was telling us was that this goal was not right for her right now, that keeping herself safe was most important and that she was making choices about how she needed to protect herself. Because child-victims often learn to feel that they are not worth protecting and can never feel truly safe, safety and self-protection had been important in the group's work.

I offered the group a new norm for endings. I said that we needed to strike a careful balance as we approached the ending, trying to work as hard as we could and risk as much as we could but also respecting each person's needs for safety. I said that if she wanted to do her disclosure we would help her, but that no one would force her to do it. Martha and the group discussed this for a while, and then Jane talked about Martha's goal and goals in general and how it was important for us to review them and take stock of the work we needed to address in the next 4 weeks.

I attempted to demand work from the group, evaluating progress and exploring feelings, but blew it by asking for too much information at once. I asked if we could spend some time right now hearing from everyone about what they had accomplished so far, what they still needed to work on, and how they were feeling about the group ending. I immediately sensed my error but didn't know how to correct it. The group was silent. Jane then said that she understood how hard it was for the group but that it was important for us to take stock of where we were. We could still accomplish a lot but we needed to know . . . Jodi burst in and said," I just feel like telling you to shut up. You both keep talking and talking about this and I'm feeling really angry. I wish you would let us move on to what we want to talk about and stop wasting time."

I attempted to address her anger directly and put it in context. I said that she was clearly feeling really angry, and that it felt to her like we were pressuring the group. I waited and then said that people often feel very angry when they face losing something that has been really important to them. I wondered if some of her anger was related to the ending itself. Rita said, "But we're not losing the group. We'll still see each other." Others agreed. I confronted the group's denial. "That's true," I said, "You can choose to continue your friendships as individuals and as a group, but this Monday night group is special, the way we work together here. It's like it has its own identity. That's what's going to end." Michelle said that she wouldn't know what to do with herself on Mondays anymore. Others joined in, saying how they would miss the group. Both workers reflected these feelings and shared their own feelings about the group ending.

I attempted to correct my earlier mistake and reach for more feelings. I said that I had asked for rather a lot at once during my earlier question about goals. This was really hard to talk about and might require some reflection. Perhaps group members could review their progress and future needs during the week and we could set aside time to discuss them next week. We would also need to talk in more depth about the final session. For now, I wondered if we could just spend some time talking about how it felt right now to be dealing with this. We discussed this for the last few minutes of the session.

September 18

I renewed the previous week's demand for work. I reminded the group that we had planned to spend some time this week taking stock of what the group has meant to people and where we needed to put our energy during these final four sessions. People had put quite a bit of thought into this, and the group spent some time evaluating and prioritizing. Martha had clarified the issue of disclosure for herself. She had discovered that, in trying to force herself to discuss the abuse before the group "audience" while feeling unsafe, she had been recreating the dynamics of her abuse as a child in which her father had taken her to bars where she had been sexually abused by various strangers while others observed. With the support and understanding of the group, she was able to carry out a disclosure related to this specific abuse, checking with the group whenever she began to feel unsafe. We credited her growing ability to protect herself while achieving her goals. Both Jane and I offered positive feedback about Martha's growth and her ability to both keep herself safe and move forward with her goals.

Later, Jane raised the issue of the final session, explaining to the group that it is generally structured around feedback, both negative and positive. She asked the group to consider a structure that has worked well for other groups, in which each group member in turn gives feedback to each of the other members and the workers. Past groups have chosen to write a special message to each individual so that the feedback would be kept and remembered. Some members were eager to do this, while others expressed considerable anxiety about evaluating themselves and others. I reached for feelings while giving the group responsibility for its own structure. I said that some people seemed eager to do this while others seemed really uncomfortable with it. Ultimately the decision of how to handle the last session lay with the group, but I wondered if we could explore how people felt about it right now. What made it seem scary, and what seemed positive about it? This was explored for a while.

Then group members asked me to review information about the local "Take Back the Night" march with them. We had told them about the march against sexual violence against women a few weeks before and, after some exploration of their fears about participating in a public demonstration, they decided to march as a group. I supported the group's readiness to act independently and support one another in new experiences. I shared with them how good I felt that they wanted to march together, and I gave them the information they needed.

September 25

We supported the group's growing independence and shared our feelings with them: As the group processed how the march had felt for them, Jane and I shared how powerful it had felt for us to see them there, marching, chanting, and singing. We also shared that it was hard for us to see them and know that the group was ending. The group was special for us, and it would be hard to let it go.

I fell for the illusion of work and let the group get off the track. Rita had been talking for some time about her problems and conflicts with her parents. At first both workers and group were active in discussing her problem, but I gradually began to feel that we weren't going anywhere and my attempts to involve the group proved fruitless. They seemed to have "checked out." I now think that some of the anger Rita was expressing was indirectly aimed at the leaders and/or the group, but I missed this at the time because she had ample reason to be angry with her parents.

I tried to regain focus by demanding work of another member. I had noticed for some time that Linda seemed very agitated and seemed to be struggling to contain herself. Rita had come to a long pause, and I asked, "What's going on with you, Linda?" Linda seemed startled: "Who me? Why? What's the problem?" I answered, "Well, Rita's been talking for a while now about her family, and I know your family has been a source of a lot of your pain. You seem really upset right now and I wonder what's happening." Linda began to talk of having a great deal of pain all the time. She said that her losses had totally overwhelmed her lately and she just didn't know how she was going to make it. I immediately felt the group come back to life. I checked with Rita that we could move to Linda's issue. It would have been better to clarify what had occurred with Rita first, but I wasn't sure how to handle it.

Linda and various group members talked for some time about how hopeless she felt. I reached for her ability to cope with her pain. "I'm just hearing that you have so much pain and sadness right now, Linda, and I wonder, what are you doing with all this hurt?" She said that she was crying a lot, just letting herself feel the sadness, and that she was also writing in her journal and writing poems. She mentioned that she had just written a poem today about her pain and where it was taking her. Several people asked her if she would read it, and she did. It was called "Children of the Rainbow," and it described how beams of light are shattered and broken as they pass through a drop of water and how they emerge to form the vibrant colors of the rainbow. The poem said that she and all survivors in recovery are like beams of light; if they can make it through their pain, they will become vibrant, beautiful, and whole. Several of us had tears in our eyes (me included) and there was a powerful silence when she had finished.

I remained silent to let the group control this moment. People thanked her for sharing such a personal, painful, and hopeful part of herself. I had been Linda's individual worker for some time and I was finding it very hard to leave her and leave the agency. I acknowledged her feelings, shared my own, and credited her ability to cope. I shared that I found the poem very moving, that I could feel that she had incredible pain, but that her art and ability to create were powerful vehicles for carrying her forward and transforming her pain. The group ended soon after.

October 2

We credited a member's growing independence. Martha told the group that she had confronted her father with the abuse since the last group. We were all amazed, because this had been a goal that Martha had not hoped to attain for several months, if not years, in the future. Her abuse had been very sadistic, and her father had continued to hold incredible power over her when he was able to have contact with her. She had been with Linda before he called and described "just feeling very powerful and safe. I was able to see Linda and my roommate right there, and I could hold the whole group right in my mind and feel you supporting me and helping me to be safe. I've never felt anything like that before. And he was weak! He was the one who seemed powerless." Martha had burned a picture of her father after the call as a way of exorcizing his control over her, and she had brought the ashes to group. Later the group gathered and flushed the ashes down the toilet. Both leaders credited Martha's incredible and rapid growth and related it to the ending and how she had taken control of how she wanted to accomplish her goals and approach the end of group. The group gave Martha feedback and discussed how it felt to be part of her sense of safety.

I missed two important opportunities to discuss anger in relation to the group's ending. Linda discussed feeling intense anger lately and feeling like she was about to explode and be violent. The group and both workers addressed her anger extensively, relating it to her abuse and her current pain and exploring coping strategies. Although I mentioned her several losses as being related to her anger, I neglected to focus on the group's ending as a major source of her pain and thus missed a potentially important piece of work.

Next, Donna raised the issue of her psychiatrist and how he had told her to get on with her life and stop indulging herself with her depression and dwelling on her abuse. The group responded with explosive anger. I allowed my own anger and the real differences between my approach and the approach of the psychiatrist to blind me to the part of the group's anger that might have been directed at me had I invited it. We did good work in helping Donna evaluate her therapy, but we missed another chance to explore the group's anger about the ending and our role as workers. I think that this group felt so special to me, and I was finding termination from individuals, the group, and the agency so hard, that I kept myself unaware of their anger.

October 16—Final Session

We assisted the group in sharing feedback and establishing closure, but we neglected to reach for negative evaluation. Each member and each worker had prepared written feedback for the other members and workers, and members took turns reading their messages to each other. (Workers passed out written individual feedback and gave verbal feedback to the group as a whole.) The material was very personal and moving and related the work of the group to strong feelings about ending. Workers assisted members in preparing to read and helped the group to respond. Some members cried and expressed deep feelings of pain and loss. Workers also responded directly to their own feedback.

A few of the women chose to hand out the personal feedback and speak to the group generally while members read the personal material. Although I believe that the material was genuine, it focused on positives only, and both workers missed the opportunity to reach for negative feedback, falling for the farewell-party syndrome. Although this important task was not accomplished, the workers did accomplish their goal of creating a safe culture in which members could risk being intimate and trusting as the group ended. I reinforced the culture that permits people to risk even as they are separating. Martha had read each note and closed with "Love, Martha." At one point, Rita said, "This is really hard, but I have to ask. You said "Love" to everybody, but you didn't say it to me. I'm sure you just forgot, but I have to say, it hurts. Don't you love me too?" She began to cry with these last words. Martha had clearly just forgotten and turned to Rita, saying, "I'm so glad you told me. I was just finding this all so hard that I didn't even realize . . . I do love you. I'm sorry it hurt that I forgot you. Here, let me write it on yours."

I asked Rita how it had felt to risk this question, and I said that I remembered that she had entered the group 6 months ago saying she never let herself be vulnerable with others. Rita responded that this was a safer place than she had ever been in before. She had shared her story, her shame, and had been vulnerable with people here. She knew she could trust us. "It's true," added Martha, "I've never been anywhere that was safe the way this is, even more than individual therapy." Michelle added, "This place is like the safe home we never had. You guys were almost like parents for us. You were honest with us and we learned to be honest with each other. And it never mattered, we could feel good, feel bad, disagree with each other and be mad, but it was OK. We could learn to be ourselves. You were there for us the way our parents should have been." Soon after, we ended the group. There was a long "group hug" at the suggestion of the members, and we ate some cake a member had ordered. The message on the cake said, "Survivors— Striving and Thriving!"

The metaphor of the poem in which survivors in recovery are viewed as "beams of light; if they can make it through their pain, they will become vibrant, beautiful, and whole" is extremely powerful and moving. It captures beautifully the struggle of these young, oppressed, and vulnerable women to free themselves from the self-image of being "damaged goods" that had been imposed upon them by those who should have been nurturing them. Their courage in joining a "Take Back the Night" march, when they felt so personally uncomfortable in doing so, was an affirmation of their willingness to fight and overthrow their oppressors. It was a social parallel of their individual revolutions against oppression described in one member's efforts to confront her offending parent. The unique power of mutual-aid groups is amply demonstrated in the content of their work together and in the "Survivors—Striving and Thriving" lettering on the cake at their final session.

In the next section, a detailed analysis of a single session in the ending phase of a group of teenagers in a residential setting completes this chapter. Many of the teens in that group have experienced emotional, physical, and sexual abuse in their families of origin. The example illustrates all of the ending phases described thus far.

A Termination Session: The Worker Leaving the Group

The following description of a group meeting with teenage girls in a residential treatment center illustrates some of the unique dynamics that emerge when the group continues and the worker leaves. The session took place 1 week after the worker told the group members that she was leaving the agency for another job. This worker in this example demonstrated both an advanced level of skill in group work and skill in dealing with endings. Of particular interest is the impact of the worker's sharing of her own powerful feelings. The entire meeting is presented, together with a detailed analysis of the skills employed. The process in the meeting is classic, as one can see elements of all the ending dynamics in one session.

Three of the girls came in with each other and seemed in a very happy mood. They said that they'd had a good week in school. I said, you know that sounded real nice and that this was one of the enjoyments of finally being a senior, and I teased about that. I asked about where Gladys and Beth were, and they said that they had to speak with a teacher about some arrangements and that they'd be there in a little while. The three of them continued talking about school and the rehearsals and the senior trip and stuff like that. Then Beth came in, and she was singing "Everything Is Beautiful," a rock-and-roll song. She took her seat and was laughing with everyone.

The good feelings expressed by the group members represented a denial of the ending. Because there was only one meeting left after this one, the worker had strategized to reach past the denial for the opposite feelings she knew would be there. The members responded to her demand for work.

After a while I said, "Hey, it's great to see everybody in such a good mood, and I hate to be a party pooper, but I feel that I have to say that this is our next-to-last meeting, and a lot of things between you and I will be drawing to an end." Margie said, "You have a hell of a nerve." I said, "You mean about my leaving?" She said, "Yeah, that and a whole lot of things." I said, "OK, let's hear them. I'm sure that my leaving and the ending of the group has caused a lot of reactions in all of you." Nobody picked up on that, and Margie said, "Are we going to have a group next year?" A couple of girls said, "Yeah, we want to have another group next year," and Beth said, "Let's have a party in honor of your leaving."

The group's anger was expressed in Margie's comment "You have a hell of a nerve." The worker acknowledged this anger and encouraged the members to continue. The anger they felt and the pain underneath it were too much for them at this point, so they backed off. They began, instead, to discuss the continuation of the group and a farewell party. The worker allowed them to move away from the anger but held them to discuss the importance of the group.

There was a lot of mixed-up talk, and I tried to pick up about continuing the group. I said, "You're saying that the group has meant something to you and that you want to continue even without me." Beth said, "Naw, the group wasn't all that good," and Margie said, "Sometimes it was and sometimes not. Sometimes the meetings were very good, and sometimes they were a waste of time." I said, "Can you tell me more about that?" Margie said, "Well, sometimes it just seemed like we weren't in the right mood and we couldn't get down to work." Jill said, "Yeah, we were just fooling around all over the place," and Donna said, "Like the mood we were in Sunday night," and they all began to talk about a riot that had happened in the cottage, and they started fooling around. I said, "Hey, can we get back to the thing about the group, and what you thought about it, and what it meant to you? I think it is important for us to take a look at it now that you're nearing the end."

The members attempted to evade the discussion once again, and the worker showed great skill in not letting them put her off. She made another demand for work and insisted that the group discuss their specific reactions to their time together. As the members described the mutual aid they had experienced, the worker attempted to explore this aspect of their learning; however, they were not ready for this discussion and still needed to express their angry feelings.

Donna said, "Well, the best meeting we had was just with three of us—me, Jill, and Gladys. That's when we really talked about ourselves." Margie said, "You mean without me and Beth, is that what you mean?" Jill said quickly, "No, I don't mean that. We did have a good meeting with everybody, but I guess that was really the best," and I said, "Well, what made it the best?" Donna said, "Because we talked about our families, and we got to understand how we were feeling," and Margie said, "Yeah, I agree. The best meetings were when we talked about our families, and the worst meetings were when we talked about the cottage and the cottage parents." I said, "How come?" Gladys said, "Because we couldn't do anything about the cottage parents or even about the cottage, and at least when we talk about ourselves and about our families we can understand more, we can know why we are like we are," and Beth said, "Yeah, we can help each other." I said, "You have helped each other a lot. Is that something important that you've gotten from these meetings?" Nobody picked up on that.

Beth began talking about a party that they had been to, and all of a sudden in the midst of a whole big discussion Beth turned to me and said, "You're leaving, you God-damned fink." And everybody stopped, and everybody looked at me. I said, "I'm leaving, and I guess that makes me a fink." And everybody began, saying, "Why are you leaving? Why do you have to leave us? Why can't you stay?" Then a whole torrent of emotion came pouring out. Finally Jill said, "Why are you leaving?" I said, "I tried to explain the reasons on Friday, but if you'd like me to I'll explain them again now. But I don't know if it's the reason that really matters. It's more how you feel knowing that I'm leaving, for whatever the reason." They said, "No, no, we want to hear the reasons, we don't understand." I said, "OK, let me try to explain. I'm leaving because I've been here for a number of years and I feel that it's time for me to move on, to move into another situation. Working here has meant an awful lot to me, and you all have meant an awful lot to me. Yet I feel that a combination of things, the long traveling, working a lot of nights, have become very hard for me and I feel like I want to work nearer to where I live, and that I want to have a new kind of experience and not work in a residential treatment school. That's pretty much the reason. If there's anything you don't understand, ask me and I'll try to explain more."

As the anger emerged, the worker struggled with her own feelings in order not to block its expression. Her acceptance of their feelings demonstrated in her response, "I'm leaving, and I guess that makes me a fink," freed them to explore the feelings of dependency and hurt that were below the surface feelings of anger. Although she had explained her reasons for leaving the week before, the group members had been too shocked to heed and understand. She agreed to explain them again while acknowledging that their feelings were what really mattered, rather than her reasons. As the group began to express their emotions toward the worker, she asked them to identify the specific things about her they had found helpful. These would be the qualities they must look for in other workers. She also stayed with their hurt feelings, and she reached for their fear about establishing a relationship with a new worker, for their sense of rejection, and for their anger. Most important, the worker also shared her own pain at leaving them. The open expression of her feelings provided the impetus for the members to respond with theirs.

Beth started to cry and said, "You can't leave. We need you." I said, "You mean you won't be able to make it without me?" Margie said, "You're the best social worker I ever had. I won't be able to talk to anybody else." I said, "We have been real close, me and every one of you, and I guess the thought of starting over with somebody else scares the hell out of you. What do you think there was about me that made it easier for you to talk to me?" Beth said, "It's because you cared about us. It's 'cause we knew that even when you were mad at us, you were really sticking up for us, and you were really with us." Donna said in a soft voice, "Yeah, but if you cared so much, you wouldn't be leaving." And I said, "That's a thing, isn't it? How could I leave you if I really care for you?" Gladys said, "We know you care for us. We know you're leaving because you really feel that you have to." And then she just kind of shrugged, and I said, "But the words don't help very much, huh? They don't take away the bad feeling." Beth said, "That's right, what good does it do me to know that you care if you're not here?" And Jill said, "Yeah, you've been my social worker for a whole year. I don't want anybody else." There was a lot more talk about the idea that they didn't want anybody new.

I said, "You're angry as hell at me. You have a right to be, and even though your anger hurts me and a big piece of me wants to say, 'Don't be angry at me,' I can understand that you are, and I know the kind of pain that must be underneath, and I feel some of that pain also. It's hard as hell for me to leave you." Beth said, "If it was hard for you to leave us, then you wouldn't leave us." Margie said, "No, Beth, that's just not the truth. It was hard for me to leave home . . ."

At this point in the session, the pain of the discussion caused the group to adopt its pattern of using a scapegoat when things got rough. Gladys, the group scapegoat, began to cry, expressing many of the emotions felt by the other members. Their anger at her was an expression of their anger at the same feelings within themselves. The worker demonstrated her group work skill, at a time when she herself was feeling somewhat overwhelmed by emotion, by paying attention to her two clients—Gladys and the group. In the next excerpt, we see an illustration of the worker's functional role, as outlined in the discussion on scapegoating in Chapter 12.

Gladys put her head down and began to cry, and one of the kids hollered, "Oh, cut it out. This hurts us as much as it hurts you." I said, "Maybe it hurts each of you in a different way, and this is how Gladys is reacting." She picked up her head and said, "Oh, leave me alone. None of you care about me," and Margie said, "Yes, we do, you don't want help. You just want to feel sorry for yourself." I said, "You're all getting so angry at Gladys, and it seems that all she's doing is acting out how you feel. Is it that you hurt so much that you don't have room for anybody else's hurt?" Jill said, "She cries all the time. Who gives a damn about her?" Donna said, "I care about her, but I don't know what to do." Beth said to her (by this time Gladys had moved away from the table where we meet and was sitting alone on a chair, crying), "Gladys, why don't you come over here?" and Gladys just shrugged, and one of the other kids said, "Aw, leave her alone," and there was kind of an uncomfortable quiet in the room, and I said, "I don't think that you feel right leaving her alone," and Beth said, "Hell, what can we do?" and I said, "What do you feel like doing? Do you feel like reaching out to her?" Beth got up and walked over to Gladys and put her arms around her and said, "You're scared because everybody's leaving, right?" Gladys nodded her head. Beth said, "We're all in that situation, too. She's leaving us, too. Miss S.'s leaving us, too. Not only you." Beth said, "But maybe it is different for

Gladys." Gladys said, "You have a mother and father. Every one of you has at least a mother or a father. Who do I have?" Beth said, "You have foster parents." Gladys said, "Big deal. They don't want me." There was a hush in the room at the pain of those words, and I said, "Wow, you really know how that feels."

The worker's trust in her group was rewarded as they reached out to Gladys to offer aid. As they spoke to Gladys, they were really speaking to each other and to the part of them that was facing the same set of problems. The faith of the worker was important at this point, because with her help they were able to experience the power of mutual aid in the peer group. As they move into their young adult years, they will have to seek out support and help from their peers; this was possibly the most important learning for them.

Beth said, "I think I know how it feels. I think I know how bad it feels. And if you want to cry, that's OK, but you gotta live. You gotta pick yourself up. You gotta face it." Gladys shook her head. "No," she said, "I can't." I said, "It seems that she can't pick herself up." Donna said, "Even when you're alone, you have to trust yourself." Margie said, "That's pretty hard to do." Beth said, "But you're not alone, Gladys, you have us. We'll help you, and somebody else can help us." Donna said, "And maybe we'll also have to help ourselves." Gladys said, "I know what you mean. I know that in the end I do have to help myself." I said to her, "But are you scared that you won't be able to do that?" She nodded her head yes, and once again she began to cry. Beth said, "We'll help you, too. Just like we did here this morning." And I had tears in my eyes, too, and I said, "Wow, you kids are fantastic." And they all kind of laughed, and somebody said, "Maybe we'll become social workers, too," and that kind of broke the tension of the moment, and we never really got back to the thing of them helping each other.

The feelings associated with endings stir deep and powerful emotions in all of us. When I use this example and the earlier ones in my workshops, workers have been visibly moved by the power of the feelings expressed; they have perhaps moved you as well. Workers also react to the degree of skill demonstrated by this worker and the workers in the example involving the survivors' group. They reflect on endings they have handled poorly by missing the cues or not facing their own feelings with enough honesty. This record represents an advanced level of skill. This same worker handled endings quite differently in her training days; she would have cut and run at several key places in this meeting. There were many group endings along the way in which she made mistakes, learned from them, and ended her next group with more skill. However painful, this process represents the only way to develop professional skill. It is a process that continues throughout a professional's working life.

Chapter Summary

The ending and transition phase of practice and strategies for intervention, as described in detail in Chapter 5, apply to group work as well as individual work. Workers help groups move through several ending stages: denial of the ending, anger over the ending, mourning, and trying the ending on for size. Helpful skills include pointing out endings early, reaching for feelings, and dealing with the farewell-party syndrome. Special dynamics arise when the worker leaves and the group continues.

Related Online Content and Activities

 Visit *The Skills of Helping* Book Companion Website at www.socialwork.wadsworth .com/Shulman06/ for learning tools such as glossary terms, InfoTrac College Edition keywords, links to related websites, and chapter practice quizzes.

The website for this chapter also features additional notes from the author and additional process recordings:

- Ending With a Hearing-Impaired Teenagers' Group
- Pregnant Teens in a Group Home: Integrating Ending Process and Content
- Welfare Mothers: Conflict in the Last Session